ACHILL ISLAND

Theresa McDonald

Achill

First published 1997.
I.A.S. Publications,
St. O'Hara's Hill,
Tullamore, Co. Offaly,
Republic of Ireland.

Editor

Jim Higgins

Design

Turner Graphics

Cover

Lithograph of the Missionary Settlement, Dugort, Isles of
Achill, 1845. Courtesy of John O'Shea.

Printed by Turner's Printing Company Ltd., Longford, Ireland.

ISBN 0 9519974 1 6 (paper)
ISBN 0 9519974 2 4 (bound)

i

In memory of my father and mother, John & Anne Kilbane, my brother Seán, and uncle, John Moran. May they rest in peace.

Hy-Brazil

I have been to Hy-Brazil,
And the Land of Youth have seen,
Much laughter have I heard there,
And birds amongst the green.

Since I have left Hy-Brazil,
Age has encompassed me,
She plucks me by the shoulder,
And will not let me be.

Dora Sigerson Shorter

Hy-Brazil, an enchanted island also known as *Tír na nÓg* is supposedly seen off Achill every seven years. Some say it is a reflection of the island in the western sky.

ii

CONTENTS

Contents

Illustrations

Achill

Foreword

There are few joys to equal the sight of the commanding majesty of Achill from the sea. There is a noble confidence about Slievemore's conical thrust as it fronts the more brooding Croaghaun, and it can light up in blue on a summer's day. Although joined to the land, Achill is very much an island, seen at its best from the sea. Like the sea, it has many moods, colours and shades, not all of which are as gentle and beautiful as the image of it that I carry.

It is a privilege for me as an outsider to preface and recommend this single handed effort at introducing us to the natural and historical complexities of the island by a skilled and enthusiastic native daughter, Theresa McDonald. Her commitment to understanding the island's people and their past is praiseworthy. Her efforts at putting the island on national and international maps of archaeological and general scholarly awareness are bearing fruit. Achill will thrive even more as an attractive visitor destination as a result of her work. That it will do so as unchanged as possible and with the minimum of self-defeating 'improvement' will hopefully be Theresa's monument and the legacy of this timely reworking of her fundamental book on the island.

I hope that future generations of visitors will share in the joy of discovering Achill as they have in the past, that it will be allowed to preserve its magic and continue casting its spell and that this book will explain the history and background of a place in so far as its unique and intangible impact can ever be captured within pages.

Patrick F. Wallace,
National Museum of Ireland.
March, 1997.

Preface

This book endeavours to provide the reader with a comprehensive account of the history, archaeology and folklore of Achill Island, the study of which has been accomplished through fieldwork, documentary research, and the research of local historians, particularly my late uncle, John Moran, Dooagh, the late Cyril Gray, Dugort and the late Brother Angelo Holmes, Franciscan Monastery, Clara, Co. Offaly. Most of the material is new but some general background information contained in *Achill: 5000 B.C. to 1900 A.D.* McDonald (1992) has been retained in the present edition.

Achill has been home to various groups of people from the Neolithic Period onwards and there is some slight evidence, as yet unverified, of an even earlier (c.7000 B.C.) Mesolithic presence on the island. Detailed investigation of the many shell midden sites along the shores of the island and on nearby Achill Beg Island may yet provide conclusive evidence for such a Middle Stone Age settlement. Achill, with its varied geology, relict flora, scenery that rivals the best Ireland has to offer, and a range of archaeological sites spanning 5000 years of continuous history, is special in many ways. This book is an attempt to document some of this uniqueness, to follow in the footsteps of those heterogeneous settlers who inhabited Achill during the pre-historic and historic periods, and to provide, where possible, details of their lifestyles so that an assessment and closer understanding of their impact on the landscape, and on life on the island today, can be made and evaluated. Life in Achill has undoubtedly often been harsh, forging in its people an iron determination to overcome the many trials and tribulations that have so often been their lot. Remoteness, lack of cohesion and a declining population could lead to where Achill would become *"a forgotten part of Ireland."* The people of Achill, however, hold the destiny of the island in their hands in that they have inherited a rich heritage which attracts thousands of visitors, annually, to the island. The development of this resource will have major repercussions for the future of tourism on the island; if sensitively developed, it can and will, provide long-term sustainable employment. Striking the correct balance between necessary development and the enhancement of this heritage will not be an easy task. The archaeological heritage is finite so any development must ensure that this resource is preserved. There is also an urgent need for more intensive study of the island's prehistoric and historic past. Environmental research relating to vegetational changes over the millennia, radiocarbon dating to provide absolute dates for major settlement phases, geological, glaciological and pedological research would greatly enhance the status of the island and would give thousands of students and visitors the opportunity to study in what many already regard as an outdoor laboratory. It is only when all of this has been accomplished, that we can say that we understand our island, our Achill. A study of Achill's geology, botany and archaeology and inshore marine life can easily provide enough material to keep many scholars busy for several lifetimes. The fascination with which foreign students and other visitors view Achill provides a glimpse of how valuable the heritage of the island is, and how it should be treasured by its inhabitants. Development *via* cultural tourism, preservation of the vernacular heritage and sensitivity in relation to new architectural development will ensure Achill remains a premier tourist resort for many years to come.

I hope that this book will prove informative to the sons and daughters of Achill and their descendants, many now living on foreign shores, as well as to the many visitors who hold Achill in high regard; may you all continue to visit and also your children's children. Writing this book demanded many sacrifices from my husband, Kevin, my daughter, Margo, and son, Redmond, to whom I owe a great debt. A special word of thanks to Margo for proof-reading; to John O'Shea, Dooagh and Jim Higgins, Galway for the excellence of their editing and proof reading, to Helen Gallagher and Máire McKay, Tullamore for help with the index, to Gabriel Harrison and Michael Byrne, Tullamore for editorial advice, and to Dr. Patrick Wallace for the Foreword. Any errors are of course mine alone.

Theresa McDonald,
March, 1997.

Acknowledgments

My research was greatly facilitated by many people who generously shared with me their knowledge of the island; local people, some no longer with us, generously gave of their time and expertise, and to all of them I sincerely acknowledge my thanks and appreciation.

A few people deserve special mention, the late Cyril Gray, Dugort, the late Captain Robert Boyd, Amethyst Hotel, Keel, my late uncle, John Moran, Dooagh, the late Brother Angelo Holmes, Franciscan Monastery, Clara, Co.Offaly. Thomas Johnston, N.T., Cloughmore, John McNamara, N.T., Dooagh, John O'Shea, F.R.I.C.S., Dooagh, Barry & Jean O'Reilly, Office of Public Works, Gerry Walsh, M.A., Mayo County Council, Dr. Patrick Wallace, Director, National Museum of Ireland, Jim Higgins, M.A., Galway, Professor Etienne Rynne, Galway, Eoin Halpin, M.A., Belfast, Maire McKay, Tullamore, June Fielding, Keel, Mary Hoban, Dugort, James McHugh, Dugort, Oswald Then, Munich, Camille Souter, Dooagh. Tom McNamara, Keel, John Toolis, Crumpaun, Keel, Joe McDermot, Newport, Richard O'Brien, M.A., Co.Tipperary, and Enda Kenny, T.D., Minister for Tourism and Trade.

I would also like to thank **The National Museum of Ireland** for permission to reproduce two photographs of artifacts from Achill; the **Ordnance Survey** of Ireland for permission to reproduce a map and aerial photographs; **Cambridge University Aerial Survey** for permission to reproduce aerial photographs. **Ursula Kavanagh** and **Douglas Duggan** for photographs contributed. **The Irish Folklore Commission at U.C.D.** for giving me access to their files on Achill, **The National Library of Ireland** for permission to reproduce photographs from the **Lawrence Collection, The National Archives, The Valuation Office, The Central Statistics Office, The Royal Society of Antiquaries of Ireland, The Henry Library at St. Nicholas' Collegiate Library, Galway, The Land Commission Surveyors, The Ulster Museum** and the staff at **Mayo County Library, Castlebar and Offaly County Library, Tullamore.**

Achill

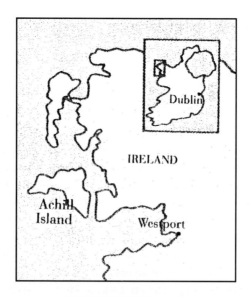

LOCATION MAP

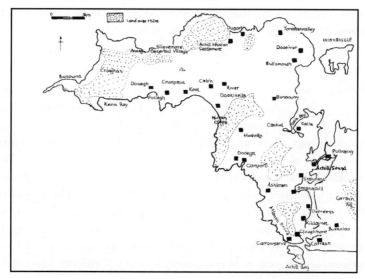

MAP OF ACHILL ISLAND, CO. MAYO. IRELAND.

Chapter 1

INTRODUCTION

Extant archaeological sites and monuments provide ample testimony of the importance of Achill during the prehistoric period, a fact which contrasts markedly with the dearth of settlement evidence for the ensuing historic period. A factor of this dichotomy may be the severance of Achill, by the sea, from the mainland, in the later prehistoric period, creating the island status which pertains today. While Achill's maritime location may have had some influence on settlement, its remote location and inaccessibility undoubtedly militated against dense demographic settlement at any time. Nevertheless, recent archaeological investigations indicate that some areas of the island enjoyed continuous settlement over a 5,000 years period, from the Neolithic Period to the present day. This fact is not immediately apparent from a study of documentary sources, which are largely silent on the later history of the island. Yet, when they do speak, they provide tantalising glimpses of an island with a vibrant and exciting past. This is nowhere more apparent than in the case of Grace O'Malley (Gráinne Uáile), the famous Pirate and Sea Queen, who seldom got a mention in the Annals but whose exploits are recorded in the English State Papers and in local folklore. In the aftermath of the Anglo-Norman Invasion, some of the the most powerful families of the day contended for control of Achill. Their exploits and those of the indigenous population of the island from the Neolithic Period onwards are the subject of this book.

Origins

Connacht has always been the poorest and most sparsely populated province in Ireland. The northern and western parts of the province have an underlying geology of pre-Carboniferous rock with Caledonian affinities associated with leached and podzolized soils and large concentrations of bogland. This area contains two mountainous peninsulas separated by Clew Bay, Connemara to the south and West Mayo on the north. The Mullet Peninsula north of Achill is notable for

Achill

its series of low, rocky islands and reefs of granite and metamorphic rocks. This contrasts with Achill and the Corraun Peninsula with their high, quartzite mountainous coastline dominated by Slievemore, Croaghaun and Corraun Hill rising to 2,214 feet (671m), 2,192 feet (664m) and 1,729 feet (524m) respectively. Despite its inhospitable physical character with high rainfall, poor soils, and constant exposure to Atlantic gales, this west Connacht area was densely settled during the Neolithic Period about five thousand years ago. The evidence for this is adequately demonstrated by the largest concentration of megalithic tombs than anywhere else in Ireland. Settlement is less clearly defined during the ensuing Bronze and Iron Ages but the Early Medieval and Anglo-Norman Periods are again rich in sites. In Achill, however, there is a hiatus between the end of the fourteenth century and the middle of the seventeenth century when, with the exception of the Tower House in Kildavnet, settlement sites are few.

The 1653 Act of Parliament assigned Connacht to the Irish. Settlers from the north of Ireland, excluding the counties of Down and Antrim settled in the barony of Burrishoole, a fact reflected in the many northern surnames in this area. *"To Hell or to Connacht"* was the ultimatum given by Oliver Cromwell to many of the rich farmers, aristocracy and general population of the more prosperous parts of Ireland, and to Connacht they came to add new strands to an already colourful and cultural western province.

In Late Iron Age Ireland, Connacht was inhabited by the *Votadini*, a Celtic British Iron Age tribe originally located near the Firth of Forth in Scotland, who had their capital (hillfort) at Traprain Law. Attacks on Roman Britain by the Picts, Scots (Irish) and their allies in the 4th Century A.D. had important consequences for these northern tribes in the frontier areas of Britain, with the *Votadini* emigrating to the West of Ireland in the late 4th Century A.D. Contact may have been maintained between these Celtic British tribes and their original homeland for several centuries as there are many references to Irish chiefs having residences on both sides of the Irish sea.

2

1. Introduction

Ptolemy, an Alexandrian Geographer, who wrote his **Geography** in the 2nd Century A.D., places the *Votadini* approximately in Co. Galway, claiming as their ancestor the mythical Fothad which may be cognate with *Votadini*. The Uaithni/*Fothad*s were supposedly of non Goidelic origin and were variously connected with the *Érainn*, the *Laigin*, and the *Cruithní*. This Laginian connection may have come about as a result of the Laginian conquest of Connacht. O'Rahilly (1976).

Connachta

An earlier name for Connacht was *Cóiced Ól nÉcmacht* meaning the Fifth (Province) of the *Fír Ó nÉcmacht*. It is possible that *Nécmacht* may be related to Ptolemy's Nagnatae, another Celtic tribe whom he located in North Connacht. The term *senChonnachta* refers to these older inhabitants. *Cóiced Connacht*, the present name of the western province is a late creation and could only have come into existence after the Connachta (Goidels from the Midlands) had conquered the province. They were made up of a group of three tribes: the *Conmaicne (Conmaicne Mara, 'the hound-sons of the sea')* the *Ciarraige* and the *Corcamoga*. At the dawn of historical time (5th Century, A.D.) we find them divided into three tribes known respectively as *Uí Fiachrach, Uí Briúin, and Uí Ailello.*

Tribes of non-Goidelic origin such as the *Laigin* appear to have entered the service of the Goidelic invaders (Connachta), who assigned them *"sword-land"* in return for military service and tribute. The barony of Gallen in Mayo bears their name and likewise, *Mag Domnann*, a district west of Killala Bay called *Irrus Domnann* or Erris in West Mayo. These Domnann were said to be related to the *Dumnonii*, a Celtic British tribe originally located in northern Britain. Tradition has it that Cruachan in north Co. Roscommon was their capital. The *Fír Domnann* were located in the district of *Cera, Uí Amalgada and Uí Fiachrach* , i.e. the baronies of Carra, Erris and Tirawley in Co. Mayo.

The Gamanrad or *Fír Domnann* of Irrus Domnann were famous for their martial qualities. They feature in **Táin Bó Flidhais** and *Fraech mac Fidaig*, the hero of this tale was one of them. The Gamanrad are also thought to be synonymous with the *Clann Úmóir*, ancestors of the

Achill

O'Malleys - the *Tuath Mic Úmóir* who were located in Umhall. A legend related in the **Dindshenchas** refers to the people of *Úmóir* and their King, *Oengus Mac Úmóir* who is said to have come from the land of the *Cruithní* (Scotland). Byrne (1987:236), however, claims that the *Partraige,* a very ancient tribe, probably descended from a pre-Celtic population, were the true ancestors of the *Fír Umaill* of Clew Bay.

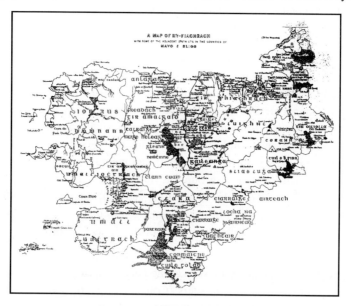

1. Map of Hy-Fiachrach, after Irish Archaeological Journal (1844)

Umhall

From ancient times Achill formed part of the territory of ancient Umhall, located around Clew Bay. This name is very old and like Achill its derivation remains unexplained. Ó Muraíle's *"Mayo Places" (1985)* says that *finum Humail* appears in Tírechán in the late seventh century A.D. *Umall* and *Fir Umaill* appear in the Tripartite **Life of Patrick.** Stokes (1887). Four to five hundred years later, during the de Burgo (Bourke) supremacy, we find the area subdivided into *Umhall Iochtarach* and *Umhall Uachtarach*. The people of Umhall are also said to be

4

1. Introduction

descended from a son of Brion, brother of Niall of the Nine Hostages, King of Ireland in the fifth century A.D. who was supposedly involved in the kidnapping of St. Patrick. The connection of the ruling *Uí Néill* dynasty (descendants of Niall) with Achill is referred to in local folklore which maintains that Cormac Mac Airt, grandson of Niall was fostered in Achill. After his birth, Cormac, was carried off by a she-wolf and was rescued by a trapper, *Lugnae Fer Trí*, who restores him to his mother. She takes him north to be fostered but on the way they are attacked by wolves and Cormac is hidden in a milk-vessel of *yew* wood. Cormac, essentially returns to the place of his birth and that of his druid grandfather in Corraun or Bunanioo *(Bun/an/ -/eo* =Bottom of the Wood where the wise man lived!).

Umhall later coalesced to comprise the territory now occupied by the Baronies of Burrishoole and Murrisk, probably *"the Owels"* of the English state papers in the sixteenth century. Called Burriswyle in the *Division of Connaught* in 1574; *Borries Owyll,* the *Burrissies alias Ballyneborieshe* in the **Ormond Deeds**, 1576; *Owles of Boroshoule* and *Boroshole,* as well as *the three Ulles: Umhall Uí Mháille, Umhall Chloinn' Philinín* and *Umhall Ioctarach.* In Browne's map of 1584, it is *'Moriske or Owles O Mayle, Boroshole, Irres* - the three commonly called the Owles.' Ó Muraíle (1985). Burrishoole was, according to the **Annals of Connacht,** designated a borough by Henry Butler in 1238 shortly after he was created Lord of Aikil and Umhall.

According to McNally (1973) Achill was always an independent kingdom, owing allegiance only to the King of Connacht. **The Book of Rights,** a **M.S.** which deals with the rights and obligations of the provincial Kings, refers to the King of Umhall sending to the King of Connacht:

" five score cows of lasting condition,

five score hogs of broad sides,

five score mantles, beautiful their texture "

In addition, Umhall also gave five steeds, five swords, five ships and five coats of mail. *Rí Oighli agus Umaill* (King of Achill & Umhall) is referred to in **Cath Maighe Léna,** while Cruchán *Oighle* is equated with Croagh Patrick in Umhall but it could equally refer to Croaghaun mountain in Achill (Holmes, *pers. comm.*)! Tírechán in the **Book of Armagh** said: *"And (St.) Patrick went to Mount Egli to fast on it for forty days and forty nights."*

The earliest chronological reference to Umhall is in the appellation of the name to the servant of *Fintan Mac Bochra,* who figures prominently in legend as having survived the Deluge, and is intimately associated with Achill in *"Fintan and the Old Eagle of Achill."* Knott (1957). Therefore both Fintan and Umhall are associated with Achill. Umhall is mentioned twice in 10th century texts and Achill seems to have been part of this territory from the earliest times. q

Umhall Uí Mháille (O'Malley's territory)

The territory of Umhall was, at the dawn of history, occupied by the *Clann Úmóir* families, from whom came *Clann Máille* but whose alleged descent from Brian Orbsen, son of the High King, is disputed in the **Book of Rights (Leabhar na gCeart).** *"With such a descent the King of Umhall would not have paid tribute"*. His full title was *"King of Aicill and Umhall"* i.e. of Highland and Lowland.

Murrisk and Burrishoole were often referred to as *Umhall Uí Mháille* (territory of the O'Malleys), while a reference in the **Annals of Ulster** (A.U.) refers to *Uí Briúin hUmil*. The Annals of the Four Masters record the death of Tadhg O'Malley, chief of his Clann in 1123 A.D. and in 1413 A.D. the near drowning of Tuathal O'Malley on the western sea. At the *Synod of Ráith Breasail* (c.1110), Umhall came under the jurisdiction of Cong or Tuam as the diocese is now called. Ó Móráin (1957).

Ó Muraíle (1985) refers to a legend dating from the 14th Century which suggests that the forebears of Clann Máille migrated from Co. Limerick sometime in the 6th Century A.D. The most famous of the Ó Máilles was Grace O' Malley (*Gráinne Ní Mháille)*, or *Gráinne Uáile,*

1. Introduction

the pirate and sea Queen, renowned in legend and folklore, but as we have seen is surprisingly not mentioned in the Annals.

2. Croaghaun Mountain and Lough Bunnafreva West © Cambridge University

Chapter 2

HISTORY OF MAYO

The name, Mayo or *Mag nÉo (The Plain of Yews)* can be traced back to the early 8th century A.D. when Bede referring to (St.) Colman's exodus from Britain after the Synod of Whitby in 664 A.D. says: *"After leaving Britain, Bishop Colman founded two monasteries in Ireland".* These were on *Inishboufind*, the island of the white cow (Inishbofin), and at *Magh nÉo* (Mayo).

The County of Mayo which comprises an area of 2,084 square miles (5,398 sq.km.) was established over four hundred years ago, following the Division of Connaught in 1574, and was comprised of the results of rough surveys which had been made from time to time.

"The County of Mayo - containing Eighter Connaught and such other counties as are under MacWilliam Eighter, and are divided into baronies to be named as followeth, but the same county is not yet divided into ploughlands by reason whereof the parishes could not be put in order of the baronies, but are written by themselves." An example is:*"Murrisk, containing Owle Imale and the lands, viz., Inishturk and Inishark, Cliara (Clare Island) and Aukilles (Achill), O'Malley chief. "*
Knox (1908:181).

Baronies

There are now ten baronies in County Mayo: Burrishoole, Carra, Clanmorris, Costello, Erris, Gallen, Kilmaine, Murrisk, Tirawley and Tireagh. The two baronies which feature prominently in this book are the baronies of Burrishoole and Murrisk, formerly called Umhall or the Owles.

Sir Henry Sidney, Lord Deputy of Ireland in the sixteenth century, maintained that Mayo at that time was in a state of turmoil, with local chieftains marauding and killing without fear of retribution. He suppressed some of the rebellions but many of the perpetrators escaped punishment. He bestowed a knighthood upon MacWilliam Eighter (Bourke), after which the latter pledged fealty to the crown on his own behalf and on behalf of his fellow land-owners:

> *"He brought with him all his Brethren, MacPhillippin, who in surname is a Borke, as he is; and besides them, a great Number of Owners of lands and castles, lying in the same country: Omaylle came likewise with him, who is an original Irish Man, strong in galleys and Seamen: he earnestly sued to hold of the Queen, and to pay her rent and service."* Knox (1908).

O' Malley was afterwards made *Seneschal* (Governor) of his own land in *Oulymaley*.

Burrishoole

Buirghís Umhaill (burgage = town), from which it is said the barony took its name is situated on the north-east shore of Clew Bay, the boundary emanating 5 miles due north of Westport. Burrishoole was later superseded by Newport Pratt, founded by a Treasury official named Pratt in the early 18th century. Henry Butler, the first Anglo-Norman Lord in the area built castles in County Mayo in 1238 A.D. and is recorded as having a *fee* of half a cantred there which was called after him *Owyll-Butler*. He is said to have built a castle there and a small town called *Burgheis Owyl*. Henry's kinsman, John Butler, still held this *fee* until 1333 after which the Butler family disappeared from Burrishoole. The de Burgos then acquired possession which they held until 1583, ending with the demise of *Riocard an Iaráinn Bourke* (MacWilliam Eighter). An inquisition between December, 1420 A.D. and January, 1421, into the Earl of Desmond's lands, said that he held the manors of *"Owlis"* (the Owles in County Mayo) off the heir of Edmund de Burgo. Curtis (1935:49). Edmund de Burgo had married Saive O'Malley in 1330 and it may have been this alliance that helped the de Burgos gain possession of Burrishoole. By 1592 the fortunes of the Bourkes were on the wane. Sir Richard Bingham, Governor of Connacht at this time commented on the lack of possessions and manpower held by the offspring of *Riocard-an-Iaráinn*. This is confirmed by the fact that Bingham was able to berth his ships in Burrishoole harbour and penetrate the islands of Lower Umhall.

Achill

After the Battle of the Yellow Ford in 1598, the victorious O'Donnells sent their soldiers with instructions to seize all the herds of cattle in Burrishoole, in retaliation for the support given by the Bourkes and O'Malleys to the English. This event is recorded in the *Annals of the Four Masters* :*"They collected all the cattle that were on the mainland outside the small islands, and though great was the gathering and collection of preys they made, they encountered no danger or difficulty on account of them, save only the trouble of removing and driving them off."*

During the reign of Elizabeth I in the late 16th century, her cousin, James (the Black Earl), became 10th Earl of Ormond and claimed to be entitled to the old Butler *fee*, based on titles which depended on the original grant, and this was provided in the *Composition of Mayo 1585*, and later confirmed in 1612 when James I:

" *granted Thomas, eleventh Earl of Ormond, exemption from all impositions on his manors and lands, including the Isles of Achill."* *McNally (1973:24).*

Thomas also got a Grant of Aughrim and Burrishoole:*"the Castle, lands and tenements of Ackille containing four quarters of land, and they were perambulated in circuit on each side by the sea-shore; all of which premises lie in said County Mayo."* Curtis (1943:51). Thus, Thomas *Dubh* (Black Tom) Butler gained possession of 5,000 acres of land in Burrishoole formerly belonging to the Mayo Butlers.

In the *Strafford Inquisition of County Mayo* in 1635, James Butler, twelfth Earl of Ormond, is recorded as being in possession of *"the castle, town, island and four quarters of Achill."* The Cromwellian Commissioners in 1655-56 dispossessed Ormond, and Curtis (1943) says:

"I cannot find that he was restored to it in any of the grants made to him under the Act ." Curtis (1943).

The Butlers of Ormond, however, retained possession of the Mayo Butler lands until 1696 when the Earl of Arran, grandson of Black Tom leased the Burrishoole Estate to Henry Bingham and at the same time leased it in *"reversion"* (the right of obtaining the estate after Bingham)

2. History of Mayo

to Thomas Medlycott, Commissioner for Revenue for Mayo and Deputy Steward of Westminster under the Duke of Ormond, for 999 years. Bingham failed to pay his rent and Medlycott acquired the estate, selling it in 1785 to Sir Neal O'Donnell for £35,598.19s.4d.

Burrishoole Abbey

Burrishoole Abbey which lies close to the old Butler castle was founded in 1469 by Riocard Bourke (the MacWilliam). In 1580 the Abbey at Burrishoole is described by Sir Nicholas Malbie as:

"an abbey standing very pleasant upon a river side, within three miles of the sea, where a ship of five hundred tons may lie at low water. It hath a goodly and large lough on the upper part of the river, full of great timber, grey marble, and many other commodities of all sides, not without great store of good ground, both arable land and pasture. Specially it hath a very plentiful iron mine and abundance of wood every way. Towards the sea coast there lieth many fair islands, rich and plentiful of all commodities; there cometh hither every year likely about fifty English ships for fishing; they have been before this time compelled to pay a great tribute to the O'Malleys, which I have forbidden hereafter till her majesty's pleasure be known. It is accounted one of the best fishing places in Ireland for salmon, herring and all kinds of sea fish." Knox (1908:189).

Murrisk

Murrisk means a swamp or sea-marsh. It formed part of the ancient territory of Akil and Umhall. It was referred to as *Muiriscc Aigli* by Tírechán in the 7th century A.D. and as *Moriske* or *Owles O Mayle* on Browne's Map of 1584. The Augustinian Abbey, established in Murrisk in the mid-15th century was built by Tadhg Ó Máille, a local chieftain. Ó Muraíle (1985). James Garvey, brother of Archbishop Garvey of Armagh was granted a lease of the Abbey in 1578 A.D. by Elizabeth I. Both Garveys were the sons of Finola (*nee* Butler) and John Garvey of Murrisk. Finola appears to have been a direct descendant of the Butlers of Mayo and may have been the last of her line.

11

3. Ireland before the Anglo-Norman Invasion, after Dalton (1910)

Chapter 3

DERIVATION OF THE NAME

Various spellings of Achill are rendered in extant texts and summarised from Westropp (1914).

Name	Year	Source
Oigle/ Aicill	*c.1250*	**Cath Maighe Léna**
Eccuill	*1235-1384*	**The Annals of Connacht**
		Italian map by Angelino Dulcert.
Akkill	*1379*	**Calendar of Ormond Deeds**
Archoill	*1351-1448*	*Portolan maps*
Ardroill/ Ardroin/ Arclon	*1450*	*Portolan maps*
C-d'aquilla	*1450*	*Upsal portolan*
C-daquil	*1500*	*Juan de la Cosa*
Karchill	*1512*	**Calendar of Ormond Deeds**
C-d'agulla	*1516*	*Portolan maps*
c-d'aquilla	*1544*	*Baptist Agnesis map*
c-dacilla	*1568*	*Domingo Olives*
Aukilles	*1574*	*Division of Connaught*
Aukylles	*1574*	*Portolan maps*
Arkyll/Akyll/Alkyl	*1590-1610*	**Elizabethan and Stuart maps**
C. d'Equilla	*1593*	*Portolan maps*
Eacuill/Acuill	*1600*	*Téige Dall O'Higgins*
Achill	*1612*	**Calendar of Ormond Deeds**
Achill	*1635*	**Strafford Inquisition**
Akil	*1655*	**Books of Survey and Distribution**

Achill

Oighle, which at one time comprised a large tract of territory extending from Killary Harbour in County Galway to Clew Bay, later contracted to a much smaller area with Cruachan Oighle (Croagh Patrick) at its centre. Oighle, the earliest version of the placename, Achill, appears in the text of Cath Maighe Léna (The Battle of Moylena), a manuscript supposedly depicting events of the 2nd century A.D. but not written down until the 12th century A.D. On the basis of the linguistic evidence, Cath Maighe Léna is, according to Jackson (1938), set in the latter half of the thirteenth century, or early fourteenth century A.D. The reference to Oighle appears in versions B and L2 of Cath Maighe Léna, version B written down in 1671-74 by Daniel O'Duigenan (Royal Irish Academy Catalogue: 586), and the L2 version written down in 1708-11 (Royal Irish Academy Catalogue:172). Cath Maighe Léna tells the story of the division of Ireland between Eógan Mór and Conn (Cétchathach) of the Hundred Battles. The story of the killing of Eógan Mór by Goll MacMorna is unknown but the death of Fraech, brother-in-law of Eógan at the hands of Conn has parallels in the **Dindshenchas** of Carn Fraech. There appears to be three Fraechs, the most famous of whom was Fraech Mac Fidaig of the Gamanrad of Iorrus.

Eccuill is the version which appears in the ***Annals of Connacht*** in 1235 when the island was plundered by the Anglo-Normans and the Irish allies of the Justiciar, Maurice Fitzgerald. Other places mentioned included *"the Dunadh Sleibi moir"* and *"the Dun maigh shliabh,"* both of which appear to have been located in the Slievemore-Dugort area. The Achill connection with ***Cath Maighe Léna*** derives from legends linking both *Fraech* and *Goll Mac Morna* with the island. The story of the killing of Eógan Mór, one of the main characters in this tale, by *Goll Mac Morna,* a Connacht champion and a member of Conn's army, came about as a result of Conn sending a messenger to Achill to enlist the help of Goll. Prior to the battle, Conn had also enlisted the help of *Eochy Whiteknee* (Eochaid Glungeal), and *Fiachaidh Whitehand (Fiachaid Laimh-Geal),* sons of *Crimhthann Culbuide, King of Aichill and Umhall,* said to be Conn's foster brothers, to present terms of settlement to Eógan Mór. Although acting as emissaries for Conn at the camp of Eógan Mór,

3. Derivation of the name

they were imprisoned and later hanged, for apparently telling Eógan that Conn, although suing for peace, did not intend to keep it!

Tírechán, a seventh century scribe and native of the district translated *Silva Vocluti*, one of the very few topographical placenames mentioned by St. Patrick in his **Confessio** as *Coill Acla* (*Ard Choill* =High Wood). This is an interesting translation if one compares it to the respective meaning of Akil and Umhall: Akil could be said to mean *Ard/choill* i.e. the High Wood and Umhall the Low Wood, which fits in with the meaning derived from Murrisk and Burrishoole i.e. highland and lowland! *Silva V(v)ocluti* (The Wood of Voclut or the Sheltering Wood); if we were to assume that the wood in question *sheltered under a mountain* and this was near the western sea (*prope mare occidentale*), one might reasonably speculate that the place of St. Patrick's captivity was in Achill!

Aicill is depicted on early maps and appears to have embraced a large area extending from Killary Harbour on the Galway-Mayo border to Killala Bay in North Mayo. Italian portolan maps indicate that Achill was on a trading route and was then pronounced broadly *Archoll* or *Archill* as depicted on maps of 1351, and 1448; "*c-dacilla*" is depicted on maps of 1568 and from 1590 to 1610. The inclusion of Achill in the portolan maps of the fifteenth and sixteenth centuries A.D. is probably an indication of its maritime importance on a main trading route, although, as yet, no definite evidence exists for this conclusion, except perhaps some rather unusual Medieval glass fragments found in Slievemore. McDonald (Interim Report, 1995).

Elizabethan and early Stuart maps depict the island as *Arkyll, Akyll,* and the *Aukilles viz* : "*the Barony of Murrisk containing Owleymale and the islands, Inishturk, Inishoirke (Inishshark), Clare and the Aukilles .*" *Akkill* appears in the **Calendar of Ormond Deeds** in 1379; *Eacaill* in the **"Colloquy between the poet Fintan and the Hawk of Eacaill"** in the fifteenth century text of the **Book of Fermoy**. In the **Books of Survey and Distribution,** (1641) *Akil* is described as the north-west portion of the Barony of Burrishoole or Lower Umhall; William Petty's **Hiberniae delineato** in 1685 depicts Achill in the now familiar L-shape. On the first

Achill

Ordnance Survey maps of 1838-1840 Achill lands include the island of Achill, Achill Beg Island, Inishbiggle Island, the Corraun Peninsula on the mainland, and the lands of Tonragee and Owenduff extending to the west of Mulranny.

The name Achill is today thought to refer to the colony of eagles which were once populous on Achill, particularly *Aquila albicilla,* the white-tailed sea eagle, now extinct in Ireland but according to Newman (1839) common on the island up to the mid-nineteenth century and the itinerant Golden Eagle seen by Lloyd Praeger in 1898. "*Yew wood,*" was also another translation and this brings us back to the derivation of Akil and Umhall, the High Wood and the Low Wood. The name of the County of Mayo is as we have seen, *Maighe Eo,* meaning *"Plain of yew trees."*

4. The Sound © Theresa McDonald

16

Chapter 4

THE ISLAND

"This sublime theatre, composed of so many great scenes informed and coloured by a mighty artist, long detained us in silent admiration. How majestic these mountains. How placid the blue Atlantic! How interesting this island, with its agriculture, hamlets and fisheries beneath the eye." Trotter (1819).

Achill has long been renowned for the magnificence of its scenery and as a well-known tourist resort but comparatively little is known about its early history and archaeology. This book endeavours to rectify these omissions in the light of present knowledge. It cannot, however, claim to be a definitive account of the island, as too many questions still remain unanswered, particularly for the period between the thirteenth and seventeenth centuries when the island was owned by a number of prominent families: O'Connors, Butlers, Bourkes and O'Malleys.

5. Dún na Glaise Promontory Fort, Cloughmore © *T.McDonald*

Achill Island is the largest island off the Irish coast and is connected to the mainland by the Michael Davitt Bridge at Achill Sound. The island is

Achill

shaped like an inverted L, and is located off the west coast of County Mayo, encircled by Clew Bay on the south and Blacksod Bay on the north. Claimed by many to be an island in name only, the Michael Davitt Bridge, only two hundred yards wide and opened in 1888, separates Achill from the mainland, although Achill Civil Parish extends to Mulranny. The island embraces an area of fifty seven square miles which includes the smaller islands of Achill Beg and Inishbiggle. It measures fifteen miles from east to west and eleven miles from north to south, narrowing to eight miles at Keel (Caol, meaning narrow quarter). Keel in Irish could also derive from *Cill*, meaning a Church! Its location at 54° North and 10° West makes it the most westerly island in Europe and according to McNally (1973) *"an outpost in terms of human settlement and flora and fauna."* Prior to the late eighteenth century there were no proper roads on the island so access would have mainly been by sea. The sea channel known as The Sound effectively separates Achill from the mainland and allows shipping passage through the Sound obviating the need to traverse the longer sea journey around Achill Head.

Two-thirds of the island is covered by peat, mainly its centre, while a large portion of coastal arable land is cultivated peat or sand. The vast majority of settlement is coastal based, a phenomenon that extends back to the Early Medieval Period. At the end of the nineteenth century, a rail line was extended from Westport to Achill Sound, facilitating connections with the rest of Ireland but this rail extension was closed in 1937. Today, the nearest rail connection is at Westport, some 38 miles away from the village of Dooagh.

The Elizabethans showed Achill as two islands with a dividing line extending from Dugort to the Minaun Cliffs at Keel, but this erroneous depiction was probably the result of viewing Achill from the sea near Inishbofin, from where the low-lying land of Keel sandybanks not being visible, the impression created was that of two islands. Known fluctuations in sea level in the post-glacial period indicate that Keel sandybanks may have been an embayment but this status was unlikely to have persisted as late as the Elizabethan period.

4. The Island

Fluctuations in sea level are indicated by the partially submerged peat banks seen along the seashore from Bunacurry to Achill Sound and at Dugort where pine stumps in the sand testify to the presence here of a once substantial forest.

Achill Beg Island, formerly depicted on maps as *Kildavnet (Kil-da-mat)* was probably cut off from the main island as a result of submergence which cut open the sea channel known as The Sound. This event also bi-sected Gubnahardin Promontory Fort and cut off Achill Beg Island from the main island. Dúnnaglas Promontory Fort, west of Achill Beg is today regularly cut off from Achill at high tide. This sea incursion no doubt is responsible for the transference of the placename, Kildavnet, from Achill Beg to its present location in the area centred on the Tower House, north-east of Cloughmore. The placename, Gubnahardia, on the other hand is today found on either side of the Sound, in Gubnahardin Promontory Fort and in Gubnahardia townland in Corraun.

Achill has many interesting features like its varied and unique geology, the lowest corrie lake in Ireland, the highest cliffs in Europe, coupled with a unique relict flora. For the tourist the island has, as Robert Lloyd Praeger so eloquently put it, *"a strange charm which everybody feels but none can explain."* The remote location of the island, at the western extremity of Ireland prompted an Achill schoolboy to describe Ireland as a large island off Achill! The Atlantic Ocean has ensured Achill's insularity and enveloped it in a time-warp, where customs and practices long since abandoned elsewhere, continue there. This extreme western location is said to have ensured that the two highest mountains in Achill, Slievemore 671 metres (2,214 feet) and Croaghaun, 664 metres (2,192 feet) at the western end of the island were not covered by ice during the last (Midlandian) glaciation of Ireland some 10-12,000 years ago. Farrington (1932). Whether or not this fact was responsible for the survival of relict flora of Arctic-Alpine, Lusitanian and North American species, many thousands of miles from their present-day habitats, is still a matter of controversy, but their presence in Achill adds to the island's uniqueness. Lough Nakeeroge East, the lowest corrie lake in Ireland, is set like a jewel in Annagh, a remote valley of spectacular scenery but accessible only on foot. This area featured in a short article entitled

Achill

"The Back of Beyond " in the ***Capuchin Annual*** . Barry (1973). Another corrie lake, Lough Bunafreeva West, is precariously perched 1500 feet above the sea at the edge of a steep precipitous cliff, on the western side of Croaghaun mountain, whose cliffs are said to be among the finest in Europe. Superimposed upon this unique geology and flora is a wealth of archaeological monuments ranging in date from the Mesolithic Period (Middle Stone Age) to the Late Medieval Period. Historically the island, although rarely featuring in the Annals, nevertheless played host to many of the great families of the day, some of whose descendants are said to be among the ancestors of the present British Crown. Achill was the last place in Ireland where *booleying*, the removal of livestock to summer pasture was practised and the extant *booley* villages, unique in the way of life they portray, are a major source of information on vernacular architecture and deserve to be studied in depth and preserved. It is hoped that the many people in Achill who care so passionately about the island and who are so well versed in its history will set up a Society (Historical and Archaeological) to monitor and preserve this valuable heritage.

The population of Achill is predominantly Roman Catholic with small pockets of members of the Church of Ireland located throughout the island, notably at Dugort and Achill Sound. The census of 1841 returned a population figure of 4,901 for the island but by 1851 this had declined to 4,075, the result of emigration and loss of life due to the the Great Famine. This however compares favourably with figures for Co. Mayo where the loss was much greater. By 1881 the Achill population had again increased to 5,060 and to 5,260 by 1911. There was a short-term decline between 1881 and 1891, due to local crop failure, which resulted in increased mortality and emigration. Population figures were maintained at a reasonable level by revenue sent back by migratory workers in Scotland and England. From the 1960's onwards the population of Achill has been decreasing steadily. This decline is particularly worrying when cognisance is taken of the age structure of the population which is largely made up of dependent children and senior citizens. How to halt this decline is problematical. Tourism, to be viable, needs the tourist season to be extended considerably, while manufacturing industries have problems of access to major markets,

4. The Island

distance and transport costs being prohibitive. Long-term sustainable employment is actively being sought all over Ireland. To compete and survive in this climate, Achill needs to mount a major review of its employment strategy.

Population Figures - Intercensal Periods

Period	Achill	Co. Mayo	Ireland
1841-51	-16.80	-29.40	-21.70
1851-61	+8.60	-7.20	-13.90
1861-71	+3.20	-3.40	-7.90
1871-81	+10.80	-0.30	-4.50
1881-91	-7.60	-10.70	-10.40
1891-1901	+3.20	-9.10	-7.10
1901-11	+9.00	-3.50	-2.30
1911-26	-1.70	-10.10	-5.30
1926-36	-2.70	-6.60	-0.10
1936-46	+1.10	-8.20	-0.50
1946-51	-0.10	-4.20	+0.20
1951-56	-8.30	-6.20	-2.10
1956-61	-9.40	-7.30	-2.80
1961-66	-12.20	-6.30	+2.30
1966-71	-12.40	-5.20	+3.30
1971-79	-1.70	+2.50	+8.00
1979-81	+0.10	+1.60	+5.70
1981-86	+1.30	+0.40	+2.80
1986-91	-10.30	-3.90	-0.40

Source: Central Statistics Office, Dublin.

Achill

Achill Population Figures, 1961-91

1961	1966	1971	1979	1981	1986	1991
4069	3958	3129	3089	3190	3148	2500

Inishbiggle Island Population Figures, 1961-91

1961	1966	1971	1979	1981	1986	1991
113	103	112	97	89	69	51

Source: Central Statistics Office, Dublin.

From 1971 to 1986 the population of Achill appeared to have stabilised to around 3,000 but, unfortunately, the latest census indicates that the trend is again downwards. The same applies to Inishbiggle, contrasting with late nineteenth and early twentieth century figures for this island which showed an upward trend: 1841 - 67; 1851 - 61, and 1911 - 149.

A high number of the population of Achill and Inishbiggle consists of dependent children and old people, supported by an increasingly diminished active category. This trend is most noticeable in the amalgamation of National Schools on the island and in the laying off of surplus teaching staff. In the past, returned emigrants helped to maintain population levels for as McGrath (1991) pointed out, in 1970, more than one-third of the pupils in McHale College had English birth certificates. Indeed, the 1974 Mayo County Council Draft Development Plan for Achill indicated that in one of four marriages, the husband lived either semi-permanently or permanently away from home. While seasonal migration is now in decline, a large number of the young people now leaving the island with third-level qualifications may never return.

In the 19th Century, Achill lay within the Congested Districts area. *The Congested Districts Board* was set up in 1891 to provide additional land for areas which had a rateable valuation of less that £1.10s.0d. per head, resulting in an inadequate amount of land to maintain life except at a very low standard. Improvement in the economy and housing were as a direct result of the *Congested Districts Board*, while the breakup of the *Rundale* system of farming necessitated fencing in and cultivation of additional

4. The Island

land. Upper Achill lies within the *Gaeltacht* with the greatest number of gaelic speaking people in Salia, Derreens, Cloughmore and Bunacurry. Lower Achill, excluded from the Gaeltacht has in recent times made strong representation for inclusion. Upper Achill and Lower Achill are said to be linguistically distinct. Stockman (1974), said that the Irish of Upper Achill had many of the characteristics of Donegal and other northern counties. The demise of the Irish language in Lower Achill is attributed to outside economic and social changes brought about by relative prosperity attained through the tourist industry. Tourism has brought many benefits to the island such as a broader more outward-looking approach to life, and relative prosperity manifested in the proliferation of hotels, guesthouses and cottage accommodation. It may well be that current tourism development will boost and stabilise the population, but attention must be given to the prevailing trend of constructing totally inappropriate buildings on the island. The vernacular house so much a part of the beauty of the landscape is increasingly being abandoned for ultra-modern developments which do little to enhance the landscape and which are unlikely to attract the more discerning tourists to the island.

Today there are seventeen villages in Achill with a population of 2,500 (Census, 1991). Six churches cater for the Roman Catholic majority on the island while the two Church of Ireland establishments are surplus to the requirements of the dwindling Church of Ireland community. Increasingly it seems the National Schools are amalgamating to cater for the reduction in school pupils. The Secondary School at Achill Sound, *"Scoil Damhnat"* and the Vocational School at the same location cater for the vast majority of second-level pupils on the island.

Long-term employment is practically non-existent, most jobs being seasonal in nature such as tourism and fishing. A number of small industries have been set up from time to time but few survive for any length of time. Seasonal employment is provided by local hotels, guesthouses and private accommodation, while fishing and farming provide additional although mostly uncertain income.

Chapter 5

GEOGRAPHY

"Foremost in grandeur and beauty of the Western islands of Ireland is seal-sentried peaked Achill."   Mr. & Mrs. S. C. Hall (1841-43).

The influence exerted on Achill island by virtue of its geographical location at the extreme western end of Ireland is further compounded by an inhospitable physical background, with the wind being the dominating climatic factor, exerting great influence on settlement and economy. This Atlantic fringe location does have one advantage in that the island rarely experiences major snowfalls or intense frost. Achill also has a long coastline where high cliffs frequently exceed 1,000 feet (303m) and which is breached at intervals by long sandy beaches. Croaghaun mountain at 2,192 feet (664m) has a two-mile precipice which extends north-eastwards before dropping abruptly into the Atlantic ocean. Five corrie lakes are located on Croaghaun, all at different elevations, ranging from fifty feet (15m) to fifteen hundred feet (454m). The now Deserted Village of Slievemore, extending across the southern slopes of the mountain occupies what is arguably the most sheltered spot on the island. Keem Bay at the western extremity of the island is sheltered by Croaghaun, the Benmore cliffs and Moyteoge. Easily the most popular bathing beach on the island, Keem, pronounced *Cím*, was in the recent past the haunt of the basking shark which attracted by the warm waters of the nearby Gulf stream in Clew Bay, was harpooned and netted in Keem by local fishermen and its oil extracted for export. The largest specimen of the porbeagle caught by rod-and-line in Irish waters was caught off Keem Bay in 1932 by Dr. O'Donnell-Browne and weighed 365 lbs. The head of this specimen can be seen lording it over the bar in the Achill Head Hotel. Other record fish caught off Achill include a Tub Gurnard caught near Bullsmouth in 1973, weighing 5.5 kg and a Blue Shark caught off Achill Head in 1959 weighing 93.4 kg (Irish Records & Specimen Weights, 1995). Clew Bay abounds with a large variety of fish, with anglers from all over the world participating in the many fishing festivals held in the area each year, probably because the largest variety

5. Geography

of sea fish caught in Irish waters have come from Clew Bay. Prichard (1987). Salmon are reasonably plentiful in season and sea bass can be caught by rod and line at Keem Bay. A Sea-Food Festival held annually in July now attracts thousands of visitors to Achill each year.

North of Keem Bay, a geological boundary separates the Keem schist from the Keem conglomerate and here at this boundary is a seam of *amethyst*, varying in colour from pale violet to deep purple, which provides many happy hours of activity for *treasure seekers,* including in 1996, the American Ambassador, Jean Kennedy-Smith.

Moving north-eastwards to Annagh, a valley with steep precipitous cliffs is dominated by Lough Nakeeroge East, at an elevation of just 15m O.D. is the lowest corrie lake in Ireland. Its moraine separates the lake from the sea. This area, rightly deserves a name applied to it by Barry (1973), "***The Back of Beyond*** " for the terrain here is indicative of an area which has been subjected to much upheaval. This is manifested in the presence of rugged hills, deep crevasses, mountain streams and glacial phenomena. Perhaps the most spectacular of the glacial phenomena is Lough Bunnafreva West, located south-east of Saddle Head and perched precariously over 1,000 feet (303m) above sea level. Adjacent to it on the west is what P.J. Joyce (1910) described as *"the most tremendous precipice in Ireland."* These massive, almost perpendicular cliffs, located on the north-western face of Croaghaun, at c. 2,000 feet (606 m)Ordnance Datum, are said to be the highest cliffs in Europe. The largest of the corrie lakes on Croaghaun is Lough Acorrymore at an elevation of just over 600 feet (181m); it dominates the village of Dooagh and provides a water supply for the whole island. The coast at this western tip of Achill is cliffed except at Keem Bay and Annagh. Behind Moyteoge Head, a narrow promontory, over one mile long and c.500 feet (152m) high called Achill Head, juts out into the sea and terminates in two sea stacks, called *Gaoí Saggart* and *Carrickakin.* Both names may be derived from the shape of the rocks which from land look like the head and torso of a man. The former is also associated with a Priest's escape during the Penal Times.

Achill

South-east of Achill Head are the Bills Rock, a natural bird sanctuary; east of Achill Head, near Keem Bay are partially submerged rocks known as *"The Daisies"* where three members of a film crew were drowned while filming *"**Shark Island** "* in 1953. The sole survivor of this tragedy, Hugh Falkus, who swam into Keem Bay for help, died early in 1996.

Inishgallon, a small island south of Purteen Harbour provides shelter for boats anchored in the harbour over winter. To the west are the villages of Pollagh and Dooagh. The small, rocky beach in Dooagh has been eroded out of less resistant rock while the village itself, originally a fishing village clustered close to the sea-shore, has been continually extended by the reclamation of additional bogland. A steep hill, the Brae, connects Dooagh to Pollagh, a small linear village and the location of one of the Roman Catholic Churches on the island. Ribbon development connects Pollagh with Keel, now the main village on the island, with shops, a post office, several restaurants and a local pottery. Keel Lake, the largest on the island covers an area of one square mile and is home to a small colony of swans. A river flows southward from this lake across Keel sandybanks before finding its way to the sea at Trawmore, an impressive beach that stretches for some two miles from east to west and which is a favourite haunt for wind-surfers, bathers and others. Strong currents at the eastern end of the beach make swimming in this area hazardous. North-east of Trawmore is Sruhillbeg Lough, a small lake dammed by deposits of sand and gravel.

Northward the towering peak of Slievemore provides shelter from the bitter north-east winds for the now Deserted Village nestling on its south-facing slopes. The village, originally comprising three linear settlements, known respectively as *Tuar, Tuar Riábhach* and *Faiche* all denote the names of fields *i.e. Tuar* meaning cattle fold/pasture or sheep-run which fits in with a derivation given to me by a local school teacher, John McNamara, Dooagh who interpreted it as: *"the walled garden (field) where cattle are kept, particularly at night." Tuar Riábhach* , meaning a striped or speckled field and *Faiche,* a meadow or green field.

The Deserted Village is linked to the village of Dooagh by a bog road which in the past provided access for the annual summer *booley* which commenced on the 1st May. The Green Road, constructed with military precision traverses the valley bottom of the Deserted Village and may have connected Keel with the Napoleonic Tower which overlooks Slievemore (*pers. comm.* J.J. McNamara). Alternatively, it may have been constructed as part of a Board of Works scheme during the Great Famine. A quartz quarry at *Leath Baile,* west of the Deserted Village was commercially mined between 1910 and 1916 by the *Irish Industrial Minerals Company* of Westport and a two feet gauge railway covered the six miles from Slievemore to Purteen harbour, where the quartz was transported by Hooker to Westport. McNally (1973). This quarry according to the geological maps contained rare deposits of tourmaline while north of the Deserted Village around the 400-500 feet contour small deposits of malachite and azurite were located.

On the south-eastern slopes of Slievemore mountain are a group of megalithic tombs, dating to the Neolithic Period some five thousand years ago. Interspersed with the megalithic tombs and the Deserted Village are a palimpsest of field systems of varying periods and remnants of hut sites of Bronze Age or Early Medieval date. Slievemore Caher, which was destroyed in the early part of the present century, was probably of Iron Age or Early Medieval date, while Slievemore graveyard contains remnants of a small Church and a number of stone crosses of Early Medieval date, together with a later *cillín* (childrens'graveyard).

The summit of Slievemore provides a *"bird's eye"* view of the whole island, although for the less energetic the view from The Star, a white quartzite boulder mid-way up the mountain, provides an equally enthralling vista. The north-east face of Slievemore which overlooks the village of Dugort and the Achill Mission Settlement is scarred by a corrie which runs from near the summit to sea level. Dugort has two magnificent beaches, the Golden Strand and the Silver Strand which are separated by drift deposits, part of which have been eroded away to form a small inlet called Porteen.

From Dugort, through the Valley and on to Dooniver, the land is comparatively low lying and consists either of bog, reclaimed bog, drift deposits or sand dunes, the latter being particularly prevalent around the Valley and Caher Point. Caher Point is the location of a *cillín*, while part of the nearby cliff edge has recently been eroded away to reveal a midden belonging to a seventeenth century settlement and associated graveyard, probably *Tóin an tSean Bhaile* (Bottom of the Old Town). To the east are the villages of the Valley and Dooniver which occupy an area of relatively low-lying bogland, interspersed with drift deposits and sand dunes. Several small lakes, Sruhill, Lough Gall, Nambrack, Lough Doo are located west of the Valley. Dooniver also has several lakes and at Bullsmouth, a sea channel separates Achill from Inishbiggle island. Westward from Bunacurry to Dookinella is a vast expanse of bog covering the central part of the island. East of Dookinella Thulis the bogland is interspersed with several small lakes: Lough Annascaddy containing a *crannóg* and Lough Naneaneen in Bunacurry. A drumlin north-east of Dookinella Church probably represents a standstill phase during the Midlandian, the last glacial event in Ireland. Between Dookinella and Bunacurry is the townland of Maumnaman, an area of poor drainage and deep bog, interspersed with small pockets of gravel and sand.

The rounded hills of eastern Achill contrast sharply with those in the west. Mweelin is a quartzite ridge running North-East by South-West extending to 1,530 feet (464 metres) at the summit. Knockmore mountain 1,112 feet (337m) is composed of schist and consequently in contrast to the quartzite peak of Mweelin has a more rounded outline with several high points, the highest on the north extends to 1,119 feet (339 m), descending to 700 feet (212m) on the south. Between Knockmore and Bunafahy mountain, whose summit reaches 941 feet (285m), is an area of wet boggy land containing the now deserted village of Bunafahy.

South of Bunafahy village is a headland containing a promontory fort which is composed of quartzite rocks which are used as decorative stonework for walls and house facades. The Atlantic Drive commences at Cloughmore, west of the harbour at Darby's Point, and traverses an area of spectacular scenery, which includes Ashleam Bay, a small sandy cove where *The Sceptre of Limerick* was wrecked and the famous *"horse-shoe"* bend which terminates south-west of Ashleam village, a clachán

5. Geography

with its ancient *"lazy-bed"* field systems. Turning westward at this T-junction the road continues through a drift-filled and boulder-strewn landscape leading to Camport Bay and the village of Dooega. Dooega is a small sheltered valley backed by Mweelin mountain on the west and bisected by the Dooega river which runs into Camport Bay. Northward is the village of Mweelin, once home to the Achill Mission Training School, together with a small settlement of staff houses, school and church. Mweelin terminates in another vast expanse of bog, with depths exceeding four to six metres in places and in which can be seen the remains of large pine stumps which belie the present treeless landscape. These pine stumps are located at least half-a-metre from the base of the bog. Their presence indicates drier conditions or a stand-still phase, intermediate between the original and later bog growth, for trees will not grow in the water-logged conditions necessary for bog growth. At the onset of deteriorating climatic conditions in the Late Bronze Age, the trees died and the stumps (largely Scots Pine) that we see in the bog today are the remains of this Bronze Age pine forest.

Cashel, the site of a prehistoric Caher, now provides access to the Booster Station which located on top of Minaun commands a breath-taking view of most of Achill. North-east of Cashel is Salia Hill at 336 feet (97m) one of the smaller of the Achill hills which overlooks Salia Bay, a narrow sea channel. On the eastern side of the hill and directly north of Achill Sound is Bleannahooey Strand. Southward towards Achill Sound, the coast is lined with huge banks of peat, eroded out by the sea and indicating major fluctuations in sea level and the comparatively recent cutting of this sea channel. Submerged peats are believed to be mainly of post-glacial age and indicate progressive submergence of the coast in the last 10,000 years. Stephens and Glasscock (1970). The depth of this channel varies considerably in places being no more than two feet at low tide and rarely exceeding six fathoms at high tide, making for critical navigation. South of Achill Sound bridge are several sand banks which in the past facilitated easy access across the Sound.The Sound sea-channel extends from Bullsmouth on the north to Cloughmore on the south and connects Blacksod Bay with Clew Bay. The island of Achill Beg, formerly called *Kil-da-mat* on sixteenth century maps is separated from the main island by a stretch of water known as the Blind Sound. The Blind Sound is bordered by huge boulders to the west, providing uncertain access to Achill Beg Island at low tide. The presence of *Cnoc na Ceasaighe* (the Wicker Causeway), located in Corraun and orientated in an east-west direction suggests a former crossing place here, providing access to Achill prior to the flooding of the sea channel. East of Achill Beg, a massive sandbank known as the *Cleigh Mhór* is avoided by local fishing boats and pleasure craft.

"Although protected by Clare Island, Clew Bay is subjected to powerful Atlantic swells and the rate of change of coastal outline can be measured accurately as spits and tombolas form and reform among the drumlin islands." Stephens & Glasscock (1970:13).

A *tombola* is a spit or sand-bar joining an island to another landmass. The *Cleigh Mhór* is such a phenomenon. Settlement on Achill Beg Island is located in a narrow valley between two hills, one of which is named The Scalp and is made up of sandstone blocks and faces south towards Clare Island. East of this is a beautiful small sandy beach known as *Trá Bó Dearg* (the strand of the red cow). Achill Beg Island has an underlying geology of schist with huge boulders of graphitic schist strewn on the northern shore. Achill Beg is now uninhabited, except for a brief period in summer, when the owners of holiday cottages take up temporary residence on the island.

Geology

The basement rocks of Achill and Corraun are pre-Cambrian in origin, formed over seven hundred million years ago and represent some of the oldest rocks in Ireland.The geology of Achill has been studied by many eminent geologists, notably Kennedy (1969) whose study of the albite schists has raised some interesting questions concerning tectonic movements in Clew Bay. Whittow (1974) dealt mainly with the question of glaciation, following in the footsteps of Charlesworth (1930-52) and Farrington (1932-53) both of whom carried on a lively debate in print concerning the glaciation or non-glaciation of the western tip of Achill as

5. Geography

well as debating the origins of the Irish flora and fauna, and the survival
in Achill of *"refuge species"*, that is plants whose place of origin was
very far from Achill. Max (1972-73 and 1974) carried out some research
on the stratigraphy and structure of Achill while recent geological
research has been carried out by Dr. David Harris of Keele University in
Britain and Dr. Jude Harkin of University College, Galway.

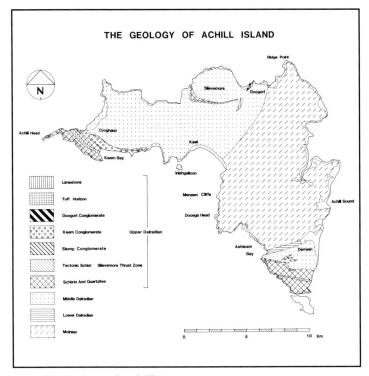

6. The Geology of Achill

Croaghaun mountain, the location of five corrie lakes and the finest
cliffs in Europe, rightly deserves the description applied to them by
Caesar Otway (1839): *"...a remnant of some lost Continent lost forever
beneath the waves."* The geological structure of Achill is composed of
schist, mica-schist, semetic schist, gneiss and quartzite, with pockets of
granite, limestone, feldspar and schistose conglomerates dispersed

throughout the island. Generally speaking, quartzite forms the mountain peaks and schist the lowland valleys. Layers of peat overlie drift deposits at many places while partially submerged peat-hags suggest a more extensive coastline in the past. The tale of *Hy-Brazil*, a mythical island supposedly seen off Achill every seven years is probably a folk memory of submergence by the sea in the later prehistoric period. Submergence in comparatively recent times was probably responsible for the destruction of a land bridge between Bullsmouth and Inishbiggle creating a channel 300 yards wide and allowing entrance to The Sound and the separation of Achill Beg Island and Corraun from Achill.

A geological fault which cuts a diagonal line between Dugort on the north-east and the Minaun cliffs on the south-west serves as both a geological and cultural boundary between Upper Achill to the east and Lower Achill to the west. East of the Minaun cliffs and stretching northeastward towards Bunacurry and Dooniver, the relief is lower and the area characterised by hummocky glacial terrain contrasting markedly with that on the west where smooth mountain slopes sweep down to the sea at Keel and Dooagh. The topographical dissimilarity between east and west or what is locally designated Upper and Lower Achill is a factor related to both geology and glacial phenomena. The moraines located throughout the island, but principally those around Lough Acorrymore, provide evidence of advances and retreats of the ice sheets, preceding and including the Midlandian, while the elevation of the various corrie lakes on Croaghaun would seem to indicate that this mountain was never entirely covered by ice but survived as a *nunatak*. According to Whittow (1974), in Lower Achill, the *"irregular kame topography of the last glaciation is missing"* and this has been taken as evidence to support the contention that western Achill lay outside the limits of the Midlandian ice sheets. Following in the footsteps of Farrington (1953) he goes on to say that Croaghaun and Slievemore mountains because of their high elevations and location in peripheral areas like Achill may have survived as nunataks throughout all the advances of the inland ice-sheets:

"The significance of these mountain-top refuges in terms of surviving pre-glacial plant and animal life must not be overstressed, for they would

5. Geography

have experienced a severe periglacial climate on the exposed summits ."
Whittow (1974).

This statement would, however, seem to contradict the present day
evidence from Greenland where hundreds of species of flora flourish in
low-lying coastal areas, adjacent to the glaciers. The question of the non-
glaciation of western Achill was first brought to public attention by the
publication of two papers by Charlesworth (1930) and Farrington (1932),
the debate continuing intermittently for twenty years and ending with two
subsequent papers in 1952 and 1953 respectively.

Charlesworth was adamant that the whole of Ireland had been
submerged beneath a glacial sea while Farrington was of the opinion that
while the Midlandian glaciation had spread from the north, the east-west
orientation of the drumlins in Clew Bay suggested local glacial epochs
and the glacial phenomena on Croaghaun indicated that the maximum
height attained by the ice during the Midlandian was no more than fifteen
hundred feet (454m).

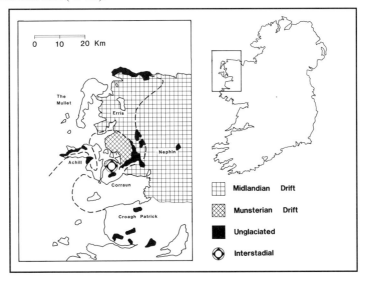

7. Glacial Drifts in North-West Mayo, after Synge (1968)

Achill

Achill does have glacial phenomena and some very interesting glacial phenomena indeed, in that the corries on Croaghaun and Slievemore provide evidence of several major glacial events such as the Wolstonian at Lough Nakeeroge East in Annagh and Corrymore which has both an outer and an inner moraine, representing early and late stages of the Midlandian. Indeed Achill is one of the few places in Ireland where this type of record exists. Other geological features with a possible volcanic origin have recently been noted by Dr. Jude Harkin in a recess of the cliffs at Bunafahy, while on the nearby beach is an excellent example of *imbrication*, in which gravel, pebbles or grains are stacked with their flat surfaces dipping towards the sea. The same geological-sedimentological processes in action today can be also be recognised in the rock record of ancient times. (Dr. Jude Harkin, *pers. comm.*). Good examples of interesting Lower Dalradian lithostratigraphy can be seen at Dugort, Kildavnet, Sraheens, Ashleam, Cashel and Minaun. It would seem, therefore, that both the physical and the cultural remains in Achill could form the backbone of a multi-disciplinary study.

Soils

The Achill soils are shallow and immature, the majority being cultivated acid peat, low in nutrients and because of the underlying parent rock of quartzite and schist, deficient in essential minerals such as cobalt and copper. This is further compounded by heavy leaching from intense rainfall, poor drainage and overgrazing by sheep. In the cool, moist climate of Achill, leaching is a major factor in the formation of iron-pan podzols and gley soils, leading ultimately to the growth of blanket bog. In nineteenth century Achill, it was common practice for boat-loads of turf to be exchanged for lime, the latter being almost non-existent on the island. Edward Nangle of the Achill Mission quickly saw that lime was an essential ingredient in the reclamation of bogland and his success is graphically illustrated by the following tribute:

"...where soils were so fertile that large crops of oats, potatoes, cabbage, savoys, sea kale, broad beans, carrots and parsnip, as well as onions and turnips were grown ." Newman (1839).

34

5. Geography

Shells and seaweed were used to make *plaggen* soils (artificially enriched soils. *Plaggen* comes from German and means 'to cut sods'. *Plaggen* soils were formed by the prolonged application of calcareous sea-sand, either alone or in conjunction with stable manure. Seaweed was often used as an organic supplement to the sea-sand. *Plaggen* soils can be seen in section in the cliff face where erosion has occurred. A classic example of this occurs at *Tra Bó Dearg* on Achill Beg Island. *Plaggen* soils were a direct response to the need for highly productive fields: its application enabled farmers to keep some fields in perpetual tillage. In the 17th century legislation was enacted to regulate the removal of sea-sand from the shore and estates with access to sea-sand were deemed extremely valuable. The period of the maximum formation of *plaggen* soils coincided with the rapid growth of population c.1780. Landlords in 19th century Achill employed bailiffs to monitor the removal of sea-sand from the shores. Analysis of the soil from excavations in the Deserted Village (McDonald, Interim Report, 1995) indicate that sea-sand and sea-shells were mixed with stable manure to aid soil fertility. The practice of making *plaggen* soils continued in the West of Ireland until the 1950's. Along the shore at Derreens and Cloughmore can be seen linear rows of boulders, the remains of *fucus farms,* or seaweed gardens; it took a period of three years for the seaweed to colonise the boulders after which it was harvested, mixed with sea-sand and stable manure, and spread on the fields.

Climate

"The constancy of moist conditions on the west coast can be judged by the presence of Hymenophyllum peltatum on the north side of Slievemore mountain ." Praeger (1934:23).

Located at the western extremity of the Atlantic ocean, Achill Island, has a comparatively low rainfall, owing to the prevalence of moist westerly winds, generally only receiving between forty and sixty inches of rain per annum. However, Achill Stations report an average of 250 days a year on which rain falls. McNally, (1973). The frequency of rain and cloud reduces the amount of sunshine received, while cloudiness and

Achill

low summer temperatures contribute to the moistness of the soil. The prevailing winds are south-westerly and the warm waters of the North Atlantic Drift ensure that temperature extremes and harsh frosts are rare. Mean annual temperature compares favourably with that for Ireland as a whole, as can be seen in the chart below. McNally (1973).

Ireland	*Achill Island*
January 4- 5 C°	5- 6 C°
July 14- 15 C°	13- 14 C°

Flora and fauna

"The striking features of the vegetation of the island are its treeless and windswept character, and the unbroken continuity of bog and heath associations; inside the narrow fringe occupied by the Halophyte groups (salt-loving), the moorland flora holds undisputed sway, save where, in sheltered places, man has reclaimed some acres from the bog."
Praeger (1904).

Two-thirds of Achill is covered by peat which is concentrated in the centre of the island, while the arable land composed of cultivated peat or nutrient deficient sandy soils is coastal based. Changes in the Achill landscape over the last one hundred and fifty years have considerably reduced the number and variety of wild life on the island. Maxwell (1832) describes a days *shoot* on Achill as consisting of *"...thirteen brace of grouse and seven hares."* The Halls (1841-43) said: *"...the shores abound in wild-fowl of every description, and the mountains with grouse. The foxes are so numerous, that the young lambs are never safe; seals are seen at times in shoals among the rocks; and the ravens and the eagles exist in astonishing numbers in the cliffs and recesses of the hills. The eagles, indeed, seemed so unconscious of fear that they remained within a short distance of us; and one magnificent fellow soared over our heads, within pistol-shot, for above an hour, keeping on our course so near that we could count the feathers on its wings ."* William Pike, a local

5. Geography

landlord and amateur zoologist provided the following account of Achill in the late nineteenth century: "...*Trees and shrubs grow here that would not grow elsewhere in Ireland.*" A good example of this can be seen today at Glendarary wood near Achill Sound. Fuchsia was said to be sixteen feet high while a near neighbour of Pike, Mr. G. Clive of Ballycroy, had camellias and azaleas! Pike reported that a live turtle had recently been washed ashore in Upper Achill; he had counted one hundred wild swans in Keel Lake; grosbeak and snow buntings were shot and stuffed; chough used to breed on the island and help to destroy vast numbers of wire-worms. Pike (1874). The Golden Eagle and the White-tailed Sea Eagle were breeding in Achill up until the end of the nineteenth century; William Pike refers to the former having laid two eggs in 1886. Westropp (1914) claims that two eagles were seen on the island in 1912. Pike (1874) also recorded sightings of peregrine falcon; hawks, merlin, sparrow-hawks and kestrel, with ouzel and water ouzel also relatively common; woodcock, merganser, the great northern diver and small black guillemot, razorbill, puffin and many varieties of cormorant and gulls whom he said were all frequent visitors. Few of this varied fauna inhabits the island today; the wild swans at Keel, rabbit and hare, the fox and a remnant of the wild goat population at Saddle Head are all that remain. The demise of this varied wildlife has occurred over the last 150 years and may be attributed to the introduction of the fox to the island, landscape changes, the demise of farming, and indiscriminate culling.

The multi-disciplinary group who accompanied Praeger to Achill in 1898, an account of which appeared in the ***Irish Naturalist (1898)***, entitled: "*Impressions of Achill by members of an Easter Party,*" provides a fascinating account of the flora and fauna of the island, unsurpassed except for Praeger's Clare Island Survey (1915). Robert Lloyd Praeger recorded 416 species of flora on Achill, the most common being heather (calluna) found throughout the island. He said that the Achill flora had a strongly calcifuge (a plant that grows best on acid soils) and that calcicole (plants that grow best on calcareous soils, e.g. chalk and limestone) were poorly represented, and that a large number of common plants were absent from the island. Plants peculiar to Achill numbered eighty-eight compared with forty for Clare Island. However, if the respective size of both islands is taken into consideration, Clare Island covering 6.5 square miles as opposed to Achill's 57 square miles, it is easy to see that relatively speaking Clare Island has a much greater variety of plants.

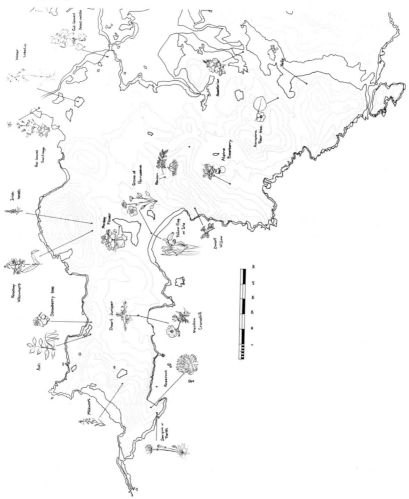

8. Map of Achill Flora, after McKay (1992)

5. Geography

The small number of island specific plants on Achill is probably related to the fact that almost two-thirds of Achill is covered by blanket bog and colonised by a small number of calcifuge species such as the ubiquitous bog-cotton, heather and several varieties of the insectivorous sundew. Juniper, once so prolific is now relatively scarce. Gorse and fuchsia are common, while *Gunnera* (often mistaken for wild rhubarb) is fast colonising large tracts of Upper Achill. Trees are rare, being confined to the wood at Glendarary at Achill Sound and around some houses.

In the Deserted Village of Slievemore, the remains of the houses are surrounded by patches of rushes and nettles, together with foxglove and primrose.

The origin of the relict flora of Lusitanian, Arctic Alpine and North American species which survived the last (Midlandian) glacial epoch on the island is unknown but heavy precipitation rather than low temperature is said to have been the chief factor in the glaciation of Ireland. The consistency of moist conditions in Achill is indicated by the presence of *Hymenophyllum peltatumun,* together with its ally *Hymenophyllum wilsonii* on the north side of Slievemore mountain. Arctic Alpine species in Achill include *Dryas octopetala* (Mountain avens), *Arctostaphylos uva-ursi* (Bearberry), *Gentiana verna* (Spring Gentian), *Euphrasia salisburgenis* (Irish Eyebright), *Calluna* (Ling), *Empetrum* (Crowberry), and *Junipericus siberica* (Juniper), many of which can be seen at specific locations such as the Minaun Cliffs and Corraun. *Vaccinium myrtillus* (Bilberry) grows in profusion on the *crannóg* in Dookinella, while *Erica cinerea* (Bell heather) and *salix* (Dwarf Willow) can be seen on moorland and around the small lakes.

Edward Newman (1839) referred to *Erica mediterranea* reaching to *"shoulder-height"* and *Pinguicula lusitanica*, stools of *Calluna* (Ling) and *Molinia* (tussocky grass) being common on bogland. London Pride *(Saxifrage spathularis)* is found in great profusion all over Achill, along with *Littorella* (Shoreweed), another common plant. Trees are not well represented, while the taller shrubs around the island include bog myrtle and the dwarf willow, *Salix herbacea.*

Achill

Isolated bands of limestone are responsible for the presence of the maiden-hair fern. At Achill Head there can be seen *Plantago maritima* (Sea plantain), *Plantago coronopus* (Buck's-Horn plantain), *Spergularia rupicola* (Rocky sea-spurrey), *Sagina maritima* (Sea pearlwort), *Cerastium tetrandrum* (Mouse-ear), *Radiola* (Allseed), *Festus ovina* (Sheep's fescue), *Aira praecox* (Early hair-grass), and *Agrostis tenuis* (Common bent grass).

Keel Sandybanks is the location of *Machair,* a term applied to flat, extensive plains of wind-blown sand which develop behind sandy beaches along the north-western coasts of Ireland. The vegetation is dominated by *Red Fescue, Bucks-Horn Plantain, Ribwort Plantain and Birds-foot Trefoil.* (Dr. John Conaghan, *pers. comm.*).

9. Children of Keel, 1932   *10. Couple of Keel , 1932*

Chapter 6

THE TOURIST'S ISLAND

"Achill is the largest of all the Irish islands and the most westerly inhabited landmass in Europe. It is a holiday island of international repute, and each summer attracts thousands of visitors from Britain, the Continent and America, as well as being a favourite resort with Irish people north and south." McNally, (1975).

Robert Lloyd Praeger visited Achill many times between 1898 and 1937 and on one occasion became quite poetical about the *"illimitable silver sea, the savage coastline, the booming waves, the singing wind."* To H. V. Morton (1930) Achill in summer was *"an island of titian-blue hills, blue skies, seas that rival the blue of Naples; but in bad weather the Atlantic waves scream on every side of them, and the winds from the east go tearing round the mountains like forty thousand devils."* He goes on to say that a weird spell hangs over the island that is uncannily captured in Paul Henry paintings: *"It is almost with a shock that one realises that the mountains are as blue as he paints them, that the sea is as blue, that the clouds are as big, that in the evening there is a space above the hills of bright green, that at certain times the whole island, land and sea, and sky, become washed in an unearthly splendour for which there are no words."* Morton (1930).

Paul Henry, shortly after arriving in Achill, while sitting on a rocky point at Gubelennaun decided that he wanted to stay in Achill and taking his return rail ticket to London out of his pocket he tore it into small pieces and scattered the fragments into the sea below. He rented accommodation in Keel and stayed on the island for another seven years. As Henry himself described it: *"I was in the grip of something that could not be argued about, something that would not be denied, I wanted to stay in Achill, and whatever reason seemed to be against such a plan was swept aside by my overpowering desire."* Henry (1951). Henry had first heard about Achill from his friend, Robert Lynd, who had *waxed lyrically* about Achill on many occasions. Arriving initially at the Colony in Dugort, Henry was not impressed with the place for *"every second house seemed to be a hotel or boarding house and the place swarmed with tourists."* He hired a Jarvey who took him *via* pony and trap, to Keel where he became so captivated with this village that there he determined to stay. The contrast between Keel and Dugort at that particular time was enormous, the former a village of thatched cottages and the latter a replica of a rural English village. Henry managed to persuade the local Postmistress, Mrs. Barrett, to put him up and a lifelong friendship developed between Henry and his hosts, John and Eliza Barrett.

11. The Back of Beyond © Tom McNamara

Many other writers and artists have subsequently made Achill their home, the German Nobel Prizewinner, Heinrich Böll, painters, Alexander Williams, Sean Keating, Marie Howet, Letticia Hamilton, Robert Henri and the current residents, Camille Souter, Margo McNulty and Margaret Morrison.

Grattan Freyer, son of Major Dermot Freyer, one time owner of Corrymore House in Dooagh, spent many happy school holidays in

6. The Tourist's Island

Achill and years later he would remember the pleasure of being able to roam freely and safely and to enjoy the myriad of delights that Achill had on offer such as *"tramping across the bog and heather to Achill Head."* He remembered Achill as a place *"you should go to before you die,"* and says *" don' t feel a summer holiday is the only possibility, spring comes early in Achill, there are no winter frosts and you can have wonderful days in March or May or June, even a bleak winter's day of blinding rain and violent storm beating against Achill's rugged cliffs, though not every tourist's dream, is an experience to remember. Achill is unique."*

McNally (1978).

Not surprisingly, the island also exerted a spell over the Reverend Edward Nangle of the Achill Mission for, shortly before his death in 1883, he is reputed to have said *"Achill may well be called the Happy Valley. In spite of all our trials, I know no place like it. "* McNally (1973).

12. Scoil Acla © Theresa McDonald

The origin of touri sm in Achill can be attributed to the Achill Mission Society, a proselytising Mission introduced into Achill in 1834. The opening of the Achill Mission Hotel in 1839 provided accommodation for travellers, before which a small lodging house on the mainland side of the Sound was the only hostelry for the island. The establishment of

Achill

the Achill Mission resulted in an influx of visitors to the island, initially to observe the work of the Mission but later to enjoy the beauty and splendour of the island, so graphically portrayed in the paintings of Paul Henry.

Prior to the middle of the nineteenth century most visitors to the West of Ireland travelled no further than Westport and as McNally (1973) points out, Dr. Pococke on his *Irish Tour* of 1752 was *"content to view Achill from a vantage point on the mainland and note in his diary a few brief items of information gleaned from local landlords."* Likewise Arthur Young in 1776 was content to view the island from Rosshill on Newport Bay. However, the beauty of Achill has always lain in its remoteness, its wild rugged scenery and unique way of life long since laid to rest elsewhere. Uncrowded beautiful beaches: *Sables d'Olonne* was according to McNally (1973) described in the *Pall Mall Gazette* in 1878 as one of *"the finest Bathing Strands in Europe"* but as he says one has only to visit Dugort to find not one but three, all far more beautiful than *Sables d'Olonne*.

Scally (1988) first visited Achill in the 1940's when Tourist Information was spread by word of mouth and accommodation was available only in small hotels and B & Bs were unknown. Tourists were met in Dooagh by girls with bicycle lamps to light the way to the various tourist establishments. Scally, himself, was very partial to Delia Gielty's (Clew Bay Guesthouse) seed cake and Cím (Keem) mutton which brought him back to Achill on many subsequent occasions. Visiting Sonny O'Malley's Pub in Dooagh he noted that the locals insisted on getting flat pints of stout, to be sure of getting good value, while the visitors got a dollop of froth out of a jug! He remembered Major Freyer and the Sunday Afternoon Tea Dances in Corrymore House when the Gunning sisters gave displays of English (Morris) country dancing. Highlights of his holiday were the walks over to Annagh and up along Moyteoge Head, the night-time at Gielty's fireside learning to pronounce the Irish placenames of the locality and the stories that went with them.

6. The Tourist's Island

13. Achill Archaeological Summer School 'Field Trip'

Achill attracts tourists from many parts of the world, many of whom return time and time again. Although the island has a number of good small hotels and guesthouses, it urgently needs a Grade A Hotel in order to compete with similar tourist resorts elsewhere in Ireland. Westport has expanded at the expense of Achill, having a greater variety of accommodation on offer, as well as more organised tourist attractions. Relatively good roads provide access to most parts of the island, although to the writer the most beautiful parts of Achill lie off the beaten track, accessible only on foot over wild and rugged terrain. Excellent hill-climbing, botanical forays, golfing, tennis, wind surfing, canoeing, hand gliding, river and sea fishing, swimming or just idly lying on the beach are some of the attractions on offer to the tourist in Achill. An additional bonus is the ever-changing colours in the landscape so zealously sought and found by the artist, Camille Souter, for although her work differs from that of her predecessor Paul Henry, both have immortalised Achill in their own way. Achill in summer is the entertainment capital of Mayo with a vibrant *"night-life"* of discos, concerts, music festivals, etc. Visitors, locals, teenagers, foreign students, the *'young at heart'*, and all who populate the island in summer generally end up having a good time and in the process contribute much needed revenue to the tourist industry.

Achill

Achill island is part of Ireland-West, a tourist region that embraces the counties of Galway and Mayo. *Mayo Naturally* now looks after tourism in County Mayo, while local information about Achill can be obtained from *Turasóireacht Acla, (Achill Tourism)* based in Bunacurry. Tourism has brought many benefits to Achill such as a relatively sophisticated outlook on life, one of the the highest YES votes in the 1996 *Divorce Referendum* being recorded in Achill. The comfortable lifestyle of residents on the island is reflected by the neatly kept dwellings and in the increasing number of new houses being built on the island. However, developments in keeping with previous architectural styles are increasingly being abandoned for non-native styles which do little to enhance the local landscape and should be actively discouraged.

Achill has many attractions which can be developed and enhanced to attract the discerning tourist and thereby provide long-term sustainable employment for young people leaving school. It is the responsibility of organisations such as *Mayo Naturally* and *Turasóireacht Acla (Achill Tourism)* to ensure that these are encouraged, adequately funded and sensitively developed.

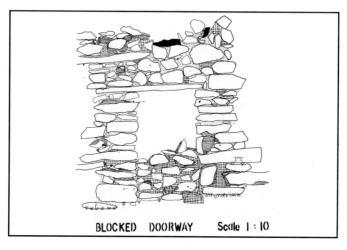

BLOCKED DOORWAY   Scale 1 : 10

14. Blocked doorway in Deserted Village © Theresa McDonald

46

Chapter 7

PREHISTORIC ACHILL

> *"It is old thou art, O Bird of Eacaill,*
> *Tell me the cause of your adventures;*
> *I possess, without denial,*
> *The gift of speaking in the bird language."*
> **Anonymous poem in the Book of Fermoy**

The absence of metal artifacts from some shell midden sites in Achill prompted Wood-Martin (1898) to speculate on the possibility that they might be of Mesolithic Period (Middle Stone Age) date. However, in the absence of scientific excavation, it is not possible to say with certainty that Achill was inhabited by hunters and fishers in the period between 5-7000 years ago. Had they been present, these hunter-fishers would have hunted wild boar and red deer in the interior of the island, then densely forested, and had their base camps along the sea shore. Many Irish Mesolithic sites have been submerged by rising sea levels in the aftermath of the Midlandian glacial some 10-12,000 years ago. On the basis of some rough calculations dealing with sea-level fluctuations, based on experiments carried out in Oronsay in Scotland, Mellars (1971), the Keel middens would appear to post-date 5000 B.C.

Red deer antlers recently found in midden sites on the Corraun Peninsula belonged to a a five year old male red deer *(Cervas elaphus Linnaeus)*, which had been shed naturally. Remains of red deer have also been found in many Irish bogs and caves, notably at two Early Mesolithic sites, Mount Sandel in Co. Derry and Lough Boora in Co. Offaly. However, red deer continued to inhabit Ireland for several thousand years after the Mesolithic. An entry written in 655 A.D. by Augustin, an Irish monk in **De mirabillibus sacrae scripturae** refers to the presence of red deer in Ireland at that time, while Giraldus Cambrensis includes red deer amongst the *"beasts of chase"* in his **Topographia Hibernica** in 1183-85. By the mid nineteenth century red deer were in decline and known only in the wild state in Killarney, Achill, Erris and Connemara. The Halls (1841-43) noted red deer in the valleys in Achill and said that a huge buck had been shot on the island a few weeks before their visit. They also remarked that deer bones and antlers had been used as trial pieces for art designs but, unfortunately none of these survived. Trial pieces were a feature of many periods but the only really datable (art-historically) trial pieces from middens (as against those from *crannógs* and water-logged medieval urban sites) is the material excavated by Professor Etienne Rynne and the late Dr. Seán O' Riordáin (1961) at Dooey, Co. Donegal and discussed by Raghnall O'Floinn of the National Museum of Ireland in an article written by him in ***Donegal: History & Society***. (1995).

The Megalith Builders

The people who inhabited the island around 5000 years ago have left ample evidence of their presence, primarily in the form of megalithic tombs, arguably the most visible archaeological monuments in the Irish countryside. They were responsible for long term landscape changes which have had repercussions down to the present day. These were the first farmers who upon arrival in Ireland brought with them domesticated sheep and goat, cultivated cereals of wheat, oats, rye and barley, and crude flat-bottomed pottery. They built their magnificent megalithic tombs on Slievemore mountain with outliers at Crumpaun and Annagh and possibly Cloughmore. The remains of a recently discovered Portal Tomb in the latter area is currently being investigated.

The Neolithic people cleared the forest to grow their cereal crops. Polished stone axes used in tree-felling have been found at Keel, Kildavnet and Monyhaig, and at three other unidentified locations. Field walls used to enclose their livestock or protect cereal crops can be seen in bog-cuttings and on Slievemore mountain.While we have no idea of the population involved, the fact that other tombs excavated elsewhere showed evidence of having been used over several generations, we can assume from demographic evidence compiled by Reed (1987-88), that by

7. Prehistoric Achill

the end of the Neolithic, around 4000 years ago, Achill had a substantial population of between five hundred and one thousand persons.

Bronze Age Achill

The onset of the Bronze Age around 2000 B.C. saw the introduction of a new technology. Metal tools e.g. the copper axe and adze made sophisticated wood-working possible, while the introduction of weapons like spears, rapiers, knives etc. heralded an inevitable slide into warfare. Hunting was probably still a major component in the life of the Bronze Age people in Achill and a barbed-and-tanged arrowhead found near Bunacurry may have been lost by a hunter chasing his prey.This arrowhead of black chert was not made of local stone (unless it came from a glacial drift deposit), but from a location somewhere in North Mayo or Sligo, suggesting great mobility on the part of these hunters. Three other arrowheads of the same material were found at Doona near Ballycroy, opposite Achill in North Mayo. It is likely that Achill was still joined to the mainland at this time, making access easy. The Bronze Age inhabitants of Achill buried their dead in cist graves, in Slievemore, Dugort and possibly Bunacurry (C. Gray, *pers. comm.*) most of which have disappeared, but some were recorded and planned by Wood-Martin in 1898. Several hut platforms of probable Bronze Age date have been noted on Slievemore, together with associated field systems and enclosures which may have been cattle corrals.

Iron Age Achill

The succeeding Iron Age around 400 B.C. saw settlement expansion throughout the island. Archaeological sites of this period consist of promontory forts, located in Dugort, facing Blacksod Bay and along the Atlantic Drive facing Clew Bay. Promontory forts consist in the main of a promontory or projecting piece of land, naturally defended on three sides but with artificial defences in the form of a fosse (ditch) or stone walls bisecting the neck or narrow part. They vary in size, from the extremely small example near Dooega Village to the spectacular site of Dún Kilmore on Achill Beg Island. These are enigmatic sites, their defensive capability suspect because of their size and location. Bunafahy on the Atlantic Drive may have had a souterrain attached but even this defensive element would not have withstood any sort of sustained attack. Associated with the coastal promontory forts are several cathairs, caiseals and a crannóg. According to Westropp (1914) the walls of the Achill cathairs were more substantial than elsewhere, being some twelve to sixteen feet thick, indicating that defence was of prime consideration.

The Achill forts are mentioned in two ancient tracts written down around the 12th century A.D. but possibly depicting events in the Iron Age. *Cath Maighe Léna* (The Battle of Moylena) mentions two sons of an Achill King slain during this battle, while a more interesting reference relates to Conn Úi Neill *(O'Néill)* of the Hundred Battles sending to Achill for help from Goll Mac Morna, a one-eyed giant and avowed enemy of Fionn mac Cumaill. Goll represents one of the supreme deities of the Celtic pantheon of gods and was supposedly leader of troops serving King Cormac Mac Airt and is primarily associated with the Connachta, originally a Leinster dynasty who in their expansion westward gave their name to the province of Connacht. In *Táin Bó Flidhais* (The Cattle Raid of Flidhais, daughter of Medb and Ailill of Connacht), a subsidiary tale in *Táin Bó Cualnge*, (The Cattle Raid of Cooley) assistance is sought by Ailill Fionn, King of the Gamanrad in Erris from Iubar, chieftain of *(Dún-Inbir-da-tonn)* a promontory fort in Dooniver: *"...from Uamma, daughter of Iubar, and the seven daughters of the majestic Iubar, from Goll Acla, fierce his valour with 400 champions."* No trace remains of this fort today; it may well have been destroyed by the submergence which cut off Inishbiggle from Achill and led to the formation of the Sound sea channel. Other places mentioned in this text which have not been identified are Rath Caim and Rath Dookinella, although the latter was probably the now destroyed site formerly known as the *Dunadh of Sliabh Mór* in Bal of Dookinella which was recorded and planned by both Wood-Martin and Westropp in the late nineteenth century.

Many of the promontory forts were re-occupied in later periods, the most noteworthy being Dún Kilmore, which has multi-period remains consisting of a large circular enclosure, over 200 feet in diameter and probably of Early Medieval date. Within this enclosure are the remains of figure of eight (conjoined) hut sites, a *leacht*, an altar or the remains of a

7. Prehistoric Achill

small church, a *bullaun* and a *cillín*. A second stone wall was constructed to the east immediately outside the entrance to the enclosure. Dún Kilmore (The Great Church), the name applied to the promontory fort would seem to more rightly belong to the Early Medieval enclosure. To the west and set within the ramparts of the promontory fort are the foundations of a Tower of Late Medieval date. Westropp (1914) referred to a second tower located on a headland which had reputedly fallen into the sea at a date unknown. West of Dún Kilmore is an isolated sea-stack, similar to Dún Briste in North Mayo, upon which are the remains of at least two hut sites.

Dún Kilmore is one of the most impressive sites in Achill and was said by Westropp (1914) to be one of the most complex of the western promontory forts. He compared it with similar sites in Brittany, while the late Professor M.J. O'Kelly on a visit to Achill in 1942 remarked on the structural similarities between the Achill, Cornish and Breton promontory forts. The Breton forts have been attributed to the *Veneti*, renowned Celtic traders and seafarers who fled to Britain and probably Ireland before the advancing Roman army. Caesar himself referred to them as excellent traders but deplored the fact that they were in collusion with the insurgent British Celts, the destruction of which was one of the main reasons for the Roman invasion of Britain. Although the origin of the promontory forts may lie ultimately in France or Iberia (Spain and Portugal), which have *Chevaux-de-Frise* in common with some Irish stone promontory forts, little information on their function, period of construction and ultimate purpose is known. Only Dún Beg in Kerry and Dún Aengus on Aran have been totally excavated; the cost proving prohibitive because of the large size of these forts and the relatively small amount of information retrieved. Barry (1987).

Another indication of a possible Iron Age site is the placename *Sheeaun*, once the location of the village of Finsheen which was demolished in the mid-nineteenth century.

Chapter 8

THE EARLY MEDIEVAL ISLAND

The Early Medieval Period began with the coming of St. Patrick in the 5th Century A.D. It heralded a great expansion in agriculture, the introduction of the coulter plough, a greater usage of iron implements, and a proliferation (40,000) of a type of dispersed farmstead, commonly called a ring-fort or rath.

Patrick, had many connections with County Mayo in the form of dedications and place names, the best known being Croagh Patrick near Louisburgh. The elusive *Silva vocluti,* one of the few place names mentioned by Patrick in his **Confessio** has, as we have seen, been linked with Achill. The Early Monastic Church which superseded the Diocesan Church of Patrick is not well represented on Achill, contrasting markedly with a wealth of sites on almost all of the neighbouring islands. The Holy Well in Slievemore graveyard is dedicated to St. Colman. St. Colman and a group of English and Irish monks left Lindisfarne after the Synod of Whitby in A.D.664 which had been convened to resolve a dispute between the Columban and Roman church over the date of Easter and other matters. The Roman view prevailed and Colman and his monks sailed for Ireland, spending some time on Inishbofin Island before finally establishing themselves in Mayo Abbey (Mayo of the Saxons), a place to which they gave their name. The dedication in Slievemore together with an upright stone cross in the graveyard, said to be similar to Cornish examples (Rynne, *pers. comm.*) may indicate that Colman and his monks spent some time in Achill, prior to establishing themselves on Inishbofin. Keem Bay, may also have been the location of an important Early Medieval site in the 5th-6th centuries A.D. for in 1942 one ogham stone and a fragment of another was found in the river bed close to the old Coastguard Station. Immediately to the east overlooking the foundations of an old village is a reconstructed Penal altar and local folklore provides a description of what seems to have been a *bullaun* stone located in the same area. Other Early Medieval sites in Achill are located at Kildavnet and Achill Beg Island. Achill Beg Island also had a substantial Early Medieval settlement. The name Dún Kilmore, meaning *great church,*

8. The Early Medieval Island

suggests that a large building, probably of wood, was formerly located within the enclosure. Another possible Early Medieval site is in Dookinella Thulis, which is the location of a *cillín* (children's graveyard), a holy well dedicated to St. Fionán, and a former Church. The dedication in Slievemore is to St. Colman and in Kildavnet to St. Davnet or Dympna while Achill Beg was depicted on 16th maps as *Kil-da-m(n)at*. The placename, *Baile*, is associated with all of the above sites, Keem Bay excepted.

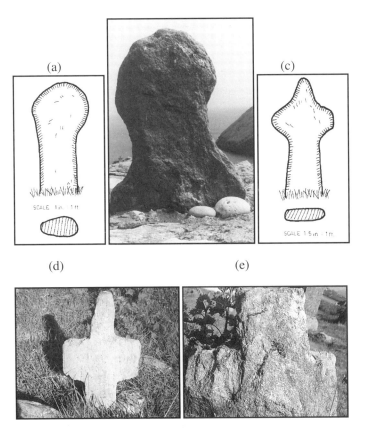

15 . *Early Medieval Stone Crosses: (A) and (C) Slievemore (D) and (E) Kildavnet and (B) Penal Altar, Keem Bay*

Chapter 9

THE RULING FAMILIES OF ACHILL

*"The kingdom of Umhall is at the head of Inquisition C, forming one great Cantred of Umhall. It is much broken up. A Butler has the northern part, the parishes of Achill and Burrishoole, which were a large native denomination called Latharis in the Taxation, which I think is **Leáth Fheurghuis**. O'Fergus was one of the three chief families of Clann Máille."* Knox (1908).

The first historical reference to Achill occurs in The ***Annals of Lough Cé*** when in 1235 A.D. the island was plundered by the Anglo-Normans under the command of the Justiciar, Maurice Fitzgerald. This incursion probably occurred because of the O'Connor connection with the island, the Normans supporting one rival O'Connor faction against the other to further their own claims of territorial conquest. Maghnus O'Connor appears to have been resident in Achill or Corraun at this time, and resisted the Normans call to surrender the island. They invaded with force, however, and Maghnus and his allies were defeated.

In 1238 Henry Butler who took part in the Invasion of Connacht in 1235 is recorded as Lord of Akil and Umhall after he acquired half a cantred in Umhall called Owyll-Butler. He built a castle at Tyrenmore (Burrishoole) and established a town there called *Burgheis Cinn Trachta*. The Butler dynasty of Umhall was short-lived and they disappear from the scene in the late 14th Century A.D. They appear to have been usurped by the de Burgo's who held the area for several centuries, *Riocard an Iaráinn*, the last MacWilliam and second husband of Grace O'Malley acquiring control in the sixteenth century. However, the Earl of Ormond, kinsman to the Mayo Butlers subsequently acquired the island, transferring it to Thomas Medlycott in the eighteenth century.

From the 12th to the 17th centuries, control of Achill would pass between the above powerful families with the O'Donnells of Donegal acquiring intermittent control at the beginning and end of this period.

9. The Ruling Families of Achill - The O'Connors

THE O'CONNORS OF CONNACHT

O'CONNOR KINGS OF CONNACHT TO 1329.

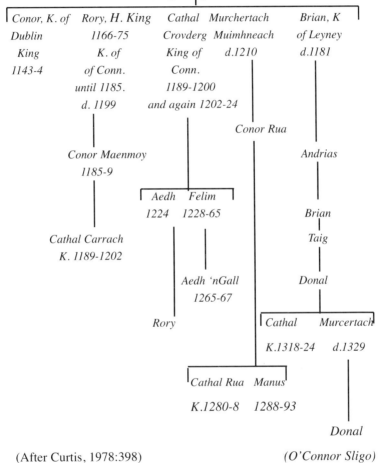

Turloch More, High King, 1119-56

| Conor, K. of Dublin King 1143-4 | Rory, H. King 1166-75 K. of of Conn. until 1185. d. 1199 | Cathal Crovderg King of Conn. 1189-1200 and again 1202-24 | Murchertach Muimhneach d.1210 | Brian, K of Leyney d.1181 |

Conor Maenmoy 1185-9

Cathal Carrach K. 1189-1202

Conor Rua

Andrias

Aedh 1224   Felim 1228-65

Brian

Taig

Aedh 'nGall 1265-67

Donal

Rory

Cathal K.1318-24   Murcertach d.1329

Cathal Rua K.1280-8   Manus 1288-93

Donal

(After Curtis, 1978:398)   (O'Connor Sligo)

Many notable families, Gaelic and Norman contended for control of Achill; documentary sources relating to these events are in the main scanty but, nevertheless, the course of events can be charted from information contained in records belonging to these families and to the occasional mention of Achill in the various Irish Annals.

Connacht remained a virtual backwater until Toirrdelbach Uá Conchobair (Turlough O'Connor) became High King of Ireland in the early twelfth century. On the eve of the Anglo-Norman invasion of Connacht, the O'Connors reigned supreme. The province had remained free from invasion under the power of the O'Connor kings and various O'Connor princeling occupied hereditary estates throughout Connacht, made up of several clanns: *Clann Murtough Mweenagh and Maghnus, Cathal Migranin, Clann Ruaidhri, Clann Cuain and Umhall.* The Anglo-Norman invasion however upset these arrangements and ultimately pushed the O'Connor family into a small tract of County Roscommon. The Clann of Murtough Mweenagh were allowed to remain in Umhall and Erris until their expulsion in 1273. Maghnus O'Connor was in Umhall when the Normans plundered Achill in 1235 and appears to have made enemies of the O'Malleys, indigenous inhabitants of the area.

One of the greatest of the O'Connor Kings, Cathal Crobh Dearg (the Red Hand), was the youngest son of the High King, Turlough Mór and half-brother of the last High King of Ireland, Ruaidhrí O'Connor. Cathal Crobh Dearg was the illegitimate son of Turlough Mór and a girl named Moran from Umhall *(Annals of the Four Masters, 1224)*, which may explain the O'Connor settlement in this area. Cathal Crobh Dearg became King of Connacht in 1201 and until the end of his reign on the 28th May, 1224 his supremacy in Connacht went unchallenged: *"the reign of the Red hand was a pleasant reign, he ruled for sixteen and twenty prosperous calm years."* After the death of the High King, Ruaidhrí O'Connor, his son, Aedh, contested the kingship with his cousin, Felim, son of Cathal Crobh Dearg. The war for the kingship was intense between the cousins and *"pitiful indeed was the tempest which God permitted to descend upon the best province of Ireland." Annals of Connacht (A.Conn.)*. Aedh, son of Ruaidhrí was King of Connacht in 1227 for we find him in attendance at a great court of the Galls (foreigners) where *"deceit and treachery were practised against him." (A. Conn.)*. Rescued by William Marshall, Strongbow's (Richard FitzGilbert de Clare) heir, he proceeded to Connacht killing many of the Galls *en route*. We are told that after this episode peace reigned for a while, although this may have been brought about as much by *"cold*

9. The Ruling Families of Achill-The O'Connors

famine and every kind of disease which occurred this year." (A.Conn). Accompanying the sons of Ruaidhrí in their foray into Connacht was MacWilliam Bourke who would wield great influence in Connacht in the ensuing period. Aedh was shortly afterwards deposed of the kingship and fled to his ally, O'Donnell, in Donegal. He had rather an unusual death in 1228 being killed by a carpenter's axe in the Court of a Norman Lord while the *"carpenter's wife was bathing him!"* The kingship was now contested by two other sons of the late High King, Ruaidhrí, and according to the Annals *"all Connacht was ruined between them."* Churches and lay properties were plundered and clerics and men of skill were driven to foreign regions! They plundered the territory of MacWilliam Bourke and the Normans retaliated by supporting, Felim, son of Cathal Crovderg who now assumed the kingship. Maghnus in Umhall supported Felim, offering him pledges and hostages. The practice of giving hostages, usually children of royal blood was common at this time.

Felim's reign was short-lived and in 1231 he was taken prisoner by MacWilliam Bourke *"because of violations of guarantees to the Normans."* The kingship passed back to the line of Ruadhrí but Felim again mounted a successful challenge against his cousins in 1233, ensuring that the kingship and sovereignty of the province of Connacht was taken from the seed of Ruadhrí forever. Peace and discipline was restored to Connacht after Felim had destroyed the castles of Aedh and MacWilliam Bourke. In 1234 heavy snow fell between the two Christmases, followed by such a heavy frost that men and laden horses walked on the great lakes of Ireland. *(A.Conn.)*. Richard, son of Earl Marshall made war on the King of England after which he crossed over to Ireland where he was opposed by all the Normans, including the Justiciar, Maurice Fitzgerald, Baron of Offaly. *(A. Conn.)*.

By 1235 the kingship of Felim was once again placed in jeopardy. A son of O'Dowd, King of the *Uí Amalgada* (Tirawley) and the *Uí Fiachrach* (Umhall) were killed in a dispute at the camp of Felim. The

Normans, under the leadership of Richard, son of MacWilliam Bourke made a hosting into Connacht burning the monastery of Boyle and stealing all its valuables. They were pursued by Felim and his army and many battles were fought! Defeated, Felim, together with the son of Maghnus and others, gathered up all their cattle and went to seek protection from O'Donnell, leaving the land of Connacht to the Normans. The Normans assembled at Doon Castle outside Westport and sent word to Maghnus, in Umhall, demanding that he accept their proffered peace terms and provide hostages. Maghnus refused both demands and the Normans sent out large raiding parties from Doon consisting of *"...the sons of Ruadhrí and innumerable soldiery, who plundered Achill and carried off great spoils before rejoining the Normans at Druimne." (Annals of Lough Cé).*

Details of the battle are given in the **Annals of Connacht**: *"Maghnus and his ships were in the Sound of this island and great fights and skirmishes took place."* The prevailing custom with regard to battles at this time was that when one or both sides grew tired, there was a respite and this seems to have occurred here, for *" the Galls drew up their ships in a recess of the great strand at that place."* Maghnus took advantage of this lull in the battle and sailing eastwards landed on Inishraher, some of his men returning to another island, Inisheany, to collect sheep from it to feed the troops. The foreigners must have followed Maghnus for *"seeing that he had not posted a guard and realising that the armies were very close carried their ships along the strand and launched them, landing on the two islands where they killed all the inhabitants."* It is not clear which islands are being referred to, Inisheany and Inishraher or the two Achills *viz "When the foreigners moreover, saw that they themselves could go towards the island and then to the other island" (A. Conn.).* There is a note in the margin of the text by Roderick O'Flaherty claiming that the islands were: *"the islands of ye Oulles praed by ye English ."* There was no love lost between the O'Malleys and the O'Connors for Maghnus reputedly said that *"if he had trusted Uí Mháille, he would have sent his ships against the Galls." (A. Conn.).* Knox (1908:86) takes this to mean that Maghnus being settled in Umhall acted oppressively towards the O'Malleys, who did not help him but rather hoped for his defeat. The Galls next landed on the islands of North Umhall *"but the commanders of the soldiery would not suffer them to kill anyone, out of respect for the Passion"* (Easter). They did not desist forever, for the Annals later tell us that:*"when the Galls had ended their sackings and plundering of Umhall, by land and by sea, they made their way to Ballysadare and there made a raid on O'Donnell because he was harbouring Felim O'Connor." (A.Conn.)* Felim O'Connor made his peace with the Justiciar, agreeing to pay him rent and tributes. The O'Connor power was, however, now on the wane, controlling only Roscommon and certain adjoining parts of Counties Sligo and Galway. The enmity between Maghnus O'Connor and the O'Malleys continued, two of O'Malleys sons being killed by Domnall, son of Maghnus on Clare Island. The O'Connor family feud continued into the next generation: *"...they raided and harassed the Galls and their enemies among the Gaels, so that the whole countryside was ruined by them alternately ."*

Maghnus O'Connor died in a *Spittal house* (Hospital) described as being located beside the *Heron's Ford* on the Yellow River. He was buried outside the Church of *Fenagh* and *"thrice the full of the Bell of the Kings of silver and thirty horses were given as an offering with him."* A beautiful monument of carved stone was set up over him but was demolished by *Uí Ruairc*, another chieftain for some real or imagined wrong. In 1248 the sons of Maghnus revolted against the Galls, burning MacHenry's (Butler) castle. The Galls marched against them, among whom was John Butler, Lord of Ballycroy and Henry's son or kinsman. The Galls plundered Umhall, north and south. MacHenry Butler came into Umhall with a great army*"for Umhall belonged to him and he lived there!"*

In 1256 a huge army of twenty thousand was raised by Walter, son of Richard Bourke to attack Felim O'Connor and his son Aedh. A great battle took place with Aedh, *"that strong sturdy Prince showing a ruler's fury, a champions endurance and a lion's prowess."* Afterwards called *Aedh 'na nGall'*, he succeeded his father to the throne of Connacht.

THE MAYO BUTLERS

"Theobald, son of Walter Butler, neither stopped nor stayed till he reached Inishowle in Lower Connacht." **A Butler Chronicler of the 18th century.**

Butler (de Buitléir). The name is derived from *Le Botiller,* the King's chief butler which was given to the family by Henry II. The first of the Butlers to arrive in Ireland was Theobald FitzWalter who accompanied *Prince John* when he landed in Waterford in 1185 A.D. and whose death is recorded in 1205 A.D. In 1215 A.D. the arrival of Henry Butler in Ireland is recorded, presumably the same Henry who later fought against Earl Marshall alongside Richard de Burgo in the Invasion of Connacht and was rewarded with a grant of land in West Mayo. Recorded as Lord of Umhall in A.D. 1238 he founded the Barony of Burrishoole. The Butlers were also known as Lords of Aicill and Umhall and may originally have had more extensive territory with John Butler owning Ballycroy. Henry built a castle at *Cinn Trachta* (Burrishoole) which was twice sacked by the O'Connors in 1248 and again in 1272, the latter occasion resulting in the death of Henry. MacHenry probably Henry's son next appears on the scene and later in A.D. 1333, John Butler, is recorded as owner of Owyll-Botiller (Butler). In the Ormond Deeds of 1380-81 a Butler is again recorded as Lord of Akyll and Owyll after which they disappear from the scene and their place is taken by the de Burgos who retain control of Achill until the 16th Century.

A Deed of Knocktopher of July 14, 1512, was a grant by Theobald, son of Nicholas Butler (*"de stirpe Owil! - the Butler race of Umhall , the Owles seems clearly indicated here"*), to William Bretnach Fitz Robert of lands in the barony of Overk, Co. Kilkenny. By this Deed it appears that Nicholas Butler *"of Karchill"* was father of Theobald and grandfather of Evelina, who married the above William Bretnach. Curtis (1935). Curtis also states that one Finola, daughter of *"Le Botiller of Burrishoole"* married John Garvey of Murrisk, Co. Mayo and their son, John Garvey, became Archbishop of Armagh in 1590. Curtis also says that Finola was described *"as of the House of Ormonde"* in the **Miscellanea Genealogica et Heraldica.**

9. The Ruling Families of Achill- The Mayo Butlers

THE BUTLER EARLS OF ORMOND

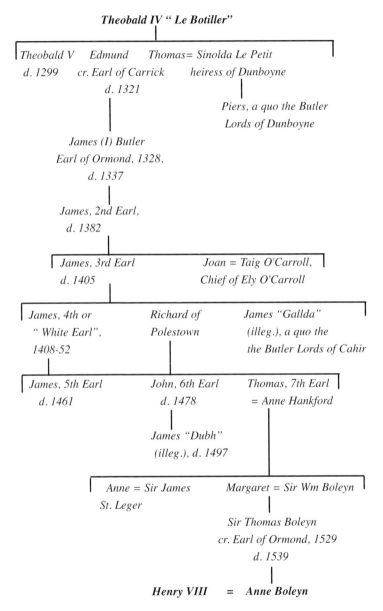

Theobald IV " Le Botiller"

Theobald V   Edmund   Thomas= Sinolda Le Petit
d. 1299   cr. Earl of Carrick   heiress of Dunboyne
d. 1321

Piers, a quo the Butler
Lords of Dunboyne

James (I) Butler
Earl of Ormond, 1328,
d. 1337

James, 2nd Earl,
d. 1382

James, 3rd Earl   Joan = Taig O'Carroll,
d. 1405   Chief of Ely O'Carroll

James, 4th or   Richard of   James "Gallda"
" White Earl",   Polestown   (illeg.), a quo the
1408-52   the Butler Lords of Cahir

James, 5th Earl   John, 6th Earl   Thomas, 7th Earl
d. 1461   d. 1478   = Anne Hankford

James "Dubh"
(illeg.), d. 1497

Anne = Sir James   Margaret = Sir Wm Boleyn
St. Leger

Sir Thomas Boleyn
cr. Earl of Ormond, 1529
d. 1539

Henry VIII   =   Anne Boleyn

Achill

Chronology of Mayo Butlers

1185-1205 A.D.   *Theobald Walter Botiller arrives in Ireland*

1215 A.D.   *Henry Butler (Pincerna) arrives in Ireland*

1234 A.D.   *Henry fought with Earl Marshall at Battle of Kildare*

1235 A.D.   *John Butler took part in Invasion of Connacht*

   John Butler, Baron & Knight of Richard de Burgo settles in Ballycroy

1238 A.D.   *Henry Butler created Lord of Aicill and Umhall*

L. 13th Century   *Henry Butler killed by O'Connors*

M.14th Century   *John Butler owner of Owyll Botiller through a grant from de Burgo. Rent £10*

L.14th Century   *Butlers disappear from Owyll-Butler*

1420 A.D.   *Owles, owned by the Earl of Desmond off the heir of Edmund de Burgo*

1434 A.D.   *Deed (indenture) between James, Earl of Ormond and Nicholas, son of Peter, son of Henry Butler, to lands leased for life in Kilkenny*

1512A.D.   *Deed of Knocktopher: a grant by Theobald, son of Nicholas to William Bretnach FitzRobert to lands in Kilkenny. "Nicholas Butler of Karchill was father of Theobald and Theobald had a daughter, Evelina, who married William Bretnach. This is the Butler race of Umhall." (Curtis, 1937).*

16th century   *Finola le Botiller, daughter of Evelina and William Bretnach, married John O'Garvey of Murrisk. Finola was described as of the House of Ormond*

E. 17th Century   *Butlers of Ormond claim Owyll-Butler*

M. 17th Century   *The most important Protestant landholder, with a large estate in Achill and Erris was the Royalist Earl of Ormond*

Late17th Century   *Ormonds dispossessed. Medlycott becomes owner of Achill.*

9. The Ruling Families of Achill - The de Burgos

THE de BURGOS (Bourkes)

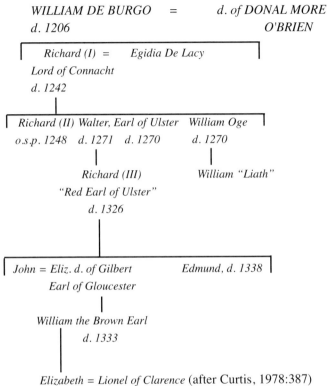

WILLIAM DE BURGO   =   *d. of DONAL MORE*
d. 1206   *O'BRIEN*

Richard (I) =   Egidia De Lacy
Lord of Connacht
d. 1242

Richard (II)   Walter, Earl of Ulster   William Oge
o.s.p. 1248   d. 1271   d. 1270   d. 1270

Richard (III)   William "Liath"
"Red Earl of Ulster"
d. 1326

John = Eliz. d. of Gilbert   Edmund, d. 1338
Earl of Gloucester

William the Brown Earl
d. 1333

Elizabeth = Lionel of Clarence (after Curtis, 1978:387)

William de Burgo was the first of the Bourkes to settle in Ireland in the 13th Century A.D. He married a daughter of Domnall Mór O'Brien, King of Thomond. He had three sons, Richard, William and Hubert; Richard became Lord of Connacht, excepting the King's Five Cantreds (which went to pacify Felim O'Connor), while William was made Sheriff of Connacht. The third generation produced two sons who would elevate the de Burgos to become the greatest family in Connacht. Those two sons, William and Walter would divide the family into two branches, known respectively as Clannwilliam (Mayo) and Clannrickard (Galway). Clannrickard formed the main line until the close of the 14th century when the title was transferred to the descendants of Richard Óg, known as MacWilliam of Clannrickard or MacWilliam Upper (Uachtarach). The hereditary succession to the MacWilliamship of Clannrickard followed the law of primogeniture until the sixteenth century. The first period of English government in County Mayo ended in 1340 A.D. and coincided with the commencement of the MacWilliamship in the person of Sir Edmond 'Albanach,' so called because he had spent some time in Scotland. Arriving in Ireland in 1335 A.D. he landed in *Umhall Ó Máille* (O'Malley's Umhall) and married Saive Ó Maille. From 1342 A.D. onwards, Sir Edmond and Clannwilliam (Iochtarach) reigned supreme. Contact and intermarriage with the local Gaelic aristocracy resulted in them becoming fully hibernicised, so that by the beginning of the 16th Century they were fighting for the succession, just like their neighbours the O'Connors. The de Burgos would retain control of the province until the Lordship of Connacht merged in the Crown in the person of King Edward I. Knox (1908:144).

The demise of English power resulted in the recruitment by the ruling families, including the de Burgos, of mercenary soldiers known as Gallowglasses, (*galloglaí*) originally enticed into Ireland from Scotland by the MacDonnells of Antrim.

Sir Edmund died in 1371 and was succeeded by his son, Thomas, who was unable to maintain peace in the province which gradually reduced the lands of the Norman lords to poverty and disorder. He eventually relinquished the MacWilliamship to Richard Óg but on Richard's death in 1387 he became the senior MacWilliam. Thomas made formal submission to King Richard II when he arrived in Ireland in 1393. Sir Thomas died in 1401 having succeeded in forming the shape of a lordship that would formally become the County of Mayo in the sixteenth century.

Walter Bourke succeeded to the title of MacWilliam but had to acknowledge the superiority of Ulick, MacWilliam of Clannrickard. From 1401 to 1503 there was constant warfare and raiding in Connacht involving both the Anglo-Normans and their neighbours the Gaelic chieftains. Walter died c.1439 and was succeeded by Edmond II the most

9. The Ruling Families of Achill-The de Burgos

warlike of the de Burgos. He was succeeded in turn by his brother
Thomas in 1458 and by Richard I in 1460, founder of Burrishoole Abbey
to which he retired in 1469. Richard II, nephew of Richard I, now
succeeded to the title and proceeded with an invasion of Clannrickard, an
indication perhaps of the hostility between the two de Burgo branches.
This is confirmed in the **Annals of Ulster (A.U.)** which record the
slaying of Richard by the sons of John de Burgh. Richard was killed in
1579 and was succeeded by his cousin Theobald, son of Walter Bourke.
The feuding between the two branches of the family continued and they
were also engaged in warfare with the O'Connors, supporting
alternatively either O'Connor Donn or O'Connor Roe and also with the
O'Donnells who were constantly attacking from Sligo. At this time, the
largest landed estate in Connacht was that of the 9th Earl of Clannrickard.

Internecine feuds were to be the downfall of the de Burgos, so that by
1566 A.D.we see Riocard (*an Iaráinn*) de Burgo making submission to
Lord Sidney, emissary of the English Crown. In 1571, John, known as
Shane MacOliverus was made MacWilliam. Knox (1908:179). That same
year Sir Edmond Fitton marched into Connacht and destroyed nineteen
castles in South Mayo. Submissions by the local lords became inevitable
and a meeting was held in Galway in March, 1572, attended by Lord
Clannrickard, his sons, Ulick and John and the MacWilliam. Lord
Clannrickard was arrested and taken to Dublin by Fitton until his sons
submitted to the Crown and peace was restored in 1574, known as *The
Division of Connaught & Thomond*. Thomond became County Clare,
Galway and Roscommon having some adjustment but basically
remaining much as they are today; Sligo contained the former O'Rourke
territory of Leitrim, and Mayo comprised the territories formerly
belonging to MacWilliam Iochtarach:

*"Murrisk, containing Owle Imale and the lands (islands) viz.,
Inishturk and Inishark, Cliara (Clare) and the Aukilles (Achill) where
O'Malley is chief. Burris, containing Owle Clann Philipin, Owle Eighter,
and Slioch MacTybbot's lands where Riocard an Iaráinn is chief ."* Knox
(1908:181).

65

Achill

The de Burgos ruled Connacht for over 300 years. The MacWilliam title had come into being to denote the head of the line of William Óg in Connacht in the beginning of the fourteenth century; it ended with the departure of the last MacWilliam, Richard Bourke, the Devils' Hook's son for Spain at the beginning of the seventeenth century. The Devils' Hook *(Deamhan an Chorrain)* was the son-in-law of Grace O'Malley and lived in Corraun.

Riocard an Iaráinn, one of the last reigning de Burgo Lords was the second husband of Grace O'Malley, the famous Pirate and sea Queen. He acquired his nickname, Richard of the Iron *(an Iaráinn),* possibly because of the iron mines on his Burrishoole lands (Corraun). They had one son, Theobald of the Ships, who was born at sea. This Theobald was created Viscount Mayo in 1625 by King Charles I and he is the ancestor of Lord Altamont of Westport House. His tomb is still extant in Ballintubber Abbey. Another famous descendant of the de Burgos is the present President of Ireland, Mary Robinson, *nee* Bourke.

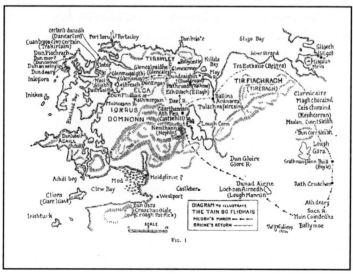

16. Routeway in Táin Bó Flidhais

9. The Ruling Families of Achill-The O'Malleys

THE O'MALLEYS

Terre Marique Potens - *"Powerful by Land and Sea"*
(The O'Malley motto).

According to the **Annals of Ulster (A.U.)** in 811 A.D. the Northmen descended on Umhall, but were slaughtered by the men of Umhall. They came again the next year and this time slaughtered the men of Umhall, killing Cosgrach, son of Flannabhrat, and Dunadach, king of Umhall. This Cosgrach belonged to the Clann Máille and represents the earliest O'Malley family reference. *Máille*, grandson of Cosgrach, who was killed by the Vikings in A.D. 812, is said to be the man after whom the O'Malley family, *Clann Máille* are called. In 1123 A.D. the name *Ó Máille* is first mentioned in the Annals. The O'Malleys are said to be true Gaels, *"Irish of the Irish"* and may have been descended from the *Patraige*, an Iron Age tribe. The name Malley comes from the Celtic word for chief, *Maglios*. The O'Malleys held the chieftainship of the two Umhalls, i.e. the baronies of Murrisk and Burrishoole until the 17th century. Their power was usurped first by the O'Connors, then by Henry Butler in A.D. 1238 and two centuries later by the de Burgos.

The Book of Rights in the 12th century lists tributes paid by the O'Malleys to the King of Connacht (O'Connor) which included 100 milch cows, 100 hogs and 100 casks of beer, the King reciprocating with *"five horses, five ships, five swords and five corslets."* Sir Edmond Fitton writing in 1575 refers to a number of chieftains who made submission to him at Galway after they had accepted the terms laid down by Sir Henry Sidney:

"to surrender their Irish tenures and take back their lands by the Queens' patent to descend by hereditary succession according to English law." Knox (1908:182).

Among those making submission were some of the principal men of the Clanndonnells, all mercenary soldiers by profession and called *Gallóglaí* (Gallowglasses), also, MacPhippipin (a Bourke) and Omayle (O'Malley), MacPhaten, Barrett, MacIvyle, Staunton, MacJordan, Dextar, MacCostello, Nangle and MacMorris. Knox (1908:185).

Achill

The Clanndonnells were regarded as the only men of force in Connacht and supported *Riocard an Iaráinn* (Bourke) as did the O'Malleys, including *Gráinne Ní Mháille* (Grace O'Malley), when they supported the Earl of Desmond in the rebellion against Malbie in 1580 A.D. Grace *(Gráinne Ní Mháille),* wife of Donal O'Flaherty of Connemara and secondly of *Riocard an Iaráinn ,* the mother of Theobald Bourke *"of the ships,"* first Viscount Mayo, was undoubtedly the most famous of the O'Malleys. We know comparatively little about her, largely due to a lack of documentary sources. Most of what we know about her life is contained in the English State Papers, in archives at Westport House, and in local folklore. In the former there is a record of *Gráinne* being constantly harassed by Richard Bingham, President of Connacht. She also fell foul of the Fitzgeralds and was imprisoned by the Earl of Desmond in Dublin Castle. Grace O'Malley's father, Owen *(Dubhdara)*, *"strong in galleys and seamen"* traded in fish with Spain and England and she herself demanded that foreign fishing fleets pay a toll for fishing in Clew Bay. Philip II of Spain reputedly paid £1000 for a 21 years lease to fish off the Irish coast.

Gráinne Ní Mháille's grandson, Lord Mayo, was executed in 1652 for his involvement in the Confederate Wars and had his lands confiscated. They were later restored to his son in 1676. The Marquis of Sligo traces his descent from the O'Malleys and the Bourkes *via Tibóid na Long* (Theobald of the Ships). His tomb, an odd mixture of styles is still extant at Ballintubber Abbey, Co. Mayo. As Sheila Mulloy (1991) points out the O'Malleys of recent times have distinguished themselves both in Ireland and in the U.S.A. Ernie O'Malley who wrote about 'The Troubles' in Ireland between 1916 to 1923; Pádraig O'Malley who was a member of the first Dáil in 1919 and the two O'Malleys from Limerick, the late Donogh and the former leader of the Progressive Democrats, Desmond O'Malley.

> " *A good man there never was of the Uí Máille but a mariner,*
>   *Of every weather they are prophets,*
>   *a tribe of brotherly affection and of friendship."*
>   O'Dugan (14th century).

9. The Ruling Families of Achill-The O'Donnells

THE O'DONNELLS

The O'Donnell's are said to be descended from Conall Gulban, a son of Niall of the Nine Hostages. Tírconnell (Donegal), the homeland of the O'Donnell's, means Conall's territory. The O'Donnells came to power in the 12th Century A.D. From an early date they collected tax and rent from the province of Connacht, setting up inheritances and inaugurating many of the ruling families in the area such as the Kelly's, MacDermot's (of Moylurg), MacDonaghs and O'Haras.

The O'Donnells of Donegal had long had an interest in Connacht.This interest was inherited from a long line of O'Donnell ancestors who had held sway over Connacht for many centuries. In 1595 Red Hugh O'Donnell, Earl of Tírconnell became involved in a dispute over the MacWilliamship (Bourkes) or the Lordship of Connacht. During this dispute O'Donnell presided over a gathering of the Lords and Barons of Connacht at Tirawley which included, Walter *(Ciotach =left-handed)* Bourke, MacCostello, MacJordan, MacDonnell, the Gallowglass, MacMaurice and O'Malley, whose prerogative it was to choose the MacWilliam, with O'Donnell having the casting vote. The island of Achill was supposedly used by the O'Donnells of Donegal as a *"penal colony"* around the 12th century A.D. but apart from folklore and a dearth of archaeological sites of this period, there is no evidence to substantiate this claim. Transgressors were sentenced to between one and seven years depending on the seriousness of their crime. Edward Newman (1839:8) may have been referring to this when he said:

"The natives of Achill are charged with being thieves and murderers; and if I were to place full credence on all I heard at the Settlement (Achill Mission), they would appear to be so. Mr. Long, however, with everything constantly exposed, walls and hedges here unknown, and living amongst a population from whom he has no power at all to defend himself, has never even lost a potato. I allude not to this subject politically; but bearing in mind solely the natural history of the island and its capability for improvement, I pronounce without hesitation, that if goodness of soil, lowness of rent, cheapness of labour and safety of property be recommendations - that no spot I have ever seen is more likely to reward

the emigrant than the island of Achill." The O'Donnells who lived in Mayo (Ross and Newport) in the Late Medieval period were descended from *Niall Garbh,* a cousin of *Red Hugh* (1572-1602). Red Hugh O'Donnell and Hugh O'Neill, Earls of Tírconnell and Tyrone led the last struggle against Elizabethan power in Ireland and were defeated at the Battle of Kinsale in 1641, afterwards fleeing to Spain in what became known as *The Flight of the Earls* . After the death of Red Hugh in Spain, *Niall Garbh* became chief and although a collaborator of the English,was lodged in the Tower of London and died there in A.D.1625. In the mid 17th Century, *Niall Garbh's* grandson, Rory, settled on a remote corner of the Ormond Estate (Burrishoole), in north-west Mayo. Rory's son, Manus, was a Colonel in the Jacobite army of King James I. Manus' son, Hugh, lived at Melcombe near Newport and is recorded as having subscribed £10 to build a Church in the town. He died in 1762 and his son, Neal, within a year of his father's death converted to the Protestant faith. This move obviously helped his career for in 1768 he became Magistrate of the District and was created a Baronet by the English Crown. Neal developed the town of Newport and became a very wealthy man. He purchased the Medlycott estate of Burrishoole, including the island of Achill, for the sum of £33,598.19s.4d. Pococke in 1752 said that the Medlycott Estate yielded an annual income of £1,700 but by 1800 Sir Neal had increased this to a staggering £8,000. He also got possession of **The Cathach,** a small book supposedly written by St. Columcille which belonged to the O'Donnell's of Donegal. His grandson, Manus, would deposit this book in a French monastery where it was later retrieved and is now in the Royal Irish Academy in Dublin. Neal, as Captain of a company of volunteers was involved in the 1798 uprising in the aftermath of which Fr. Manus Sweeney from Achill was hanged in Newport. Neal died in January, 1811 and in 1817, his son, Neal Beg inherited the estate. In 1827 when Neal's son Sir Richard assumed ownership, the Burrishoole estate was in decline. Sir Richard was known as a *"Darbyite",* a member of a religious sect affiliated to the *Plymouth Brethren*. In 1852, the island of Achill was sold to the Achill Mission Society for the sum of £17,500, £10,000 being paid by the Mission and £2,333.33 each by Messrs. William Pike, Thomas Brassy and Samuel

9. The Ruling Families of Achill-The O'Donnells

Holme. The remaining townlands in the north-east were sold separately in the same year. Dooniver continued under the proprietorship of the Marquis of Sligo who held it on lease from Sir Richard O'Donnell and the old McLoughlin lands in Bunacurry went to Dr. John McHale, Archbishop of Tuam, while the Valley and Corraun were purchased by William McCormack. In 1873, the Valley became the property of the Earl of Cavan and in 1888 the Dowager Duchess of Cavan sold this estate to Mrs. Agnes McDonnell, who later featured in the Lynchehaun saga (Famous Characters Section). Sir Richard O'Donnell died in 1879 and the O'Donnell residence in Newport became Newport House Hotel.

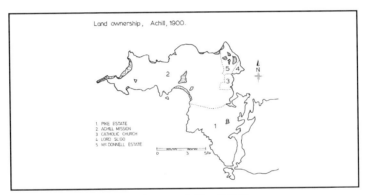

17. Landlord Division, after McNally (1973)

18. Lazy beds (ridge-and-furrow) oats ridges, Bunafahy

Achill

DUKE OF ORMOND HOLDING - 17TH CENTURY				
Owner	*Profitable Land*	*Unprofitable Land*	*Total*	*Townland*
Duke of Ormond			*4 Quarters*	*Akil*
	310	13,514	1 Quarter	Kildawnagh/ Kildawmod
	80	4,882	1 Quarter	Slewmore
			1 Quarter	Carrowgarve/ Achill Beg
	40	4,600	6 Bals	Dookinella
	40	5,300		Quinn
Total acreage:	470	28,296		

Source: Books of Survey and Distribution Mayo (1636-1703).

Chapter 10

THE LATE MEDIEVAL ISLAND

The Tudor Conquest of Ireland around 1600 heralded great changes in the landscape and in the way of life of the people. The Gaelic Lords, including MacWilliam Bourke of Galway, eventually and at various times for irregular periods swore allegiance to the British Crown and agreed to obey English Law. In the Composition of Connacht in 1585, compiled by Sir John Perrott, Lord Deputy of Ireland, the Gaelic Lords had surrendered their lands to the Crown but later received them back as a feudal grant. As a result of this, the independent peasant farmer now had the status of tenant; failure to pay rent resulted in confiscation of land with consequent fluctuation in ownership. It was during this time that the Earl of Ormond acquired, through his connection with Queen Elizabeth I, the Burrishoole lands of the Mayo Butlers. This suggests that either he or Elizabeth were familiar with events in remote Burrishoole, and that they also probably knew that the Mayo Butler line, in the absence of a male heir, would become extinct with the demise of Finola Garvey (*nee* Butler).

The Books of Survey and Distribution compiled in the seventeenth century (1636-1703), refers to Achill as: "*a Parish in the Barony of Burrishoole with the arable land in the valleys and near the shore, ownership of the island being vested in the Earl of Ormond.*" Simmington (1956). Land units, e.g. *quarter, trine, cartron or gneeve*, were common in Achill as elsewhere in Mayo and represent acreage units. However, the system of valuation related not to quantity but to quality as in the Duke of Ormond's holding, as shown in the Table on page 72. The *Baile* was the largest land unit which in the land assessment of the sixteenth and seventeenth century, roughly represented the modern province of Connacht. McErlean (1983). In the ***Books of Survey and Distribution*** Achill equalled four quarters. Quarters were sub-divided into sixteen cartrons, or twenty-four gnives. *Baile* (bally) and *rath* are two of the most common Irish placenames. MacAirt (1955) maintains that where *baile* placenames are common, the pre-Celtic farmers had been left in occupation of the land, even if relegated to bondsmen, while

73

raths accommodated the Celtic immigrant population who were generally freemen of superior social status. Price (1963) has argued that there is no evidence for the use of *baile* as a placename before the twelfth century and that the name may simply mean a *"piece of land"*. While the *Baile* represented the total estate, the fractional divisions within this were *"closely adapted to the subdivision and periodic rearrangement of property among the owning group."* McErlean (1983). Townlands said to be the oldest land units were divided into *"quarters"* (*ceatháir*) anglicised as *"carrow"*, meaning into four parts, as for example the townland of Carrowgarve, in Upper Achill. There is also variation in the amount of land contained in a *"quarter,"* as in the Earl of Ormond's holding, shown in the Table on page 72. There was no breakdown into arable and pasture until 1729. The ratio of unprofitable to profitable land during the tenure of the Duke of Ormond would suggest widespread pastoralism or transhumance, with a dominance of livestock over cultivation. This is in line with trends elsewhere in Mayo, a picture eloquently put to Walsingham, the English prime Minister by John Browne, Sheriff of Mayo, who said that *"...little corn was grown in the west of the county where the people lived mainly on the milk of their livestock."*

In the west, Gaelic Lords copying their Norman overlords built large Tower Houses like that in Kildavnet, while the majority of the population, which in former times had grouped their dwellings around the *rath* or ringfort, now clustered around the castle or tower house. By 1776 the practice of taking holdings in common, the Rundale system, was universal in the west of Ireland. This led to nucleated settlements called *clacháns,* although this word was not introduced into Ireland until the early nineteenth century, by a Scot named John Donaldson. Proudfoot (1959). *Baile Ailt,* now deserted, located west of the tower house in Kildavnet may be such an example. The *clachán* consisted of clusters of dwellings of related family units grouped together without formal plan and differing from the nucleated villages in the east and south of the country with their associated Churches and nearby Tower Houses. Interestingly, however, in the Kildavnet example, we find the Tower House located in close proximity to *Baile Ailt* and to an Early Medieval

10. The Late Medieval Island

Church and graveyard! Writers of the Late Medieval Period describe rural dwellings as primitive cabins with no chimney, door, stairs or windows. The houses in *Baile Ailt* are in the main large, substantial buildings, more akin to the medieval long-houses than to the examples cited above. The *clachán* evolved from a system where sons and daughters, acquiring land from their parents, tended to group their houses around the original homestead, eventually forming small nucleated settlement units. Intimately linked with the *clachán* was the system of Rundale, where land was held in common by all the people of the village and periodically redistributed as population increased until by the nineteenth century most of the units had become totally unviable. Subdivision of land had been encouraged by the absence of good management on many estates, such as the securing of labour *in lieu* of land allotment, the need for landlords to increase their political prestige by increasing the numbers of freeholders on their estates, and by the practice, described above, of granting land to family members upon marriage. Consequently large farms were broken into smaller and smaller plots, resulting eventually in unprofitable holdings. In Mayo at the advent of the Great Famine, subdivision of land had been carried to extremes; there was almost complete dependence upon the potato and agricultural methods were primitive; metal tools being totally unknown in Achill and other parts of the county! The famine totally destroyed this way of life:

"In many districts nothing is left but a vague recollection by old people that their fathers had told them how a dozen chimneys smoked where none is to-day, that whole villages once stood and people clustered "as thick as stars" where nothing but a slight unevenness in the fields and a forlorn sceach (bush/briar), or two is to be seen." Edwards & Williams, (1994:435).

Place names harbour echoes of long forgotten villages e.g. *Tóin ant Sean-Bháile, Finsheen, Tamnaghmore, Tamnaghlaur, etc.* Names of fields and houses dimly recall people who lived over a century ago. e.g.*The Scotch House,* in Annagh, *Teách na Man,* in Cloughmore, *Darby the Runner* in Dugort and *Brian a Stalkire* in Bunowna. Who were they? Only in folklore are they remembered!

Chapter 11

PRE-FAMINE ACHILL

"Seven *thousand people, connected to Ireland by a narrow bridge, live on the Isle of Achill in the shadow of blue mountains and in the gloom of brown peat bogs, they think in Irish and they speak in Irish.*"

H. V. Morton *In Search of Ireland* (1930).

Church organisation in the West of Ireland in the late 16th century was in disarray and most churches were roofless or in a state of dilapidation. Englishmen made up the clergy of the Established Church and the Irish clergy who had lost their livings joined the underground Church. Repression against Catholics carried on during the reign of William & Mary was followed by the Penal Laws during the reign of Queen Anne (1702-1714). Connacht in the eighteenth century was the most remote and most Catholic part of Ireland, reserved for 'delinquent' Catholic landowners banished by Cromwell to the West. The Catholic population outnumbered Protestants by a ratio of fifty to one. Simms (1958-59).

Penal Laws

The Penal Laws prohibited Catholics from entering parliament, holding government office, entering the legal profession and from holding commissions in the army and navy. The end result of this was that many of the Catholics in the professions and those with landed property, including Browne of the Neale, had become Protestants. According to Wall (1967:220) by 1778 out of total annual rentals in Ireland amounting to £4,000,000 Catholic proprietors were in receipt of only £60,000 per year. Among the mass of the Catholic peasantry, whose condition had been brought about by a rising population, was a resultant keen competition for land, despite escalating high rentals. Agriculture was the main source of livelihood and there was increased dependence

11. Pre-Famine Achill

upon the potato. The introduction of the Penal Laws had inflicted an oppressive, unjust and degrading lifestyle on the bulk of the population, and impoverished the vast majority of Irish Catholics. In addition to the above restrictions, they were not allowed to own property, and were prevented from practising their faith, so that by the end of the eighteenth century, living conditions, particularly for those resident in the west of the country, had degenerated into a state of abject poverty, degradation and ignorance. The Penal Laws were partly repealed in 1780 but Catholic Emancipation did not take place until 1829.

Economic progress set in train by the Napoleonic Wars (1794-1815), left the west largely unaffected and the despairing peasantry eventually resorted to rebellion in 1798. However, *pikes and pick axes* were no match for the English soldiery and the rebellion was quickly put down, despite an initial victory known as *"The Races of Castlebar."* The aftermath of the rebellion saw virtual annexation with Britain in the form of the Act of Union in 1800, which was of no benefit to the bulk of the population for instead of expected emancipation and prosperity, further calamity was to lie ahead. Edwards & Williams. (1994).

Rural Irish society was a complex hierarchy where each section had its allotted place according to the size of holdings. At the top of the pyramid was the landlord who set the rent paid by the tenant. Many of these were absentee landlords who had little interest in the welfare of their tenants, exacting as much rent as possible to finance their lifestyle in London, Paris and Rome. The resident landlords were in many cases as impoverished as their tenants, eventually losing their estates in the *Encumbered Estates Court*. A good example of this was the O'Donnell's of Newport and the McLoughlins, both landlords in Achill. The average holding of the tenant farmer was small: in the West 50% of holdings were under five acres. The conditions of the tenant farmers were little different to that of the cottier or agricultural labourer, for the landlord could increase the rent *at will* and all produce grown, with the exception of the potato, went to pay the rent. The labourer did not pay rent which was offset against labour performed at the behest of the landlord. Population increase exacerbated poverty, evictions were common and many people took to the roads as beggars. Edwards & Williams (1994).

Achill

Tithes

Tithes consisted of a tax levied on the entire population for the support of the clergy of the Established Church and as Catholics outnumbered Protestants by a ratio of fifty to one, tithes were unacceptable to the majority of the population. Resistance to the payment of tithes resulted in the Tithe War which saw the rise of secret societies, such as the Whiteboys, who terrorised the countryside keeping the police and military occupied. The government harried on all sides enacted the *Tithe Bill* of 1838, reduced the tithes and converted them into a charge on the land, payable by the landlord. O Muirithe (1972).

Population

On the eve of the Great Famine the population in Ireland totalled, according to the 1841 census, 8,175,125, five million of whom were dependent upon agriculture. 45% of farms were under five acres in size with only 7% being in excess of 30 acres. Connacht in 1841 had a population of 1,418,859 and possessed 43% of the six million acres of all the uncultivated land in the country. 78% of the population of Connacht were dependent on agriculture with 64% of holdings ranging between one and five acres in size (Edwards & Williams, 1994:89). Between 1821 and 1841 the population of County Mayo increased by over 100,000. Statistics for Ireland indicate that there were 217 people per square mile of arable land; in Connacht this rose to 386 people per square mile and in Mayo to 475, more than double the national average!

The Cottier tenant paid a rent of between £1.10 shillings and £2 per annum for land and a dwelling-house.The houses were generally wretched with the annual income of the labourer being £8 to £16 per annum. The pre-Famine economy was based upon fishing, kelp (seaweed) farming, cattle rearing and on the flax/linen industry. The potato, introduced at the end of the sixteenth century, was the mainstay of the vast majority of the population. The chief agricultural implement was the *loy* or spade, or the *gowl-gob* (primitive spade) used in Achill and north Mayo. The trenching method *(lazy beds)*, was the most favoured for sowing potatoes, the same as it had been for wheat and oats. The potato beds ranged from two feet to six feet in width, with the intervening trenches one foot wide by about two feet deep. The seed potatoes were laid on the surface of the ground and earthed up from the trenches. This resulted in providing a very efficient drainage system as well as dredging nutrients from the trenches and making them available to the newly sown crop. As the shoots appeared the crop was again moulded up from the trenches. This method of *lazy bed* cultivation allowed steep hillsides such as Slievemore to be cultivated, as well as areas where plough cultivation was not possible. A common practice was the *burning and paring of land* for potato cultivation and in Achill the *soot houses* were used to manufacture nitrates as an aid to cultivation. *Burning and paring* also enabled cultivation of mountain and bogland. The narrow potato drills only became possible after the introduction of the plough which was not introduced into Achill until after the mid nineteenth century. The popularity of the potato as a food source was facilitated by its ability to thrive on marginal land, a commodity which the west of Ireland has in abundance. Curwen (1818), maintained that *"...by counting the ascending range of cabins on a mountainside, a tolerably correct computation might be formed of the generations from its first settlement ."*

Communal sharing of work was normal with men working in groups called a *meitheal*, a communal or co-operative system, to bring in the harvest, cutting turf, fishing, building a house, etc. The women were occupied in weaving, knitting and cooking. Food was shared amongst the people in the village. If a large catch of fish was brought in, everyone got their share, and likewise in the killing of a pig, cow, sheep etc. The communal spirit extended to social life which centred around the *céili* (singing and dancing), held in various houses during the year. Wakes and weddings also involved participation by the whole community.The rapid industralization of Great Britain in the early nineteenth century provided employment for Irish emigrants and cheap and fast transport between Britain and Ireland. After the Napoleonic wars the price of wheat fell and rents became harder to collect. There was little work, and seasonal employment in Scotland and England became the norm. Economic decline followed upon the ending of the Napoleonic wars; absentee and self-seeking landlords discouraged intensive farming and sub-division of holdings made farming totally uneconomic. Irish economic and social life between 1800 and 1840 was undoubtedly poor but nevertheless during this period an effective Police force was set up; the National School system of Education was introduced and a Poor Law set up to cope with destitution.

Catholic Emancipation

The Act of Union did nothing to alleviate the plight of Catholics for King George III refused to comply with the wishes of William Pitt, his Prime Minister who had intended that Catholics would be given equality of rights under the Act. Daniel O'Connell founded the *Catholic Association* in 1823, the first fully democratic political party and twenty years after his election to the English Parliament, the Catholic Emancipation Act was passed into law in 1829.

Rundale

Rundale is defined as a system of joint tenure or tenure in common. The origin of the system is obscure. Edwards and Williams (1994), maintain that in 1845 it was estimated that there were almost two million acres of land in Ireland held in common or by joint tenancy. Much of this was probably grazing land and not tillage. The Rundale system centred around the village which with the attached land usually formed a townland. Each family had their holding of arable land scattered amongst those of their neighbours, sometimes in as many as thirty or forty plots. The now Deserted Village in Slievemore was a good example of this, where one tenant held several small strips of land at various locations throughout the village, some no bigger that one quarter acre in size.There were no fences and the strips of arable land were divided by stone walls or balks about a foot wide. Grazing was held in common and consequently all decisions relating to improvement required communal

11. Pre-Famine Achill

approval. The basic unit was the *sum* or *collop*, a land measure of use rather than of area. The *sum* equalled the quantity of grass necessary to support one cow (called cow's grass), two heifers or six to eight sheep. The family's holding was in direct proportion to the share of rent he paid to the landlord. A hierarchical social system existed by virtue of the fact that the townland was rented by one or two individuals from the landlord and a village headman or elder (the King) presided over disputes, collected taxes such as the county cess and generally oversaw the work of the community. An example of this can be seen in the Medlycott and O'Donnell Estate Rent Rolls from 1756 onwards, showing how land was rented on behalf of tenants in various townlands. By 1845 Mayo was the only county where Rundale still remained the dominant form of tenure.

Since the listing of the Earl of Ormond's Burrishoole Estate in the **Books of Survey and Distribution** (1636-1703) to the first Medlycott Rent Rolls, considerable sub-division of the original five townlands appears to have taken place, with new ones being carved out of the existing townlands. Records of these would probably be in the Medlycott Estate Papers, location unknown. There are no records of subdivision in the *Manuscript Collection* in the National Library. Similar alterations took place in the post-Congested Districts Board period, the Achill townlands undergoing further change, with new ones appearing and old ones disappearing. It seems that it was during this period that certain families became associated with different townlands e.g. Dookinella Calvy and Dookinella Thulis, etc.

The Rent Rolls on pages 82-84 would seem to confirm what Praeger (1904) noted at the end of the 19th century i.e. the dominance of pastoralism over arable cultivation on the island which must have a long history. Rents, to judge from the Rent Rolls are relatively high for the period, with variation in the rents paid in particular townlands. Sub-letting was the norm with high rents being common. Freeman (1957) indicated that rents ranged from between £6 to £10 per acre in the West of Ireland. The value of respective Fisheries and Kelp (seaweed) is indicated by the high rents they commanded; even the Encumbered Estates sales advertisements emphasised the desirability of acquiring an estate with a Fishery and/ or access to seaweed.

RENT ROLLS - ACHILL & CORRAUN - 18-19th CENTURY

YEAR	TOWNLAND	TENANT	RENT
1756	Tonragee-Tonatanvally	R. Geonty & Partners *	£48
1756	Corraun	Jm. 'Boy' Gallagher *	£50
1756	Dooega-Carrowgarrow	Ed. McNamara & Ptns. *	£56
1758	Dookinella-Gortnamanragill	Denis Sweeney *	£25
1758	Dookinella-Gortnamanragill	John McLoughlin *	£25
1761	Pt. of Slievemore (lease)	Thady O'Mulloy	£44
1761	Duaghmore & Crin & Gortakeel		
	Sparrow island	Chas. & Owen O'Malley *	£65
1770	Kildaunet	Neal O'Donnell	£58
1772	Kilguin?	John McLoughlin	£70
1772	Owenduff-Dooniver	John Mulloy	£16.3.6.
1776	Kildavnet	Owen O'Malley	£24
	Achill Beg	George O'Malley	£22
	Dooega+ 1/2 Carrowgarrow	Bryan Muloogo (Mulloy ?)	£29.11.11.
	Dookinella, etc	Bryan Mulloy Jn.	£37
	Dugort-Quinn-Dirk	John O'Malley	£43.11.11.
	Kildavnet	Col. O'Donnell	£55.11.11.
	Slievemore-Quinn-Tonatanvally-OTHER		
	Gortagill & Mill-Dooniver		
1776	Dookinella-Corraun-		
	Owenduff	J. McLoughlin	...
	Kildavnet-Achill Beg	Neal O'Donnell	...
	Dookinella 2.	Denis Sweeney	...
	Dooega	F. Sweeney	...
	Dugort	Owen O'Malley	...
	Doughmore	John O'Malley	...

11. Pre-Famine Achill

YEAR	TOWNLAND	TENANT	RENT
1788	Dookinella 1.	John McLoughlin	£26. 5. 0.
	Dookinella 2.	Denis Sweeney	£26. 5. 0.
	Owenduff	R. McGowan	£16.0. 0.
	Dookinella 1 & 2.	Rent increase	+ £47.10. 0.
	Kildavnet	Hugh O'Donnell	£58
	Kelp shores-Newport & Achill	Sir N. O'Donnell	£100
	Corraun (Gortmarle)	Pat McLoughlin	£110
	Dooega	Tenants	£95
	Dugort	Tenants	£34.13.0.
	Dooagh	Tenants	£68. 5. 0.
	Slievemore	Tenants	£46. 4. 0.
	Achill Beg	Tenants	£42.10 0.
		Tenants	£40
		Tenants	£80
	Fishery-Do(u)na	Sir N. O'Donnell	£100
	Kelp Shores	Sir N. O'Donnell	£150
1794-6	Achill Beg	Edmund Kilbane	£60
	Carrigorriff	Brian Heary	£50
	Dun Kinella	Terence Thavley	£54. 5. 0.
	Dun Kinella	Edmund Caffery	£54. 5. 0.
	Cashel	Neil Lynchan-P. McNulty.	£50
	Doogort	Pat & Owen O'Malley	£72. 2. 7.
	Keel	Thady Mangan & Co.	£150.15.0.
	Cloghmore	Brian Kilbane & Co.	£30
	Dereen-Kildavnet	Martin McHugh	£60. 8. 0.
	Saile	Pat Cafferkey	£30. 0. 0.
	Henly More (Slievemore?)	Loughlan O'Molloy	£100. 0. 0.
	Claggan	H. McMenamon	£40. 0. 0.
1798	Achill Beg	F. Gallagher	£30
1810	Dookinella 1.	Calvy & Company	£25
	Dookinella 2.	Thewlys and Company	£25

Achill

YEAR	TOWNLAND	TENANT	RENT
1810	Dooega	M. Lavelle	£95
	Dugort	Owen O'Malley	£35
	Carrowgarriff	John Kilbane	£25
	Keel	A. Molloy	£60
	Kildavnet	Gallagher & Company	£15
	Kildavnet-Cloughmore	John McLoughlin	£15
	Derreen	Quin & Company	£3
	Polranny	Lynchion	£12-15
	Polranny	Sweeney	£30
	Salia	McGreal & Company	£9
	Slievemore	Malley & Company	£46. 4. 0.
	Cashel	P. McNulty	£25
	Priest's dues	Quinn & Co. 0. 1Yr. Rent	£2.10.0.
1831	Achill Beg	J. Gallagher	£59. 1. 7.
	Carrowgarriff	Villagers	£47. 4. 1.
	Cashel	P. McNulty & Company	£46. 3. 1.
	Dooega	J. McShane	£175. 7. 9.
	Dugort	Owen O'Malley	£66. 14. 4.
	Keel	Richard Mangan	£138.12.10.
	Ballinacarriga	Kilbane & Company	£27.13.11.
	Cloughmore	Pat McLoughlin & Co.	£27.17.11.
	Derreens-Kildavnet	Pat McLoughlin	£56. 2. 9.
	Priest's Acres	M. Lyncheane & Co.	£4. 12. 4.
	Polranny	Lyncheane	£42. 0. 0.
	Polranny	Sweeney	£55. 7. 10.
	Slievemore	Owen O'Malley	£92. 6. 2.
	Kildavnet	E. Kilbane	£27.13.11.
	Salia	Andrew Dever	£27.13.11.

* *Residues of Estate (Medlycott) not included in conveyance to Earl of Altamont.*

11. Pre-Famine Achill

ACHILL 4 QUARTERS - 1729 (acreage)			
Townland	_Arable_	_Mountain/Bog_	_Pasture_
CORRAUN	69	3538	
KILDAVNET	173	1149	2044
CARROWGARROW	193	2050	1178
DOOEGA	9.2	1104	160
DOOKINELLA	62.2	1313	836
TONATANVALLY	67.2	1661	459
GORTAGILL & MILL	34	1715	148
DUGORT	89		237
DIRK, PART OF			
SLIEVEMORE			256
QUINN & DOOEGA	32	2228	520
DOONIVER	17	373	
GORTAMANRYGILL-			
PART OF SLIEVEMORE	20		62
DOEGHMORE			
(DOOAGH?)	65		482
REST OF SLIEVEMORE HELD BY			
ED. O'MALLEY	183.2	1776	228
PLUS SPARROW ISLAND			
IN DOEGHMORE TOWNLAND			8.2 ACRES

Source: Manuscript Collection, National Library of Ireland.

Achill

Townlands and acreage units as per Townland Index, 1851.

Townland	*Acres*	*Townland*	*Acres*
Bunacurry	*1226*	*Srahmore*	*353*
Cashel	*1687*	*Bal of Dookinella*	*189*
Dooniver	*767*	*Dookinella Calvy*	*1935*
Maumnaman	*569*	*Dookinella Thulis*	*793*
Salia	*1898*	*Belansally*	*833*
Tonatanvally	*2068*	*Dugort*	*226*
Carrickildavnet	*184*	*Dugort East*	*2034*
Carrowgarve	*206*	*Dugort West*	*1659*
Claggan	*173*	*Keel East*	*1644*
Cloughmore	*168*	*Keel West*	*4071*
Derreens	*1770*	*Slievemore*	*3722*
Dooega	*3761*	*Mweelin*	*1444*
Sraheens	*2207*		

Achill Land Owners, 1876.

	Acres	Valuation
John Carr, Mweelin	*125*	*£ 38. 00.*
Earl of Cavan, Dugort	*1900*	*£126. 00.*
Frank Gallagher, Bolinglanna	*210*	*4. 00.*
Owen Gallagher, Bolinglanna	*18*	*10s.*
Domnick Grehan, Tonragee East	*9*	*2. 5s.*
Michael Malley, Bolinglanna	*105*	*2. 10s.*
Michael Malley, Tonragee East	*6*	*1. 10s.*
Pat Malley, Bolinglanna	*14*	*3. 5s.*
Bryan Pat Patten, Bolinglanna	*26*	*10s.*
William Pike, Glendarary	*10,697*	*£673. 00.*
Trustees of Achill Mission Estate	*19,155*	*£1,011. 00.*

Chapter 12

TRAVELLERS' TALES - PRE-FAMINE

Dr. Pococke, 1752

Historians tend to rely on primary sources, i.e. first-hand accounts of events. The following account of Achill which would appear to fall into this category was however obtained by Dr. Pococke on his ***Irish Tour*** in 1752 from a local landlord, probably Sir Neal O'Donnell, for Pococke himself never actually visited the island: *"The inhabitants have a kind of sheep here with a coarse wool fit for yarn stockins, which they spin and knit and sell the stockins, to French seamen at Dugort, for about ten pence a pair; and with this produce they pay their rent. They have oats and potatoes sufficient for their own use."* Stokes (1891)

Arthur Young, 1776

Arthur Young writing about the great stock farms in County Mayo in 1776-77, viewed Achill, without any great interest from Rosshill on Newport Bay, and provided the following account of the island: *"The cottages of the Irish, which are called cabins, are the most miserable looking hovels that can well be conceived. The furniture of the cabins is as bad as the architecture; in very many consisting only of a pot for boiling their potatoes, a bit of a table, and one or two broken stools; beds are not found universally, the family lying on straw."*

19. Beehive Hut, Keel c.1900 A.D. © Lawrence Collection

Achill

James McParlan, 1802

James McParlan, writing about Achill in 1802, remarked on the subdivision of land which ranged between four to eight acres and which he maintained was a traditional feature of the Achill landscape.

J. B. Trotter, 1817

A first-hand account of Achill comes from J.B. Trotter who visited Achill in 1817. Sir Neal O' Donnell was the landlord when Trotter and his party called upon him in Newport. Sir Neal's father, also called Neal, who had met with Dr. Pococke during his visit to the area in 1752, had died in 1811. Trotter paints a picture of a thriving Burrishoole community with a vibrant linen industry, a weekly market where an average of two hundred pieces of linen were sold, exceeding previous sales going back fifteen to twenty years! Trotter saw Sir Neal as a generous and improving landlord who had given his tenantry a great deal of flax seed to sow and who *"lately had constructed a Linen Hall."* The Fisheries were also said to be excellent with great quantities of salmon and mullet being caught.

In Newport, Trotter met up with a group of Americans who had arrived by boat and decided to join them on their journey to North Mayo *via* Achill. He regaled his American friends with a potted history of the Achill people, saying: *"we are going to visit a relic of the ancient aborigine race, if it ever existed."* Where he obtained this snippet of information is unknown, as he does not elaborate. At Achill Sound, the journey was interrupted owing to a sudden hurricane and with wind and tide proving contrary, a landing was effected on Achill Beg Island. They were most favourably impressed with their welcome and the hospitality offered to them by the islanders in a nearby cottage where " *a snowy white tablecloth was spread on the table in their best room and excellent potatoes, milk, eggs and butter set out before us and no payment was accepted for the meal."* The people of Upper Achill have always been renowned for the generosity of their hospitality as was pointed out to Dr. Gerry Stockman. Stockman (1974).

12. Traveller's Tales - Pre-Famine

Trotter observed that the people were *all Irish speakers but also understood English*. He said the island was inhabited by ten to twelve families who cultivated, *oats and barley, flax and potatoes, had some sheep and cows, and fished to supplement their income*. Although the people had no surplus, their rent being paid in one *sum* in common, meaning that a single individual leased land from a landlord and then sublet to other tenants, as outlined in the Rent Rolls. The visitors expressed sorrow that these islanders had not more comforts e.g better gardens, out-houses, cattle and more fowl! *"Free, however, from fever (a blessing at the moment), and free from any of the miseries attending extreme poverty."* Trotter, (1819)

A Mr. Conway, agent to Sir Neal O'Donnell lent the party his boat to cross to the main island (Achill). Trotter was impressed with Achill, saying that it formed a small republic in itself : *"A large island of singular situation, with 5000 inhabitants, the sole property of Sir Neal O'Donnell. The people manufacture woollen stockings and cultivate with great care all the available arable parts of land. Great quantities of stockings form stacks in many homes."* Trotter (1819).

He pointed out, however, that there were grievances among the islanders at petty traders who came to the island to buy all the stockings together with linen-webs, butter and other commodities at low prices and then later sold them elsewhere at much higher prices!

"The islanders are very civil with comfortable habitations and tolerable farms. The island consists of several Hamlets, chiefly on the seashore, whose houses, built with round stones and without gables, have a very significant appearance. They cultivate some flax, have an abundance of (firing) turf, are cheerful and contented but some complain of high rents. The fertile ground is let in a sort of tenantry in common: the Hamlet divides a portion of land among the inhabitants and all are bound in one lease to pay a certain rent (sum) which equalled the amount of grass a full grown cow could eat in one season. As a result of this there is less improvement and continual discord. A portion of land can be given to a stranger or inherited, a new division is then called for which the

Achill

landlord may grant and the whole Hamlet is them thrown into confusion. This custom is ancient." What Trotter (1819), so eloquently described was the Rundale system,widespread throughout the west at that time. Beef prices were 1d (penny) per pound, mutton 1d per pound, geese and turkeys 6d each and ducks 2d each.

He said that the people were less well provided for on the spiritual level, for there was no priest on the island and going to a place of worship was rendered logistically impracticable. Tithes were however paid by the islanders despite the fact that all were Catholic, with many having never seen a Church or Minister! He was particularly taken with the young women, saying that *"the young women have a Grecian or foreign beauty which differs from English or indeed from people of Leinster and Munster. Black eyes and hair, so common in those areas are not to be found here at all."* He described an unusual sight at night, namely torches, made by placing burning turf on poles which the wind kept flaming and bright to light the way ahead.*"Achill has small but bad roads. There is no Doctor or Lawyer on the island but yet the people are healthy and submissive to the laws. There are few diseases, but fever is beginning to make some ravages. There is no Dispensary or Hospital within thirty miles. The people are extremely intelligent and have a love of information. They are respectful, tolerably educated, have reverence for the laws and are quiet and loyal. In 1798 a few young Achill men did join the rebellion but none returned. An Achill man will go to Castlebar in one day and return the next, on foot!"* Trotter (1819).

The people were said to be exceedingly hospitable, married young and had comfortable dwellings. As *"mountaineers they were naturally very active, had an independent manner but were were very agreeable to meet. They fished in summer but lamented the absence of a local market town."*

Seaweed was abundant and used as fertiliser but Trotter and later Edward Nangle of the Achill Mission claimed that bad agricultural methods, common to Connacht, were practised in Achill. *Burning and paring* was probably one such method. This method ensures abundant growth for a few years but leads ultimately to soil degeneration and erosion.

12. Traveller's Tales - Pre-Famine

The party walked over the bogs towards Minaun Head: *"as we reached rising ground, many comfortable cottages presented themselves and in one of them, with very humble accommodation, indeed, resided the priest of Achill."* It is not clear if the gentleman in question is a Protestant Minister, or a Roman Catholic Priest. Trotter was impressed with his library which contained some historical French works and which seemed to be the *"chief society"* he had in this sequestered spot! *"His emolument cannot exceed £20-£30 per annum."* The Rev. Joseph D'Arcy Sirr, writing in 1845, said that Achill was originally in the Parish of Burrishoole but *"owing to some visitation entries, the Archbishop considered it a distinct parish, and on dissolving the Union of Nenagh in 1830, he presented the supposed Rectory, as an honourable superannuation to the old Curate whom he found in the union, the Rev. Charles Wilson whose income was £100 p.a. There was no curer of souls, no Protestant congregation, no Church, no Glebe. It was seldom visited but by the landlord, the late Sir Neal O'Donnell, who sometimes took up his quarters there in a cabin."* Later accounts in the Achill **Missionary Herald** indicate that a Reverend Charles Wilson, Protestant Minister, was resident in Newport c.1831 while the **Tithes Register** place a Rev. Stoney in Dugort around the turn of the nineteenth century. Sirr's account would seem to be at variance with J.B. Trotter's eye-witness account of 1817:

"Remote from all the civilised hours of man, shut in by the sea and without even the ameliorating residence of one respectable person in the island, it was not supposed that the poor unenlightened inhabitants, who were even ignorant of the English language, could resist the allurement of superstition, or learn to improve either their social or moral condition." Trotter (1819).

At Minaun Head, Trotter and his party viewed the Atlantic ocean rolling its blue waves to the rocky shores or sandy beaches of Achill. *"Numerous villages, small but populous, and reduced to a diminutive size from our elevation; lakes, rivers and cultivated patches of fertile land, and intervening small mountains were spread immediately around us below."* On the summit of Minaun the party found a small heap of stones (cairn) to which Mr. Bald, (1836-40), Engineer and Surveyor,

Achill

resident in Mayo had added varieties of the greenest moss and the plant *"London Pride"* formed a couch of great beauty around them:

> *"Upon leaving Achill, we took leave of our friendly, young priest. Placed in this most remote and sequestered isle, without any society suiting the education he had received, he was performing sacred duties to his fellow creatures and following the example of his great master. Rowing us back out to our ship anchored in the Sound, a journey of one hour, the boatman spoke in Irish and sang songs. Other boats from Achill crossed the Bay to approach the ship with provisions."*
> Trotter (1819).

John Barrow, 1836

By 1836 when John Barrow visited Achill economic and social conditions had deteriorated dramatically: *"Its inhabitants are said to number 3000 to 4000 and to support themselves by planting potatoes, rye, barley, and oats; some few possess a cow and a pig, and some, in addition, a few sheep, but they are represented to be miserably poor and of course superstitious. In 1831, when relief was sent from England, most of them were in a state of starvation, many hundreds subsisting chiefly on seaweeds, mostly on the Fucus saccharifera, known in Ireland by the name of sloke - and the typhus fever raging among them."* Barrow (1836). This was probably due to the famine in 1831 which was exacerbated by extremely bad weather with violent storms and heavy rainfall.

Baptist Noel, 1837

Baptist Wriothesley Noel, writing about Achill in 1837 said: *"Its surface is mountain, moor and bog, interspersed with patches of potato-grounds, from which the inhabitants derive a poor and precarious support. There are sheep and cows on the island; but in severe winters many of these animals die of starvation.The houses are formed either of loose stones, rudely piled upon each other, without cement, or of sods dug from the bog, the roofing being often heath, laid upon bogwood. The inhabitants are small and have an emaciated look. There are no trees and there is little cultivation."* Noel (1837)

12. Traveller's Tales - Pre-Famine

Dr. Edward Newman, 1838

A description of Achill by the Dr. Edward Newman in 1838 refers to the island as *"more like a foreign land than any I have visited: the natives reside in huts, which a good deal resemble those of the Esquimaux Indians."* Newman (1839) counted sixteen villages, including booley (transhumance) villages, on the island with clusters of between twenty and eighty houses in each:

"These houses are summer residences only, are entirely deserted in winter, others winter residences only and deserted in summer." Newman (1839).

20.   Cabins in Cashel c.1850 A.D. © Ulster Museum

John O'Donovan, 1838

John O'Donovan in *The Ordnance Survey Name Books*   (1838-40) referred to the inhabitants of Achill as being mostly the descendants of the *Kinel-Connell* family who emigrated with O'Donnell, (from Donegal) about 200 years ago; *"they are shrewd and intelligent, and are well able to understand the motives of Nangle in telling lies of them ."* He refers to a Mr. McLoughlin who was said to be making some improvements on the island, teaching the natives the use of the plough of which they knew nothing! McLoughlin was said to be of the northern stock, a traveller and a man of great intelligence. Referring to Edward Nangle and the alleged worship by the Achill people of a stone God he said: *"There is no such thing, and Conor Patten tells me that Nangle invented it out of his own head. Who could believe him said Conor when he stated publicly that there are 365 islands in Achill in which the word of God was never heard!"* There are, however, 365 islands in Clew Bay!

Slievemore is described as being bounded on the north by Dugort West townland and the sea, on the east and south by Keel East townland, and on the west by Keel West. The townland of Slievemore was said to contain 3,722 acres, three roods and twenty one perches, including twenty six acres, one rood and ten perches of water, the property of Sir Richard O'Donnell, with the rent from tenants £100 per annum. In the townland were three villages: *Slievemore; Tonragee and Dooagh;* 300 acres were cultivated, set mainly in rye and potatoes.

"In the townland of Slievemore there is a Killeen or small graveyard which contained a Church dedicated to a Saint Colman. In the north-east part of it stands a mutilated cross, the arms of which are said to have been broken off by four tyrants, Coman, Cuimin, Henry and Puca who made an incursion into Achill and at the same time burned down a house of one Dubhdara (Dudley) O'Malley which stood near the western extremity of this churchyard"; but O'Donovan said he could get no account of who the quartet were or when they lived. O'Donovan (1838-40). A hollow flag *(bullaun)* which the pilgrims used to fill with water for the pattern lay close to the Holy Well, *"but O'Donovan did not see it."* Mason (1967).

G. Fairholt, 1843

A sketch by Fairholt (1843) in the ***Irish Independent*** described Dooagh village as a cluster of about forty cabins with not one chimney, *"the walls of uncemented sea stones, thatched with heath."* Home improvements were said to lead to further *rack-rents*, so that there was no initiative for improvement but,*"inhuman as were the prevailing living conditions of Achill's land serfs at that time, they were palatial compared to others elsewhere."*

12. Traveller's Tales - Pre-Famine

21. The Village of Dooagh, c.Late 19th century © Lawrence Collection

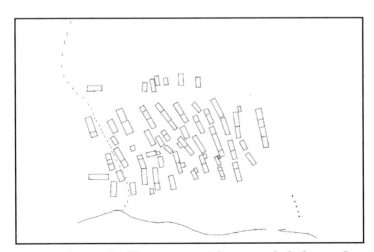

22. Plan of Dooagh Village, c.Late 19th century © Ordnance Survey

Chapter 13

THE GREAT FAMINE - 1845-1849

"Almost as many people emigrated from Ireland during the famine as died." Goodbody (1995:21).

The Great Famine caused the most sweeping changes in Ireland's social and economic structure. At the onset of the Great Famine the population of Ireland numbered 'eight million.' Except for a small industrial base in the north east, Ireland was mainly an agricultural country and from the eighteenth century onwards Irish labourers and small farmers became increasingly dependent upon the potato. It was perhaps inevitable that reliance on a single crop would lead to disaster; hardships experienced during previous famines, involving localised failures of the potato crop, between 1739 and 1741, 1800-01, 1816-17, 1822 and 1831 should have heralded warnings to the Government that a more serious failure would have catastrophic results for the general population. John McHale, Catholic Archbishop of Tuam wrote to Earl Grey, the British Prime Minister after the 1831 famine saying that *"unless the source of misery is checked by some vigorous legislative provisions, it will come again and again and be fraught at each returning visit with some new accumulation. Corn is being exported while the people are starving, the linen-trade which formerly employed large numbers of women is extinct. The people are digging up seed potatoes recently planted. "* Costello (1939). Predictably, however, there was no response and no precautions were taken so that when the potato blight *(phytophthora infestans)* struck, the country was taken by surprise, whole sections of the Irish population were decimated and the landscape of the country was irrevocably altered. In the aftermath of the Great Famine, it was estimated Ireland had lost one quarter of its population as a direct result of famine, disease and emigration.

The Great Irish Famine which devastated the country occurred between 1845 and 1849 as a result of a previously unknown disease *phytophthora infestans,* which produces black spots on leaves and a whitish mould on

13.   The Great Famine - 1845-1849

the underside of the leaf. The mould contains spores which can be transported by wind, rain and insects to other plants e.g. the potato. Once the fungus is established in the plant, the potato tuber in the soil becomes black around the edges and gradually becomes totally rotten and turns into a foul-smelling mush. While the initial blight was serious, the Relief Commission set up by the Government helped to limit mortality but in mid 1846, *The Times* reported that *"...what was last year but a partial destruction is now total annihilation; and it has become very general belief that the month of December will not find a single potato in the country. Ireland is, therefore, doomed to suffer a recurrence (if it should not rather be called a continuance) of that distress which has well nigh pauperised the whole population."* Goodbody (1995:3).

Sir Robert Peel, the British Prime Minister who would visit Achill after the Famine sent experts to Ireland to diagnose and to see whether it was possible to remedy the potato blight.

By 1847 the potato blight had spread to most parts of the country and distress was acute. An English Quaker, William Bennett, arrived in Dublin in 1847 and set out for Mayo and Donegal to distribute seed for green crops: these consisted of turnip, swede, carrot and mangel-wurzel, flax, parsnip and cabbage. His description of the extreme poverty being experienced in the west is graphically illustrated in the following extract:*"We entered a cabin. Stretched in one dark corner, scarcely visible, from the smoke and rags that covered them, were three children huddled together, lying there because they were too weak to rise, pale and ghastly, their little limbs - on removing a portion of the filthy covering - perfectly emaciated, eyes sunk, voice gone, and evidently in the last stage of actual starvation. Many cases were widows whose husbands had recently been taken off by fever, and their only pittance, obtained from the public works cut off ."* Goodbody (1995:26).

Another Quaker, William Forster, a Minister from Norwich armed with money to help relieve stress, and accompanied by a party of friends which included James Hack Tuke, toured some of the worst affected areas of the West, establishing links between the Central Relief Committee, set up by the Quakers in 1846, and local bodies to coordinate the distribution of aid. A letter from a member of Forster's party describing scenes in Co. Mayo was published in the United States arousing great sympathy and resulting in the receipt of large shipments of food and clothing, costing several hundred thousands of pounds and substantial cash donations towards Famine relief. Below is an extract from this letter:*"In the parts of Mayo which I visited, the failure (of the potato) is complete, and the destruction of the cottier population is total. They have nothing. The public works do not employ one quarter of them. There is no other employment. The wages of those who do get work are quite insufficient to support a family at present prices. They have been unable to purchase their usual supply of winter clothing, and a number had been forced by want to pawn any good clothes they had. The pigs are gone; the poultry are eaten or sold; the very dogs have been drowned, lest they should eat anything that would support human life. "* Goodbody (1995:22).

The principal relief agencies were the British Relief Association set up in London on January 1st, 1847 by the Rothschilds, Barings and others and the Central Relief Committee. The aim of the British Association was to relieve the *"very numerous class of the sufferers.....who are beyond the reach of of the Government"*; assistance was to be *"afforded by the distribution of Food, Clothing and Fuel; but in no case shall money be given to the parties relieved."* Woodham-Smith (1962:169). Government relief during the famine was based on the employment of labourers to build roads throughout the country; by 1847 the total number of labourers involved in these work projects had reached three quarters of a million, representing three million people if dependants are included. Goodbody (1995:20). Wages were close to or below starvation level so that the really destitute, paupers without land-holdings, vied for places in the Poor House, the majority of which were filled to capacity. This led to a change in Government policy so that the public works were abandoned in favour of Soup Kitchens with three million people being fed daily by the Government. Like the British Association and the Achill Mission, the Quakers were of the opinion that gratuitous relief was ultimately bad for the recipients. Therefore it became Government policy to provide loans

13. The Great Famine - 1845-1849

and/or grants to help set up various industries, such as kelp-processing, woollen manufacture, etc. throughout the country.

Irish Poor Law Act, 1838

The Irish Poor Law Act divided the country into 130 districts known as Poor Law Unions, each administered by a board of Guardians. 650 Relief Committees were set up to administer employment schemes, some of which were grant-aided and others financed by local loans. The Poor Law Amendment Act increased the number of Poor Law Unions from one hundred and thirty to one hundred and sixty three. According to James Hack Tuke the province of Connacht had nineteen of these Poor Law Unions. From 1843, a valuation scheme was introduced which made landlords responsible for the rates of all holdings under £4.

Fisheries

The Central Relief Committee (C.R.C.) set up by the Quakers encouraged fishing as an industry, particularly in the coastal areas of the west where fishing was an important mainstay of the population. Fishing stations were approved for Achill Sound, Galway, Belmullet and Clifden. Clifden and Achill Sound never got established and the other two were deemed unprofitable within a year. These fisheries administered from Dublin ran into basic organisational problems and local private enterprise was non-existent:

"A sum of three hundred pounds was made available to a single individual who was to remain responsible for it. With this he purchased fifteen boats along with the requisite nets, lines and other equipment at a cost of £14.10s.0d. per boat. He also bought ten currachs at £4 each and spent £42.10s.0d. on equipment for them, enabling some eighty to a hundred fishermen to return to work. The loan was secured on the boats and tackle and they were to remain the property of the C.R.C. until the loan was repaid, after which the ownership would transfer to the crew according to a formula set down by the C.R.C. This enterprise was established in November, 1847 and continued until October 1849 when the C.R.C. wound up the operation on the grounds of mismanagement by the proprietor." Goodbody (1995:23).

Achill

During a crisis, such as the Irish famine, articles tend to be sold or pawned in order to obtain money for food and these often include the very equipment needed for obtaining an income. On his journey to Connacht early in 1847 William Forster found that the fishermen in the tight-knit community of the Claddagh in Galway were unable to put to sea as they had pawned their nets and had no money to repair their boats. He made grants to them to remedy this. Goodbody (1995:22). James Hack Tuke (1848) records a similar situation which occurred in Achill:

"standing on the magnificent cliffs of Achill, we saw deep inlets and bays filled with shoals of mackerel and herring, the whole surface of the sea seemed completely alive with them. Around us an inexhaustible supply of food, but the people were wholly unable to procure it to allay their cravings." Nets and tackle had been sold *"to buy a little meal."* Tuke (1848).

He said that one fishing boat and three currachs only were engaged in fishing and that money was urgently required to develop the fisheries which would provide hundreds of people with employment. *"One of your correspondents"* (probably Robert Savage, a local Quaker and proprietor of the Achill Mission Hotel at Achill Sound) said that: *"with a loan of £100 he would be able to have 10 currachs built and fitted out with lines, etc. Ten boats would provide employment for a number of people."*

Tuke said that a small *curing station* had been established at Achill Sound which could preserve any quantity of fish not required in the district. This was an important development as even if large quantities of fish had been caught they could not be preserved or sold. This curing-station was probably the *"salt-pans"* referred to by Edward Nangle of the *Achill Mission* which were subsequently renovated by Alexander Hector of whom we shall hear more later. It seems that the Quakers did provide the requested loan to procure the currachs and fishing gear for Robert Savage in a letter published in the **Mayo Constitution** in 1847 confirms that a donation of £40 had been received *"to buy currachs for the poor fishermen of Achill."* One hundred dispossessed people from Achill were taken from the Work House in Westport and employment given to them as a result of this enterprise. The loan was repaid by 1848.

13. The Great Famine - 1845-1849

Tuke was obviously correct in his observation that shoals of fish were available for the taking and within the space of three weeks over 90,000 herring and mackerel were caught. The currach, however, is suitable only for in-shore fishing; deep-sea fishing required more substantial craft, so despite the abundance of fish in Clew Bay, the Achill fishermen risked life-and-limb to bring in large catches. The *Mayo Constitution* carried another article by Robert Savage detailing a major tragedy which had occurred in Achill on Monday, 8th November, 1847 when fishermen from the village of Keel after setting out from Portnaluinge (Boatport) in six boats ran into a violent storm which resulted in the drowning of nineteen men and boys. They left behind fourteen widows and thirty eight orphans. In addition, five Achill fishermen returning from Achill Head at the outset of the storm were swamped and all were drowned, making a total of twenty four Achill fishermen drowned. Dr. Adams of the Achill Mission writing in the *Achill Missionary Herald* said that:

"the cries resounding from the cabins in Keel, the wild screaming of the orphans, and the tears of the aged, made it one of the most distressing sights he had ever witnessed."

Food

Oats was the chief grain crop, rye being used for thatching cabins. Turnips and *mangel wurzel* were unknown in Achill before the Famine, and when introduced the people had to be taught how to sow them. *"In some places the mangel wurzel is good; elsewhere, there is a lack of knowledge of the cultivation of this crop so that farmers and cottiers sow the seed like grass, omit thinning, resulting in growth that takes place on top with a little taper root like a radish."* Tuke (1848). Indian meal, the chief food during the famine, was widely distributed, but again lack of knowledge in its preparation and cooking led to severe outbreaks of dysentery in many places.

In Connacht the quantity of corn and green crops sown was small. One quarter of the population lived on a diet of turnips and boiled half-decayed potatoes. A typical meal during the famine might have consisted of boiled turnips and fish or boiled oatmeal or Indian meal and milk. The origin of *boxty* may have been derived from the usage of blighted potatoes after the blight had been scraped off. Near the sea-coast, in places like Achill, seaweed and sand-eels supplemented the diet.

Connacht was divided into 19 *Poor Law Unions* and half the population of the province were said to reside at this time in mud cabins of worst description, with only one room. Tuke (1848). There were 67,000 labourers. Waste land comprised 1,906,000 acres, 46,000 farms of reasonable size and 44,000 farms under 15 acres in size. The net annual valuation was twenty shillings per head compared to £3 in Leinster.

Food stealing was common during the famine, although Achill appears to have had an exemplary record in this regard. In some parts of Connacht, people stored seed-potatoes in the floors of houses, others built *botháins* (huts) in the fields, and some sat up all night watching their stores. Sheep stealing was widely practised and in this sphere Achill was not immune. Seven years transportation was the usual penalty for sheep stealing. Robbery of food supplies was however generally rare, even in the west where poverty and hunger were endemic.Visitors to the Achill Missionary Settlement during the famine complimented the Achill people for allowing cart-loads of grain to travel, unmolested, throughout the island, without fear of robbery. There were one or two instances of theft but these were extremely rare.

Housing

Tuke (1848) during his visit to Connacht in 1847 provided graphic details about living conditions and also how whole villages had been deserted:

"This is no doubt in part owing to the decrease in population which is much more perceptible than I had anticipated; the inmates of whole villages have been swept away, and in Mayo alone the diminution of the population, by death or emigration, is estimated by many persons at 100,000, or one quarter of the whole." Tuke (1848).

Soup Kitchens

Soup kitchens had been used previously in the famine of 1739-41 and were later set up by the Society of Friends and other Relief agencies

13. The Great Famine - 1845-1849

again during the Great Famine. Recipients were vetted by the local Relief Committee who then assessed their needs. The relief consisted of a quart of soup and either bread or Indian meal. Tickets could be bought by charitable organisations or other agencies such as the Achill Mission for distribution to the poor. Funds to finance the soup kitchens came from voluntary donations, including Britain, the U.S.A. and Canada. There was criticism that unwholesome food was added to the soup resulting in dysentery and so rice was added as a preventative.

After the establishment of the Soup Kitchens, the Government abandoned the Public Works and £50,000 was lent to landlords to buy seed for distribution to their tenants. The very poor were classed as *paupers* and given outdoor relief paid for out of local rates.This was easier said than done. In 1844, the warship, *Stromboli,* and two Revenue cruisers stood by in Clew Bay to intimidate the people into paying their rates. Woodham-Smith (1962) said that Dean Kirwan, Catholic Dean of Mayo calculated that *"each shilling had cost a pound or more to collect"*.

Large boilers were used to prepare food for the soup kitchens. When set up in the open, the huge fires set underneath them gave rise to clouds of smoke which attracted people from neighbouring areas. This soup was distributed *via* a ticket with a name or number on it and entitled the recipient to a daily ration of this food. Often the relief food was of poor quality consisting of perhaps a sack of Indian meal or turnips, funds or supplies having been diverted elsewhere by members of Relief Committees. The bitterness felt by people receiving relief was the association of food distribution with proselytising activities, particularly so in areas like Achill and other parts of the west. The distribution of food by these proselytising societies was a strong inducement to the local population to attend bible-reading classes and/or send their children to the Mission schools.

The Poor House

At *Westport Poor House,* of the one hundred admitted in one day, *one half* were evicted tenantry from Keel and during the previous week seventy five people were admitted, also from Achill, nearly all of them

103

evicted by the same landlord! Tuke (1848) querying this with Sir Richard O'Donnell was told that Sir Richard was only the *"nominal owner"* of the island! However, tenancies were held *at will* i.e. for one year only, so eviction was easily obtained against defaulters. In addition, improvements carried out by the tenants reverted to the landlord with no claim for compensation, so there was no incentive to improve a holding.

On the 1st December, 1845 Mr. T.L.Wood visited Achill and subsequently wrote to Sir James Dombrain with his findings. He said that the potato blight was making a sad harvest, particularly in the northern part of the island. Visiting Achill Beg he observed a man opening a potato pit in the fields: *"...the sod which they place between the top covering and the potatoes, five out of every seven potatoes were found to be diseased."* On the 24th June, 1846 a letter to the Relief Commissioners stated that Sir Richard O'Donnell *"..in the absence of Lord Lucan has appointed a local Committee for the Temporary Relief of the Poor in this neighbourhood (Achill) consisting of the the following gentlemen:*

Reverend Edward Nangle, Achill Mission, Chairman,
Rev E. Lowe, Achill Mission, Rev. French, Achill Mission,
Rev. Fr. Dwyer, Parish Priest, Achill Sound, Rev. M. Monaghan,
Rev. W. Binkey, Mr. J. Campbell, Mr. Domnick McLoughlin, Achill,
Mr. John McLoughlin, Achill, Dr. Neason Adams, Achill Mission,
Treasurer and Mr. T. L. Wood, Secretary."

The Achill Relief Committee rapidly ran out of funds and all road works were suspended. Two hundred and seventy five people had been employed on the scheme until the money ran out.

The soil and climate of Connacht was particularly suited to the growth of flax, 2,499 acres were sown in 1847, half near Newport upon the estate of Sir Richard O'Donnell. Over one thousand people had been employed in the industry, mostly women. Tuke (1848) noted the disparity between what Sir Richard paid tenants for flax (5-7 shillings) and the market price of 15-20 shillings per acre. Sir Richard told Tuke: *"..that flax grown on his estate was sown too late and resulted in a poor crop - hence the low price."* Flax seed cost 25s ; 2 diggings 28s and rent 30s - 35s, so profit margins were extremely tight. Tuke (1848) condemned the Mayo

13. The Great Famine - 1845-1849

landlords for exacting high rents which tenants were unable to pay and for allowing the bailiffs to practice *"canting"* (selling by auction), small patches of oats or potatoes. Seizure of crops *in lieu* of non-payment of rent was often followed by eviction, with the roofs of houses being removed to prevent re-occupation. The following describes one such instance: *"Whilst upon the island of Achill, I saw a memorable instance in the course of proceeding, at the wretched fishing village of Keel, belonging to Sir Richard O'Donnell: here, a few days previous to my visit, some twenty families had been evicted, making, as I was informed, with a previous recent eviction, about forty evictions. "* He described a scene in Keel witnessed by him personally: *"One grey-haired old man bearing his bed-ridden wife in his arms pointed to his now roofless dwelling, the charred timbers of which were scattered in all directions. He said that he owed a little over one year's rent and lived in the village, which had been home to his forefathers, all his life. Another man, with five motherless children, had been expelled and their boiling-pot sold for 3s.6d. From this village alone one hundred and fifty persons had been evicted, owing from one half to one year's rent ."* Tuke (1848).

23. Maria O'Malley , Keel , 1932   Pat Weir, Keel, 1932

105

Chapter 14

THE ACHILL MISSION, 1831-1886

Background

The relative prosperity of the eighteenth century was drastically reduced in the aftermath of the Napoleonic wars (1795-1815), after which a majority of the Irish population experienced great poverty and a huge reduction in income. An increased demand for grain, leading to a rapid increase in the price had distorted the economy. The potato, for long the mainstay of the bulk of the population, had, during the war, been superseded by the production of grain. Grain was a 'cash crop', with attendant benefits going exclusively to landlords or wealthy tenants, the only people who could afford the higher rents being obtained as a result of the increased demand for land. To meet this almost insatiable demand for grain to feed the armies, there had been a shift from pastoral to tillage farming, involving a larger labour force but with the resultant benefits being offset by a rising population, increased demand for land, housing and employment. More and more Irish grassland, the traditional base of the Irish peasant farmer, had been broken up and tenants in possession of sizeable leaseholds had been able to set up as landlords themselves by creating under-tenancies. Green (1967:266). It became common practice for individual tenants to lease land and then sublet it, often at inflated rents. The Achill Rent Rolls of the eighteenth century mirror this trend very well. Landless men had no recourse but to reclaim the mountain and bog and colonise these areas. Therefore, peace when it came in 1815 had major implications for the Irish economy; Ireland was devoid of an industrial base and increased competition with Britain, plus monetary deflation until the amalgamation of the exchequers in 1826 all exacted their toll. The income of both landlord and peasant was drastically reduced while population continued to rise, unemployment soared, and emigration became an increasingly attractive option. By 1841 the census show that only 7% of holdings were over thirty acres and 45% under five acres. In Connacht this latter figure was as high as 64%. There was little

14. The Achill Mission, 1831-1886

sustainable work, repeated minor famines took their toll, and bereft of agricultural initiative by the Rundale system which involved constant subdivision of holdings, together with massive over-population and total dependence on the potato, life in rural Ireland deteriorated dramatically.

The *Treaty of Limerick* in 1691 had marked the onset of the Protestant ascendancy and the now almost exclusively Irish Protestant Parliament restored members of the Established Church of Ireland to dominant positions in society; Protestant nonconformists and Catholics became liable for the payment of Tithes (taxes) towards the upkeep of the Established Church and new anti-Catholic laws were passed.The people had nowhere to turn as the banishment of the Catholic clergy in 1697 forbade their return to Ireland under pain of death, and severely decimated the number of active priests in Ireland who were now fugitives from the law and dependent upon the Catholic population for food and refuge. Churches and chapels fell into disrepair and places of worship were few in number, the priests having to say Mass in private houses and at Mass Rocks. *The Act of Coercion* in 1765 further alienated the peasantry and encouraged in *"the masses of the rural population a spirit of non-cooperation with the ruling authorities, and a total lack of faith in legal methods and institutions as a means of redressing their wrongs."* Wall (1967:229). Despite denunciations and threats of excommunication by the Catholic clergy the people began to support secret societies such as the Whiteboys, proponents of agrarian violence, whom they obviously felt were better able to address their grievances. Eventually, the Catholic Church did manage to reorganise and by the middle of the eighteenth century had all but returned to full strength. The people who had endured the restrictions and persecutions of the Penal Laws had scarcely adapted to their new-found freedom of worship after Catholic Emancipation secured by the liberator, Daniel O'Connell in 1829, when proselytising stations now began to appear in some of the most socially and economically depressed areas in Ireland. The Achill Mission was one such organisation.

In the 1830's and 40's the Established Church of Ireland was still pre-eminent, encompassing within its membership the majority of the landed classes, many of whom had little sympathy with their tenantry. Prominent in this category would be the erstwhile Lord of Burrishoole, Sir Richard O'Donnell who had inherited the estate in 1827 upon the death of his father, Sir Neal O'Donnell. Sir Neal, had purchased the estate from Thomas Medlycott, Commissioner for Revenue for Mayo and Deputy Steward of Westminster under the Duke of Ormond. During the Medlycott tenure, the estate was producing in the region of £1100 per annum, but after Medlycott sold the estate to Sir Neal O'Donnell in 1798 that income rose to £8000 per annum, an incredible increase which reflects the economic benefits accruing from the increased demand for food during the Napoleonic Wars. The O'Donnells had a large flax plantation near Newport and also encouraged tenants on the estate to grow their own crops which they subsequently purchased, although as we have seen at well below market value. Tuke (1848). Some economic advantages do seem to have filtered down to the general population which were described by Trotter (1819). The inhabitants of Achill Beg were described as residing in clean, comfortable dwellings and living on their own produce. They had no access to a ministry and attendance at church was said to be logistically very difficult. Schools, apart from those privately instituted (Pay schools), were non-existent until the National Board of Education was set up in 1831 in order to establish a network of schools throughout Ireland. In the west of Ireland, this move was strongly opposed by Dr. John McHale, Catholic Archbishop of Tuam on the grounds that these schools would be non-denominational and implicitly support a British ethos.

That the Burrishoole estate of Sir Richard O'Donnell was seriously in debt by the 1830's is without question and local folklore is full of stories of emigration, and eviction in the wake of the downturn in the economy. Rent arrears became common, swiftly followed by evictions as witnessed by Tuke in Keel, with Sir Richard unaware of what his bailiffs were doing. He would also implicitly if not explicitly support the proselytising efforts of the Achill Mission, the result of his *"Darbyite"* leanings and anti-Catholic sentiments.

14. The Achill Mission, 1831-1886

O'DONNELL RENT ROLL 1829 -1831

DENOMINATIONS & TENANT ARREARS

	Arrears	Paid	Bal. due.	Rent p.a.
ACHILL BEG:				
John Gallagher & Co.	£214. 11. 2	£170. 3. 5	£44. 7. 9	£59. 1. 7
CARRAGARRIFF:				
Villagers	£165. 4. 3	£123. 2. 0	£42. 2. 3	£ 47. 4. 1
CASHILL:				
Pat McNulty & Co.	£168. 18. 7	£135. 0. 1	£33. 18. 6	£ 46. 3. 1
DOOEGA:				
James McShane	£613. 17. 1	£392. 9. 11	£221. 7. 2	£175. 7. 9
DOOGURTH:				
Owen O'Malley	£249. 4. 7	£186. 0. 7	£63. 4. 0	£ 66. 14. 4
KEELE:				
Richard Mangan & Co.	£524. 11. 2	£414. 2. 6	£110. 8. 8	£138. 12 . 0
KILDAVNET:				
E. Kilbayne	£106. 14. 1	£69. 17. 3	£36. 16. 10	£ 27. 13. 11
BALLINACARRIGA:				
Kilbane & Co.	£104. 16. 10	£71. 11. 10	£33. 5. 0	£ 27. 13. 11
P. McLoughlin & Co.	£102. 1. 4	£96. 18. 8	£ 5. 2. 8	£ 27. 17. 11
DERREEN/KILDAVNET:				
Pat McLoughlin & Co.	£209. 1. 6	£157. 10. 3	£51. 11. 3	£ 56. 2. 9
PRIEST'S ACRES:				
Mick Lyncheane & Co.	£18. 9. 3	£11. 10. 11	£ 6. 18. 4	£ 4. 12. 4
POLRANY:				
Lyncheane	£153. 17. 1	£103. 13. 9	£50. 3. 4	£42. 0. 0
POLRANNY:				
Sweeney	£193. 17. 1	£127. 8. 6	£66. 8. 6	£55. 7. 10
SALA (SALIA):				
Andrew Dever	£99. 11. 4	£58. 14. 7	£40. 16. 9	£ 27. 13. 11
SLIEVEMORE:				
Owen O'Malley	£341. 16. 7	£290. 10. 11	£51. 5. 8	£92. 6. 2

Source : Rent Roll Ms: 5745

Achill

General conditions on the island in 1831 were described by Edward Nangle (1837) of the Achill Mission, Fr. Connolly, Parish Priest (1834) and Mr. & Mrs. S.C. Hall (1841-43). These descriptions indicate a poverty-stricken population, said to be existing without the ameliorating influence of either social or religious support. *"A supply of driftwood for fuel and of seaweed for manure, while a shoal of herrings occasionally brought them a great influx of wealth!"* Nangle (1837). He described the Achill people *"...with few exceptions, as being on the verge of poverty, brought about by a recent minor famine and appalling weather conditions of gales, snow, sleet and freezing conditions."* There was but one *"Pay School"* at Achill Sound, with few pupils in attendance, and it was claimed that very few of even the most respectable farmers could read or write. There was no resident priest on the island and the people were said to be very superstitious, placing great faith in amulets of every kind and even worshipping a stone for their God! *Achill Missionary Herald (1837)*. Other accounts, including that of Dr. McHale confirmed the economic and social deprivations of the people. Dr. McHale maintained that a Bishop visited the island once every year and that one or possibly two priests ministered on the island. However, they do appear to have been non-resident. Fr. Connolly in his assessment of conditions on the island, said: *"following years of difficulty and distress the people are starving and reduced to the lowest ebb of misery by the exaction of immense sums of rent,"* mainly arrears, which had accrued over fifteen years. *"The leases of those who could not meet this demand of the landlord were broken, their lands stripped, and of course the rent raised, and their houses tumbled in the most inclement season of the year."* , *Achill Missionary Herald (1837)*.

Nangle claimed that the people of Achill were without skills of any kind, even metal tools being a rarity on the island. Houses were described as being constructed of rough cobbles and turf, some having no chimney, and the door being the only outlet for the smoke from the fire. The island had few trees *"..nothing higher than an osier"* (willow) - the vegetation consisted mainly of heath, juniper and coarse grass. The superstitious nature of the islanders was cause for comment: *"it was a common*

14. The Achill Mission, 1831-1886

practice among them preparatory to the building of the Colony to find people swearing "by Slievemore " and worshipping a stone altar at the foot of Slievemore which tumbled down last year, as another piece of idolatry." The latter may be the Portal Tomb in Dugort West. Worship of a *Stone God* circulated by Edward Nangle would later be contradicted in an anonymous article in the **Freemans Journal** (1850):*"regarding the ignorance of the people adoring a large stone set up as idol for public worship. Was this a deliberate falsehood? The Islanders are well instructed in the faith, the intelligence and shrewdness of their character renders the thing quite absurd."* Achill may have become confused with Inishkea Island. Worship on Inishkea of the *Naomh Óg*, a stone idol, kept wrapped in flannel, was well known. A priestess from a particular family looked after the idol which was brought out on ceremonial occasions. Ritual involved the supplicant kneeling before the idol, its face having been sited towards a point where the wind was blowing, repeating seven *paters and aves*, after which the requested favour would follow! Idol worship and other idolatrous practices would be excuse enough for Edward Nangle to commence his proselytising mission.

Origin

"A man of deep personal piety, and animated with a burning zeal for the glory of God. Liberal in his views - nothing of High Churchiasm. Sound in his theology. In controversy he was adept but indulged in invective. He was impulsive and obstinate and a fearless champion of the truth. A man of self-denial and sacrifice." Armstrong (1906).

The Reverend Edward Nangle was born at Kildalkey, Athboy, County Meath in 1799, the son of Captain Walter Nangle who had been married three times. Edward Nangle graduated from Trinity College in 1823 and the following year was appointed as a minister in Athboy but after a short while he was transferred to Arva, in County Cavan where he became indisposed as a result of illness. This illness involved a nervous breakdown and thereafter he was prone to severe bouts of manic depression. Induced by perusal of **Anderson's Historical Sketches of the Native Irish (1830)**, he decided to study the Irish language during his convalescence. In 1828 he married his first wife, Eliza, whom he had met in Arva: in the same place he also met Dr. Neason Adams who would become his lifelong friend and ally. For five years he lived in comparative poverty, seeking patronage from various establishment sources until, eventually, he was made secretary of the Sunday School Society and literary assistant in a religious tract office in Dublin. Bowen (1970).

Hearing about an abortive attempt by the Baptists to set up a school at Achill Sound in 1830, he began to lay down plans for the establishment of a Mission on the same plan as that used by the *United Brethren* (Moravians) whose main aim was to convert Catholics to the Protestant faith. The main objective of the Mission was a proselytising one and this was clearly stated by Edward Nangle himself in **The Origin, Progress and Difficulties of the Achill Mission (1839)**, and *reiterated by the statement: " ..we never made any secret of it."* Edward Nangle had been greatly influenced by the Methodists whom he considered more liberal than the Calvinists and the United Brethren were an off-shoot of the Methodists and more importantly they were also *missionaries*. Bowen (1970) quoting Monck-Mason, Secretary of the Irish Society, said that from the outset Nangle displayed banners of opposition to existing superstitions, leaving the Irish Society, the slower job of undermining them!

In 1817 and 1819 the first of a number of famines hit the west coast of Ireland and these were followed in 1831 by a much more severe famine which brought in its wake cholera and dysentery. Probably at the instigation of the Rev. Stoney, Rector of Burrishoole, Edward Nangle and his wife decided to accompany a cargo of Indian corn on board the *The Nottingham* which was being sent to Westport by a Relief Committee in Dublin. The Tithes Register contains the name of a Rev. N. B. Stoney with an address in Doogurth, Achill, in 1788, the recipient of £100 per annum in *tithes*. The Rev. Stoney who met Edward Nangle in Westport was then in his early thirties and was probably a son of the Rev. N.B. Stoney. Both father and son would undoubtedly have had considerable knowledge of local conditions for Nangle *"...hearing of the great distress being experienced in Achill he decided to visit the island."* His reconnaissance complete, Edward Nangle returned to Dublin and set in

14. The Achill Mission, 1831-1886

train plans to set up a Mission on the island of Achill, the first such Mission to use the Irish language as a means of converting Catholics! Whilst in the West in 1831, he had received encouragement for his venture from Sir Richard O'Donnell, landlord of Achill who agreed to grant him a lease of mountain land in Dugort at the nominal sum of *one shilling* per annum.

Edward Nangle's first encounter with Achill was favourable as it confirmed his thesis that the island was ripe for a proselytising Mission. The arrival of the Achill Mission must have had a certain appeal to the islanders with a promise of work, schools for children and no doubt anticipated future prosperity. Bonfires were lit on the beach in Dugort to welcome him to the island. The *Achill Missionary Herald* confirms this belief saying that there was free and friendly intercourse between the Mission and the locals for about three months until the Catholic Church intervened, referring presumably to the visit in 1835 by Dr. McHale. That these good relations would have been maintained is unlikely to judge from the following contemporary statement of 1842:

> *"...we receive little encouragement to believe that, even if the plan and conduct of the Mission were wise, humane, charitable, and, in a word, Christian, its purpose has been worked out in such a manner not at all commensurate with the large amount of monies expended in its formation and sustainment."* Halls (1841-43).

Years of neglect and indifference by the Catholic Church, together with the absence of support from the Established Church probably led to a certain religious ambivalence amongst the Achill people, which was compounded by the injustices of the Penal Laws, the imposition of Tithes, and the execution of Fr. Manus Sweeney in Newport in 1798. Suddenly, in both the religious and political sphere, they were confronted by two opposing factions, both vying for their support. The mass exodus from the Catholic Church during the Great Famine was no doubt exacerbated by *"hunger and thirst"* with the provision of food for children attending Mission schools no doubt a powerful incentive for recantation from Rome, but the loose ties seen heretofore between the people and that Church probably made such recantation less problematical than previously supposed. Edward Nangle himself cited *"neglect of the people by the Catholic Church"* as one reason for the initial success of the Mission. The Catholic clergy on the other hand claimed that the large *"coffers "* of money being sent from England to the Mission during the famine placed it in a financially unassailable position as far as inducements to converts were concerned.

Setting up the Mission

"Dugort where in ages dreary,
Nangle bold Apostle came,
To comfort the sick and weary,
Wastes of darkness to reclaim."

Schools Manuscripts Collection, Irish Folklore Commission, U.C.D.

Edward Nangle, having secured a lease of 130 acres of land in Dugort proceeded with his plan of establishing a Mission on Achill. He formed a committee to oversee the work of the Mission which would use the medium of the native Irish language to convert the islanders. Two main objectives were stated: religious conversion and the social improvement of the tenantry on the Mission estate. In practice, the latter aim was largely ignored. A steward was engaged and sent to Achill in the summer of 1833 to supervise the reclamation of a wild tract of moorland and erect houses for two families. This land was drained and reclaimed over a period of two years. A farm was soon enclosed under the supervision of a superintendent, a church erected, followed by seven slated houses, an infant school, a printing office and a small dispensary. Soon the Mission grew into a village on the barren mountainside with cultivated fields and gardens. A schoolmaster was sent to the island that same year and was followed shortly by a scripture reader and another house was erected. Edward Nangle, arrived in Achill in July 1834, accompanied by his family. He was followed within a short time by another Minister and three more Scripture Readers. The initial population in the Settlement included a Clergyman, Minister, Four Scripture Readers, and a Superintendent and Steward.

14. The Achill Mission, 1831-1886

Communications at this time were by sea as there were few roads on the island. Nevertheless, despite the difficulty in getting supplies, reclamation and agricultural activity proceeded rapidly:

"a small field of oats was reaped on our mission farm, the grain is of the finest quality. The ground where it grew was a useless bog three years ago. A limestone quarry which a friend lately discovered in the immediate neighbourhood of our Settlement, will greatly forward our agricultural work, as we find by experience that lime is the best manure for the bog-land, indeed it cannot be effectively reclaimed without it. Our potato crop is remarkably productive, and we are happy to say that it is generally so throughout the island." **Achill Missionary Herald (1837)**.

Spade cultivation was the norm at the time so presumably there were some metal tools on the island, as demonstrated by the numerous pre-famine lazy beds in Slievemore, Bunafahy, Ashleam and elsewhere on the island. The people initially associated with the Achill Mission appear to have come from a variety of backgrounds and included many of the coastguards and their families already resident on the island. One of the coastguards, Mr. Reynolds, a chief officer resident in Keel had already served one term in Achill and was now serving a second term. He claimed that the Mission had in a short space of time effected great improvement in *"the cultivation of land and in the provision of schools,"* and said that some of the islanders were more respectable than others! Charles Bridger, who arrived with his family, was employed as the Achill Mission Steward at a salary £40 p.a. He was originally from the south of England but had been resident in Ireland for eleven years before being recruited by the Achill Mission to work in Dugort. Thomas Ralph, a convert was employed as a Scripture Reader at a salary of £24 p.a. and came to Achill in 1834 after meeting Edward Nangle in Ballina, Co.Mayo, having previously worked for a Mr. Blest in Sligo. Others included John Gardiner, Thomas Williams, Mr. Bradshaw, the Rev. Joseph Baylee and Thomas McNulty, the latter a bible reader but employed as a labourer by the Mission. He had originally come to Achill as a servant boy to Mr. Bridger. James O'Donnell, foster brother of Sir Richard O'Donnell, formerly with the coastguards but after dismissal from this body for alleged involvement in Ribbonism, became a schoolmaster in Dugort. Accompanying Edward Nangle was his wife, Eliza, a skilled bookkeeper who would save the Mission book-keeping fees over many years! A contemporary description refers to her as a frugal woman:

"...her first house was scanty and consisted of a sitting room which was also the assistant Missionary's bedroom. The house was situated on the side of an uncouth mountain. A small patch of ground was turned up to grow stunted vegetables. Food only available at Newport, and no roads to the Settlement." Her encounter with Asneath Nicholson (1847) indicates a dour, suspicious woman. She died in 1850 and was buried in Dugort along with five of her children. She was survived by her husband and three boys.

Dr. Adams and his wife, Isabella, whom Edward Nangle had met in Arva in 1828 and who became his lifelong friends, accompanied him to Achill and set up a Dispensary in Dugort. It appears that Dr. Adams may have been present during Nangle's first nervous breakdown as there is mention of the fact that Dr. Adams cared for him (Nangle) when no one else would.

Mission Schools

The National Board of Education established in 1831 had met, as we have seen, with initial resistance from the Catholic Church, particularly from Dr. John McHale, Archbishop of Tuam who opposed its introduction on the grounds that the schools would be non-denominational, schoolbooks would have a decidedly British content and the Irish language would not be compulsory. He eventually, if reluctantly, accepted the idea and later became adept at availing of the attendant financial benefits to set up several National schools in Achill to counter what he saw as the proselytising efforts being undertaken by the Mission schools. On his instructions, Fr. Connolly, Parish Priest of Achill in 1835, applied to the National Board of Education for permission to set up six National schools on the island. Edward Nangle had opened his first school in the village of Slievemore on the 23rd December, 1834 with

14. The Achill Mission, 1831-1886

forty-three children in attendance, several more turning up the following day. By 1836 schools were established at Dugort, Cashel and Keel which were attended by four hundred and twenty children. Nangle, needless to say, strongly objected when rival National schools were erected, not as one might have expected throughout the island, but confined to those areas already occupied by the Mission schools. This led to innumerable verbal and physical disputes between the rival denominations, many ending up in Court. Nangle assailed the religious principles of Fr. Connolly and the Catholic Church, while Fr. Connolly retaliated by stirring up his congregation against the Mission.

Mission Schools: 1835

Slievemore	*140 pupils*
Dugort	*160*
Keel	*40*
Cashel	*80*

Later other Mission schools would be established at: Dooega, Bunanioo, Polranny , Mweelin, Cloughmore and Derreens.

Edward Nangle placed great emphasis on education and contrasted the Settlement with the rest of the island: *"It is a distressing sight when walking through the villages in this island to see children, dogs, pigs and poultry congregated at the doors, or basking in the sun, all receiving the same education. The mind unavoidably turns to the Colony where sixty one children in the Infant school may be seen daily committing to memory, their scripture exercises and learning to sing the praises of God through redeeming love."* In 1837, the first year of issue of the **Achill Herald,** an advertisement was placed for a Schoolmaster at one of the Mission schools at a salary of £150 per annum.

The people

The friendly relations that existed initially between the local population and the Mission were shattered when Dr. McHale visited the island in 1835 and shortly afterwards appointed a Fr. Connolly to succeed Fr. O'Malley as Parish Priest. In dealing with the Mission, the policy of the Archbishop was to fight *fire with fire*, and the succession of priests sent by him to Achill all exhibited strong militant tendencies. Fr. Connolly upon his arrival immediately denounced the Mission from the pulpit of the chapel in Dookinella Thulis, after which local labourers refused to work at the Settlement. Within a short time Edward Nangle claimed that a *"furious persecution"* had been organised against the Mission at the instigation of Dr. McHale. Fr. Connolly added fuel to the fire by sending a letter to the Achill Mission which was subsequently published in the ***Achill Herald*** claiming that the *"...Colony was opened up to the drunkard, the sheep stealer and the adulterer; the poor were tempted with bribes, the naked were promised clothing, the hungry, food, the able-bodied, labour, the homeless, a cottage, in a word everything provided they apostatized from their faith ."* There are several references to a Chapel in Dookinella Thulis, located in the now derelict villages of *Baile Thuas* and *Baile Thios.* Patrick Comerford *(Scoil Acla Lecture, 1996),* claims that Kildavnet was the only Church in use in Achill in the 1830's and that there were two priests ministering on the island, but there is no mention of Dr. McHale visiting this Church during his first (1835) visit to the island while on a subsequent visit he confirmed children in Dookinella Church *"...because the Church in the south of the island was closed! "*

Controversy

Mr. & Mrs. Hall visited Achill in 1842 and despite Nangle's claim that their stay was of short duration, they nevertheless managed to acquire substantial information concerning the activities of the Mission:

"The establishment of the Colony commenced in 1833 for the avowed purpose of converting Romanists; a tract of reclaimable land (being, however, nearly the worst upon the island and most inauspiciously selected), was obtained, and work commenced on August 1st, 1834. The Colony is supported by donations and subscriptions. The 7th and 8th Reports are before us (1841) and from these we receive very little encouragement to believe that, even if the plan and conduct of the Mission were wise, humane, charitable, and in a word, christian, its purpose has been worked out in a manner not at all commensurate with

these large amount of moneys expended in its formation and sustainment" Halls (1841-43). They said that the Colony was composed of fifty families numbering three hundred and sixty five individuals, out of which, eleven were originally Protestant, the remainder being Roman Catholic converts, of whom nineteen were from Achill, "*...others come from distant parts of Ireland and some even from England! Out of a population of 6000 in Achill, only ninety two were converted by the Mission in nine years .*" According to the Halls what Achill needed was not a proselytising station but a colony of men "*... who took a human view of the human wants and human feelings of these poor islanders.*" Freeman (1957) quotes from the 1838 Report of the Mission: "*We likewise built a number of small cottages and when persons present themselves, expressing a desire to be sheltered from the tyranny of the R.C. priests and their police, and to receive scriptural instruction for themselves and their children, we let them one of the cottages with a plot of ground attached to it, at a fair rent.*" The Halls claimed that the principal feature of the Settlement was the Orphan school, an issue which more than any other, inflamed the passions of the Catholic clergy, including Dr. McHale. These orphans were generally of Catholic parentage taken in by the Mission and brought up as Protestants in the Dugort orphanage. Although the Halls saw the education of children as a worthwhile project, they were not encouraged by the 1841 Mission report concerning the fate of pupils (converts), who had left the Mission schools:

3 female orphans sent into service
8 boys learning trades
3 supporting themselves.

A boy named Hart, whom the Halls had picked up on the road after being expelled from the Mission had his good clothes taken away before leaving and given three shillings for his journey from Achill to Sligo. In Newport a local Church of Ireland clergyman brought out five other orphan boys who had been expelled from the Mission. The Halls also enumerated the methods used by the Mission to obtain funds. Collections

were made under different categories but all were controlled by Edward
Nangle and the Achill Mission Committee.

Fund-raising categories:

1. Mission

2. Orphan asylum

3. Dispensary

4. Bible Society

5. Donations of clothing

6. Relief of distress

7. Infant school

"*The average collection is £3000 per annum, managed by the Mission
Board of Guardians, many of whom have never visited the Settlement.*"
Halls, 1841-43).

Although Edward Nangle would claim that the account of the Mission
published by the Halls (1841-43) was the result of a twelve hour visit to
the island, much of it seems to have been true and indeed appears to be
confirmed in Edward Nangle's own writings in the ***Achill Missionary
Herald.*** According to the Halls the principle objective of their visit to
Achill was an inspection of the Colony "*of which we had heard opposite
accounts:*" for example, "*...a bundle of firebrands;*" "*...a sanctuary for
the oppressed?*" Halls (1841-43)

The Colony

The Halls provided a contemporary account of the layout of the Colony
as it was and is still called today: "*The Colony is situated on the northern
part of the island near the village of Dugort, at the foot of Slievemore and
at the mouth of a small bay. It consists of a terrace, at one extremity of
which is the school, with the offices connected with it; at the other are the
infirmary, the mill and the dispensary and in the centre are a small hotel,
the printing office and the residence of the missionary-in-chief, the Rev.
Edward Nangle. The dwellings of the labourers are built up the hill at the
back of this terrace, which seems to be occupied exclusively by the
official personages of the mission; some of the workmen have also*

14. The Achill Mission, 1831-1886

residences in Dugort. The period of our visit was an unfortunate one; a contagious disease was raging, the school was, for a time, deserted in consequence and we may, no doubt, assume that this accounts for the absence of neatness and cleanliness upon which we had calculated, as marking the distinction between the colonists and their less favoured neighbours." Halls (1841-43). Asneath Nicholson (1847) visited the colony and found that while there had been some improvement in the living conditions of a few people, the majority continued to live in desperate poverty: *"The neat white cottages and the pleasant roads make a striking contrast with the hurdles about Molly Vesey's, but I do not speak sarcastically when I say that the manners of the people in the shop where I waited, and in the the parlour of Mr. Nangle, were not in so good keeping with christian refinement as were those in the cabin of Molly. I had looked in the cabins of many converts in Dingle and in Achill, and though their feet were washed cleaner, their stools scoured whiter and their hearths swept better than in many of the mountain cabins, yet their eightpence a day will never put shoes upon their feet, convert their stools into chairs, or give them any better broom than the mountain heath for sweeping their cabins. It will never give them the palatable well-spread board around which their masters sit and which they have earned for them by their scantily paid toil."* Nicholson (1847). Nangle, predictably, attacked Mrs. Nicholson in the *Achill Missionary Herald and Western Witness* for creating a spirit of discontent among the *lower orders,* making them see their superiors as unfeeling oppressors!

The Achill Missionary Herald and Western Witness, 1837-1864.

The Achill Mission had been in existence for six years prior to the publication of the *Achill Missionary Herald and Western Witness,* the previous six years having been spent setting up the Mission, reclaiming wasteland and constructing buildings for staff, converts and orphans.

The first issue of the Achill *Missionary Herald & Western Witness* was produced in July, 1837, the editorial comment by the editor, the Reverend Edward Nangle, would set the tone for succeeding issues of which there would be prolific output; the frequent controversial content would bring notoriety to Achill and ensure that the island became well known to people in many parts of the world. The famous and not-so-famous would visit the island over the years in order to observe the work of the Mission at first hand. The *Achill Missionary Herald and Western Witness*, a monthly journal would bring news of the Mission to those who were unable to visit so that they too might follow the exploits of Edward Nangle as he pursued his proselytising activities.The following extract is taken verbatim from the first issue of the *Achill Missionary Herald and Western Witness* of 1837 which will hereafter be referred to simply as the *Achill Herald*:

1837

"The Achill Missionary Herald and Western Witness, a monthly Journal, exhibiting The Principles and Progress of Christ's Kingdom and exposing the errors and abominations of that section of The Rival Kingdom of Antichrist, commonly called The Papacy; together with a practical exposure of the civil, social and political delinquencies practised by the Pope's emissaries in attempting to re-establish his wicked usurpations throughout the world generally, and especially in this kingdom ." (Achill Missionary Herald, 1837).

Extracts from the section entitled *Local and Provincial News* in the *Achill Herald* graphically record the economic and social conditions prevailing on the island over a forty year period, including the Great Famine. *"The battle for souls,"* was carried out against a background of famine, social and economic change and the beginning of the separation of Ireland's link with Britain. Incidents depicted illustrate the defining roles of the two main protagonists, the Achill Mission and the Catholic Church, the outcome predictable by even a remote insight into the psyche of the native Irish. The first issue of *The Achill Herald* was published on July 12th, 1837 No. 1. Vol. 1. The publication was delayed due to *"important engagements and remoteness."* A woodcut *vignette* was placed on the front page and shows a view of the newly constructed Settlement. Several other woodcuts would provide different views of the Settlement as it responded to enlargement and change. Subscription for the *Achill Herald* was four shillings per annum, postage paid.

14. The Achill Mission, 1831-1886

Two topics of interest, the weather and the crops appear throughout the various editions of the Achill Herald and are of particular interest as they cover both pre-and post-Famine times in Achill. They are incorporated in the text where appropriate, particularly where climatic conditions are clearly seen to have had an impact upon the prevailing economic conditions on the island. An example from an early issue is outlined: *"this part of the country has been favoured with a long continuance of dry warm weather. The crops consequently exhibit a peculiar appearance of luxuriance, and promise a speedy supply to the islanders, many of whom are suffering severely at this time from scarcity of provisions."*

Extracts are taken on a year by year basis so that the changing social and economic conditions on the island can be charted and the progress and setbacks of the Mission outlined.

24. Old Dugort © Lawrence Collection

Within a short time after the establishment of the Settlement in Dugort, the Mission also claimed that they had acquired an additional 500 acres:

"the greater part of this land is contained in an island (Inishbiggle), c. 6 miles distant from the Settlement. "

Inishbiggle (*Inis Bigil*) actually contains 637 acres.

Achill

1838

The Mission claimed that upon their arrival on the island, implements of iron were unknown; they do not mention the *gowl-gob*, a wooden spade with iron shoes which had been widely used in Achill and parts of North Mayo for generations. The Mission engaged in intensive agricultural activity, sowing oats, rye, potatoes and a variety of vegetables. They reclaimed tracts of bogland, using sea sand and lime. The potato crop of 1838 gave cause for concern for although an abundant harvest had been anticipated, the results on the Mission farm and elsewhere on the island were disappointing. However, this *"partial failure of seed was compensated for by luxuriant oats and rye."*

Work now commenced on the building of a Corn mill and Tuck mill (for thickening frieze), at a site leased from Sir Richard O'Donnell, the mills and kiln costing £200. The location of these two mills is not given but there was an existing Corn mill and a Tuck mill in Belfarsad, erected during either the McLoughlin or Medlycott tenure in Corraun. There was also a reference to Mills in Dookinella.

An advertisement by Edward Nangle for a *"...faithful, orderly Protestant to work in house,"* would seem to indicate that local labour was not the preferred choice. However he did for a time employ a local girl, for whom he appears to have formed an attachment but who, because of family opposition, was subsequently sent to Dublin causing predictable scandal, orchestrated, according to Edward Nangle, by the Catholic clergy. A governess was also employed to teach English, French, Music, Drawing and Needlework and also *be able to cut-out dresses and take charge of a wardrobe.* Salary £25 per annum.

In May, 1838 the Archbishop of Tuam confirmed twenty eight young people at the Settlement, nineteen of whom were said to be the children of former Roman Catholics. Previously Fr. Connolly with an address at Achill, Newport Pratt, had claimed that there were twelve adults and twenty three children (apostates) in the Colony. Edward Nangle disputed this, publishing the names of sixteen families, totalling sixty four persons. He also said that ninety four children were examined in Sunday School by the Archbishop, the Church being filled to capacity. Prior to his departure, the Archbishop made a donation to the orphanage. On the Monday following Confirmation, the people from the *neighbouring village* refused to sell potatoes to the Mission settlers, on the orders of the Catholic priest. The neighbouring village which is mentioned on numerous occasions was either Slievemore or Finsheen. In 1852 when the Mission acquired two-thirds of the island, they evicted the tenants and demolished the dwellings in Finsheen, a village of about twelve dwellings, where the present St. Thomas's Church was erected and opened in 1854. (John O'Shea, *pers.comm.*).

There were some changes in personnel at the Mission, Rev. Joseph Baylee being replaced by the Rev. Mr. Coneys who was said to be one of the foremost experts on the Irish language. A Catholic curate, Fr. William Roche arrived on the island and immediately became embroiled in controversy, assaulting John Connors (for which he was later convicted), a Mission schoolmaster stationed at Bullsmouth.

There was an *anti-tithe* meeting in Castlebar and Newport which, according to Edward Nangle was instigated by Dr. McHale. The meetings were covered by the **Mayo Telegraph** which reported that several resolutions had been proposed and seconded by Achill people who because their names were prefixed by the title "**Mr.**" in the newspaper were ridiculed for being pretentious, particularly, as it was said, they could neither read nor write! This reflects Edward Nangle's contempt for the native population and is at variance with his subsequent laudatory praise for those who recanted from Rome.

In October, the island fell into a state of anticipated excitement awaiting the arrival of Dr. McHale, the Catholic Archbishop of Tuam. A Fr. Henry, possibly the same priest who would later become parish priest of Achill was sent to prepare the island for the visit, and he allegedly began by cursing all converts from the altar of the Chapel in Dookinella Thulis. Fr. Henry was described by Bowen (1970) as *"a caricature of a narrow-minded and authoritarian R.C. cleric."* On the Sunday following the arrival of Dr. McHale, a large crowd gathered under the Minaun cliffs where Dr. McHale, after mass was over, addressed the congregation. According to the **Achill Herald**: *"He was dressed in rich canonical robes*

125

Achill

with a mitre on his head and a crozier in his hand " . McHale, sometimes referred to as *"the Lion of Judah"* was a formidable opponent having spent several years in litigious conflict with Bishop Lyons of Killala. He was particularly incensed about the Orphanage which had been set up by the Mission and immediately began correspondence with Sir Robert Peel and other notable English politicians in an endeavour to halt the Mission's proselytising activities.

The *Achill Herald* carried a story concerning the Rev. James Dwyer, a priest of Achill also *"...residing at Newport Pratt "* who had claimed that while on a visit to York in England he had seen a poster in a shop claiming that fourteen Roman Catholic orphans were being fed, clothed and educated by the Achill Mission. He maintained that this was totally untrue and invited Nangle to supply further details of these orphans. Nangle in his reply was evasive, claiming that: *"...not all children in the orphanage were natives of Achill, six were from Achill and another six from the mainland near Achill. "*

He said that there were a total of twenty one children of Catholic parentage in the orphanage and appended a statement signed by several witnesses to that effect.

In November a tremendous gale caused damage to the roofs of houses in the Settlement. A young man, the *"son of one of the chief persons on the island "* was said to have become a convert. A boat from Inishkea island, laden with fish landed at Dugort but the crew refused to sell fish to the *"Jumpers."* A *"Jumper"* is a derogatory term and means a person who *"jumps "* from one religion to another while a *"Souper"* indicates a person who changed their religion for soup or other food.

In December, an advertisement was posted advising that the cargo of the wrecked *William & George* of Dumfries would be auctioned in Keel at 12 o'clock on Friday, 28th December, 1838. On the 17th December prior to the auction, Thomas Roberts, a constable on duty in Keel and in charge of the cargo from the *William & George* was relieved of duty around midnight and went to bed. At 2 a.m. he was awakened by the sound of a shot. A neighbour claimed that Mr.Reynolds, a coastguard had become involved in a row over an alleged theft from the wreck.

14. The Achill Mission, 1831-1886

Reynold's had been struck (seemingly in self defence) with a spade called a *gub* and died of his wounds a few days later. A couple from Keel were arrested and charged with this offence, but later acquitted by the judge on the grounds of self-defence.This story features prominently in Achill folklore with claims that Reynolds either beat up a brother of the people with whom he had the row or allegedly ordered other people to do it for him. Reynolds left a widow and eight children for whom a fund was set up by the Mission. He is said to have been buried in the Settlement. A violent storm raged on the night Reynolds died which was afterwards compared with *Oidhe na gaoithe Mora* (the night of the Big Wind) andnamed *Oidhe Randall*. Houses were unroofed in the neighbourhood and heavy losses were sustained. There was however no damage to Mission property.

1839

Relations between the Mission and local people appear to have deteriorated: windows of cottages in the Settlement were broken by stone throwing and several other minor incidents were recorded.

The opening months of the year brought more wet weather and agricultural work was delayed. By May, however, a house for the *reception of visitors* was completed. In June there were reports of distress in Achill and the price of potatoes has risen to 6d-7d a stone (14 pounds) and oatmeal to £1.4s. per cwt. (hundredweight), the former due to the failure of the 1838 potato crop. Provisions for the Mission had to be imported because of *exclusive dealing, a practice similar to boycotting!* Achill labourers working for the Mission were being paid 8d per day, roughly enough to buy a stone of potatoes, while the unemployed consistently faced starvation in the event of crop failure. It would be the practice of the Mission, except in one single instance, not to engage in gratuitous relief, whatever the circumstances. In fairness, it would have to be said that the Society of Friends and the British Relief Association also adopted this practice. The Mission recorded its first request for relief this year which was said to have come from *neighbouring villages* and this one must remember is *five years* before the Great Famine! Snow and hail in the middle of May was followed by warm sunshine and drought in June. Nevertheless there was *abundant sowings* and no evidence of seed failure as in previous years! Potatoes were still 6 pence per stone, but the price of oatmeal had dropped to 14s. per cwt. The Achill Sound Hotel opened on the 1st July, 1839 complete with a Ferry Boat and *float* to transport guests across the Sound.

Behind the scenes the Catholic clergy were active, two orphans were coaxed from the orphanage with the promise of *tea, bread and butter, meat and fish,* compared to their diet of *plain but wholesome food at the Mission!* On the 27th July, Lady Anne Wynne laid the foundation stone of a House of Recovery for the orphans and other children at the Settlement who were now said to number one hundred and sixty five, a substantial increase on the previous year and which probably reflects the near famine conditions being experienced on the island.

Another drought was followed by heavy rain. The new potatoes were dug, which seems to suggest an early crop and four acres of oats were sown, manured with *local lime*, a commodity very much in short supply in Achill. Distress was not confined to Achill. The dire conditions in Connacht prompted the Government to carry out an investigation and a Captain Chads of the Royal Navy visited the Settlement where he donated £40 towards relief which was matched by a corresponding amount from Sir Richard O'Donnell. The money went towards the employment of labourers to construct two roads, one in the north and one in the south of the island. The Mission again claimed that local priests were trying to starve them out by *"exclusive dealing."* Funds were however received from christian friends and used to good effect with *"...poor neighbours visited with famine fed from these funds."*

One hundred people were now employed on the Mission farm. The priest tried to stop people going to work at the Mission and successfully cut short *"...the resumption of friendly intercourse between the people and the Mission."*

The Sunday Mass sermon was devoted to imprecations against Mission personnel (scripture readers were particularly detested) and numbers at the mission dwindled. In addition, it was alleged that the priest and a schoolmaster were keeping watch on people working at the Mission with the result that people would hide from view behind turf stacks and in bog holes until they departed!

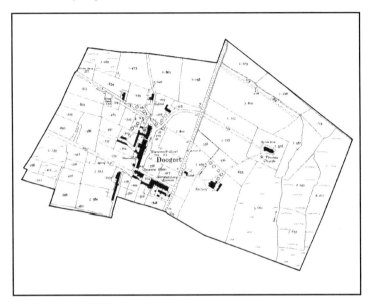

25. Plan of the Settlement

Correspondence commenced in the ***Achill Herald*** between the Rev. James Dwyer and Edward Nangle. Nangle in this type of situation had few equals, *"the pen is mightier than the sword"* was a maxim to which he enthusiastically subscribed, and few were his equal. He delighted in ensnaring people into making injudicious comments, revelling in the many derogatory comments expressed against himself and the Mission, all of which he published verbatim so that readers of the ***Achill Herald*** could no doubt sympathise with the image portrayed i.e. that of an embattled clergyman, striving to enlighten a recalcitrant island community. Money poured in from overseas, in this year alone, £910 came from England and £138 from Ireland. As well as engaging in acrimonious written debate, he also turned this to advantage by later publishing the correspondence in pamphlet form, the revenue from which went into the Mission coffers. He did this with the correspondence between himself and the Marquis of Sligo and needless to say with that from Dr. McHale. He was an adept master of debate and used this to good effect in the *Achill Herald*, inflaming the passions of the readership and at the same time guaranteeing for himself and the Mission a never ending supply of funds. The colony was projected to the readership as an embattled enclave, precariously holding on to a foothold in a *"godless island."* Nangle's *Achilles heel* was his total belief in his own omnipotence and like many such before and after him, the edifice he had so carefully built up came crashing down when he came into conflict with Joseph Napier, a Trustee of the Achill Mission who, unfortunately for him, happened to be a former Lord Chancellor of Ireland. The ensuing court case would nearly bankrupt the Mission and result in its eventual demise.

Fr. Dwyer, having been *ensnared* into an open debate within the pages of the *Achill Herald,* no doubt hoping to extricate himself gracefully suggested an open discussion to be held in Dugort so that people from the Settlement and from the *"...large neighbouring villages of Keel, Slievemore, Dookinella and Dugort would be able to attend ;* it was said that there were *"... thousands of people in these villages !"*

Mrs. Reynolds, wife of the late Coastguard Reynolds produced a posthumous child and among the contributions received was one from the Grays, a family whose history would be intertwined with that of the Mission for a long time to come. It was reported that:

"..on the 1st October, a flood, the greatest in living memory did considerable damage to the Mill dam, drains and fences of the Settlement. The immense torrents which rolled down these mountains on that night seemed to be rather the effect of a large water-spout than that produced by ordinary rain ."

The corn was, however, harvested safely and the oats kiln dried and ready to be ground:

"A total absence of husbandry among natives means that local grain crops are shrivelled and the return small."

14. The Achill Mission, 1831-1886

In November, the body of a dumb young man was found near the cliffs. When found the body had been lacerated by eagles. Two species of eagle, the Golden Eagle and the White-Tailed Sea Eagle were recorded in Achill as late as the 1890's.

"The village of Keel, the scene of poor Reynold's murder and of the burnings of the Holy scriptures has been severely scourged by the prevalence of a malignant fever. 2d per house was collected by the priest to avert the pestilence by a Mass ."

Fr. Dwyer, now well in Edward Nangle's sights was accused of blasphemy, having said Mass on Keel beach and prayed for the return of herrings! The herrings did return but not for some time and then not to Keel but to the colony, 300,000 being caught off Dugort in 1846 which *"were sold at a fair price."* Fr. Dwyer was also accused of sending his brother to Keel, Slievemore and other adjoining villages to prevent people from signing applications for the construction of school-houses in these villages.

1840

The year began well with mild weather and the *polyanthus* was said to be in full bloom! This was however, followed by gales, cold rain and sleet but the weather, there was no rain for six weeks, creating excellent conditions for agricultural work. Despite this, the Mission alone succeeded in completing Spring work, conditions on the island generally appearing to have deteriorated with the absence of sowing being attributed to insufficient funds to buy seed!

Heated exchanges continued between Edward Nangle and Fr. Dwyer, the latter maintaining that several people had left the Mission and that one convert had only been induced to the Settlement by extreme poverty. There were reports of violent assaults on Mission personnel and rewards offered for the apprehension of the culprits responsible. Fr. Dwyer also claimed that the orphans at the Settlement were starving and that several had died. Nangle admitted that two children had indeed died and another two were suffering from *dropsy*. One hundred orphans were said to be housed in four houses under the supervision of married couples. Fr. Dwyer now forbade people to work on the recently acquired Mission farm in Dooega but his instructions were ignored for the **Achill Herald** reported that people from Dooega were working on the farm despite the priests warning "*...they are presently burning land preparatory to planting potatoes.*" Cashel village, the location of a Police Barracks and now also the location of Fr. Dwyer's residence, seemed to cause particular odium to Mission personnel and would feature prominently in subsequent editions of the **Achill Herald**, Cashel women were accused of singing obscene songs at Mission staff as they passed by.

In May the first tourists visited Achill, something not previously possible owing to a lack of accommodation. Now, however, there was a good hotel available at Achill Sound which had been considerably enlarged by the proprietor who was also, "*...running a car once a week between Achill Sound and Westport.*" In this same month severe gales blowing from the east and north-east did considerable damage to crops and gardens but *poor neighbours* of the Mission reaped a substantial supply of *sea-wrack* blown in by the gale. This would not be Slievemore, but was possibly Old Dugort. In June a young man from Dugort herding his cows fell ninety feet into the sea and was drowned. "*Fr. Dwyer, representative of the Anti-Christ lies dangerously ill of malignant fever in Tuam. He has been succeeded by a priest named Gallagher, a native of this island.*" Fr. Dwyer recovered from his illness and returned to the island in September. His return seemed to coincide with more heckling in Cashel!

The weather continued tempestuous with severe gales blowing from the west and north, badly affecting the potato crop and causing much distress on the island where food had become increasingly scarce. Potatoes of native growth were said to be exhausted and the importation of new supplies was impossible because of a lack of money. Sir Richard O'Donnell and his wife paid their annual visit to the Settlement and must have witnessed the distress amongst their tenants. August commenced with a very bad storm, gales and heavy rain leaving the oats and early potatoes water-logged. The Mission managed to save most of their corn because it was claimed that an " *...early sowing is the best way to avoid damage to crops.*" Despite the bad weather the potato crop on the island was said to be good.

14. The Achill Mission, 1831-1886

November was a very stormy month, the *"wind nearly stripped thatch from one of our cottages, threw down a rick of hay and killed two geese, carrying them twenty feet in the air and then dashing them on to the ground ."* December saw the formation of a *Catholic Confraternity* on the island after which children were withdrawn from Dooega school by their parents.

1841

On January 20th a tremendous gale from the north caused considerable damage to the roofs of houses in the Settlement. A schooner, the *John Lloyd* docked in the bay to avoid the storm. Also avoiding the storm was a large mullet (or conger eel!), five feet one inches long by two feet nine inches in circumference and weighing five stone, which was *triumphantly* caught in Dugort. There was a report of a *"faction fight "* between two sections of the congregation at Kildavnet Chapel, with the priest having to quell the riot. This is the first mention of Kildavnet being operational and it coincides with the arrival on the island of Fr.Gallagher, a native of Achill whose tombstone is prominently located in Kildavnet cemetery. In February there was a serious incident which would cause a lot of ill-feeling locally. During the construction of a new Catholic Church (the present Dookinella Church), it was alleged that the building had been maliciously damaged by Mission personnel. Charges were preferred but the culprits were acquitted. The Mission however said it would take its own action to discipline the perpetrators. However, as the result of representations by a local priest, the Lord Lieutenant ordered a retrial with the alleged perpetrators being summoned to attend Court at Achill Sound. Fr. Dwyer went to England to collect money for the repair of the Church and was castigated upon his return for not disclosing how much money he had collected and how it was to be disbursed. Fr. Dwyer retaliated by advising Catholics to sell goods to a shop recently opened in the Settlement at exorbitant prices but otherwise not to patronise it. A Post boy taking mail to the Settlement had his bag set on fire by a prankster and the already bad relations between the Mission and the local community deteriorated further still.

Achill

The weather was reported fine but after the oats and potatoes were sown it became wet and stormy. A vessel, the *Sceptre of Limerick* , was wrecked off the coast and a Hooker going from Westport to Clare Island went down and all aboard were drowned. Subsequently the body of Sergeant Bloxham, a passenger on this ship was washed ashore at Dooega and buried at the Settlement. April continued incessantly wet and stormy and little work was done. On Sunday 25th April the tops of the mountains were covered with snow. *"Because of the continued bad weather the Spring sowing was very late ."* The weather seems to have improved and the sowing was completed; the early oats and potatoes were said to be showing promise while new potatoes *(early ash leaf kidney)* were of good size and quality when dug in the Mission garden!

Tourism

The first known advertisement relating to the promotion of tourism on Achill appeared in the *Achill Herald*, inserted by Robert R. Savage of the Achill Sound Hotel thanking his patrons and informing them of the provision of tours, fishing, trips to caves, other haunts and the Druids' Altar (a megalithic tomb on Slievemore mountain). The weather however would not have encouraged tourists, July being wet and stormy with little sunshine. The inhabitants of Achill were said to be very poor and wretched.

In October a tremendous gale blew from the north-west. The villages of Bunacurry and Dookinella were badly hit and the new chapel seriously damaged. This was followed in November and December by an outbreak of *scarlatina* at the Settlement, causing several deaths. The year ended as it had begun with another storm, which blew down the roof of the chapel in Dookinella again!

1842-1845

Life in the Settlement had a decidedly English ethos, so that it was normal for *"a special dinner "* to be organised so that the school-children could celebrate the baptism of the infant *Prince of Wales*. The year began with a *"tremendous storm which tumbled corn stacks and removed thatch from houses. The Orphan boy's house was badly damaged and roof-ridge tiles torn down."* The sea off the Dooega coast was said to have been

14. The Achill Mission, 1831-1886

blessed by a priest who was paid ten shillings by the villagers. A few days later a woman collecting *sloke* (seaweed) on this beach was drowned prompting the **Achill Herald** to comment "*...so much for the blessing !*" Another tremendous gale did much damage to the Settlement and there was a continuance of storm and rain. A young woman named Rogers from Slievemore was found dead on the beach, having fallen from the cliffs.

A report in the **Achill Herald** claimed that numerous poor on the island were reduced to a state of extreme want, potatoes were very scarce and expensive, making it impossible for them to purchase seed and/or sow their land. A fund was set up for the poor and upon receipt of funds, the Mission said it would initiate a road-building programme to provide much needed employment. Mr. Glendenning, agent for the O'Donnell Estate, provided the poor with a quantity of oatmeal for which they had to provide signatures and security. The conditions were: No security! No food! The very poor were now reported to be turning to the Mission Fund for help but, the **Achill Herald** clearly stated that the Mission "*...gives no food to those who are not incapacitated by age, infirmity or sickness!*" Seemingly, *multitudes* had sought assistance but only *sixty* were selected from among the most destitute who were then employed making roads and fences in the farms belonging to the Mission. The Halls (1841-43) published a letter in the **Evening Packet** claiming that out of a population of 5000 in Achill, 4000 were starving. Edward Nangle said this was exaggerated but this was confirmed by Dr. McHale who claimed, that at least two people on the island had died of starvation! An indication of how wretched many of the inhabitants of Achill were is illustrated in extracts from letters written on their behalf by some of the better off and literate people on the island:

Keel, 16th June, 1842
"Dear Sir,
The bearer, is in greatest want. Has 7 in family ."
Keel 19th June, 1842
"Dear Sir,
Bearer in great distress. Has 5 children. No Cattle. One horse."

135

Achill

Keel, 19th June, 1842

"Dear Sir,
Bearer has a mother and father, both on sick frame for some time and
desolate for food."

An alternative to the extreme poverty experienced in Achill and
elsewhere in the west was emigration. A list of the numbers of emigrants
from Westport to Quebec on the 3rd June, 1842 indicates that this
alternative was fast gaining popularity: 158 persons aboard the
"Jubilee;" 169 on the **"Warrior; "** 357 on the **"Brittania; "** 161 on the
"Mary Alice " and 161 on the **"Bruce. "**

26. Kildavnet Graveyard

In August, *The Achill Herald* reported that stress was at an end,
potatoes were plentiful and there was promise of a good harvest. It was
claimed that although the priests did nothing for the poor while they were
starving, they had again, now that food was plentiful, ordered the people
to discontinue working for the Mission. A grant of £100 was given by the
Inspector General to erect a Boat Pier at the end of the island (probably
Kildavnet). In September the prediction of a good harvest was confirmed

and things settled back to normal. Patrick Hughes, late Sergeant Major of H.M. forces, was appointed the new manager of the Achill Mission Hotel. In October the bad weather returned with gales blowing from the north and north-west but the breakwater of the unfinished boat harbour seemingly survived the storm.

1843

The stormy weather continued and the Boat Pier which had survived the earlier storm was now destroyed. In addition, three fishermen were drowned at a sandbar (*Cleigh Mhór*) off Achill Beg Island; another was saved by Mr. Robinson, chief boatman of Achill Beg coastguard station. A letter appeared in the **Brighton Gazette** claiming that the people of Achill greeted the arrival of the Mission by lighting bonfires on the shore and initially sent great numbers of children to the Mission schools. The difficulty of setting up the Mission because of lack of funds, access to the island in the absence of roads, the roughness of the sea journey and the difficulty of obtaining food were emphasised. The progress of the Mission, although hampered by opposition from the Catholic Church could however claim that there were one hundred and seven orphans in the orphanage, three hundred and fifty two converts in the Settlement and two hundred and forty children, including the orphans, attending Mission schools. There was mention of Dr. Adams, who it was said had given up a thriving practice in Dublin to come to Achill and who was said to be ministering free to the local community. It could be said that Dr. Adams' brand of Protestantism, liberally spread with christian charity, ameliorated the more strident aspects of Edward Nangle's evangelism. While this may be true, Dr. Adams wholeheartedly supported his friend in the evangelization of Achill, but, at the same time, dispensed relief from donations received without any apparent strings attached.

A fire, said to have occurred accidentally in the orphanage dining room and kitchen did much damage; the female school and a room occupied by the printer and three store rooms were totally consumed. A young orphan subsequently died in another accidental fire which seemingly occurred shortly after the first.

Achill

Although the weather was said to be good, there was a report of the failure of the potato crops throughout the island but the oats and rye were harvested successfully.

In September, the Lord Bishop of Tuam confirmed seventy four children in the Settlement. However, there appears to have been some resistance to the Mission's proselytising efforts: a convert and the *only* Protestant was forced to live in a neighbouring village although ostracised by his relatives, "*...because the missionaries were not sure of the sincerity of his conversion* " and he died without the benefit of any Church. This is but one instance of the rigidity of attitude which was a hallmark of the Mission.

The Mission made much of the fact that a plot had been uncovered to *strangle* Nangle and other Missionaries in their beds, the information being leaked by a person who seemingly had refused to become involved in the plot but who was subsequently suspected of being in league with Nangle. It was claimed that some of the people involved had got relief from the Mission in 1842. There was also a report of a *"break-in "* at a house in Dooagh, the intention being to force the owner to join an illegal confederacy!

1844

The New Year saw the establishment of a Mail Car run on Tuesdays, Thursdays and Saturdays from Newport to Achill, the opening of a Post Office in Dugort and the commencement of work on a new Hotel in that village. Passenger fares on the new Mail Car were outlined in the *Achill Herald* :

Dugort Post Office - Achill Sound	1s.	0d.
- Mulranny	2s.	6d.
- Newport	3s.	6d.

Children under 10 years half-fare. No dogs!

A letter written by the Halls was published in *The Times* which defended the people of Achill against Nangle's conspiracy theory (relating presumably to the abortive attempt to strangle him), which they claimed was an attempt to inflame the English against the Irish, and

14. The Achill Mission, 1831-1886

which they pointed out occurred, coincidentally, prior to Edward Nangle's proposed English fund-raising trip. They also pointed out that the Settlement, isolated amidst 6,000 Achill people, was vulnerable to attack but yet none had occurred. Having visited Achill in 1842 when the people were starving, the Halls said that the houses in which the people of Achill lived "...*would not be good enough for English pigs,*" yet no sheep were stolen from the mountains and there was no injury to any Protestant. The people "...*lived solely on their own guidance with no magistrate and no gentleman within 20 miles.*" Yet, the Mission labelled these people idolators and loaded them with abuse, while on the other hand offering them food, clothes and comfortable lodgings on the sole and easy condition of becoming converts ! The report of the attack on the Mission was a "*foul slander*" according to the Halls, and it was no coincidence that the attack came immediately before Edward Nangle began his circuit of English towns, the result of which would be a "*freightage*" of English gold for his small colony on Achill. Nangle replied immediately, refuting the allegations and saying that the Mission had given work to one hundred people per day during the famine of 1842 but nevertheless Mission staff were subject to threats, and constant "*hootings.*" He referred to a report published by a committee of the House of Lords in 1837 regarding a sermon given by Fr. Connolly where this priest allegedly exhorted the people of Achill to attack Mission staff. The editor of the **Mayo Telegraph,** the Honourable Frederick Cavendish, a Catholic convert, also treated the account of the conspiracy as a fabrication. It should be remembered that Edward Nangle was a manic depressive, alternating between periods of elation and of depression, and probably seeing conspiracy where there was none.

In February, 1844 another letter from the Halls appeared in **The Times** relating to the *murder* of coastguard Reynolds. The Halls claimed that Reynolds had been killed by a blow from a "...*pair of tongs in a drunken attempt to kill a poor islander into whose cabin he had burglariously entered.*" The Halls pointed out that the Judge had ordered the immediate acquittal of the persons charged with the offence. In March, the alleged conspiracy case came before Castlebar Assizes and several witnesses gave evidence, including Robert Savage, a Protestant who maintained

139

that the accused were *"respectable, correct men."* The case was transferred to the summer session as the Jury could not agree on a verdict. In May, the Rev. Solomon Frost, a former Catholic priest arrived at the Mission to study for the Protestant ministry and to preach about the errors of Catholicism. In June, a flood threatened the Settlement. In July members of the ***Devon Commission*** (1847) headed by the Earl of Devon, and including Sir Robert Ferguson and Messrs. Wynne, Hamilton and Reddington, Land Commissioners, arrived at the Settlement. *The Devon Commission* was set up to report on the occupation of land in Ireland *(Parliamentary Papers, 1845),* and provided valuable information on the Rundale system and associated settlements. Nangle told the Devon Commission that he had tried to change the joint tenantry (Rundale) form of land-holding found on the island.

In August, *H.M.Vulcan* came ashore and landed Sir Edward Blakeney, Commander of Forces in Ireland, General Thompson, Colonel Foster, Captain Conry and the Honourable Mr. Plunket, all stayed a short while at the Settlement before proceeding to Killary Harbour. In September, Dr. McHale again visited Achill and according to the ***Achill Herald*** conducted himself peaceably! It also stated *"...that the prosperity of the Settlement must be galling to McHale as he predicted in a letter to the Bishop of London in 1835 that the Mission would be a failure."* The reason for Dr. McHale's visit was seemingly *"the consecration of the shells of two chapels ! "*

Another (accidental) fire occurred in the carpenter's workshop at the Settlement, and all of the wood including the material for the new hotel was destroyed. There is a reference to the village of Finsheen which was subsequently cleared and demolished by the Mission: *"neighbours from Finsheen and Dugort came to help."* It also seems to indicate that there were good relations at this time between the Settlement and these villages! This good deed was reciprocated later that year when *" ...a cabin in the nearest Romish village to the Settlement caught fire,"* and the people from the Settlement helped to put it out!

On this the eve of the Great Famine there was an abundant harvest with the potato crop being unusually good and oats likewise. The weather remained dry and calm, the best in the living memory of the oldest inhabitant. In October, the *Achill Herald* reported that the Rev. George McNamara, a curate in Kilcomman had been received into the Church of England. There was consternation at this momentous happening with a Catholic source suggesting that Fr. McNamara had been suspended prior to his defection. Nevertheless, the conversion of Catholic priests must have been relatively common for the *Achill Herald* carried a request for donations to build a house for these lapsed priests and subsequently reported the laying of the first stone of a house which would be used by Catholic clergymen who had converted to Protestantism! In attendance at the ceremony were the Rev. Mr. O'Brien, Mr. Frost, Mr. McNamara, Mr. Lowe and Edward Nangle. An individual from Cashel village, the location of the Catholic curate's residence, requested that the Mission open a school in that village and was allegedly later cursed from the altar by the priest!

1845

In January, the National Board of Education was said by Nangle to be antagonistic to the Settlement as they were setting up schools in the same areas as those of the Mission, even going as far as setting up a school in the immediate neighbourhood of the Settlement! Another Mission school established earlier and located about eleven miles from the Settlement in the house of a respectable Roman Catholic peasant had a new schoolhouse erected in the vicinity. A convert said to be a National school teacher from outside Achill was reported to have sought asylum in the Settlement.

Scandal and farce erupted in Achill when a local priest who had previously entertained his congregation by publicly admonishing a young man, a convert, from the altar of the Catholic chapel was now allegedly carrying on an affair with the wife of a local man and was also said to have solemnised the marriage of cousins from a neighbouring village, without first securing the requisite dispensation. Nothing more is heard of the alleged affair but questions did arise concerning the validity of the marriage, the husband seemingly called on the priest saying that as the marriage was invalid, he now intended marrying another and would not be applying for a dispensation. The Priest was *aghast* and seemingly said: *"of course you are married,"* to which the husband replied: *"well then I need not pay for a dispensation!"* All this no doubt provided entertainment for readers of the **Achill Herald.**

In August, a new hotel opened in Dugort. In the same month, the **Achill Herald** carried a report concerning a poor man who had left the Mission to seek admission to the county home in Castlebar because he had been thrown out of his lodgings when it was discovered he had come from the Mission! This incident, together with a previous one involving an old convert forced to reside in his own village, seems to suggest that there was a policy whereby people who could no longer support themselves were forced, despite converting, to find accommodation elsewhere, a policy subsequently confirmed by Nangle when accused of enticing converts with the promise of accommodation, food and clothing. As he himself said: *"...anybody unable to be self sufficient would not be welcome at the Settlement! "* The death was reported of two orphans, one of whom had received a *classical education,* preparatory to entering the ministry. A petition was organised at the Settlement to protest at the endowment of Maynooth as a Catholic Seminary. This would suggest that Nangle did not confine his anti-Catholic activities to Achill.

An additional wing was added to the Church in the Settlement to accommodate the one hundred and twenty people now resident in the Colony. Divine service was celebrated at the Mission Settlement in Mweelin by the Rev. George McNamara. Seemingly *en route* to the ceremony the Rev. McNamara encountered Fr. Dwyer who seemingly stopped him in the middle of the road, took off his hat and crossed himself to intimate *"...to Mr. McLoughlin and his family who followed him on their jaunting car,"* that the presence of an *unfrocked priest* obliged him to protect himself from spiritual harm!

Mr. James Sherwood was appointed as manager of the new Hotel in Dugort and large numbers of tourists were said to have visited the district. In September, the Mission was *"...assailed by falsehoods and rumour that £1500 had been embezzled and was missing from asylum funds",* after a person (unknown) had absconded from the Mission.

14. The Achill Mission, 1831-1886

Famine

The ***Achill Herald*** in October carried the first report of the potato disease:

"We are thankful to say that the potato disease has not made its appearance in this island, although parts of the neighbouring district are suffering severely from its prevalence." On November 26th this situation was reversed: *"Since we last published, we regret to say that the potato rot has given unequivocal proof of its presence in this island. But, so far, the immediate damage done is small, bearing no comparison with the loss sustained in other districts."*

A letter contained in Relief Committee files from T. L.Wood to Sir James Dombrain said that the *potato blight was making great inroads in Achill, particularly in the northern part of the island."*

In December the Rev.William Bourke, formerly a Catholic Curate arrived at the Settlement to superintend the Reformed Priest Asylum. The year closed with a report that: *"...a fearful tempest visited the island. The roof of a new schoolhouse was damaged. In Dooega several corn stacks were thrown down and boats drawn up on the beach were broken. This gale was more severe than the one in 1839."*

1846

The onset of the New Year was greeted with optimism which would unfortunately be of short duration. A shoal of herrings totalling some 300,000 were landed in Dugort, the largest catch in living memory, which were sold at *fair prices,* averaging 1s.3d. to 3s. per 100. This was followed in February by the appearance of the *" potato disease"* which was said to be making rapid strides on the island, the open pits displaying a mass of rotting pulp.

By March the disease was widespread throughout the island and resulted in the price of potatoes *"increasing beyond the reach of the population"* and Indian meal having to be imported to relieve distress.

The *Horticultural Society* predicted that things would get worse. The British Consul in Washington reported that the potato disease had first been detected in America in 1843, so it had taken just two years to reach Ireland. The decimation of population by death and/or emigration which it would leave in its wake would change the face of rural Ireland for decades to come.

In 1807 Ireland was the most densely populated country in Europe but by 1860 the opposite was the case. A cure for the potato blight, *phytophthora infestans* was not found until 1885 i.e. a solution containing copper sulphate sprayed onto the stalks prevents invasion of the fungal spores. O'Shea (1996). Conditions locally were further exacerbated by a large fall of snow which completely covered the whole island and within a short period fifteen persons were said to have renounced popery. A letter in the *Relief Commission Files* from J. R. Ward, Secretary of the *Achill Island Relief Committee* dated the 24th June, 1844 is reprinted below:

"Sir,

With reference to your letter of the 13th inst. to the Rev. Edward Nangle, I have to acquaint you that Sir Richard O'Donnell of this county in the absence of Lord Lucan has appointed a local committee for the Temporary Relief of the Poor in this neighbourhood."

£130 was provided to construct a road from Newport to Dugort which it was claimed would shorten the distance between the two areas by two miles. There was also mention that Sir James Dombrain had visited the island and was aware of local conditions.

A letter to Mr. Stanley of the *Relief Commission* was received from Colonel Arthur Knox-Gore (who owned lands in Corraun) also recommending the commencement of *"Relief works"* between Newport and Achill as *"employment for the destitute poor was urgently needed."*

Knox-Gore complained that the *Board of Works* had promised to have a *Public Work* commenced in the district but people had waited in vain for this to happen, even though similar works had subsequently been approved in other parts of Mayo, where distress was not as bad as in

14. The Achill Mission, 1831-1886

Achill! He claimed that many of the people in Achill had not had potatoes of their own since January. Worse was to come and is outlined in a letter from the *Achill Temporal Relief Committee* to the *Relief Commissioners:" The exhausted state of funds has led to the suspension of public works, pending receipt of further funds!* Another letter received from Sir Richard O'Donnell stated that a further £200 had been received for the road in question (Newport to Dugort) and that a *memorial* (recommendation) to that effect had been forwarded. The attention of the Commissioners was drawn to the fact that while two hundred and seventy five people had been employed, they were dismissed when the money ran out, and these people were now left without any means of support. It was stressed that help was urgently needed for the starving population of this remote district.

In July the **Achill Herald** reported that the: *"scarcity of food becomes more distressing and had the Government not taken the precaution of storing meal in the Coastguard Stations many people must have perished of famine."* Thanks was acknowledged by the committee for money received *"to give employment to neighbours."* It was claimed that the priests had done nothing to help the people. This was contradicted in a story relating to a tragedy which occurred in Bullsmouth when two crew men drowned while landing a cargo of Indian meal, seemingly imported by the Catholic Church, for the **Achill Herald** claimed that "the distribution of this cargo throughout the island resulted in a statement saying: *"...people who renounced popery have returned to their own Church."*

Faith in the new potato crop partially mitigated the fear of further distress but ominous portents were voiced by the Relief Committee that the current crops, even if they were free from blight, would not feed the people for more than two months. The Relief Commissioners hired a building at the Settlement to store Indian corn which was placed under the supervision of the coastguards. Distress was now acute, with people offering to sell their beds to purchase food. Subscriptions were requested from the readership of the **Achill Herald** to help alleviate distress on the island. Another tragedy occurred which resulted in the death of a convert who drowned while landing a boat load of turf at *Inishbiggle*. This sad incident, because it occurred on a Sunday prompted the following comment from Edward Nangle: *"Remember the Sabbath day to keep it holy! "*

In October the **Achill Herald** carried extracts from a letter from Dr. McHale seemingly authorising one of the priests on the island to *fundraise* to build churches and schools in Achill, although Nangle claimed that the existing *"Mass houses on island are not yet finished."* This seems an extraordinary statement considering the dire poverty on the island. If people had no money to eat, how could they afford to contribute to church building! By the end of the year conditions on the island were grim, the total failure of the potato crop, and the prediction in the **Achill Herald** that: *"reclaimed land at the Mission would only provide food for one sixth of the population."*

A meeting was held in Castlebar where the magistrates agreed to advance the sum of £75,350 to the Barony of Burrishoole to feed the people for nine months, a sum (according to Nangle, who obviously did not approve), was twice the yearly income of the barony! He doubted if the County Cess would be able to repay this sum and feared that the *"country would be bankrupt and landlords ruined."*

A relief deputation to the Mission from Cashel village alleged that a Miller there was making £100 per day by selling meal. If this is the same miller who lit a fire on the capstone of the Portal tomb in Dugort West to detach a portion of the stone with which to make a millstone, his subsequent fate (he was dead within six months), some said, may not have been undeserved!

In November the *Lydney Lass,* a large schooner, freighted with a cargo of provisions costing £3,000 sailed from Dublin. These provisions *"would be stored at the Mission and which people could buy at a fair price."* Indian meal was now selling for £10 per ton in Liverpool and £15 per ton in Ireland, a factor which inspired Nangle with the idea of the Mission freighting cargo from England. This was, however, circumvented by a decision of the Government to supply Achill with meal for which they had now leased a store. The cargo from the *Lydney Lass,* because of bad weather, was landed at Westport and transported to

14. The Achill Mission, 1831-1886

Achill *via* three Hookers, resulting in some damage to the cargo. A fierce storm blew up when the Hookers were trying to land at Dugort, one did so but the other two had to go on to Bullsmouth and to Salia. Although people from the Settlement stayed on the beach all night, some of the cargo from the first Hooker was lost. The lack of a pier at Dugort was said to be a severe drawback and a request was immediately sent to the *Board of Works* asking that they construct a pier for the Settlement. In the meantime, a generous English (Protestant) gentleman offered to defray costs amounting to £25 towards the production of a preparatory survey, as well as £200 towards the work, despite the fact that he had no connection with the island.

The supply of meal was inadequate and the people were once again said to be starving. For whatever reason, Dr. McHale, advised the Government to exclude the Mission and only supply meal direct to the poor. He claimed that the *Relief Association* in Dublin was composed entirely of Protestants. Nangle retorted by saying that the Catholic Church was doing nothing for the Achill poor.

In December, Nangle apologised in the ***Achill Herald*** for not replying to correspondents, due to an unprecedented increase in correspondence because of the famine. He said that he felt shattered and his health had suffered. The weather was unusually severe even for December, with sleet, snow and gales sweeping the island. The mail car was delayed for five hours, having been involved in an accident in Cashel due to thick snow. Dr. Adams appealed for "*...frieze and brogues for the naked Achill labourers .*" In the ***Achill Herald*** he claimed that poor people attending the Achill Dispensary could not avail of *Public Works* because of lack of clothing.*"For 6-7 months they have bought no clothes and are now selling their pigs, poultry, sheep, etc. (even blankets) to buy food. Yet carts with provisions pass through the island, not only unmolested, but assisted by the islanders."* Again we see evidence of Dr. Adams brand of charity with no apparent strings attached.

1847

When James Hack Tuke visited Connacht in 1847 he said it consisted of an area of 4,392,043 acres, a population of 1,418,859 and a Poor Law valuation £1,465, 642.17s.6d. By the end of the famine the population of this area would be halved. The *Achill Herald* in January was able to report that no deaths from starvation had occurred in Achill, a fact attributed to the cargo of Indian meal which had arrived on the *Lydney Lass,* just in time to prevent a catastrophe! Funds became available and work was given to 4,458 labourers on the Mission farm of which 2,066 were said to be Catholic. This was disputed by Catholic sources and subsequent clarification of the numbers involved, indicated that the Mission was employing people on a rotational basis, at an average of one hundred per day. Using this system, the Mission would have had influence over two-thirds of the population of the island and could exercise its authority at will. The alternative to this was almost certainly starvation. The Mission was supplying two meals per day to six hundred children attending schools on the island, including one hundred orphans. A persistent claim made by the Catholic clergy in Achill was that unless children attended the Mission schools, neither they nor their parents would qualify for relief. If this was true it would seem to indicate that the Catholic clergy had little input into the distribution of relief *via* the *Achill Relief Committee,* despite the fact that Dr. McHale had a great deal of influence with the relevant authorities. Religious conviction would have had to be very strong indeed to watch children die when food was available, albeit at a price. Conditions on the island continued to deteriorate as is evidenced by the following comments: *"Famine increases in intensity on the island. All resources are now consumed and all are dependent upon imported goods."* The poor were said to be eating limpets and seaweed (forever to be remembered in folk memory as *"famine food "*), to maintain life. The desperate conditions are reflected in the fact that when a Hooker belonging to General Thompson of Connemara put in at Achill Sound it was plundered by the here-to-fore law-abiding natives. Even Edward Nangle seemed surprised, saying that *"the good conduct of the islanders has always been deserving of the highest commendation."* There now appeared a report of the appearance of both fever and dysentery on the island and this further disaster was compounded by a heavy fall of snow. In February, the *Achill Herald* ominously predicted that the New Year was pregnant with disaster.

14. The Achill Mission, 1831-1886

Edward Nangle addressed an open letter to the people of Achill, saying that despite Dr. McHale and the priests cursing the Settlement and the fear being instilled in the local Catholic population that houses would be *"thrown down* " if they apostatized, yet nothing had happened. He asked: *"Who helps Achill now?" "Not Dr. McHale and the Roman Catholic Priests but Protestants in the Settlement!"* He referred to the tens of thousands of pounds sent from England to help the Irish famine poor and asked for more converts, referring to *God's* dreadful *"famine in Ireland as a punishment for sin."* The character and religious belief of Edward Nangle are graphically illustrated in these words. By way of contrast, Dr. Adams, of the Achill Dispensary and Hospital was distributing, *unconditionally,* 175 frock coats and waist coats, 27 monkey jackets, 277 pairs of brogues and 400 yards of frieze.

Dr. Adams drew attention to the plight of the sick, aged and infirm who were destitute; people were dividing *last morsels* equally between themselves in order to survive, while at the same time carts with provisions were passing, unmolested, through the island. In addition to the hardship being experienced through famine, the weather became extremely bad with snow, frost and extreme cold. In the midst of all this the famine increased in intensity and soon all reserves of food were consumed leaving the people wholly dependent upon imported food: *"...distress is so great that the people are attempting to maintain life by eating limpets and seaweed ."* The situation was somewhat relieved in February when a supply of Indian meal went on sale at a Government store. At the same time, the *Expedition of Milford ,* a small sloop laden with sixty tons of food and five tons of seed oats, arrived at the Settlement from Dublin, funded by donations to the Mission relief fund. It was claimed that the Mission was now free to send sacks of meal throughout the island without fear of molestation. The *John of Dublin* arrived in Dugort, laden with thirty six tons of food, three tons of *guano* and one ton of seed potatoes.

950 persons were now employed daily by the Board of Works.

214 were employed on Mission farms.

1266 children were receiving two meals of Indian corn per day.

149

Achill

Despite help from the Government, it was claimed there was still considerable distress among the people and private benevolence, chiefly through the Mission was essential: "...the *people have pale faces, emaciated forms and dejected countenance, eloquent with misery.*" While it was claimed that no deaths could be directly attributed to hunger, mortality was without doubt above average; reports of internment indicated that more had occurred during the preceding two months than in the previous two years. Dr. Adams claimed that a major cause of death was *insufficiency (hunger)* and *unwholesome food,* also remarking that it was very difficult to feed 6000 people on a remote island!

Some indication of how dire conditions were can be seen by a statement in the **Achill Herald** saying that Catholic neighbours of the Colony were no longer reluctant to hear the Bible and that many had applied to read recantation in the Church in Dugort. All had been refused. Edward Nangle told the people that he would feed them, teach their children and after the famine was over, they would be welcome to come forward and make public confession. He said that now was the time for instruction not proselytising! This seems a remarkable statement and complete *volte face* if one takes into account previous remarks and his unremitting proselytising zeal. It would seem to have occurred in one of his more euphoric moods!

Cultivation and sowing on the island was now said to be at a full stop, except on the Mission farm, the reasons given were that the people could not afford to buy seed and that furthermore they did not understand the methodology involved in the cultivation of green crops!

Dr. Adams paints a harrowing picture of conditions in Achill at this time, referring to the " *...bloated and emaciated figures on roads tottering on to procure food or calling to the Dispensary for medicine. These roads that usually at this season were covered by cheerful boys and girls mounted on their ponies going to collect seaweed for their potato beds. Now fever, dropsy and dysentery, all of which have become more frequent so that the numbers can no longer be counted.*"

150

14. The Achill Mission, 1831-1886

Nangle asked the Government to supply a vessel so that he could personally procure one hundred tons of potato seed to be sold at cost to the natives but the Government declined his request. In May, Dr.Adams again penned a graphic picture of just how bad conditions were: *"Give us a ticket! Give us a ticket!"* This was a cry frequently heard from people begging for food. A food ticket entitled people to a small daily ration of food from the *soup kitchens*. The Public Works had been virtually suspended since 1846 and other means of employment was non-existent Dr. Adams said that *"...many of our neighbours whose best efforts were often directed against the Mission are now employed on the Mission farm, receiving a practical fulfilment of the divine precept, of doing good to them that despitefully use you and persecute you! "* He again appealed in the *Achill Herald* for help on behalf of the most needy from whom he was receiving daily requests, examples of which are appended below:

> *"Sir,*
>
> *The bearer is in great distress, has seven in family and they haven't anything to eat, only seaweed. They lost three cows and a horse this spring. They did not get on the road this year and four of them are sick."*

> *"Honoured Sir,*
>
> *We do hereby certify this woman has been a nurse of six persons lying in a fever who has no means of support but depends on your Honour."*

Dr. Adams also reported that *fever, dysentery and anasarcous swelling* were becoming very common, the former now increasing in severity. He prescribed a diet of solution of crystals of tartar, nitrous *æther and tincture of sguiles* to remove dropsy and recommended *Dovens power plus Nutt galls* for dysentery, unless the person was old or had a *shattered constitution.*

Distress on the island continued but was alleviated somewhat by the expansion of out-door relief (Soup Kitchens). Because of this the Mission felt it prudent to reduce meals from two to one per day for children attending the Mission schools! The *'famine boilers '* used in out-door relief can be seen at the Settlement in Dugort, one in a garden a few doors away from the Slievemore Hotel and a second in another nearby

garden. There was a report that thirteen currachs fishing off Achill Head
were seized by H. M. Customs and carried to Belmullet with fishing lines
and large quantities of fish confiscated. These boats were seized because
they were not registered or numbered! Obviously nobody told them there
was a famine raging throughout the country!

The Mission planted twenty one tons of foreign potatoes, *French,
Spanish and Dutch* with no sign of the potato blight present. However,
agricultural work throughout the rest of the island had virtually come to
a standstill; some turnips had been sown but the wet weather which
prevented the burning of the land proved to be a serious handicap. Much
distress was predicted because of this lack of sowing. The *Achill Herald*
claimed that the Public Works were a sham, being confined to the winter
when the weather was bad, while they ceased in summer. It was predicted
that the population would die of starvation unless food was
imported: *"...even the resources of the more comfortable class of peasant
are now gone and the whole island is now reduced to a state of utter and
universal pauperism."* Reports of the activities of the Mission began to
filter out of the island and resulted in a Mr. Bourke, an employee of the
Board of Works, writing to Edward Nangle to ask a number of questions,
viz:

*"Is it true that some hundreds of Roman Catholic parents are fed (from
funds subscribed to you) on condition that their children should attend
daily at Protestant schools?"*

In his reply, Edward Nangle claimed that in 1845 he had discovered
that wages paid to Protestant labourers were insufficient for their wants
so he had, *in lieu* of additional payment, undertaken to feed their children
attending Mission schools; subsequently this relief was extended to two
schools, attended principally by Roman Catholics. He also claimed that
people were asking for more schools despite the fact that his views on
priests and popery were well known. Nangle claimed that relief given to
children in the schools had saved thousands from starvation. He said that
some Roman Catholic parents refused to move their children from the
Mission schools even on their deathbed! It is however likely that concern
for their children's well-being rather than religious fervour was their

14. The Achill Mission, 1831-1886

prime motivation.The Poor Law Extension Act of June, 1847 proposed that funding for outdoor relief would be paid for *via* rates. As this burden would have fallen mainly on the landlords, a clause was inserted whereby anyone who held more than a quarter-acre of land was excluded from relief. The end result of this was that the Poor House could no longer cater for the destitute.

In July, it was claimed that out of a population of 7,000 people on the island, 5,000 were receiving daily relief, an indication of how bad things were. There was a rumour, unsubstantiated, that some poor people had been violently dispossessed by a Catholic proprietor on the island! The **Achill Herald** pointed out that many people had been obliged to sell cattle and even blankets; others had cattle confiscated for rent payment. Disease was rampant and another year of famine was predicted, heralded by the re-appearance of blight on the potato crop.

In September, Dr. Adams claimed that fever and dysentery had returned under more severe forms and that a schoolmaster had died of yellow fever. He was bitter that the Board of Health refused to give any assistance. The harvest as expected was poor, even the turnip crop was a failure except for a plot on the Mission farm. The results were predictable, to quote Dr. Adams: *"From daylight to night time the cries of the sick and starving seldom cease at my window ."* He was concerned that only 500 of the inhabitants were capable of feeding themselves until the Spring; the Mission was now feeding fifteen to eighteen hundred children per day in the Mission schools and eleven new schools were planned. The *Island Society* provided funds for teachers' salaries and it was anticipated that six hundred extra children would be added to the above number. It was reported that in order to provide additional relief *via* work schemes, Sir Richard O'Donnell, agreed to give to the Mission as much *"wild land as we can cultivate in the vicinity of each village. This land will be leased for three lives or thirty one years to me as agent of the Achill Mission Society." **Achill Missionary Herald (1847)**.

It was anticipated that the poor would be employed in fencing and reclaiming the land and building a schoolhouse upon it, and that payment would not be in money but in food! Payment for a day's labour was *one quarter stone of meal* and it was assumed that this combined with the food given to the children in the schools would be adequate to support a poor family. The cost of one quarter stone of meal was 3 pence so this was the wage paid by the Achill Mission to people on the verge of starvation. Justifying this policy, Edward Nangle said that:

"...gratuitous relief was ruinous, especially to those whom indolence and imprudence was habitual. A low rate of wages would allow modest relief to many more families. A low rate of wages was the best security against imposition." It was felt that "a payout in wages would encourage the numbers of people looking for work from the Mission."

He further maintained that the poor would receive permanent benefit by the creation of a Scriptural school in the village; *"...for the houses erected and land reclaimed by their labour would suffice with a very small salary to support a teacher ."* He suggested that joint collections be made in England to enable a small vessel to be sent from Liverpool freighted with Indian corn.

The Catholic Church retaliated in an article which appeared in **The Tablet** in June saying that Achill was *"...the scene of the grossest attempts at seduction and coerced perversion ."* It was further claimed that the island was being exploited by Nangle, the *'soul-buyer'* and that nothing was *"given of all the money that comes from England and elsewhere, for the relief of the poor of Achill, except that which is given in exchange for consciences ."* It went on to say that although donations had doubled because of the famine, no one got anything unless their children attended the Protestant schools. It maintained that the wretchedness of the people could be measured by the following incident: *H.M. Frances,* a vessel bound for Greenock in Scotland while passing Achill was boarded by thirty men in nine boats who sought cargo and were apparently very disappointed when they discovered that the cargo on board consisted of sugar, rum and molasses, which the Captain offered but which were refused. The Captain was then compelled to produce stores which was devoured by the party who acted *"like famished wolves. "* Their hunger appeased, they left the vessel peaceably. Captain Eliot described the appearances of these wretches as being *"very pitiful with countenances* *wild and haggard and clothing scanty .*" It seems they had a small quantity of fish in the boats, some of which they gave to Captain Eliot. He offered them money but all they wanted was food. ***The Tablet*** went on to say that the Achill people did not ask for charity until the last of the mountain sheep had been consumed and all resources depleted. The ***Achill Herald*** maintained that discrimination was practised by the Catholic clergy during the famine, that they refused the last rites until payment was made, and that their Church was in decline since the onset of the famine.

The tumult exemplified in the above was reflected in the weather when the island was again visited by severe gales blowing from the north-west which continued for two days and did much damage to standing corn and also that which was reaped, throwing down stacks and carrying sheaves through the air.

A request for a pier on the north shore in Dugort was again taken up with the Board of Works. However the Board considered the expense involved too great for the amount of traffic using such a facility. The Mission wrote back saying that the bay at Pollowaddy was well sheltered and that the part of the coast where a pier would be more practical was located four miles south of Pollowaddy, at Bullsmouth. They pointed out that there was a pier in Achill Sound and yet another five miles to the south in Cloughmore; the east and south sides of the island being sufficiently provided for, the Mission saw Dugort as being the best spot for use by the people in the villages of *Toneylanwalla, Toneynant, Dugort, Finsheen, Bealnasally, Slievemore, Dukinelly and Keel!* An Englishman who worked in Achill during the famine claimed that *Pollowaddy* was an ideal spot as it had a line of roads leading to it which would be useless if no pier was erected. Mr. Gibbons, an engineer with the Board of Works said that there were few boats in the locality, *"All true, said Nangle, for the obvious reason that there is no pier here."* Emphasising his point, he said:

"A few years ago there was not one cart in the whole island and if the roads had not been made until the natives provided carts to run upon them, we should have no roads! "

Achill

His opinion of local industry was obviously not very high! The Board of Works was asked to contribute £1,200 towards the cost of the pier to be added to the £400 donated by a well-wisher. The Mission agreed to pay the cost of a survey providing it did not exceed £25. Another problem arose concerning the materials to be used, Barry Gibbons claiming that mica slate was unsuitable. Edward Nangle said that there was a splendid quarry of red granite at Tarmon on the opposite side of the bay which had been used in the construction of some of the Mission houses!

The *Ness of Dublin* freighted with seventy six tons of Indian corn, imported by the *Benevolent Friends of the Mission*, was anchored in Dugort. It was regretted that sufficient funds were not available for the three hundred tons previously envisaged. Guernsey jackets sent by the Society of Friends (Quakers) were said by Dr. Adams to have afforded great comfort to those recovering from fever and dysentery. Three plots of waste land were procured and three hundred and twenty six people were deployed to work on land reclamation. The location is not specified. Mr. Domnick McLoughlin, a member of the *Achill Relief Committee* incurred the displeasure of Edward Nangle by going to England to raise funds, without, it was claimed, permission from the *Relief Committee*. Upon his return he was further castigated for failing to provide details of the amounts collected. Obviously furious at the insinuations against his character, he wrote quoting from the Minutes of a Committee meeting at which the following resolution had been passed:

"That the awful state of this island and parish present to the eye of the beholder at the present time a most gloomy picture, the inhabitants are not only reduced to the lowest extremity from the want of food; deaths from starvation (are) frequent, fever and dysentery prevailing to an alarming extent, but what appears still more frightening is that the land, with very little exception, will be shortly reduced to its primitive sterility, for want of seed and means to cultivate it, unless some active and immediate measures are taken. Domnick McLaughlin as Member and Treasurer was duly requested to go on a deputation to Dublin and London to represent the wants of the Achill poor.

Dated, Cashel, 27th day April, 1847 and signed by:-

14. The Achill Mission, 1831-1886

Patrick Greene, C.C. John French, Domnick McLaughlin and John McLaughlin."

Later Domnick McLoughlin in a reply to the aspersions cast upon his character claimed in a letter published in the *Achill Herald* that:

*"Everything in **The Tablet** is true. So would every man in Achill say, even the supposed converts if their true sentiments were known, as many of them have told me. But alas! poverty; no not even this, but famine, starvation, the clinging to life compels them to act otherwise than they would. You may show that you gave some nominal relief to Catholics: you are too experienced after nine years fruitless efforts to gain followers among the islanders (previous to the famine), to cast the hook without the bait. Yes, half a pound of meal to the innocent children to induce them to attend your schools. Can you, even after eleven years state that you gave relief alike to the Catholics without tampering with their religion, for do not your tract-readers take every opportunity of feeling their way and use the means within their reach? Why did you not act during the season of distress, as that truly charitable body, The Society of Friends, the Evangelical Society and your worthy colleague, Dr. Adams, who, there is no doubt is a sincere Protestant, and would have no objection to converts, but gave relief and clothing, and without interfering in their religion. Were not some children at your schools dismissed and refused relief because their parents would not sign some document about popery and the Blessed Virgin."* Domnick McLoughlin said that £61.19s. 6d. in total had been incurred by him on expenses and that the formal meeting at which he was to provide details of his trip was deferred until the return of Mr. Greene, another Committee member who was doing duty in another parish. He claimed that children in the Mission schools were only getting a half-penny's worth of food per day and that adults were getting three pence and working for it as well! In conclusion he stated: *"I think I will have less difficulty in showing the expenditure of £61.19s. 6d. than you will have in the sum of £7,800 as stated by a member at one of the meetings of the committee, that you received within the last year."*

157

Achill

Edward Nangle said that the adverse comments about him and the Mission emanated from the **The Tablet** and said that four hundred Catholics were in daily employment at the Mission, and to name one who had been refused employment! He also asserted that converts names were marked for exclusion from public relief (by Rev. Greene) and that poor families were dispossessed from holdings on Mr. McLoughlin's land because they called at the Protestant Mission when sick. He denied that £7,800 had been collected. He had receipts for £3,384 and a balance of £850 remained at the end of the year.

The month of November would bring further tragedy for the people of Achill:

"This month, even for this boisterous climate has been unusually tempestuous. On the 8th at 4.p.m. a furious gale suddenly arose from the north west, nineteen men from the village of Keel had gone out in six boats to fish for herrings: they were not far distant from the shore when the gale set in, but it blew with such violence that they could not row against it: they were carried out to sea, where every soul perished. Thirty eight children were orphaned. The Society of Friends have sent a ton of meal to Dr. Adams for the widows and orphans. Had the gale sprung up half an hour later, the loss of life would have been still greater as all fishermen in the village were prepared to go to sea. The Irish cry resounding from the cabins, the wild screaming of the orphans, and the tears of the aged made it one of the most distressing sights I have ever witnessed." Neason Adams.

Distress continued without mitigation but that afforded by voluntary aid or benevolent individuals. Four hundred labourers were now employed by the Achill Mission on reclamation, with another sixty working on Mission farms. One thousand, three hundred and forty nine children were being fed in the Mission schools, the food given out had all been grown on Mission farms *viz.*

14. The Achill Mission, 1831-1886

Item:	Tons:	Cwt:
Potatoes	5	5
Turnips	18	12
Carrots	1	6
Parsnip	-	1

Although the potato crop was defective, the rest of the harvest was abundant. Labour has again been rewarded:

"...we mention this to show our friends that the poor are not maintained by us in idleness!" Another extract says: *"Although, through God's mercy, fever and dysentery have abated considerably, the sick, the aged and infirm, in the Hospital, attending the Dispensary and through the island, require assistance as much as at any period since the famine commenced. The Poor house is upwards of 30 miles from Achill and many who accustomed to very warm cabins cannot bear the excessive cold at this season, have returned with their wives and families in a terrible state."* Neason Adams.

Education

There were now said to be thirty nine Protestant schools in the district of Achill and Ballycroy, all of which had been excluded from public relief by Mr. Richard Lynch, agent of the British Association who had now run out of money. It was also claimed that there was discrimination in the amount of relief distributed viz:

> *Protestant: one half pound of meal per day.*
>
> *Catholic: 10 ozs bread, broth and clothing.*

From this Edward Nangle drew the conclusion that school children were being seduced from Protestant schools by more food! An example of the tables being turned! This prompted him to make a formal complaint to the Marquis of Sligo who had little sympathy for the plight of the Mission saying that Mr. Richard Lynch was held in the highest esteem by the *British Association* and that neither National nor Mission schools were now getting relief. He felt that Nangle's accusation of a Catholic *proselytising* effort: *"comes ill from the Protestant Mission Settlement where temporal advantages have long been considered as an inducement to starving peasants to desert the faith of their fathers ."* *Marquis of Sligo*.

Undeterred by this rebuff, Edward Nangle wrote to the *British Association* on behalf of seven hundred and one families asking why relief had not been extended to the Mission schools. According to him, these families represented two-thirds of the population of Achill. There must have been some unease in official quarters regarding the distribution of relief by the Mission for Mr. Lynch, the Poor Law Inspector, to cede the local distribution to Fr. O'Malley.

On the 22nd December, a small schooner, the *Clyde of Glasgow,* bound for Westport ran ashore one half a mile from the Settlement and was totally wrecked.The weather was said to be cold and stormy, distress acute, and fishermen could not go to sea because of the bad weather.

1848
Transportation
An article appeared in the **Mayo Telegraph** regarding sheep stealing and comparing the respective sentences for this offence in England with Ireland, the former favouring two to three years imprisonment and the latter seven years. Two men (almost certainly converts), were convicted of this offence, and the local parish priest recommended to the authorities that seven years transportation be imposed in expiation of their crime! Representation by Edward Nangle to the Lord Lieutenant resulted in mitigation of the sentence from transportation to two years imprisonment. It was reported in March that food shortage and distress continued, the *Poor House* now being overwhelmed by demand. Out-door relief was said to be totally inadequate and people were dying of hunger on the roads and in houses. The Board of Works was castigated by the Mission for offering relief *via* work on roads as this meant that cultivation was neglected.

14. The Achill Mission, 1831-1886

A further downturn in the plight of the needy was the decision by the *Poor Law Commissioners* to discontinue out-door relief to paupers. The Mission said this decision was catastrophic for Achill where there was no employment and people were totally dependent upon relief. In the landlord clause of the *Poor Act,* persons possessing or owning one quarter acre of land were not deemed to be eligible for relief. People were said to be in a dire state pending the harvesting of the new season's crops. Some were selling their holdings as they could not wait three months for the harvest.

By May, Edward Nangle had reason to believe that the inhabitants of Achill were willing at last *to decry popery.* The Confessionals were said to be empty and the priest had got a grant of £100 to supply seed with the aim of enticing people to rejoin the Catholic Church. There was jubilation at the decision of the Board of Works to erect a pier in Dugort which was to cost £1200. A grant of £900 was authorised and an application made for additional assistance to the *Society of Friends "for their well-known liberality and desire to promote the fishery."* Surprisingly, however, the request was rejected. A note of optimism was struck by Dr. Adams who said that: *"...the cheering prospect of the coming harvest and the out-door relief have in mercy checked the progress of disease on the island."* There were only two cases of fever and two of dysentery, *"...one severe bite of a dog, and one of pleurisy admitted to the hospital during the past month."*

In August, it was reported that the *Mary & Jane* had left Dublin with freight containing twenty tons of Indian meal, *"to help with our system of relief until the harvest is brought in! "* By the end of the month prospects were again gloomy as the fatal *blight* had again made its appearance and people were now really in extremity having borrowed money and sold cattle and furniture to pay for seed. With predictable sensitivity the **Achill Herald** reported that:

"our neighbours now recognise the hand of God in the fearful visitation which has affected them for three years - and divested them of all their property - this conviction has wrought such a change in them that the christian teacher in now sure of a welcome in every house."

161

Achill

There was a report on the Achill Orphan Asylum from Rev. E. Lowe, Superintendent of the Mission. Edward Nangle who had been Superintendent was temporarily transferred to Skreen in Co. Sligo. Lowe claimed that of the one hundred children in the orphanage, ninety nine were of Catholic parentage.The elder boys would be apprenticed to trade and the girls trained in usefulness! The orphanage was now in debt and urgently needed funding. At the same time it was reported that the Mission had acquired a site of forty acres for a Church and a Glebe House at Achill Sound, the new site being nine miles from the Settlement and five miles from the new chapel at Mweelin. The Catholic clergy were said to be getting worried about the progress of the Mission, five of them visiting the island during the month.

By September the weather had undergone a favourable change and Edward Nangle, upon his return to Achill, carried out examinations in all of the Mission schools. The previous gloomy prediction was fulfiled with the report that all but the grain crops had failed. Work at the Mission continued, for it was reported that a workman, while digging a drain in one of our premises, *was buried for twenty minutes beneath a heap of clay* before being eventually rescued from his ordeal. In November, the barque *William Kennedy* freighted with two hundred and twenty tons arrived from Philadelphia after a sail of thirty days. It contained a full cargo to feed the two thousand poor children attending Mission schools and cost £2,200 which was paid for out of donations received. The Mission was now enjoying its most successful period so far and hopes were expressed that Achill might soon become a Protestant island!

A pamphlet was published by Nangle containing the correspondence between himself and Lord Sligo under the title: " *The case of the Achill Mission Schools and the British Association.*" By September the Indian corn from America was ground and distributed to schools. The local population were said to be subsisting on a diet of turnips! The weather was tempestuous and other cargo *en route* to the Settlement had to be landed at Achill Sound. The Post Office had withdrawn the Mail car between Newport and the Settlement, substituting a *"Foot Post"* instead.

14. The Achill Mission, 1831-1886

1849

Two painful incidents, both concerning the Mission occurred in January:

1. "Plunder of one of our boats by persons in the south of the island, one of the perpetrators is in gaol on information received from Mission schools. "

2. Concerned the Rev. Lowe and the Orphanage and the theft of a box containing school funds from his house.

In February, the Mission was employing one hundred and seventy two men in the preparation for cultivation of two large tracts of mountain land for which a supply of Indian meal was paid *in lieu* of wages. Dr. Adams was said to be dispensing rice to the poor to add to their diet of limpets, seaweed and Indian corn.

It was claimed that there were now a total of thirty four schools in Achill including Ballycroy and Inishbiggle.The children were said to be making progress, unlike when the Mission first arrived - then they were wearing *"...amulets or charms, called gospels and scapulars, which were sold by priests to simple people ."*

Divine service was now being celebrated in Dugort, Mweelin, Achill Sound and Bullsmouth and plans were advanced to open another station for preaching the gospel in Duagh (Dooagh). In addition to the normal Sunday service there were week-day lectures in six other villages. There was said to be a serious decline of Catholic influence on the island. Eight Protestant clergymen were employed in Achill, five churches had been constructed, another was in progress, and there were five stations where divine service was celebrated.

"When the Achill Mission commenced operations here 15 years ago there was but one church and one minister in the whole district ."

At this stage in its history, the Mission was without doubt, extremely successful. The fact that the conversions proved to be temporary indicates a miscalculation on the part of the Mission regarding the strength and opposition of the Catholic Church and of *"old allegiances,"* forged over many generations, despite periods of appalling neglect.

In June it was announced that there would be an extension of the railroad from Westport to Mulranny, greatly facilitating the journey to Achill. The Secretary of the *Shipwrecked Fishermen and Mariners Benevolent Society* visited Achill and the Rev. Seymour of the Achill Mission was appointed honorary agent.

Satisfaction was expressed that every village in Achill now had a Scripture School. Young people in the schools were said to be very intelligent and some would be trained as teachers. It was felt that there was a need to establish a training school on the island. It was however anticipated that training fifty students would require an annual expenditure of £8 per boy and donations were required for this and also to feed the poor who would otherwise have to go to the Poor House.

There was consternation over an *illegal marriage* between a Protestant and a Catholic, solemnised by Rev. Peter O'Malley and now before the courts. The case was, however, dismissed. Autumn saw a reappearance of the *potato blight* and the Mission was now said to be feeding 1800 children and Indian meal had been reduced in price to £6.10s. per ton.

There was a report on the design of the proposed Training school in Mweelin: the building would contain a school room for fifty boys and three apartments for the teachers; the scholars would be lodged in cottages in the immediate vicinity, six in each cottage at a fee of £5 per annum for board and lodgings; payment for accommodation would be sourced from the scholars who would be employed in agricultural work under the supervision of the Steward of the Mission; wages accruing for this work would pay for their accommodation; an average term of two and one half years was thought to suffice to qualify as a teacher. Subjects to be taught would include: English - reading, writing and grammar, Geography, General History, Maths, Surveying and Mensuration and a thorough acquaintance with the Bible.

14. The Achill Mission, 1831-1886

The Bishop again visited the Settlement to confirm four hundred persons, twenty eight of them Protestant, the remainder Catholic, some aged but the majority children. Seven hundred and fifty people were present at the ceremony and another five hundred outside. There was a bonfire in the Settlement by way of celebration, after which the bishop laid the first stone of the new Church at Achill Sound, which was attended by between twelve and thirteen hundred people. The weather was said to be unusually fine and the corn doing very well.

In October, Dr. Adams, *via* the ***Achill Herald***, thanked subscribers for clothing received. He said that wool was now being bought and a number of women would be employed in spinning. *"Ireland cannot produce better frieze, or at a lower price than can be manufactured in the Isle of Achill ."* In December an advertisement was placed in the ***Achill Herald*** for four school-teachers at a salary of £15 per annum, with lodgings.

1850

The January edition of the ***Achill Herald*** reported the renewal of altar denunciations by Catholic priests, including threats and curses on people sending their children to the Mission schools. *The Douay Bible* was publicly burned after which the number of children attending the Mission schools declined to sixteen hundred. There was mention of seven female schools where the teaching of embroidery had been introduced. More donations were required if the Mission was to feed the children until the harvest was reaped.

Violent incidents against Protestants in Aughrim, Louisburgh, Clifden and Tuam were reported in the ***Achill Herald.*** There were also references to Catholic *lubrication* of ***The Tablet***, now with an elegant and impressive style and no more vulgar ribaldry that distinguished previous Roman Catholic outpouring!*"We exult in the appearance of this Journal."*

In February, a severe gale from the west was accompanied by the most terrible squalls ever experienced, even worse than *"Oidhe Randall "* in 1839. Houses were wrecked to their foundations and many windows

Achill

broken. Dugort and Mweelin suffered great damage. In Mweelin the roof of the Church was blown off and some houses were completely destroyed. In Dugort the printing works was wrecked, glass in the orphanage and in the school was broken and the house of the Rev. Lowe and Mr. Langley stripped. Edward Nangle's house had fifteen panes of glass broken in windows while in Mr. Hughes' house the ceiling fell in and the roofs of several other houses were partially damaged.

Clothing was distributed to five hundred boys and to three hundred girls. The priests were said to be quiet, maintaining that the children would leave the Mission schools when the food ran out. A report in April claimed that Mission funds were exhausted and unless replenished, eighteen hundred poor children would have to go to the Poor House. A second hospital was also required, the original hospital now being in existence for nine years. This would cost about £200, the building to be of stone and lime with a slated roof.

The Mweelin development was said to have made excellent progress:

"there is a rectory, a handsome little church, a stewards house, a long row of cottages (to house 15 families in all), a school house for 40 scholars (children of converts and those from neighbouring villages). 60 boys selected from 30 schools in parish will be trained as teachers ."

An advertisement in the *Achill Herald* offered a *Furnished House to let* containing two sitting rooms and seven bedrooms, plus servants quarters. Apply Mr. Langley, Dugort.

"Board and lodgings for one week including servants: £1.5s. 0d.
Jaunting cars and ponies for hire - 6d, 8d, 10d per mile.
Ponies 1s.6d. per day."

In May there was intense diatribe against the Catholic clergy for their *heartless neglect* of the poor of the parish. They were said to be demanding payment for services during the famine. It was during this period that the Achill Estate of Sir Richard O'Donnell came before the

14. The Achill Mission, 1831-1886

Encumbered Estates Court and was sold in various lots. In the *Report of the Devon Commission*, Frederick Cavendish of the **Mayo Constitution** in 1849 commented on the embarrassed state of the landlords when the fall-off in rents had made an already perilous state a critical occurrence. Absenteeism was largely responsible for encumbrances and as matters deteriorated it became incumbent upon the Government to arrange the sale of estates so that new money could be invested in Irish agriculture. Bailiffs employed by some landlords were accused of practising usury while they grew rich on the gains extracted from poor farmers, while the tenantry were rack-rented on pain of eviction.

New Landlords

The Achill Mission purchased three-fifths of the O'Donnell Estate in the *Encumbered Estates Court*. The purchase price was £17,500, £10,500 being contributed by the Mission and £2,333. 6s. 8d each by Thomas Brassy, William Pike and Samuel Holme in return for small estates on the island. Archbishop McHale and William McCormack purchased the remaining lands of Bunacurry and Corraun respectively, while the Marquis of Sligo retained his lands in the Valley. The purchase by Dr. McHale of Bunacurry townland was extensively covered in The **Tablet**, **The Mayo Telegraph** and the **Freemans Journal**. It was claimed that this act would gladden the heart of Catholics and all decent Protestants, because it was high time to strike a blow at the*"falsehood, intrigue and misdeeds of the proselytisers in Achill ."* An excerpt from **The Tablet** in 1850 refers to the Archbishop's intentions:

"We understand his Grace (Dr. McHale) intends immediately to set about building extensive religious establishments on his estate in Achill, in order to save these poor islanders from further persecution. He hopes to erect, in the first place, a monastery for a community of the "Christian Brothers and also another for the Franciscan Monks. The Christian Brothers, it is hoped, will attend exclusively to teaching and educating, whilst the other monks will also employ themselves in reclaiming and tilling this mountain tract, and will thereby, of course, afford employment to hundreds of those who are at present exposed to death from hunger or damnation from relief. His Grace also expects to erect a convent for the

Achill

Sisters of Mercy in Achill, and a large Hospice or House of Refuge, attached thereto." The reaction of the Achill Mission to the above development was predictable:

"We shall encounter the Monks with the only weapon of our warfare, the sword of the spirit; which is the word of God."

A monastery was to be erected at Dugort on the south side of the road going west to the colony, where the Franciscan Monks would reclaim and till a large area of the mountain side, thereby providing employment for a large number of people *"whose souls were in danger from the Mission soup and stirabout."* The Mission counteracted this move by calling upon the Orange Society to protect the Protestants in Achill: *"we will call them to our aid in this spiritual warfare - they have what we need, organisation, determination and zeal."* A number of persons employed in carrying stones from the townland of Cashel, part of Achill Mission land, to Bunacurry townland, the property of Dr. McHale, were warned against the illegality of this action. Workmen continued to take the stones and even went as far as pulling down a number of unroofed houses on Mission property. In the *Battle of the Stones*, the priest's faction was not strong enough to wrest the stones from the Achill Mission group, so the dispute was halted by both parties signing an agreement to leave the matter to the legal authorities to sort out ownership. At the request of Edward Nangle, Sir Richard O'Donnell, the local magistrate, arrived on the island, accompanied by a sub-inspector and eight men to mediate in the dispute and to oversee the removal of the stones by Mission personnel. Leaving the island Sir Richard O'Donnell and his party met a group of men from Corraun seemingly coming to aid *"McHale's men."* This *"lawless"* mob was headed by Ryan, editor of the **Catholic Vindicator**, a member of the *"Irish Mineral Trading Company "* and an associate of William McCormack, owner of Corraun.

"...who is spending the money of some English company in Corraun, professedly in reproductive labour, but really trying to advance the cause of popery ."

Ryan was said to be intoxicated and Sir Richard and his party decided to stay on the island to prevent further trouble. The remains of stones were collected on Monday and left within the boundary *"where we plan to build a new Church and schoolhouse."* The stones were, however, again removed by Fr. Gallagher and his men and the Mission decided to go to Dublin to seek legal assistance. The *"Battle of the Stones"* held up work for several months, the Courts were unable to decide ownership, and in the meantime Dr. McHale was incurring considerable expense in order to protect his claim to the stones. Eventually work was abandoned and a new site in Bunacurry was chosen. Edward Nangle, needless to say, was delighted that *"the Monkery"* had to go and claimed that the *"the proud ecclesiastic, Dr. McHale, could not stand up to the Mission.* " The **Achill Herald** reported in July, 1853 that:

"...the doctor has removed the site of his monastery to the other extremity of his land, at the greatest possible distance from the Protestant territory and in the centre of that small portion of the island which has fallen into Roman Catholic hands. How mortified this haughty ecclesiastic must feel under such falsification of his prediction of the down-fall of the Achill Mission ."

In the meantime the Pope had written to Dr. McHale asking why so many Catholics in the Archdiocese of Tuam were forsaking their religion. Dr. McHale replied that while this was true of Achill, he was taking steps to remedy the situation by increasing the number of clergy and building a monastery for Franciscan Monks, both of which would help to keep the people faithful and bring back to the fold those who had defected. When Dr. McHale visited the island to confirm children it was claimed by the Mission that only one hundred and ninety six children were confirmed compared to four hundred confirmed at the Settlement the previous year. Dr. McHale's reception was said to be poor, only one hundred and fifty people turning out to welcome him, a very different reception to that afforded him in 1835, according to the **Achill Herald.** Dr. McHale's visit involved a procession from Achill Sound to Cashel where the parish priest had his residence. *En route* three young Protestant youths overtook the procession and it was claimed that: *"..the crowds closed around them spalling the aprons and shawls which they carried as banners on the end* *of poles on their horses faces. The youths fearing for their lives appealed to Dr. McHale who did nothing, but Fr. O'Malley intervened and let them go free.*" Dr. McHale later heard confessions and said Mass in the Chapel (Dookinella) near the Settlement with between two hundred and two hundred and fifty present. He promised more schools for the island and also promised to visit every year from then on.

Despite the above setback the Achill Mission Estate was now virtual owners of three-fifths of the island, ownership being vested in the trustees appointed by the Mission. These included Edward Nangle, the Hon. Somerset Maxwell, the Hon. Joseph Napier, William Brooke, Master in Chancery and George Alexander Hamilton. Upon completion of the legal formalities, the Mission was said to be "...*contemplating the immediate improvement of a large tract of land which has fallen into our hands in the vicinity of the Settlement .*" Thus began the demolition of the village of Finsheen! Funds were needed for the reclamation work and it was envisaged that one hundred and eight persons would be be employed in this undertaking.

William Pike, the new owner of Sraheens, Carrickildavnet and Derreens, and later a magistrate on the island had come from England where he had been chairman of the *Committee of Birkenhead Improvements*. Pike encountered quite a lot of trouble in Achill, from both sides of the religious divide, i.e. Edward Nangle and Fr. Henry and from various illegal organisations. He was accused by Fr. Henry of ordering his bailiff, to serve *Notice to Quit* on the tenants of Derreens Village. He would allow them to keep their crops and give a moratorium on rents owing from the previous year; if they did not agree to surrender possession, they were to be evicted forthwith. Pike had the right of vacant possession from the *Encumbered Estates Court* which allowed him, under the law, to clear his lands of tenants. He later claimed that he possessed an injunction to turn out eighty four families from his estate but had not done so, only evicting some of the more obstructive characters! The advent of the landlords had encouraged the setting up of a branch of the *Ribbon Confederacy* in Achill and Pike duly received a threat from the "*Molly Maguires*" to *stop wasting the lands of Achill and compelling poor Roman Catholics to leave their homes and lands.*"

14. The Achill Mission, 1831-1886

Similar threatening notices would later be served on Murray McGregor Blacker and Captain Charles Boycott in Keel West townland which they had leased from the Achill Mission. Pike blamed Fr. Henry for inciting the tenants against him claiming that the priest had promised them, in the event of eviction from the Pike estate, that he would procure them lands on the McCormack Estate in Corraun.

The McLoughlin Estate which William McCormack had purchased was in 1850 in a condition of hopeless decadence, *"a wild and pauperless tract of 6,878 acres of which 5,925 acres were mountain, held by tenants in common and subject to a fee farm rent of £193 per annum."* William McCormack was a member of the *Irish Beetroot and Sugar Manufacturing Company* and the tract of land purchased by him in Corraun had for long been considered part of the Mission demesne. The acquisition of this land caused alarm in the Colony, particularly when it was learned that McCormack had forbidden people to give lodgings to Protestant teachers and that he was employing five hundred labourers reclaiming wasteland. Hearing of Dr. McHale's plan to build a monastery in Bunacurry, McCormack immediately offered £200 together with ten to twelve acres of land in Corraun for the construction of a Church in that area.

Visitors to the Settlement this season included Samuel Holme, now owner of Carrowgarve, Dooega, Claggan and Cloughmore townlands who was accompanied by his son and daughter. Sir Richard O'Donnell also visited the island as well as a Mr. Wilde, probably William Wilde, father of Oscar, who subsequently wrote a very interesting article on *booleying* in Achill in the nineteenth century. The *Achill Herald* reported that the suffering of the poor in Achill had increased rather than diminished when in the autumn there was again a reappearance of the potato *blight*. In the meantime, the Franciscans and the Catholic clergy had begun their counter-reformation. Dr. McHale, when visiting the island, had demanded that the people stay clear of the *proselytisers* and refuse to send their children to the Mission schools. The Mission responded by threatening eviction and persecution of all those who refused to comply but this was so unjust that several members of the

Mission Board resigned in protest. When the Rev. Nangle left Achill in 1852 the Mission was in decline.

1851

In January, the contract for purchase of the Achill Mission Estate was nearing completion.The estate contained 24,000 acres with a net annual income of £400. A list of all contributions was prepared and Edward Nangle asked them for support for another two years when he envisaged the estate would be self-supporting. In February, a letter appeared in the *Edinburgh Review* complementing Sir Richard O'Donnell on improvements carried out by him around Newport and saying that he had now commenced work in Achill by:

"thoroughly draining 437 acres,
clearing 537 acres and
constructing 52 miles of fencing."
"...how much more praiseworthy Sir Richard O'Donnell's actions than that of the Protestant Mission."

The author of this article, a Mr. Elwood, seems to have got his facts wrong for the Mission were now owners of the O'Donnell Estate. Edward Nangle claimed that Sir Richard O'Donnell had enclosed seventy acres of land with a good stone fence and partially levelled the land within this enclosure but that the Mission was the main improver on the island with major works being carried out at Bal, Dugort and Mweelin. He refers to a letter received from Sir Richard O'Donnell some years past when he said that the Mission lease would be renewed because of the good work being done on the island!

Lord Clevenden was praised in the *Edinburgh Review* for sending agricultural improvers to Ireland. One visited Achill and he was said to be astonished by the improvements carried out in the Colony, especially in the cultivation of grain crops and with turnips and carrots better than in Dublin. In March, it was claimed that distress on the island was never more severe than now. A school, one mile from the Settlement, was deserted, the children having gone to the Poor House, others to the sea-shore to alleviate their hunger. Is this the beginning of the desertion of Slievemore? In August, it was reported that the potato blight was still

14. The Achill Mission, 1831-1886

prevalent on the island. On the 13th inst. the *Susan of Galway* appeared off Achill Beg with a cargo containing twenty one tons of meal which was safely landed. This relief was provided by Samuel Holme of Liverpool, the recent purchaser of a small estate in Achill.

The first stone of the new hospital at Mweelin Valley was laid. The Training school in Mweelin was now said to have fifty four boys in residence. The Mission had also established an agricultural college on a farm near the Settlement which was to be an asylum for poor youths who otherwise would have to go to the work-house and be re-converted to Catholicism! The farm was to be worked under the superintendency of boys *"...who will acquire such skill and habits of industry as are unknown among the peasantry of this island."* Agricultural operations were carried on vigorously, fences on the farm surrounding the Agricultural school were nearly completed and thorough drainage was going on. A large piece of land in the same village was now being dug, preparatory to putting in a crop in the Spring. Drainage continued at Mweelin. One hundred acres of oats were to be sown there the following year. The average number employed on the farm was one hundred and forty nine. *"Every shilling spent enhances the value of land, now the property of the Achill Mission ."*

The Training school at Mweelin was examined by an Inspector of the Church Educational Society. A Training school for females was also proposed because several girls of superior talent were now said to be in the Mission schools and it was proposed that they be domiciled at the Settlement and placed under immediate instruction. An eminent architect had agreed to provide plans free of charge to construct a Master's dwelling, dormitories, school and dining rooms and farm yards and offices. The cost for one year was estimated at £1,000.

September saw the beginning of a long spell of dry weather; the harvest was gathered but the potato crop was found to be partially destroyed. The model farm produced several green crops, together with turnips and carrots of *White Belgian* and *Altringham* varieties. This farm was said to be thoroughly drained and practising the most improved methods of cultivation, unlike the *native* method of agriculture where there was no

173

meadow and where the furrows of tilled land had never been turned up; *"the seed being sown year after year in the same exhausted soil and but for the super abundance of sea-manure employed by them would yield no crops at all ."* A bit of local news involved a Priest on the island who married a couple at *midnight* when the bridegroom was intoxicated! £1. 2s. was paid to the Priest for this service.

27. Keem Bay © Ursula Kavanagh

An advertisement in the **Achill Herald** offered to let a Hotel and forty acres of land at Achill Sound. The Hotel was said to be on the shore and had a good supply of seaweed nearby. Another advertisement is listed below which would attract the attention of one of the most infamous characters in Irish history and Achill folklore, *Captain Charles Cunningham Boycott:*

TO BE LET: *"...the mountains and valley of **Keem,** the most picturesque spot in Achill. The mountains of Keem are celebrated for the excellence of the mutton fed on them. There is also in the bay a **Salmon Fishery,** which if worked by a skillful fisherman would yield from nine to ten tons of salmon in the season. There are also other unoccupied lands."* Details from Mr. Isaac Johnston, Dugort.

14. The Achill Mission, 1831-1886

In December, 1851, there was a notice in the **Achill Herald** to the effect that money was needed for the Achill orphans for, despite the purchase of the island by the Achill Mission, it was not still not financially secure. If funding was not received the orphans would have to go to the Poor House.

1852

A letter dated 6th January, 1852 in the **Freemans Journal** from Dr. McHale reads as follows:

"The public and especially the English portion of it may judge what credit the Achill questors may take for zeal for education, when it is informed that some of those colonists had violently and illegally seized heaps of stones which were purchased for the purpose of erecting a monastery and schools for the young, during the coming season of spring and summer. Independently of annoying the clergy and illegally depriving one at least, of the men of his liberty for some time, those emissaries of religious impiety and social discord scrupled not to put us to an amount of expense in vindicating our legal right, which would have considerably helped to forward those institutions." Another letter in the same Journal contained the following information:

"I visited the site of the new monastery selected by his Grace. The building is to be on the south side of the road leading to the Protestant Colony of Dugort. The monastery is destined for the Monks of the Third Order of St. Francis, large schools for the gratuitous education of the poor children of the surrounding villages are to be attached to the establishment, and, I am told, it is their intention to lay out a model farm for the institution of the boys in all the improved modes of agriculture, and especially such as will be found suited to the natural position and soil of the island." **Freemans Journal**, 8th January, 1852. On the 26th of January, Dr. McHale also published a letter in the **Freemans Journal** thanking the people of Achill for donations to counteract the work of the Achill Mission.

It was reported that because of a late alteration to the *Poor Law*, each electoral division would now be liable to taxation only for its own poor. Desiring to avail themselves of this enactment the Achill Mission sent a bailiff to ascertain the number of paupers for which they would be liable but the master of the house refused the requested information. With the aid of friends, the Mission said it would hope to give relief to the destitute and employment to the able-bodied so that *"our poor-rate will be reduced so low as to be no longer, as it is at present, an incubus on the industry of this district."*

In March, there was a request from Dr. Adams asking for donations for Mweelin Valley Hospital, in the form of *"a half-note, the least troublesome way of sending money through the post."* The death of an Achill convert in the Poor House was notified to the Mission by the Rev. Stoney, Castlebar. It was noted that two monks had arrived on the island belonging to the Franciscans or *"bible burning"* fraternity!

In June, the Rev. Joseph Barker was nominated as Rector of Achill, Rev. Edward Nangle having been appointed to the living at Skreen in Sligo but who planned to spend three months of the year in Achill.Upon the departure of Edward Nangle the *Society for Church Missions* undertook the maintenance and support of the whole Missionary agency including ministers, scripture readers and also the entire support of the Mweelin Training school. No reason is given for this administrative change but it may be that Edward Nangle's health had become a problem. Financial problems were also indicated in that large arrears due to Missionary agents and labourers were noted, as soon as the new arrangements took effect. It was claimed that a variety of circumstances contributed to this embarrassment, notably the famine having created a drain on funds. Money also dried up after the purchase of the Achill Mission lands and despite monies having been paid to the *Encumbered Estates* in April 1851, conveyancing was still ongoing and therefore rents could not be collected. Arrears also accrued on the Poor Rate, and County Cess and all work was discontinued, pending completion of the sale so as to avoid incurring further debt. Notwithstanding this, eighty orphans and one hundred and twenty destitute children were fed. However, the Achill orphan refuge was placed under the auspices of the *Achill Temporal Relief Committee,* made up of Protestant ministers and chaired by Dr. Adams. Its duties involved providing for destitute children and orphans, feeding schoolchildren with half a pound of Indian meal bread per day and the relief of distress. This committee was limited to the care of the recently purchased estate, and income received there from was to be expended in labour to benefit the tenants. The introduction of an improved system of cultivation was promised. That Edward Nangle would agree to this new departure was unlikely, as proved to to be the case when it was brought to his attention.

August was a month of unusual activity in Achill - the hotel was crowded, the Bishop visited on the 7th and consecrated the new Parish Church at Achill Sound, confirmed children and laid the foundation stone for a new Church at the Settlement, the present St. Thomas's Church. One hundred and sixty seven children were confirmed and upwards of eight hundred people assembled for the service. Dr. McHale, also in Achill on the same day, presided over confirmation in Dookinella Chapel as the chapel in the south of the island (Kildavnet?) was closed! Dr. McHale stayed in Cashel.

A letter in the **Connacht Ranger** praised Dr. McHale's visit and castigated the Achill Mission for the persecution, extermination, proselytising etc. of the Catholic population. It claimed that children had been enticed to Church on Confirmation Day by the promise of a feast! In September, a reader of the *Achill Herald* wrote suggesting that Edward Nangle compile a history of the Achill Mission. The year ended with several small incidents involving locals and Mission personnel, many of them having to be sorted out by the Courts. There was consternation in the Mission upon learning that the Marquis of Sligo had contributed £1 towards the Sisters of Mercy fund for distressed young women. Dr. Adams claimed that children who left the Mission after Dr. McHale's visit were now returning "*...as they prefer food, clothing and bible reading to hunger, nakedness and ignorance.*"

1853

A major *fracas* occurred in January involving the death of a convert who had requested burial in the Mission graveyard, a decision violently opposed by his nearest relatives. William Pike, the landlord in the district was asked to intervene in the row and opted for a compromise solution i.e. burial in Kildavnet with a Service read by the Rev. Barker of the Achill Mission. Although there was initial agreement on this course of action, scuffles broke out during the ceremony, preventing the Rev. Barker from officiating, and people were reputedly beaten with sticks, whips and stones by Scripture Readers in the graveyard. William Pike had some Catholics arrested but let them go shortly afterwards which caused great offence in Mission headquarters. Pike said that he had tried to restrain fanatics on both sides!

There was a riot in Keel and a house occupied by the Mission (Female) schoolteacher had windows broken. A schoolhouse in a village which belonged to the Mission was taken over by a *papist,* a tenant of the Mission, prompting the following response:*"We have now determined to clear the estate of a lot of these lawless fellows ."*

The Tablet (1853) carried an extract from Dr. McHale's Pastoral Letter: *"We hear from the clergymen of Achill the consoling assurance that the schools of the proselytisers to which hunger alone attracted destitute children, were becoming deserted every day while the schools of the monks were numerously attended."* The battle was not yet over. An advertisement appeared in the *Achill Herald* for a Superintendent for the *Achill agricultural school* with the proviso that *"he must be married as his wife will have to take charge of the dairy."*

In March, a boat laden with seaweed struck a rock between Bullsmouth and Inishbiggle. Two men on board were rescued by the coastguards. The counter reformation commenced in earnest with the appointment of a new parish priest of Achill, Fr. Henry, who was alleged to have urged his congregation when encountering Mission personnel to *"scold them, and scald them."* Fr. Henry had already been convicted for assaulting a Mission employee and was now out on bail! He became Nangle's greatest enemy and a thorn in his side for many years. He sent a letter to the *Mayo Telegraph* claiming that:

"Nine Protestant schools had closed in Achill during the last eight

14. The Achill Mission, 1831-1886

months. Four teachers (converts) had been re-admitted into the Catholic Church."

In its reply the **Achill Herald** explained that the *Irish Church Missions* had decided to cut down expenses and concentrate pupils in fewer schools. Some schools had already closed as they were located in townlands now owned by Dr. McHale. The school at Dooniver closed because Patrick McHugh had obtained a lease of that townland from the Marquis of Sligo and refused to permit continued usage of that building by the Achill Mission. A similar situation pertained in *Sruffaunbee* when William McCormack acquired land in that townland. In addition, the Mission's school in Corraun closed *"when Ryan broke it up!"*

The Weekly Telegraph in June, 1853 published another letter from Fr. Henry: *" ...let us hope that those who occasionally send clothing to other poor localities will follow the example of this charitable lady by not forgetting the naked little ones of Christ in Achill, and thereby give them an opportunity of receiving a liberal and religious education suited to their state of life, from the good brothers of the Order of Saint Francis who are here giving employment to the poor and educating the children."*

In July, the *Bianconi* car carried travellers between Mulranny and Achill and contracted to convey mail to Achill on alternate days. In response to Dr. McHale's letter in the **Telegraph**, Edward Nangle on his annual break in Achill claimed that there were:*"39 children in the Protestant school at Achill Sound, 78 children in the Infant school in the Settlement; a mixed school was being held in a temporary Church and had 72 scholars; the female orphan house had 44 poor children and the Mweelin training school had 44 boys in training."*

It was regretted that work on the Church in the Settlement had been discontinued because of lack of funds. £700 had been collected but a further £1,250 was needed for an endowment. Divine service was held at Inishbiggle, Mweelin, Dooagh and Achill Sound. Edward Nangle, accompanied by some visitors (possibly Boycott & Blacker), toured Keem Bay and Bunowna:

"En route to Kim the party visited the schools in Dooagh, conversing

*freely with the villagers on popery. Having feasted our eyes on the magnificent scenery of Kim we headed towards Bunowna and saw former human habitations. A rude wall had been raised to meet a great rock projecting from the side of a hillock; in this wall was a door so low that to enter it we were obliged to creep on our hands and knees. In this rude habitation about 200 years ago lived a man named **Brian a Stalkire**, who lived on the wild deer which at that time abounded on the island."*

Returning home, the party stopped at Rockfield, midway between the villages of Keel and Dooagh, where Nangle's friends selected a site for a schoolhouse and place of worship to service the two villages. The party attended divine service at the wild and remote village of Dooagh where the sermon and service were conducted in Irish. One hundred and twenty four people were present. In August, it was claimed that twenty acres of land were to be reclaimed to build the schoolhouse at Rockfield. The following appeared in the *Achill Herald:*

"The small portion of the population of this island who live under the more immediate control and instruction of Dr. McHale and his monks, on the lands of Bunacurry deport themselves in a manner which is not very creditable to their masters. The young people frequently shout after the Protestants and converts as they pass along the public road, and some of their seniors, instead of teaching them better manners, encourage them in this unmannerly conduct by their example. Nothing in a temporal way is so much needed for the people of this island as training and habits of industry."

An extract from the *Mayo Constitution*, entitled *Bright Prospects for Mayo,* concerned the activities of William McCormack and Mr. Ryan, the new owners of the old McLoughlin Estate in Corraun. Their estate:

"...consists of a few huts at Corraun Manor while the marine cottages, splendid and commodious harbour, stores, dwellings, hotel, chapel and monastery....all exist only in the fertile imagination of Mr. P. B. Ryan of Corraun Manor House, alias of the flourishing City of Eden! This exulting capitalist rubs his hands...he has a royalty on the mines and 8,200 acres of land." There appeared to be some doubt as to whether Mr.

14. The Achill Mission, 1831-1886

McCormack and Mr. Ryan proposed to carry out the improvements outlined.William McCormack, it was said, had reserved:*"10 acres for a Chapel and Monastery, 3 acres for two National schools, 10 acres for charitable building and 160 acres for domestic and summer residences."*

An advertisement appeared in the *Achill Herald* offering *shooting* on 23,000 acres of mountain (Mweelin) carefully preserved for two years, and well-stocked with game. In November, two boats laden with people landed in Achill, one at Annagh and another at the Settlement. Seemingly, they were *en route* from Sligo to the U.S.A. aboard the emigrant ship *California* when one hundred and fifty miles from land the vessel sprung a leak and the passengers had to take to the boats, spending four days at sea without food or water. The passengers were taken to the hospital in Dugort and it was not long before a Franciscan monk arrived at the hospital to tend to the needs of the shipwrecked. He was refused admission as was Fr. Henry when he arrived. The medical officer in charge was Dr. Montgomery and he subsequently featured in the enquiry set up to establish why the two clergymen had been refused admission to the hospital. Numerous donations were received from well-wishers to aid passengers of the *California* and among the donors was one from Mr. & Mrs. Blacker, the new tenants in Keel West townland who each contributed £1 together with clothes towards the collection. Funds for three hundred orphans were again being solicited in December.

1854

In January, Fr. Henry, *"the notorious Priest"* whom the Mission claimed had been convicted for violent assault wrote to the *Telegraph* calling on the *Poor Law Commissioners* to dismiss Dr. Montgomery. The battle for souls continued unabated between Fr. Henry and the Mission. There was some support for the Mission amongst locals which is confirmed in a letter to the *Achill Herald* from a convert in Dooagh who claimed that:

"slanderous and false reports concerning my reasons for separating from the Church of Rome have been circulated among the ignorant and misguided inhabitants of this island."

The main reason given was upon reading the *Douay Bible,* prohibited by the priests, he became concerned for his immortal soul and although he knew he would be held up as an object of scorn and contempt by neighbours and parishioners, nevertheless he was prepared to follow his conscience! In Inishbiggle, the islanders in a letter to the *Mayo Telegraph (1854)* asked Fr. Henry for re-admission into the Catholic Church:

"which during the years of famine and starvation, we were compelled to abandon in order to support life."

Fifty one panes of glass were broken in Cashel schoolhouse. This was compensated for by the erection in March of a capacious building between Keel and Dooagh for a Mission school and Church, together with forty acres of land which was being reclaimed. By May, the new Church at the Settlement had been roofed and slated, thanks to the generous individual who had supplied funds for the building.

In June, the Hon. Frederick Cavendish converted to Catholicism, Samuel Maynard (late of England) became the new proprietor of the Achill Mission Hotel and Sir Richard O'Donnell was again in the *Encumbered Estates Court*. The Catholic Church appeared to be making inroads for Fr. Henry claimed that there were now ten Catholic schools on the island and that twenty seven poor families from Inishbiggle had been reconciled to his Church. The Mission disagreed saying that there were only twenty two families in total on Inishbiggle Island composed of *12 converts, 1 Protestant and 9 Roman Catholics*. In August, the Rev. John Vickers, a Missionary at the Settlement, Dr. Montgomery and John Carr were in court for riot and affray connected with the refusal to admit Fr. Henry and the Franciscan monk into the hospital to minister to the passengers of the shipwrecked *California*.

Fr. Henry also brought in help from outside the island in the form of a group of Catholic missionaries some of whom, *Rinolfe and Vilas,* appear to have been Italian! The October edition of the *Achill Herald* carried an appeal for funds to construct a Glebe House at Achill Sound. A letter in the *Mayo Constitution* from the Rev. Stoney castigated the Sisters of Mercy for the alleged cruel treatment of Protestants in the Mayo

14. The Achill Mission, 1831-1886

Infirmary. In November, three persons renounced *popery* in St. Thomas's Church, one of whom had studied at Tuam and Maynooth! In December, *Ribbonism* was said to be active in Achill. A reference to the Mission referred to those *"who used every device to bring strays back to fold."* Fr. Henry wrote to the **Mayo Telegraph** regarding William Pike who had allowed hand-bills to be circulated amongst his Catholic tenants alluding to the £50 offered by the Superintendent of the Achill Mission regarding a treatise on the *"doctrine of transubstantiation."* William Pike's life was threatened and a notice was sent to him saying: *Death! death! death!* and ordering him to quit the island. The Government offered £50 reward for information on the person who wrote the letter. Some locals also offered £134 for the apprehension of the culprit(s) who sent the *Rockite Notice* to Pike. Contributions were received from:

Mr. McG. Blacker, £20.	Charles Boycott, £5.
David McHale, £1.	Joseph Clarke, £1.
Henry McLoughlin, £1.	Honor McHale, £1.
Henry Meehan, 10s.	Patrick Sweeney, £1.
Dr. Adams, £10.	John Carr, £10.

1855

The **Achill Herald** celebrated seventeen years of existence this year. Letters were received from the community on *Inishbiggle island* asking for money to enlarge their schoolhouse and place of worship. They obviously had a change of mind with regard to rejoining the Catholic Church! *The Society of Irish Church Missions,* the new administrators of the Achill Mission Estate published a report on the progress of the Mission on the island. The Mission was now facing strong opposition from the Catholic clergy who had a spy system in operation in the villages to report on recantation; fears were expressed about *Ribbonism* which was said to be making progress on the island and a stipulation was laid down stressing that anybody attempting to influence religious liberty on the Achill Mission Estate would face expulsion. There was concern at the number of people emigrating but prospects on the island looked good.

Achill

A letter from Fr. Henry in the **Freemans Journal** referred to the eviction of a village by a Sheriff and a *posse* of Police. Parents of some of those evicted refused shelter to their children for fear of offending the landlord! Some of the evicted families were said to be living in Kildavnet chapel and schoolhouse. The village in question was probably *Baile Ailt* located on the Pike estate. The lease of this area had ended upon the sale of the O'Donnell Estate and it was incumbent upon William Pike, the new owner, to enforce his legal rights to the property. Although some of his tenants were restored to their tenancies, he also seems to have availed of this opportunity to get rid of so called *families of bad character.* The Mission went one step further saying that he should also have exercised the same right over the Kildavnet chapel, also on his land.

There was an appeal for funds for the *Claremont Institution* in Glasnevin, a home for deaf and dumb children, including some from Achill. A familiar name on the committee was one W.R. Wilde, M.D. A new Church was consecrated by the Bishop of Tuam in August.

In March, the Rev. Joseph Barker was soliciting funds for the *Achill Mission Patriotic Fund.* He claimed that three quarters of the population of Achill were Catholics and that these, with the exception of the landlords, were the wealthiest people on the island, but yet the Protestants had contributed six times more than the Catholics but, neither Dr. McHale nor the people of the townlands of Dooniver and Tonatanvally, had made a contribution, both townlands being under *popish* landlords!

14. The Achill Mission, 1831-1886

28. Cemetery north of Settlement © Theresa McDonald

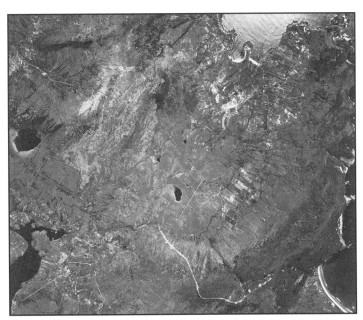

29. Aerial view of Upper Achill © Ordnance Survey

Achill

CONTRIBUTORS TO THE ROYAL PATRIOTIC FUND FOR CRIMEAN WAR WIDOWS AND ORPHANS.

GLENDARARY £10. 13. 0.

W. Pike	£5. 0. 0.	Anne Scott	£1. 0. 0.
Louise Tile	£3. 0. 0.	James Egan	£0. 2. 6.
Catherine Kelly	£1. 0. 0.	John Scott	£0. 2. 6.
Julia A. Chadwith	£0.10. 0.	Pat McNulty	£0. 2. 0.
Bridget McNamara	£0. 2. 6.	Owen Lavelle	£0.10. 0.
Bridget McHugh	£0. 2. 6.		

DUGORT COLONY £12. 17. 0.

M.M. Blacker	£5. 0. 0.	Richard McKeon	£0. 2. 6.
A. Adams	£5. 0. 0.	Margaret Ruddy	£0. 2. 6.
J. B. Atley	£0.10. 0.	Thomas McNulty	£0. 2. 6.
Emily Atley	£0.10. 0.	A. Lendrum	£0. 2. 6.
Mary E. Atley	£0. 2. 6.	Bridget Ralph	£0. 0. 6.
Henry McLoughlin	£0.10. 0.	Mrs. Stubbs	£0. 0. 6.
Samuel Maynard	£0.10. 0.	Michael McGinty	£0. 0. 6.
George Awe	£0. 5. 0.	T. McManamon	£0 . 0. 6.

MWEELIN £4. 7. 6.

Rev. J. Barker	£1. 0. 0.	Catherine Henly	£0. 0. 6.
Rev. J. Conerney	£1. 0. 0.	Ellen Bourke	£0. 1. 0.
John Carr	£1. 0. 0.	M. Cafferkey	£0. 1. 0.
John Stewart	£0. 10. 0.	M. Cafferkey Jn.	£0. 1. 0.
Audley Brown	£0. 2. 6.	Michael McCann	£0. 1. 0.
Elizabeth Brown	£0. 2. 6.	Anth. Cafferkey	£0. 1. 0.
A. B. Dillon	£0. 2. 6.	Edward Gallagher	£0. 1. 0.
Anthony Lavelle	£0. 1. 0.	Matthias Baynes	£0. 1. 0.

DOOEGA £0. 14. 0.

Anthony Lavelle	£0. 10. 0.	Mrs. Barry	£0. 2. 0.
Michael Lavelle	£0. 0. 6.	Mrs. Connor	£0. 1. 0.

SRAHEENS £0. 5. 0.

Frank Moran	£0. 1. 0.	James Kilbane	£0. 0. 6.
Daniel Cafferkey	£0. 1. 0.	M. Cooney Jnr.	£0. 0. 6.

14. The Achill Mission, 1831-1886

SALIA	**£0. 17. 6.**		
Pat Kilbane	£0. 1. 0.	Michael Kilbane	£0. 1. 0.
Hugh McTigue	£0. 1. 0.	John Gallagher	£0. 0. 6.
Michael Kilbane	£0. 0. 6.	John Kilbane	£0. 1. 0.
Pat Dever	£0. 0. 6.	Thomas Cooney	£0. 1. 0.
James Kilbane	£0. 1. 0.	Daniel Cafferkey	£0. 0. 6.
Lawrence McNulty	£0. 1. 0.	Sally McTigue	£0. 0. 6.
Terence Dever	£0. 1. 0.	Pat Ginty	£0. 1. 0.
Thomas Corrigan	£0. 1. 0.	Bryan Masterson	£0. 1. 0.
Martin Patten	£0. 1. 0.	Pat Gallagher	£0. 1. 0.
DERREENS	**£0.13.11.**		
Michael Lynchecan	£0. 1. 0.	Hugh McNulty	£0. 0. 4.
Pat Corrigan	£0. 1. 6.	Thomas McCann	£0. 0. 3.
Mrs. Corrigan	£0. 1. 0.	Anthony Kilbane	£0. 1. 0.
Bryan Masterson	£0. 1. 0.	Pat Kilbane	£0. 1. 0.
Pat Patten	£0. 1. 0.	Pat Corrigan	£0. 1. 0.
Pat Lynchecan	£0. 1. 0.	Martin Patten	£0. 0. 6.
James Ginnelly	£0. 0. 6.	John Quinn	£0. 0. 6.
Neal Lynchecan	£0. 1. 0.	Pat McLoughlin	£0. 0. 6.
Thomas Gallagher	£0. 0.10.		
ACHILL SOUND	**£0.15. 0.**		
Robert Jeffrey	£0.10. 0.	Henry Galbraith	£0. 5. 0.
CASHEL	**£0.10. 6.**		
Martin Gallagher	£0. 1. 6.	Henry McLoughlin	£0. 0. 6.
Widow Gallagher	£0. 0. 6.	Daniel Corrigan	£0. 0. 6.
Samuel Cochran	£0. 1. 0.	Owen Gallagher	£0. 0. 6.
A. Gallagher	£0. 0. 6.	John Gallagher	£0. 0. 6.
Denis Gallagher	£0. 0. 6.	John English	£0. 0. 6.
Anthony McNulty	£0. 0. 6.	Pat Cafferkey	£0. 0. 6.
John Cafferkey	£0. 0. 6.	Denis Gallagher	£0. 0. 6.
Thomas McNulty	£0. 0. 6.	Matthew English	£0. 0. 6.
DOOKINELLA	**£0. 8. 0.**		
Edward Calvey	£0. 0. 6.	Anthony Patten	£0. 0. 6.
John Gallagher	£0. 0 .6.	Thomas Cleary	£0. 1. 0.
Kelly Gallagher	£0. 0 .6.	John Cleary	£0. 1. 0.

Achill

Hubert Barrett	£0. 1. 0.	John Gallagher	£0. 1. 0.
Conor Patten	£0. 1. 0.	Edward Gallagher	£0. 1. 0.
KEEL	**£0.14. 0.**		
Mrs. Mulloy	£0. 1. 0.	Peter McNamara	£0. 0. 6.
Pat Barrett	£0. 0. 6.	Mick Fadian	£0. 0. 6.
Pat Patten	£0. 1. 0.	Thomas Murphy	£0. 0. 6.
E. McNamara	£0. 0. 6.	John Mangan	£0. 0. 6.
Thomas Lavelle	£0. 0. 6.	Geo. McNamara	£0. 0. 6.
Pat Calvey	£0. 1. 0.	Thomas Mangan	£0. 0. 6.
Anthony Mangan	£0. 1. 0.	Edward Whibbs	£0. 0. 0.
Edward Lavelle	£0. 0. 6.	Thom.McNamara	£0. 0. 0.
Anthony Lavelle	£0. 0. 6.	Pat Lavelle	£0. 0. 0.
John McHugh	£0. 1. 0.	Martin Lavelle	£0. 0. 0.
Pat Lavelle	£0. 1. 0.	John Lavelle	£0. 0. 6.
SLIEVEMORE	**£0. 2. 0.**		
Michael English	£0. 0 .6.	Mich. Lynchecan	£0. 1. 0.
Anthony Malley	£0. 0 .6.	Pat Corrigan	£0. 1. 0.
POLRANNY	**£0. 4. 6.**		
Pat Sweeney	£0. 10.0.	Mich. Lynchecan	£0. 1. 0.
Frank Sweeney	£0. 16.0.	Pat Corrigan	£0. 1. 0.
ACHILL COASTGUARD & OTHER RECEIPTS			**£3. 18.0.**
Joseph Cafferkey	£0. 2. 6.	John Cafferkey	£0. 2. 6.
Michael Mannion	£0. 1. 0.	Joseph Clarke	£0. 3. 0.
Thomas Connor	£0. 2. 6.	Bernard Boyle	£0. 2. 6.
Phelim McNulty	£0. 1. 0.	Pat McNamara	£0. 2. 6.
Thomas Raftery	£0. 2. 6.	Catherine Lavelle	£0. 2. 6.
Thomas Raftery	£0. 2. 6.	Mrs. Meehan	£0. 5. 0.
John Byrne	£0. 0. 6.	Mrs. A. Law	£0. 2. 6.
David McHale	£0. 2. 0.	Honor McHale	£0. 2. 6.

In June, a roadway was under construction to the Monastery. In July, Dr. McHale visited the island and said Mass in Dookinella Church. The death occurred of Isabella Adams, wife of Dr. Adams who had spent twenty years in Achill and was superintendent of the infant school. The couple were childless. A large funeral followed her coffin, including the

14. The Achill Mission, 1831-1886

Roman Catholic parish priest and Catholics from remote parts of the island, an indication of the respect in which she and her husband were held on the island.

1856

The new Church in Dugort was still awaiting an incumbent. After Edward Nangle's removal to Skreen in Co. Sligo there was a notable decline in the fortunes of the Mission. In February, the magistrates court sat to hear a case involving Thomas Clarke of the Monastery, Bunacurry, and Charles Boycott of *Cím* (Keem). William Pike, the magistrate, refused to adjudicate. Thomas Clarke stated that he went to see Mr. Boycott at his residence in *Cím* to ask for the payment of a debt which he alleged was due by another party! Mr. Boycott told him to go away as he owed him no money, and said that he would summon him for unlawful trespass. The case was dismissed.

In June, Edward Nangle paid his annual visit to the island, and compared it to the island of 1831. In 1831 transport in Achill was by pony. The island was wholly under the domination of the priests; there were no human habitations in the vicinity of the Sound, *"nothing except the remnants of a building which had been a salt factory,"* giving an impression of failure and desolation! It was difficult to get a boat to the island and the only shelter from the elements was the above roofless building. Improvements to 1856 included a mail car running from Newport to Achill.

"The ruined salt factory had been converted into an Hotel and a taxi car west of the Sound took passengers to other parts of the island. There is a fine Glebe House at Achill Sound and on land reclamation near the Glebe were two slated cottages and two schoolrooms, together with apartments for teachers. Forty five children were now enrolled in the school. Approaching the Hotel the visitor could see the spire of the Mission Church rising before him, a major feat considering there were no Protestants here in 1831."

There was a fine estate on the side of a rocky hill at Glendarary,

Achill

belonging to Mr.William Pike:*"The benefit of having a gentleman resident on the island is incalculable."* Mweelin contained a Church, a Minister's residence, schools, and a hospital (erected by Dr. Adams). This Church had a congregation of one hundred and twenty and the training school offered opportunities to boys seeking a career in teaching or the ministry. Unfortunately, the latter establishment had recently been removed to Dublin which Nangle found deeply lamentable:

"Leaving the Crossroads at Mweelin and returning to the main road to Dugort the visitor will see on rising ground before him, surrounded by a field of reclaimed land, a substantial slated building. This is Cashel schoolhouse named from the scattered village in the immediate vicinity. There are forty to fifty pupils in this school despite the fact that Cashel has been the residence of the parish priest for many years. In 1831 the villagers were all papists, most are now Protestants with the congregation numbering over one hundred. Cashel was very popish and the people used to abuse and harass the missionaries and Mission staff as they walked through the village. The foundations of a handsome Church were laid in this village but lack of funds prevented completion. Further on is the monastery of the Franciscan monks. The monastery has no influence beyond one village. Above the monastery on rising ground is another slated building, the residence of the notorious Fr. Henry. Two miles further on is the Romish Chapel (Dookinella). Space does not permit tales that could be told about the erection of this building."

Dugort occupied an area of one hundred and twenty acres and was the location of a prosperous village, the Settlement, which had a hotel, shop and post office, a hospital, printing office, agricultural school, farmyard, and three schools, (male, female and infant), a Church with the residence of the minister adjoining it and a congregation numbering two hundred. He lamented the fact that the physical aspect of the Settlement had deteriorated since his removal to Skreen. Emigration had thinned out the congregation and the schools, with over one hundred people leaving the area in recent years and *"the lack of a resident gentry who could have supplied work for these people was sorely felt."* Nangle extended an invitation to enterprising gentlemen to come and live in Achill, a request that would be acted upon almost immediately. He reiterated this in

14. The Achill Mission, 1831-1886

August, 1856 in a *"Letter to Friends of Achill "* published in the **Achill Herald**:

> *" Fifteen people should form a Committee and each subscribe £100 to lease for 20 years a plot of land from the Achill Mission Estate. The first crop would cost £15 per acre with an estimated return of £7 per acre. If the plan was implemented on an extensive scale, gravel could be extracted to build a movable railway using hand carts. A man and one hand cart would equal twenty men with baskets and the cost ratio would be 1s:20s. (1:20)."*

1857

An attempt by two Methodist Scripture Readers to entice converts from the Achill Mission was met with stiff opposition. *The Poor Law Guardians* were elected to the Achill Mission Estate. This, according to the **Achill Herald** was the result of collusion between William Pike and the Parish Priest to oust the agent of the Achill Mission Estate who had previously filled this post. An election was held where it was claimed intense canvassing took place with a *"monstrous falsehood circulated locally that Mr. Boycott, and his friend, Mr. Blacker, had lately purchased from the Trustees of the Achill Mission, the lands on which the voters reside! "* Murray MacGregor Blacker and Captain Charles Boycott had recently arrived on the island, leasing the townland of Keel West from the Achill Mission. The name of the *lessee* however was William Blacker, who may have been the famous agriculturalist.

In May, there began an ominous rumbling which would have serious consequences for the Mission. Edward Nangle writing in the **Achill Herald** from Skreen in Co. Sligo reviewed the work of the *Society of Irish Church Missions* which had taken over the running of the Mission Estate upon his transfer to Sligo in May, 1857. While acknowledging that this move had saved the Mission from destruction, he also said that some proceedings of that society were not calculated to advance the work of the Mission, such as their delay in appointing an incumbent to the Church in Dugort, and then only filling the vacancy on a temporary basis. In what he considered a gross misinterpretation of the *Deed of Trust,* the trustees wanted to expend the whole or part of the income from the estate, derived from rents on *temporal* improvements, resulting in little or no money being left for missionary purposes! As a member of both the committee of the Achill Mission and a trustee of the Achill Mission Estate, Edward Nangle strenuously objected to this saying that not a *single farthing*, beyond the necessary charges on the estate, could be dispensed with in this fashion. As far as he was concerned the income from the estate was to be used *exclusively* for missionary purposes. As a result of this, the *Irish Society for Church Missions* withdrew from administration of the estate saying they would resume work on the island only if the trustees won the argument. Edward Nangle claimed that the views of the society were unreasonable and he referred to the purchase of Achill:

" *When the property came into the Encumbered Estates Court, the Mission appealed for funds to purchase the whole of the O'Donnell Estate, including the two townlands on the mainland of two thousand acres, plus the whole island with the exception of three townlands on the eastern shore. The price agreed was £17,500 and contributions of £11,000 were received.*"

It would seem that he regarded the Mission as his creation, which in a way it was, and deeply resented any administrative interference such as that proposed by the trustees. This action would lead to a serious rift between the trustees and the committee of the Achill Mission and would ultimately involve a major court case which would nearly bankrupt the Mission. The reasons behind Edward Nangle's transfer to Skreen are not known but in leaving Achill, the Mission lost an able administrator, as is confirmed by the following description of the Mission, a comparatively short time after his departure:

"The Mission Estate had deteriorated in appearance. Agricultural work had been terminated and labourers forced to leave the island. Fifty people had left Dugort in the last three to four months and some converts had returned to popery. The dilapidated cottages gave a derelict appearance to the Settlement. An attempt had been made to do away with rundale."

The schools were said to be badly attended and the breaking up of the training school at Mweelin had caused a great blow to education in that district. The Mission needed a third Minister, proficient in Irish to minister to the *"old people,"* many of whom could not understand English.

"A great number of persons who converted from popery in this place have left it, going to Australia, the U.S.A., India, Africa and Great Britain."

In June, a letter was published in the **Belfast Mercury** concerning Nangle's proposed fund-raising trip to Britain. It pointed out that because of his conduct, his own son-in-law, John Wilson, had been forced to sever connections with the Mission. Upon completion of the purchase of Achill by the Achill Mission Estate, Edward Nangle was alleged to have proposed at a committee meeting in Dublin that all natives residing on the estate should be evicted if they did not send their children to his schools. It pointed out that the *Society of Irish Church Missions* had now withdrawn from the island and that Nangle was seeking £120 for a non-existent agricultural school which had for long been broken-up and the land and stock sold. Adding insult to injury it continued:

"A little bird tells me the land situated in the very centre of the colony is now in possession of Roman Catholics at a rental of £75 p.a."

The **Belfast Mercury** also pointed out that in January 1851 Nangle had asked for support for two years only but now six years on he was still asking! It claimed that although he had been working in Achill for twenty years, his achievements were few. This seems a little unfair for there was no doubt but that his achievements were considerable, even if few would agree with his methods. The question was posed: *"Who owns title to Achill - Edward Nangle or the trustees?"* It also suggested that accounts for the Mission should be produced going back over twenty years!

Edward Nangle's reply was terse. He demanded the names of any family who had been evicted by him. Solicitation of funds for the defunct agricultural school was needed to pay off a debt of £1290 incurred by the school which was still liable even if the school had closed. The net annual amount available for Mission purposes was £400. He pointed out that the management of the Achill Mission Estate was vested in four trustees, of whom he was one, and that the annual reports contained full details of the accounts.

In August, it was reported that the potato crop had been seriously damaged by *blight* and the potatoes were given to the cattle. In November, the Achill orphan home was removed to Mweelin where the Reverend Joseph Barker now resided. However, Rev. Barker subsequently moved to the Glebe House at Achill Sound and the orphans were returned to Dugort under the supervision of the Rev. Nassau Cathcart. It was stated that the purpose of this orphanage was to rear females as Protestants and to prepare them to be servants. The annual upkeep for one orphan was £5 per annum and subscriptions for this purpose were urgently needed. William Pike wrote to Edward Nangle complaining of an alleged attack on him in the *Achill Herald* and asked that the allegations be withdrawn or legal proceedings would be initiated. Nangle, predictably, reiterated the allegations and told Pike to go ahead and sue the Mission. The dispute concerned a claim that William Pike had found a Constable Lougheed, drunk on duty and had allegedly threatened to have him thrown out of Achill. The Mission defended Constable Lougheed saying he was of *"blameless character."* They also cast aspersions on Pike's principal witness, claiming that he had been expelled from the Mission for embezzlement.

1858

January, 1858, saw publication of the accounts for 1857. Included in these was a payment to Dr. Adams for his house in Achill, the sum involved was, however, not disclosed. Other items of interest included:

1. Building a house for John McDowell	£12. 0. 0.
2. Labourers making road to Church	£7. 1. 6.
3. Quarrying gravel	£3. 19. 8.
4. Gravelling road	£3. 19. 6.
5. Reclaiming land	£ 5. 3. 4.
6. Allowances to converts	£10. 0. 0.

14. The Achill Mission, 1831-1886

In April, the hotel at Achill Sound, together with forty acres of land and *"a good supply of sea manure"* was again advertised for letting. In August, it was reported in the *Achill Herald* that the Marquis of Sligo had married the daughter of Anthony Nugent, a Roman Catholic by special licence in Galway. It was claimed that enemies of the Achill Mission were allegedly circulating slanderous reports about the society e.g. *"the Achill Mission was now almost entirely in the tenantry of Catholics and that ninety one out of every one hundred Catholics had recanted. £700-£800 per annum had been donated to the officials of the Achill Mission and none had gone to support the schools."* The October issue of the *Achill Herald* outlined the current state of the Achill Mission which indicated a serious decline in its fortunes:

"The School house in Sraheens which had been built by the Society for the Irish Church Missions had closed temporarily; there was a considerable falling off in Church congregation with services in Cashel and Mweelin discontinued; there was poor attendance in Inishbiggle; the orphan house in Dugort had fourteen female orphans in residence; the school at Rockfield built by a friend of the Mission had been discontinued; ten Protestant children were attending a national school in the neighbourhood but received instruction once a week from a minister; the Mission property was falling into disrepair and the corn mill was idle." All of the above ensured that the year ended on a dismal note for the Mission, with decline setting in rapidly.

1859

In January 1859, it was claimed that missionary work was suffering due to the prolonged absence of the Rev. Joseph Barker who was temporarily resident in Ballinasloe where his wife was seriously ill. An advertisement for a temporary replacement at a salary of £100 per annum, plus a house appeared in the *Achill Herald.* In February, there was a reference to the fact that a local convert had returned to Rome! In June, a priest in Dookinella Church denounced an artisan and his family who were working in the Settlement and, for good measure, included anybody subsequently daring to employ him. It was suggested that the trustees *"level the Mass House"* in Dookinella, which now occupied land owned by the Mission. On the 21st August, Dr. Neason Adams died, aged 84 years. Edward Nangle was greatly upset by this sad event having known Dr. Adams and his wife, Isabella, since 1825. Dr. Adams had adored his wife, Isabella, who had died in 1855 and, as we have seen, he had her remains interred above ground in a cemetery in Dugort and later removed to the family burial place at Knockbride, Co. Cavan, after which he broke up his estate in Dugort.

"The Origin, Progress and Difficulties of the Achill Mission " written by Edward Nangle by popular request was advertised for sale. At the same time, another advertisement appeared in the *Achill Herald*, inserted by a newcomer to the island, notably, Alexander Hector, *Fish Curer to the Queen for Scotland*. Hector had come to Achill in 1855 and set up fish curing and processing plants at various locations throughout the island which provided employment for several hundred local people. The year ended with reports of riots in Tourmakeady and Ballinrobe.

1860

The year began with more trouble for the Mission. An English visitor, Vere Foster, having spent ten days in Achill wrote privately to a friend on the island, the contents of which were *"leaked"* to Mission personnel, causing great offence in the Settlement. Foster claimed that analysis of figures published in the *Achill Herald* indicated that the Mission was in serious decline, *viz.*

2000 children in 1849
1600   1850
878   1851

He also claimed that the Mission would not lease land to Roman Catholics despite the fact that nineteen out of twenty people were Roman Catholics; the Mission owned three-fifths of the island and there were 8000 inhabitants in Achill; the granting of a lease by the Achill Mission Estate forbade the exercise of Catholic rights of worship or education; all Protestants on the island were imported; many natives converted to Protestantism during the famine but had since left; £500,000 was spent on proselytising; the training school at Mweelin was uninhabited with

14. The Achill Mission, 1831-1886

slates falling off the roof and windows broken; the hall and other houses were used as a granary by a neighbouring farmer; there was no proselytising since Edward Nangle left the island and Protestants and Catholics were now living in harmony.

Edward Nangle trenchantly refuted the above in the *Achill Herald* and took great delight in subsequently being able to show that Vere Foster had made a donation to a Catholic establishment in Tourmakeady, thereby showing his true colours! Pointing out the ignorance of the writer regarding local matters he said that none of the natives who were influenced by the teaching of the Achill Mission could, except at hazard to their lives, give expression to their convictions! To put an end to this persecution, the Achill Mission acquired land on the island and the natives were informed that no Roman Catholic should have a lease on land, in order that the trustees could remove *at will* people infringing the religious liberty of a neighbour. He assured the readership that no Catholics had been dispossessed on account of their religious beliefs and he challenged anybody to point to a single instance of eviction. He said that Protestants made up 25% or a quarter of the population of the Achill Mission estate. There were 480 tenants and 129 Protestants. The total population of the island at the last census was 4400. There was no clause forbidding the exercise of Catholic rites but there was a clause forbidding the building of churches, monasteries and schools on Mission lands. In summary he said that there were:

134 Protestant families i.e. 630 individuals
31 families always Protestant
16 families converts.

87 families were natives and there are also many Achill converts in other parts of the world. The amount spent on proselytising was one fifth of the £500,000 mentioned. Schools were set up at the request of the natives. Mweelin Training College had closed because its activities were moved to Dublin. Serious disturbance, not harmony, had been the norm in Achill since his departure. He further claimed that Foster's letter was full of falsehoods and that he did not know of the "*hair-breadth*" escapes of the missionaries on the island or the threatened destruction of lives and property!

Achill

As if the trouble with Vere Foster was not enough the island was visited by the severest gale known for a number of years. The buildings in Mweelin were stripped of slates and tiles. During the gale, the homeward bound barque, *The Neptune of London* was wrecked on the rocks under Minaun Head. It had tried to anchor off Sparrow island (Inishgallon) near Purteen, but was unable to do so. One of the crew was washed overboard and a boy of 13 years was also lost. Both were subsequently buried in the Mission graveyard. The captain and the crew of ten climbed to the rigging and were eventually brought ashore by locals and taken to the Mission hospital to be the cared for by Dr. Carmichael. Aid for the stricken crew was received from the *Shipwrecked Mariners Society.*

On March 20, 1860 at Castlebar Assizes, John Carr, agent of the trustees of the Achill Mission estate appeared to defend himself against the plaintiff, Mr. Boycott, "*who holds a tract of mountain land from a Mr. Blacker, one of the tenants of the estate.*" The case concerned wrecks off Achill and the ownership of salvage. Captain Boycott claimed the wreckage of a ship in a bay on his property and John Carr wrote to the *Receiver of Wrecks* at Westport informing him of the situation, *viz.* "*Mr. Boycott's men were found this morning early, in his presence, breaking up a wreck and conveying iron to his house.*" Boycott claimed that Carr's letter libelled him and he also claimed that he had permission from Carr to take goods from the wreck. Carr said that he had been informed by his bailiff (O'Donnell) that he saw Boycott and his men looting the wreck. The case was dismissed as the jury could not agree on a verdict.

In May, there was a *genial change in the weather* but unusual distress was experienced by the locals. It seems that the late spring left many cattle without food and some had perished. The poor had to give food to the cattle, some of which consisted of seed potatoes and they were now obliged to obtain meal for the summer, six weeks too early and available only at exorbitant cost. In June, there was said to be fearful distress in the Barony of Erris. Sir James Dombrain (formerly of the coastguards and familiar with the west coast), sent a cargo of meal to be sold at cost price. The local priest said sums of money collected should be given gratuitously to the people as this would be a more effective way of relieving distress. Edward Nangle said that the money was more likely to go to the priests or to the Pope's Treasury! The Achill Mission however donated £200 to the Dombrain Fund for *"gratuitous relief, for the very first time and only in these exceptional circumstances."*

1861

The Rev. Nassau Cathcart left to take up a position in Guernsey. The weather was very stormy and wet with hail stones. A gale struck the colony and manure spread on the fields was carried like a shower into the air. Water was swept from streams and yet not a cloud was visible, and the sun shone. The storm lasted for two hours and the back of the old Church was stripped and the roof of the new Church damaged. The roof of the infant school was also damaged and *"...the house of our oldest convert completely wrecked."* Many people in Achill were injured in this storm, the worst for years.

The Rev. Skipton was appointed as the new incumbent in Dugort. The April and May editions of the *Achill Herald* had a notice to the effect that Achill orphan boys were now available as servants. A local census indicated that there were 759 Protestants in Achill and Ballycroy. In June, the Catholic population of Achill thanked the Achill Mission for feeding the poor during the famine. A visit by Dr. McHale was said to have been largely unattended so much so that when mass was said in Dookinella, many remained at work in the fields nearby. It would seem that all this was wishful thinking for the evidence on the ground would strongly suggest that the tide had turned. The potato crop was again poor, two thirds short of normal yield, a fact that was said would make heavy demands on the *Temporal Relief Fund,* so again there was an urgent need for funds.

By October, the Mission charities had collected only one third of one month's expenses and it was pointed out that arrears, amounting to £600 were overdue in subscriptions from the *Achill Herald*. That the readership had fallen off was not surprising for after Nangle's departure for Skreen, the content, particularly with regard to local and provincial news about Achill went into serious decline and was substituted by increasingly large treatise on religion, not the most absorbing of topics for the general reader! The Mission felt seriously rebuffed when Sir Robert Peel visited the island and did not either announce his visit or pay a courtesy call at the Settlement. Sir Robert Peel, founder of the British Police Force had been responsible for the *Repeal of the Corn Laws,* before which imports into Britain were levied with tariffs to protect English farmers. He stayed overnight with William Pike at Achill Sound, leaving again first thing the following morning. Either Sir Robert Peel or relatives of his subsequently owned a house in Corraun, one of three now derelict houses of non-native design. The year ended with a lament that the quantity and the quality of the potatoes from the years crop was poor.

1862

The year began with the Reverend Edward Nangle engaged in a contentious debate with a Priest in Coolooney in Co. Sligo. The death of Prince Albert was announced in the *Achill Herald*. In April, a meeting of the *West Connacht Church Endowment Fund* was held. On a motion proposed by the Rt. Hon. Joseph Napier the chair was taken by Lord Plunket, Bishop of Tuam. Joseph Napier, a former Lord Chancellor of Ireland was also a trustee of the Achill Mission and had come into conflict with Edward Nangle over disposal of Mission funds for the temporal relief of tenants on the Achill Mission estate, an initiative strenuously opposed by Edward Nangle who maintained that this revenue was solely for missionary purposes. Edward Nangle's animosity towards Napier had not abated to judge from the following remark: "*a double-minded man is unstable in all his ways,*" seemingly casting doubts on Napier's allegiance to Protestantism.

In May, Edward Nangle recalled that thirty one years ago he had met an Evangelical Minister in Sackville Street (O'Connell Street) in Dublin who upon hearing of his intention to go and live in Achill said that he was off on a wild goose chase and that "*...the priests would blow him out of Achill in six weeks.*" It took a little longer than that but they eventually did, being led into the battle by the *"Lion of Judah,"* Archbishop McHale, and assisted by the Franciscan Monks in Bunacurry.

In August, a letter from Fr. Henry was published in *The Pilot*, an American newspaper claiming that there was no employment available

14. The Achill Mission, 1831-1886

on the island. Edward Nangle challenged this saying that the Achill Mission estate was providing employment and that a gentleman at the western extremity of the island was willing to employ labourers *at one shilling per day and could not find any to work!* Nangle was also worried that Fr. Henry had lately started to make himself agreeable to the Protestants on the island. In September, the agent of the Achill Mission estate wrote to Edward Nangle claiming that Fr. Henry was showing favouritism in his distribution of relief, the majority of food going to Roman Catholics and provided details of the amounts involved:

*"**Family No. 1:** Comprising four people. This tenant pays £2 per annum rent, he has seven cows, 2 horses and three sheep, and was a papist. A convert and now a pervert! Allocation: **6 stone of meal.***

*   ***Family No. 2:** Pays £2 per annum rent. Has seven cows, one horse and sixteen sheep. A papist who lends money on credit at 30-40% interest. Allocation: **2 stone of meal.***

*   ***Family No. 3:** Comprises eight in family. A convert. Pays £1. 15s.0d. per annum rent. Has two cows and two sheep. Allocation: **1.5 stone of meal** ."*

Fr. Henry maintained that the tenants were poorer now than before the Achill Mission purchased the estate. Edward Nangle disagreed, pointing out that in 1851-52 when the Mission purchased the island in the *Encumbered Estates Court,* the greater portion of arable land lay waste and the tenants had few cattle:

"Take the townland of Slievemore where fever was most prevalent, and consequently the greatest destitution prevailed. This townland consists of upwards of 3000 acres, with 120 families residing on it, 20 of whom have no cattle or sheep, and very small holdings, with rents so low as 5s. per annum. The remaining 100 have 226 head of cattle, 78 horses and 395 sheep; the total rent for the land and houses is £180 or an average of £1.10s. each; the tenants are allowed the grazing of one cow for every £1 of rent they pay and are charged 2s.6d. p.a. for the remainder."

Achill

Fr. Henry pointed out that the Marquis of Sligo had but one tenant, Mr. Patrick McHugh, *"the most comfortable man on the island!"* Without both his and his brother's assistance, many Achill Mission tenants would have starved or have had to go to the work-house. Fr. Henry also said that the poor had to pay 4s.7d. per pound *poor rate* which was very high compared to that levied elsewhere. The agent of the Achill Mission Estate pointed out that lands in his management were let at a reasonable rent and but for the various dues payable to the Catholic clergy, the tenants would be more comfortable. This was said to be the principal cause of poverty on the island! In the autumn the potato crop was said to be deficient, the weather was *fearfully inclement,* oats and rye were poor but plenty of turf had been saved. The food prospects however looked gloomy. Another letter from the agent of the Achill Mission to the Editor of the **Achill Herald** concerned Fr. Henry's allegation that the Mission had done little to improve the lot of tenants. He maintained that when the trustees acquired possession of the island, the wealthy tenants on each townland had portions of stripes sublet to the poorer classes and were charging three times the amount of rent being paid by themselves. This was reported to the trustees who gave instructions to have all the townlands *re-striped* and every man given his own portion at a fair rent. This re-allocation had been done where practicable.

It was said that some comfortable farmhouses had lately been built, partly at the expense of the trustees and two more were in the course of erection:

"in which neither cows nor pigs are allowed to live in common with men, women and children. Fr. Henry knows this and also knows that there is not a single dwelling house among the tenants of Dr. McHale or Mr. Cavanagh to equal them in comfort and cleanliness. The townlands of Dugort and Slievemore were held under old leases which expired in 1859 and 1860. The lands were then striped and every man got a portion of it and if Fr. Henry looks he will see great improvement here and if not, let him ask some of the oldest men in each village and they will tell him there has been more improvements in making fences, drains and reclaiming land since the leases expired. These improvements are going

202

on in every townland owned by the Achill Mission estate except one which has an old lease still in existence. Where then is the dread of eviction and constant service of NOTICE TO QUIT!" It was pointed out that although Mr. Cavanagh had a thriving tenantry he had not granted a lease to the one Protestant in his townland and there were no Protestants living in townlands where Catholics landowners had control. It was also claimed that two-thirds of Fr. Henry's flock were tenants of the Mission and some tenants expelled some years ago kept asking to return!

In November, a storm and heavy winds hit the island, the worst in living memory. Some of the corn crop which had not been cut was lost. The poor were said to be deeply in debt and the potato crop had again failed. In December, the house of a supposed convert was selected in which to hold the annual *Stations*. This incensed the Scripture Readers who blocked Fr. Henry's approach to the house, forcing him to retreat and seemingly causing much local amusement.

1863

In the Spring, there was said to be considerable destitution on the island, some people having gone to the U.S.A. leaving wives and children behind. Some converts had only one meal per day. In consequence of distress after three bad harvests, the trustees, at the suggestion of the agent granted the tenants a reduction of 25% on one half-years rent due. In May, Fr. Henry left the island and the new curate almost immediately wrote to the Mission complaining that there had been a threat to evict some tenants unless they sent their children to the Mission schools, an allegation totally rejected by the Mission. By July, there was said to be great destitution in Achill. Dr. Brodie, a Poor-law inspector was sent to investigate complaints made by the new curate, Fr. Thomas regarding evictions. By August, the Relief Fund had enabled people to buy seed potatoes but it was said that successive years of failure had reduced some families to penury. One man who had owned eight cattle three years ago, now had none. The potato blight again reappeared. In September, ninety nine children were confirmed, eighty one said to be from Achill. In November, a storm and heavy winds hit the island. Some of the corn crop which had not been cut was lost. The poor were said to be deeply in debt and the potato crop had failed.

1864

Demise

These were momentous years for the Mission and commenced with the resignation in January 1864, of the Rt. Hon. Joseph Napier, following a very expensive court case instigated by Napier against Edward Nangle, and the Achill Mission.The case is outlined in great detail in two pamphlets both entitled, *Case of the Achill Mission Estate, (1864).* The background to the court case involved a Deed of Trust, drawn up upon the purchase of *The Achill Mission Estate* which Napier said was defective, as it did not provide for the filling up of vacancies in the committee occasioned by death or resignation. He questioned the legality of the committee to appoint new members upon the death of existing members, and the resultant dispute between himself and Nangle plunged the Mission seriously into debt. In 1855 the committee of the Achill Mission had entered into a formal arrangement with the *Committee of Irish Church Missions,* without consultation with the Trustees and seemingly at the instigation and approval of Edward Nangle who was both a leading committee member and also a Trustee. Nangle, having secured the resignation of Somerset Maxwell one of the four Trustees, endeavoured to solicit the resignation of Joseph Napier and George Alexander Hamilton on the grounds that they lived outside Achill and seldom attended meetings, leaving himself as the sole representative Trustee. Napier and Hamilton resisted stating that as their proper function as trustees was said to be purely nominal they had employed a local agent on the estate, together with a solicitor in Dublin to manage the property. Amalgamation of the two bodies seems to have been Edward Nangle's objective in the event of the resignation of Napier and Hamilton. At a meeting of the committee on the 14th December, 1860 those present decided without prior consultation that members who had not attended the last four meetings would henceforth cease to be members. This affected the Dean of Emly, Charles French, the Reverend B. Stoney, the Rt. Hon. Joseph Napier and George Alexander Hamilton. When Napier and Hamilton became aware of this in early 1861 they strongly objected *"believing in the importance of independent proprietary management."* They consulted forthwith with Sir Hugh Cairns, an advocate regarding their legal rights and he recommended the intervention of the *Court of Chancery*. Meanwhile Edward Nangle had preferred charges against Napier and Hamilton claiming that they had no connection with the Achill Mission Society until after the Trust Deed had been set up in 1848 and that the present dispute occurred because of rights claimed by them to exclusive control and distribution of rents of the trust estates. Edward Nangle's council would later claim that the funds of the society were confined to the committee of management and not to the trustees and because of this the committee resolved to let the trustees become members of the committee at a meeting on the 23 July, 1857. Napier and Hamilton refused to resign until such time as the Trust was protected by law and the Charity with which it was constituted had been secured. The animosity between Napier and Nangle can be traced back to 1857 when the committee of the Achill Mission queried the right of the Board of Trustees to apply any part of rents collected for the improvement of the estate. The committee headed by Nangle maintained that the Trustees only had nominal proprietary rights and nothing more. Conversely, the Trustees claimed that the function of the committee was to oversee the conduct of the Mission while they as Trustees were charged with managing the property of the estate. Edward Nangle said that it was the committee's duty to disburse the net proceeds received by the estate while the Trustees had the actual management of the estate. Napier and Hamilton on the other hand maintained that *"the proprietary management should be by an independent body of trustees, so as to be kept clear of questions of religious controversy."* Nangle said that since Napier had been appointed a trustee in 1850 he had abandoned the principles for which he was elected, backing the system of *National Education*, attempting to divest the Committee of all authority and to monopolise the exclusive power of distributing the income of the *Achill Mission Estate* by endeavouring to use these funds for temporal relief. He said that the Mission had suffered severely from its connection with Napier. Napier's crime was that he placed the *"greatest importance upon measures to keep the management of the property clear of all controversial squabbles and the tenants fairly and equally treated - without any form of partiality whatever."* Relations between the two took a further serious downturn when it became known that Napier had met with Fr. Henry at the latter's request, concerning a school the priest proposed setting up in the village of Dooagh on the property of the Achill Mission estate. Relations between Nangle and Fr. Henry had never been good with legal writs flying backwards and forwards between the two. To Nangle therefore, the meeting between a Trustee of the Mission and his arch enemy, *"Priest Henry,"* amounted to treason! The Court found in favour of Nangle, but Napier was highly respected and supporters of the Mission were deeply concerned. Newspapers expressed concern that so little had been done by the Mission to help the poor of Achill. A new committee of management was instituted to administer the affairs of the Mission and three new Trustees were appointed. The costs of the court case were crippling for the Mission and Edward Nangle predictably said that they should be paid by Napier as he had originated the case in the first place. The Mission was now in serious decline and converts began to relapse.

After 1864, reports of the Mission were intermittent and in 1874 the **Church Advocate, 1864-74** and later the **Irish Church Advocate, 1874-87** superseded the *Achill Missionary Herald and Western Witness.* In December, 1874, the Reverend T.S. Treanor became the incumbent in Dugort and he published details of expenditure on relief which totalled £165.9s.10d. Payment of £24.2s.5d. to the agent of the Mission was expended upon a mason and labourers opening, clearing and preparing a sewer at the rear of the north building in the colony; the purchase of a boat load of limestone, the construction of a lime kiln; an addition to the schoolhouse in Cashel and the provision of three gulleys to settlers' houses in Mweelin. Edward Nangle resigned as a Trustee of the Achill Mission in 1873. He went to live in Monkstown in Dublin in 1879. *The Irish Church Advocate* continued until 1887 but there was little or no mention of Achill or indeed of Edward Nangle and the Achill Mission, except to mention the death of Edward Nangle in 1883, aged 83. In 1886, the Rev. William Fitzpatrick published a short paper entitled:*"Achill as it was compared to what it is,"* a report on a visit to the island which had been undertaken in order to:*"enquire into the circumstances of the tenants on the Mission Estate and to make certain important arrangements for the benefit of the estate and those resident upon it and to enquire into the Mission work carried on in Achill and in the adjoining areas."* Fitzpatrick claimed that the Achill Mission had been a great success until 1882 when a serious blow had been dealt to the Mission by the introduction of the *1881 Land Act* which led to a reduction in the rental rate of between 30% and 40%. In addition the *Arrears Act* cancelled a large amount of arrears and the *No Rent Manifesto* of the *Land League* had a further detrimental effect upon the income of the Estate.

The Mission was wound up by the Trustees and the Irish Society once again undertook the management of the Mission. Some interesting cameos of life in Achill in post-famine times were penned by the Rev. Fitzpatrick. Visiting Inishbiggle island he was appalled at the extreme poverty of the islanders: *"Bags of periwinkle were being got ready for export; earnings were 4 pence per day for collecting periwinkle, the people obtaining meal and barter for their labour."* He refers to a co-operative which had been set up with goods being brought in by Hooker (a large cutter-rigged boat of ten to twelve tons). He referred to the toll bridge at Achill Sound which had cost in the region of £1000. He said that although the hotel at the Settlement was temporarily closed during his visit, there were plans to produce a ***Tourists' Guide to Achill*** to advertise the attractions of the island. An interesting article in this guide provided details of the *Climate and Ornithology of Achill,* documented by William Pike, who resided in Achill for over twenty years.

Fitzpatrick claimed that the absence of consumption in Achill could be attributed to the climate and by way of an aside said that there were no incidents of *distemper* in dogs! Potential tourists were referred to several good houses in Dugort and throughout the island. The resident gentry also got a mention: *"Now there is the residence of Major Pike where the Earl of Cavan spends part of the year and the house of the Rev. G.W. Weldon in Dugort with a resident physician, a summer lodge of a Dublin solicitor and house of the agent of the Achill Mission, a hotel at Achill Sound and another in Dugort."*

Achill

Great changes were said to have occurred in Achill since the advent of the *Land League,* the priests now having great power in Ireland. Rents owing to the Mission were forcibly withheld, with severe retribution *(cutting off ears)* to any who dared pay rent on the Mission Estate. *The Irish Society,* (formed in 1818) had expended £600 per annum on the estate but in 1882 handed it back to the Trustees.

30. Visit of Parish Priest to Dooagh Village, after O Muirithe (1972)

From 1865 onwards, the congregation had dwindled considerably after which very few Achill children attended the Mission schools, a far cry from former expectations.

14. The Achill Mission, 1831-1886

Achievements

The people of Achill benefited in many ways from the Mission in that the *Achill Herald*, circulated widely abroad, brought people from many parts of the world to view the work of the Mission; their reports containing as they did references to the scenic beauty of Achill (there was one suggestion that it become a National Park) resulted in huge numbers of tourists arriving annually on the island, a trend which continues to the present day.

According to Bowen (1970) another of Edward Nangle's contributions to Achill was his *"nurturing of the Irish language" via* William Neilson's *Introduction to the Irish Language* which was printed in Dugort in 1843. Another was the considerable improvement in health services, courtesy of the work of the indefatigable Dr. Neason Adams, together with the publicity generated by the *Achill Missionary Herald and Western Witness*, which made Achill known to the wider world and which has perhaps only been surpassed by Heinrich Böll's, *Irisches Tagebuch - Irish Journal*, *(c.1957). First English edition (1967)*, in which he painted a graphic and haunting description of the Deserted Village in Slievemore.

Edward Nangle also instituted land reform, endeavouring to dispense with the Rundale system which had for long prohibited agricultural initiative on the island. Another important contribution was the part he played in re-invigorating the Catholic Church, particularly with regard to Achill, an area which prior to his arrival had been shamefully neglected by Church authorities.

The contribution of the Mission to the educational advancement of the people of Achill is not straightforward. According to McGrath (1991) 83.9% of the Catholic population over 5 years of age in 1861 were illiterate compared to 29% of Protestants. This imbalance was adjusted somewhat by 1891 when the respective figures were 52.5% and 9.8% and can, perhaps, be attributed to the proliferation of schools on the island, both Catholic and Protestant, in the latter half of the nineteenth century.

Only the name of the Mission remained in 1882 and in 1886, the Mission schools were placed under the care of *The Irish Society for the Promotion of Education of the native Irish through the medium of their own language*. Today, the Settlement in Dugort stands witness to the endeavours of Edward Nangle and the Achill Mission Society. Although few descendants of the original settlers remain, there is still a strong sense of identity with the Settlement and all that it represents. Indeed, many descendants of former settlers return annually for summer holidays. Relations between the two communities are excellent, both respecting the other's traditions. The church-going congregation in Dugort is small, averaging a maximum of ten during the winter months so that services are alternated between Dugort and Castlebar. Only during the summer months is St. Thomas's well attended when an influx of visitors inflate, for a short time, the small congregation.

The lay out of the Settlement with its neat street plan, central square and enclosed *"village green"* resembles an English country village and is testimony of its non-native origin. On the opposite side of the road at the end of a long tree-lined driveway, is the Church of St. Thomas; a sign on the gatepost invites *all denominations* to enter freely; had this practice been adopted by Edward Nangle, who knows what might have happened! A portrait of him in St. Thomas's Church in Dugort depicts the one-time *Apostle of Achill,* as an autocratic, stern-faced man.

Edward Nangle devoted his life to the promotion of the Achill Mission and by so doing opened a new chapter in the island's history, for good or ill, it is up to individual readers to judge for themselves. His removal to Skreen, probably for health reasons, undoubtedly slowed down proselytising endeavours on the island, but it is unlikely that the final outcome would have been any different, particularly once the Catholic Church was forced into abandoning its lethargy towards the people of Achill and mounted a successful counter-reformation. The Franciscan Monks who identified and no doubt reinforced the nationalistic

14. The Achill Mission, 1831-1886

aspirations of the population played a major role in this counter-reformation. (Bro. Angelo Holmes, *pers. comm.*).

Seddall (1884) in his biography of Edward Nangle said that:

"Mr. Nangle was doubtless at times headstrong in forming his opinions, stubborn in holding them, and harsh in giving them expression."

He also said that:

"...the almost total collapse of all missionary work - the absence, at any rate of late years, of any missionary success in Achill was a great sorrow to him ." Seddall (1884).

Edward Nangle's over zealous and unorthodox method of enlisting converts was his downfall. His poor health and absence from Achill for long periods was also a contributory factor in the failure of the Mission. His Dublin Evangelical friend was correct in his prediction that the priests would run him out of Achill, but his complex personality, together with the rigidity of the Protestant ethic which he forcefully applied, was anathema to a people nurtured in a different ethos.There appears to have been mutual incomprehension between Edward Nangle and the Achill people and his failure to use less of the *stick* and more of the *carrot* was a serious error. Failure to appreciate the strong ties of the people to the land, particularly in the case of Slievemore and Finsheen, led to strong resistance and antagonism.

The counter reformation instigated by Dr. McHale and implemented by the Franciscans, together with Edward Nangle's fragile health and removal to Skreen, contributed to the downfall of the Mission.

Edward Nangle died in 1883. Like many people before and after him, he succumbed to the charm of Achill, for on his deathbed he is reported to have said:

"Achill may well be called the Happy Valley. In spite of all our trials, I know no place like it." Edward Nangle.

31. Going to Mass, c.Late 19th century, after O Muirithe (1972)

32. House in Bolinglanna © Theresa McDonald

14. The Achill Mission, 1831-1886

The Rev. Edward Lowe composed the lines of the song below before leaving Achill for Sligo:

I

Slievemore, Slievemore, *you are standing there,*
With your head so high and your sides so bare,
Rising sublime from the dark blue sea,
an image and a type of eternity.

II

At the foot of Slievemore is our childhood past,
But far, far away our lot be cast;
Wherever we roam in the world so wide,
Its dear old form in our hearts we'll hide.

III

And we'll remember the days of yore,
the friends whom we loved, but may n'eer see more,
The old seashore which our young feet trod,
and the house where we gathered, to worship God.

IV

The infant school where we worked and played,
Till the walls seemed to rattle with the noise that we made,
May thoughts such as these through life's daily scenes,
Freshen our hearts to their vernal green.

V

The orphan house and the old flagstaff,
will make us in turn both to weep and laugh,
While the mountain top in the mind appears,
Dimly to be seen through the mist of tears.

VI

Well, we hope there will yet come a day,
When sorrow and sin will both vanish away;
then, may we meet those that we loved of yore,
In the valley at the bottom of the Old Slievemore.

(Sung to the tune of The White Cockade).

213

Chapter 15

ENCUMBERED ESTATES AND ACHILL LANDOWNERS

"Thomas John Medlycott seized in fee amongst other lands of all that and those the farm and lands of Corraun, Tonlegee, Tonatanvally, Knockmullen and the Bleachyard (Newport), situated in the County of Mayo and being so signed." **Medlycott Estate Papers, 1776.**

There was marked contrast between the large wealthy landowners of the midlands and the impoverished landlords in Mayo, the former provided aid for building, supplied plans for cottages, laid out roads and organised drainage operations, erected lime-kilns, employed agricultural experts and endeavoured to check sub-letting; the latter, like the O'Donnells of Newport, were to be found in 1840 clinging tenuously to their estates, with incomes eaten away by increasing sub-division of unviable settlements, living like the poorest farmers, but scorning to bring up their children to any sort of business, and screwing out of their miserable tenants in addition to rack-rents, produce such as butter, eggs and fish. (Edwards & Williams, 1994). The Famine affected all classes of society, rents were not paid, so the income of the landlord was reduced, there was a reduction in trade, and few houses were built so tradesmen suffered, and the reduced income of the landlord meant that fewer servants could be employed. The Encumbered Estates Court was set up in 1848-49 to facilitate the sale of bankrupt estates. Either the owner of the estate or a creditor could petition the court to sell the estate.

The Medlycott Estate

Thomas John Medlycott acquired the Burrishoole Estate from the Earl of Arran in 1696. Medlycott leased the estate to the O'Donnell's of Newport, the Marquis of Sligo and to Patrick McLoughlin, a Dublin Draper, who was his cousin and also his Estate Manager. Sir Neal O'Donnell purchased the Medlycott Estate in 1785. The Marquis of Sligo leased lands from the O'Donnell's and also acquired ownership of a

15.   Encumbered Estates and Achill Landowners

number of townlands in Achill. There were disputes between Medlycott and McLoughlin, between Medlycott and O'Donnell and between the O'Donnell's and the Marquis of Sligo, and also within the McLoughlin family after the death of Patrick McLoughlin and his son John. Thomas John Medlycott of Rockhill, Co. Dublin and his son, John Thomas Medlycott of the first part, Frances Phillipa and Susanna Medlycott of the second part, John Buxton of the third part, John Thewless and Samuel Pa(e)tters of the fourth part, and John, Earl of Altamont, of the fifth part, conveyed *"amongst several other lands, the lands of Corraun, Tonlegee, Tonatanvally, Knockmullen and the Bleachyard, a lease of three lives with a covenant for perpetual renewal of the premises so conveyed"* by lease and release bearing the date, 15th-16th July, 1776 between John Thomas Medlycott and Patrick McLoughlin of Francis Street, Dublin City (Woollen Draper) the lands as outlined above:

"to have and to hold unto the said Patrick McLoughlin, his heirs and assigns for the lives of the said Thomas John Medlycott and Thomas McLaughlin, son of said Patrick McLaughlin and of his Royal Highness, George, Prince of Wales."

The Medlycott Estate leased on the 6th July, 1776 to Patrick McLoughlin for three lives was renewable for ever on payment of a peppercorn renewal fine.The last renewal bears the date 28th September, 1832, and is from Sir Richard O'Donnell, Baronet to the Reverend Peter Browne, Earl of Altamont, now Marquis of Sligo and James de Burgh Browne and Prince George of Cumberland, now King of Hanover. A second lease and release bearing the date 15th-16th July, 1777 was made between John Thomas Medlycott and Sir Neal O'Donnell of Newport Pratt of the lands of Corraun, etc. On the 20th December, 1777 Thomas Medlycott granted a lease of lands from this date to the 29th September, 1784 to Patrick McLoughlin of Dublin and his son, John, merchant of Newport Pratt at an annual rental of £135.9s. 0d.

The McLoughlin Estate

Patrick McLaughlin had made a will in 1776 bequeathing various lands to his sons: John and Patrick acquired Newport Pratt with John also getting Knockmullen, the Bleachyard and the lands called Red Hill; in

215

the event of John's death the lands were to revert to Patrick, his second son. Peter got Corraun, Henry, Tonragee and Thomas, Tonatanvally and Bunacurry. John McLaughlin died in 1815 and his eldest son also called John, before his death in 1839, bequeathed the lands of Tonatanvally and Bunacurry, which he must have inherited from his brother, Thomas, together with his own lands Knockmullen and the Bleachyard, to Domnick John McLaughlin. Peter died in 1810 and his lands in Corraun went to John and Domnick. After the acquisition of the Burrishoole Estate by Sir Neal O'Donnell the fortunes of the McLoughlin family declined. The famine brought ruin to the McLoughlins when their tenants absconded or were unable to pay their rents. Family feuding over ownership of the estate led to bankruptcy and the estate was sold in 1850-52 in the Encumbered Estates Court. Analysis of the acreage units assigned to tenants on the McLoughlin estate indicates a range of holdings from one acre to a maximum of twenty six acres with tenants leasing lands from year to year i.e. *"at will."* The total estate contained 12,733 acres, one rood and thirty six perches and the gross rent per annum was £1,477.18s. 1d. The net rent per annum was £1, 245. 6s. 6d.

John's will in 1840 bequeathed all his interest in the lands of Knockmullen and the Bleachyard, Red Hills, Tonatanvally and Bunacurry *"and that said Domnick John McLaughlin should in like manner convey to said John McLaughlin his interest in said lands of Corraun all of which was agreed."* On the 14th March 1846, there was an indenture between John McLaughlin and the Reverend Peter Browne (later Marquis of Sligo) relating to the lands outlined above. On Tuesday, 26th March, 1850, the estate of John McLaughlin of Corraun and Domnick John McLaughlin, *"The Lodge,"* Achill came up for sale. This included the lands of Corraun, sub-denominations of Ards, Bolinglanna, Belfarsad, Knocknamona and Mweewillin, together with the lands on Tonlegee East (Tonragee), including the village of Pull, Tonlegee West, the village of Shrughanbee, the houses and premises in and about the town of Newport Pratt, said lands being the property of John McLoughlin; also the lands of Tonatanvally, Bunacurry, Gortwaile, otherwise Knockmullen, and the Bleachyard, said last-named being the property of Domnick John McLaughlin. In all eight lots were sold.

15. Encumbered Estates and Achill Landowners

Details of the estate indicated that £100 had been expended in Corraun under the Land Improvement Act. This lot was said to have a large supply of sea-manure and a right to take turf (turbary).There was anchorage for vessels of one hundred and fifty tons burden within a few perches of a store built recently and capable of containing three hundred tons of grain. A Mill and a kiln and two National schools had been erected at considerable cost, and there were sites for two other mills. The sea was said to abound with fish and there was game of every description and a large rabbit warren on the estate. Two new roads through the centre of Corraun were nearing completion at an expenditure of £4,000. The Tuck Mill and another mill were located in the townland of Belfarsad close to the old National school. Bunacurry was advertised as adjoining a handsome colony established by the Reverend Edward Nangle: *"It has superior grazing and a large supply of shell-sand, seaweed, of kelp type by which a Scotch gentleman, within the last few years realised a considerable profit."* This townland was purchased by Archbishop McHale.

The O'Donnell Estate

Niall Garbh's grandson, Rory, was the first to settle on the Burrishoole Estate in the mid-seventeenth century, then owned by the Duke of Ormond. His great grandson, Neal, after the death of his father, Hugh, in 1762 converted to the protestant faith and was subsequently made a Baronet in 1768. In 1777, Neal acquired a lease on lands in the Burrishoole Estate from John Thomas Medlycott, son of Thomas John Medlycott who had acquired the estate from the Earl of Arran. Sir Neal is recorded as purchasing the Medlycott estate in 1785. Upon his death in 1811 his son, Neal Beg, inherited the estate. Neal died in 1827 and was succeeded by his son Sir Richard who would end up disposing of the bulk of the Burrishoole Estate in the *Encumbered Estates Court* in 1854:

"The Lordship and Manor of Burrishoole (The Newport estate of Sir Richard O'Donnell) held part in Fee simple and part in Fee farm. No quit rent payable out of the estate."

Achill

Four valuable Chief rents of: *£23. 1s. 5d.*   *£9. 4s. 7d.*

                             £104. 6s. 2d.   *£92. 6s. 2d.*

payable by the Marquis of Sligo who holds under Sir Richard O'Donnell by leases for lives renewable forever.

The estate was made up of the following lands: Knockeeragh, Tonlagee East, Tonlagee West, Owenduff, Tonatanvally, Part of Bleachyard (Newport), Knockmoyle, Cuilaloughaun, Shramore, Gubnahardia, Belfarsad, Mweewillin, Bunanioo, Bolinglanna, Dooniver, Bunacurry, Knockmullen (Gortawarla). The estate contained 33,000 acres of arable, pasture and mountain lands. £25,000 has been expended on the Estate since the Griffith Valuation by way of drainage, fencing etc. Richard Griffith was employed on Famine Relief Schemes from 1846 as a special commissioner for the Board of Works. There was little difference between the valuation of Griffith and the Commissioners:-

           Griffith's Valuation: *£844. 8s. 6d.*
           Commissioner's Valuation: *£909. 12s. 6d.*

The Marquis of Sligo

The estate was held under a Fee Farm Grant *"pursuant to the Renewable Leasehold Conversion Act, from the most Noble George John, Marquis of Sligo to Sir Richard A. O'Donnell, Baronet, bearing the date 1st day of May, 1852, in lieu of a certain lease dated 28th September, 1832."* This lease is that referred to above between Sir Richard O'Donnell and the Reverend Peter Browne, Earl of Altamont and later Marquis of Sligo.This lease conveyed to Sir Richard O'Donnell all the loughs, dams, weirs, rivers, water-courses, fisheries, fairs, markets and the tolls, customs and accustomed duties thereof. Also the sea-shore, seaweed or sea-tank, woods, underwood and timber. The rent was £808. 12s.3d. per annum payable half-yearly. A note penned by an unknown hand reads:

"The tenantry are a thriving, orderly class of people and the district is one of the most quiet and peaceable in Ireland."

15. Encumbered Estates and Achill Landowners

The O'Donnell Estate was sold in the following lots: Keel, Slievemore, Doogort Mill Plot, Doogort, Mweewillin, Meen Mweelin, Cashel, Polranny Lynchecan, Polranny Sweeney and Inishbiggle Island and were conveyed by the commissioners on the 31st July, 1852, to the Reverend Edward Nangle for £10,500. Achill Beg Island, Cloughmore, Claggan and Salia were sold to Thomas Brassy for £2,333.6s.8d. Carrick, Kildownet, Derreens and Sraheens, otherwise Ballynacorriga went to William Pike for £2,333.6s. 8d. Two undivided thirds parts of the lands of Carrowgarve were sold to Samuel Holme for £2,333.6s.8d. Corraun and sub-denominations was advertised as having an income of £92. 6s. 2d. from rental per annum.

A description of the Corraun lands is of interest: *"This lot is a chief rent reserved out of a large tract of arable and mountain land held in perpetuity and producing a considerable interest to the Lessee, several excellent lodes of copper and sulphur ores exist on this portion of the estate and the value of the property will be vastly increased on the minerals being duly developed. Proceedings are pending in the Courts of Chancery to decide the right to the royalties which Sir Richard O'Donnell claims to be entitled to, as being reserved out of the original lease to John McLaughlin and out of the last renewal to the Reverend Peter Browne, as trustee for the Marquis of Sligo."* It seems that Sir Richard O'Donnell and the Marquis of Sligo were both claiming ownership to minerals lately discovered in Corraun. These mines with extensive deposits of sulphur ore, copper and haematite were very valuable and of the highest quality as was borne out by a Mining Engineer, George Henwood: *"a better sample of gozzan (a true index of the mines), cannot be anywhere seen."* The Red Cove, containing ferruginous mica slates, through which ran veins of rich haematetic character iron ore, were said not to be commercially valuable. Corraun was, however, a valuable property which also contained a licence from the Fishery Commission for the establishment of oyster beds in Achill Sound. The roads through the estate, were said to have been skillfully and systematically laid and constructed.

Sir Richard O'Donnell had conveyed, by lease, the above lands to the Reverend Peter Browne on the 28th September, 1832, and in the

219

Achill

Encumbered Estates Court, the Marquis of Sligo is named as tenant and representative of Patrick McLaughlin. The connection between Patrick McLaughlin and the Marquis of Sligo is not clear. However, in 1853, in the *Encumbered Estates Court,* Sir Richard O'Donnell is said to be in receipt of rent amounting to £92.6s.2d. per annum for Corraun, the tenant was the Marquis of Sligo, representative of Patrick McLaughlin.

William McCormack

William McCormack purchased the lands of *Tonragee East and Tonragee West, Bolinglanna* with sub-denominations *Knocknacasse, Bunanioo* and sub-denominations, *Knocknamona and Glossilaun,* otherwise *Glossilaun, Mweewillin, Belfarsad and Gubnahardia* which were subsequently acquired in the *Encumbered Estates Court* by William M. Dickens and the Hon. & Reverend Alwyne Compton. In the valuation registers of 1882 Charles H.B. Dickens has title of the above lands from the *lessor*, the Marquis of Sligo. Other *lessees* in Corraun are Canon Armstrong, Mrs. Anne Clive and Sarah J.P. Knox-Gore. *The Irish Land Commission* acquired all of these lands early this century. The *Cushlecka* and *Dooghbeg Salmon Fishery,* which in 1886 was said to have been worked at a loss for the previous five years, was purchased by Alexander Hector and upon his death reverted to his wife, Anne Hector and their son, also called Alexander.

33. Pier at Kildavnet c.Late 19th century © Lawrence Collection

Chapter 16

POST-FAMINE ACHILL

"If we were to look back to 1850 B.C. we would see a well-wooded Ireland, and in clearings we would see a Bronze Age population enjoying a standard of life equivalent to that anywhere in western Europe. If instead, we look back to A.D. 1850 we see a ruined landscape, almost destitute of any woody growth, and with the fertility of much of its soils grossly depleted by endless repetitions of potato crops. Those of its people in whom any element of élan vital had survived had only one goal - to seek a higher standard of living elsewhere. And it is on the foundations of that ruined landscape that much of what we see around us today has been built." Mitchell (1976).

This description fits the post-Famine Achill landscape very well. In many cases, pre-Famine villages were deserted and with them the old way of life disappeared forever.

J.E. Howard, 1855.

J.E.Howard visited Achill in 1855 shortly before these changes began to take place and his impressions of the island bear testimony to the appalling conditions of the people at this time and to the apathy which prevailed among them:*"The Achill folk are hopeless in the direction of improvement. Having the example of the Achill Mission for several years, they have not moved an inch in the same direction. Contrast between two Dugorts: one under Slievemore neat and clean; one on the opposite cliff dirty, frowsy and disorderly. The example of a decently housed Settlement has had no effect on the Achill people. The Achill houses are mostly filthy, the people having cattle which live with the family. There is only one room with a big turf fire, creating an intolerable atmosphere. In one house, a bed filled one-third of the floor, most of the remainder being occupied by two cows. A rough deal table near the bed comprised the furniture and visitors must sit on the bed. The Poor Law Guardians kept cattle in houses themselves! It is the prevailing custom! Wherever you go in Achill, you will find cattle in the houses, along with the family sharing*

221

the same room. A civilised Irishman said: "two cows, two clean cows only, and you're surprised at that! Where have you been? Where were you brought up? A large landowner built some good cottages for them and offered them rent free, on condition that they would not live with the cattle. The people would not accept, so they got the houses at last on their own terms, and took the cows with them as before." Howard (1855). Howard described local marriage customs . When a young man fancied a girl, he went to see her father and asked: what will you give with her? The answer was usually three cows and one calf plus a sheep and a lamb! On death, he wrote: *"They bury their dead in the old savage way, without any funeral rites, except as the relatives may have in their minds. The priest says no prayer, reads no service, does not attend in his official character, unless specially engaged and paid."* Howard (1855). The following extract would seem to indicate that Howard was receiving his information from a source prejudicial to mainstream Achill:

"The Papists deny the right of Protestants to be in the island at all. Stories of wrong-doing, probing and spoliation which the peasantry claimed against the Achill Mission were untrue. A Brother Bonaventure of the Franciscan Monastery forbade retribution against the colony by the Achill Land Leaguers. Howard's driver told him about the Protestant Settlement on the island, made for the purpose of introducing Christianity: *"people here, some years ago, were quite like a set of heathens, living idly on what the ground produced and going neither to church, chapel, nor meeting.* He also said that : *The pastures were excellent as denoted by the Keem-fed mutton celebrated throughout the West! An English gentlemen (Blacker) is living in Keem in an Iron house similar to those which are sent to Australia and is beginning to erect by its side a substantial stone-built dwelling. He has another iron house for his steward or herdsman. Peasant habitations in Keem consist of miserable huts."* Howard (1855). There is a also a description of the Penal Altar:

"a heap of stones in a pyramidical shape forms a sort of rude altar; one of the stones resembles a receptacle used for holy water in a church.

16. Post-Famine Achill

This may have been a *bullaun* stone, usually found in Early Medieval sites. Also found here were the remains of an ancient village, ogham stone(s), Penal altar and a stone cross.

34. Castle-Tower foundations in Dún Kilmore © T. McDonald

Rev. Thomas Armstrong, 1902.

The Rev. Thomas Armstrong visited the island in 1902 and provided this picture of Achill, quoting liberally, like J.E.Howard, from the **Achill Herald**: *"The population of Achill in 1831 was 6,000, of which only 76 were Protestant, of whom the greater proportion were coastguards and their families. There was no school on the island and those who could read had acquired the art from a hedge-schoolmaster. Under the regime of the priests, the vast majority were not merely devoted Roman Catholics but were characterised by the grossest ignorance and superstition. Masses were said on the seashore to procure a supply of seaweed and fish."* Armstrong (1886). Seddall (1884) was correct when he said that Achill, prior to the coming of the Mission, was almost unknown to the outer world but this changed when the island became the scene of spiritual conflicts and exploits:

"During the last 50 years it has had a history so thrilling, so romantic, so full of incident, that one can only wonder how it has come to pass that it has so long escaped notice." Seddall (1884).

Chapter 17

EMIGRANTS AND MIGRANTS

"Oh, the far tawtie fields are calling me away,
An' the stretching in the bothies on the straw,
An' the old men moanin' at the breakin' o' the day,
An' the trekking when the mornin's in the raw. "

O'Dowd (1991).

Booleying

Booleying or transhumance was widely practised in Achill, and provided a safety valve in that it allowed maximisation of available resources. Seasonal migration to Scotland and England superseded this ancient system and went hand-in-hand with more permanent emigration to the U.S.A. Booleying had alleviated pressure on the growing crops and provided fresh pasture for livestock, while the migratory worker to the potato fields of Ayrshire or the Lothians, earned sufficient income to allow him and his family to live at home for most of the year. Economic problems are endemic to small island communities with limited resources so that any imbalance between population and resources, necessitates remedial action, such as booleying in the past and migration and emigration in the present. The main resources of the island, agriculture and fishing, are inadequate to sustain economic viability for more than a small percentage of the population. Hence, the present dependence upon tourism which helps to limit emigration, particularly amongst the younger generation. The average holding in Achill is approximately five acres, insufficient to maintain a family for more than a portion of the year. Recourse to some form of relief from population pressure has therefore been endemic to Achill for generations. Booleying or transhumance is defined as the movement of livestock, usually cattle, from a permanent lowland village to summer pasture in the mountains. The practice is quite old and probably goes back to the Early Medieval period or earlier. Spencer (1596) referred to the practice and said: *"People keep their cattle and lyve themselves the most part of the year in Bollies, particularly upon the mountain and waste wild places and removing to fresh pasture as required"*.

17. Emigrants and Migrants

Booleying is mentioned in the Brehon Laws and Chapman (1979) noted a connection between transhumance routes and the location of megalithic tombs in Spain. Today is it practised by the *Vlah*s, shepherds in Greece, and by other groups in the Swiss Alps. In Ireland it is generally associated with the Rundale system of agriculture where unenclosed fields necessitated the removal of livestock to the mountains so that the crops could grow undisturbed.

Booleying was a very efficient way of maximising resources and was an integral part of the farming system; summer pasture in the mountains was available for one season only but both the altitudinal and horizontal distance between the permanent village and the booley necessitated the construction of temporary dwellings or booley huts in the mountains, for dairy cattle cannot be moved over such terrain on a daily basis.

In Achill, booleying was practised up until the 1940's. O'Donovan of the Ordnance Survey (1838) noted that the people of Achill owned houses in two townlands, one of which was a booley: *"It is a great habit among the people of the island to have two townlands and houses built on each where they remove occasionally with their cattle. The townlands are held under one lease and one of these farms is called a Bouley. Bellanasally is a boulay of Dookinella, part of which stretches to the top of Slievemore mountain, where about 130 acres are cultivated."*

O'Donovan (1838-40).

The extant booley houses in Achill are oval in shape with a rectangular interior, similar types being known from Wales and dated to the 14th century A.D. The **Annals of Lough Cé** mention large herds of cattle in the vicinity of Achill in the 13th century A.D. but by the 19th century A.D. Tuke (1848) recorded that the average number of livestock per household was two cows, three sheep, with 25% of the population also owning a pony. The demise of booleying came about in the 19th century when incoming landlords began to *impound* livestock which trespassed on their property. Retrieval fines were prohibitive and there was a consequent reduction in the number of cattle kept. After removal from

Achill

Slievemore to Dooagh in the second half of the 19th century, the people subsequently re-occupied the now Deserted Village on a seasonal basis.

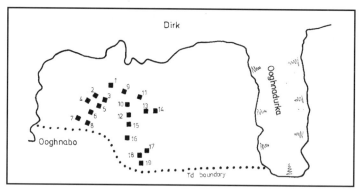

35. Sketch Plan of Dirk Booley Village © Theresa McDonald

36. Bunowna Booley Village © Lawrence Collection.

Tattie Hokers

A prophesy by *Brian Rua Ó Cearbháin* of Erris said that *"carriages on iron wheels"* would carry dead bodies to Achill on both its first and last journeys. He was referring to the extension of the railway line between Westport and Achill and his prophesy came true, for in 1894 thirty two young people were drowned in Clew Bay on their way to the

17. Emigrants and Migrants

"tattie hoking" in Scotland, while in 1937 the bodies of ten young people, who died in a fire in a bothy in Scotland, were brought back to Kildavnet cemetery for burial. The bothy fire alerted the government to the necessity of providing some protection for Irish migratory workers and resulted in a provision contained in the Scottish Rural Housing Bill in the British House of Commons. There was also much talk within Irish Government circles of formulating a plan to provide work for the migrants in Ireland but apart from the initial response to the tragedy, nothing more was heard of this plan. There was some local initiative. Peadar O'Donnell (1937) recounts how *"a little while ago a few lads from Achill working in the Cheshire Gardens got the idea that if Glass Houses with heating were set up in their island a good part of the local migratory labour problem could be solved."* The scheme was put to the Fianna Fail Government and the Minister for Agriculture and was rejected. Peadar O'Donnell was a frequent visitor to Achill, staying on occasion with the McHughs in Bullsmouth where he finished writing *"The Islandman."* (James McHugh, *pers. comm.*). He encouraged the migratory labourers to organise so that they could negotiate with the Scottish Potato Merchants to fix wages and conditions. While these negotiations were going on some Gaffers (heads of the tattie squad) made secret contact with the owners of the Scottish farms where the tattie hokers were employed, and despite protests and withdrawal of labour little was achieved either in working or living conditions. Migration had been a feature of Irish life for centuries but only became the norm for people from Mayo during the eighteenth and nineteenth centuries.

"Mayo furnishes England each year with the largest proportion of reapers; eleven hundred men and women from Achill in England and Scotland." O'Dowd (1991).

The 1662 Settlement Law in Britain followed an earlier statute of King Henry V in 1413 which ordered the removal of all Irish vagrants from Britain, suggests that even at this early date, Irish migrant workers were seeking seasonal employment in Britain and would continue to do so following every harvest crisis in Ireland. O'Dowd (1991). The Settlement Law of 1662 *"provided the Government with the authority to remove all those likely to become paupers after forty days of their arrival in the parish."* O'Dowd (1991). O'Dowd also says the acceleration of Irish seasonal migrant workers to Britain occurred only during the population pressure of 1780-90, which had forced many people to abandon their homes for large portions of the year. Seemingly, harvest failure in 1782-83 brought many people to their knees, and without the safety valve of seasonal work, many would undoubtedly have faced eviction and possible starvation. The onset of the Napoleonic Wars brought about relative prosperity with exports bringing in much needed revenue, but the subdivision of holdings still proceeded at an alarming rate during the war, as tillage acreage expanded, leaving many holdings unviable. This led, inevitably, in the aftermath of the war, to an increase in the number of migratory workers leaving Ireland for Britain, and was, as O'Dowd claims, responsible for the establishment of the first regular passenger steamship to Britain in 1815 to cater for the increased numbers of migratory workers. Potato failure in 1817 and 1819, coupled with very wet weather, brought destitution to many areas, with 30,000 people leaving Mayo for Kildare in search of work, but despite all this, the population still continued to rise.

Haris Stone (1906) wrote that:

"in the harvesting time the young men nearly all go to Scotland and Lancashire to work as agricultural labourers, in order to earn enough to keep their families home."

From Dooagh alone some 200 departed annually to the *tattie- hoking*, some as young as fourteen years of age. The main destination was Ayrshire where the squad remained together to work as a unit throughout the early potato season. In 1906 the *Royal Commission of Congestion in Ireland* reported that 2,000 people, roughly two-fifths of Achill's population were engaged in migratory labour in that year.

Kirkintilloch

The lot of the migratory worker was harsh in the extreme and often culminated in disaster such as the *Kirkintilloch* fire of 1937. Ten young people were burned alive in a *bothy* in Scotland and brought home for

17. Emigrants and Migrants

burial on one of the last trains to operate between Westport and Achill, fulfilling the prophesy of Brian Rua Ó Cearbháin. This tragedy is outlined in detail by the late Peadar O'Donnell (1937) in an article entitled *"The Bothy Fire and all that."* The Commission set up by the government after this tragedy was said by O'Donnell to be nothing more than *"a scratching post"* to stop public disquiet and was soon forgotten. James McHugh of Dugort who was himself a *"Gaffer"* in Scotland for many years recalls that:

"Many Achill boys and girls from fifteen years and over went to Scotland to earn their living at the "tattie hoking ." The work was hard and involved kneeling on the hard ground for ten hours per day picking potatoes into two baskets, one for the big potatoes and one for the smaller ones. Wages were six pence per hour. These boys and girls were hired each year at the Hiring Fair. Maura Rua from Corraun was only eleven years of age when she went to Kilmarnock to the tattie hoking. The person in charge of the squad of tattie hokers was called the Gaffer. Some Gaffers were better than others: where wages were 5p. per hour. One named Kilcoyne from Keel paid an extra penny per hour." (James McHugh, *pers. comm.*).

37. Clew Bay Disaster Memorial © Lawrence Collection.

229

Chapter 18

FAMOUS CHARACTERS

William Blacker

The Devon Commission was set up in 1847 to assess land usage in Ireland. The Secretary of the Devon Commission, Pitt Kennedy took as his base the calculations of Richard Griffith, the valuation commissioner that there were over one and a quarter million acres in the country which could be brought under cultivation and another 2,330,000 which might be drained for coarse meadow or made fit for grazing by sheep and young cattle. Pitt Kennedy claimed that the land could provide eight-acre holdings for 192,369 families and enlarge the holdings of another 133,720 families to the same acreage, thereby permanently reducing the number of labourers in the market by 500,000. A fundamental criticism of Kennedy was made by the peasant farmer who said that Kennedy's thesis was based on the assumption that all that was wrong with the country was a shortage of land and that the country suffered from under-production rather than over-population. Other drawbacks to the proposed scheme were related to the proposed extension of arable areas through reclamation of marginal land and how long these could continue to be farmed, together with the danger that a State-sponsored reclamation of waste land would act as a spur to population growth thereby intensifying the population problem.

The most practical proposals were made by William Blacker. His aim was to intensify the cultivation of existing arable land which would increase the income of the individual farmer, leading ultimately to a higher standard of living, the hitherto absence of which had led to subdivision and the growth of population which had outstripped the demand for labour. Blacker was said to have started out with the orthodox Irish assumption that *"a pauper population must be employed or it becomes dangerous, and when they cannot get work they must get land."* Edwards & Williams (1994). Having accepted the necessity for subdivision, Blacker set out to prove that its effects could be countered by the introduction of green crops and house-feeding on small holdings and that the agricultural output of Ireland could be increased threefold. Before publishing his schemes, Blacker had already put them into practice with considerable success on the large properties which he managed in Co. Armagh. Did he possibly do this in Achill too? William Blacker was an Armagh land agent who published a ***Prize Essay*** in 1834 which he had previously submitted to the *Agricultural Committee of the Royal Dublin Society* on the management of landed property in Ireland. A William Blacker leased the townland of Keel West in Achill from the Achill Mission Estate in the mid-nineteenth century which was farmed by a Murray MacGregor Blacker and Charles Boycott. Reports contained in accounts of Achill by various antiquaries: *"where soils were so fertile that large crops of oats, potatoes, cabbage, savoys, sea kale, broad beans, carrots and parsnips, as well as onions and turnips were grown."* Newman (1839). He also hinted at the presence on the island of a competent farmer. Parts of Achill, notably Keem Bay and Dugort, appear to have been intensely cultivated in the nineteenth century giving rise to the speculation that the William Blacker of Achill may have been none other than the famous agriculturalist.

William Blacker resorted to empirical research to test his theory and followed this up with the employment of an agricultural instructor from Scotland, to advise the tenant farmers on how to adopt a proper system of crop rotation, instead of exhausting the land with successive corn crops. He provided loans so that tenants could obtain sufficient lime for their first crop using the new methods. Edward Nangle, in a remark relating to reclamation and cultivation of the Mission farm in Dugort, mentioned that a friend of the Mission had located a small deposit of lime in the vicinity of the Settlement which proved invaluable in reclamation! Blacker also provided his tenants with clover and vetch seed on six-months credit if they undertook to sow the former with their first grain crop and the latter instead of a second grain crop. The result was heavier yields: *8-10 tons of potatoes; 16-18 cwt of wheat and 17-19 cwt of oats to the acre.* He claimed that tenants with between two and a half to five acres were now able to keep cows for the first time! His advocacy of the merits of a mixed system of plough and husbandry were adopted and his contribution to Irish farming practice immense.

Achill

Captain Charles Cunningham Boycott

Captain Boycott (1832-1897), who gave his name to a new word in the English language, was twenty five years of age when he arrived in Achill in 1857. He was accompanied by a Murray MacGregor Blacker and both were tenants of William Blacker who had leased the townland of Keel West from the Achill Mission Estate. Murray MacGregor Blacker and Charles Boycott (who may have been related) immediately set about enclosing their estate in Keel West and initially built a large Iron House in Keem. Although it is difficult today to envisage this area covered with cultivated fields and meadows, the remains of field cultivation ridges indicate that this was the case. The methods of cultivation described, closely echo those outlined above by William Blacker and it may well be that either he or Murray MacGregor Blacker were responsible:

"the soil was tilled to sow rye and women were employed at three pence per day haymaking and collecting heather and sedge for bedding, the latter having to be carried from Corrymore lake in creels on their backs. The rye crop was rotated with potatoes and meadow, and the labour load was offset by the importation of modern machinery ."

Irish Folklore Commission, U.C.D.

The Blacker Estate consisted of 2,000 acres of land in Keel West townland which was rented at £42.10 shillings per annum. McNally, (1973). Keel West townland comprised the area from Achill Head to the river which flows west of O'Malley's Pub in Dooagh. The townlands of Keel East and Keel West are separated by the townland of Slievemore but originally Keel West may have been a *booley* of Keel East. The remains of houses in Keem Bay are however very similar in plan to those in the *booley* village of Bunowna in Keel West townland and may be contemporary. Both villages predate the nineteenth century. The Keem Bay house built by Murray MacGregor Blacker and Boycott was burned down and Boycott moved to Corrymore House, while Murray MacGregor Blacker emigrated to the United States of America.

Boycott seems to have been a brutal landlord, exacting fines on the hapless tenants if their livestock strayed on to his lands; even fowl such as geese were in danger of being run down by his side-car, or horse, if

232

18. Famous Characters

they were caught grazing along the roadway, west of the river. Workers were fined if they were late, the fines sometimes exceeding the wages. He tried to prevent local fishermen from fishing in Keem Bay and was even brought to Court by the Achill Mission Estate for laying claim to a wreck in this area. Boycott had a large stock of cattle as well as huge flocks of sheep; it was reported that during the annual sheep-shearing it used to take twelve men a full day to shear his sheep.

Boycott enlarged Corrymore House each year until it became a substantial residence built around a courtyard, the back wing consisting of outhouses, offices, etc. Boycott's wife supposedly visited the island once and is reputed to have worn *"huge earrings, almost touching her shoulders."* According to the Irish Folklore Commission files in U.C.D. she liked the poteen imported from Inishkea and was *"a different character altogether from her husband!"* Boycott was to remain on the island for twenty years, Murray MacGregor Blacker only staying for six years. Boycott's departure to Ballinrobe to work as a land agent on Lord Erne's Estate was not regretted in Achill. In Ballinrobe, Boycott met his downfall at the hands of Michael Davitt and the Land League when he refused to reduce tenants' rents during the land agitation of 1879-80. Labourers on the Erne Estate refused to work for him and local suppliers refused to sell him food, *"boycotting"* him and it was this action that gave a new word to the English language i.e. *to boycott = to shun!*

Alexander Hector

Alexander Hector arrived in Achill around the same time as Murray MacGregor Blacker and Charles Boycott, probably in response to a request from Edward Nangle in the **Achill Herald** in 1852 for *enterprising Protestant gentlemen* to come and live on the island to provide work for the local population and at the same time benefit from an able work-force and cheap labour. In 1856, the **Achill Herald** announced the arrival of Alexander Hector from Bervie in Kincardinshire in Scotland: *"An enterprising Scotsman, Alexander Hector,* has leased from the Achill Mission Estate *the principal part of the shores of this island for the purpose of carrying on a Salmon Fishery, on an extensive scale ."* The **Achill Herald** claimed that hitherto *"the salmon had been* *left in undisturbed possession of the deep,"* an unlikely scenario for Edward Nangle had himself referred to a local salmon fishing operation in Keem in the 1852 edition of that newspaper. However, there is no mention of salmon fishing during the Great Famine, a fact attributed to the lack of suitable fishing gear. This omission would be dramatically rectified by Alexander Hector for having been employed in salmon fishing in Scotland since his youth, Hector had a large fund of experience at his command and more importantly he brought to Achill a peculiar net called a *"bag-net"* which had been invented sometime before by his father. With the arrival of Alexander Hector, it was claimed that the quantity of employment, which the working of his fishery would create, would be of great benefit to the natives and he was wished every success in his endeavours by Edward Nangle and the Achill Mission.

The venture proved to be very successful, particularly as the *bag-net* proved to be a very efficient method for catching large quantities of salmon and Hector's first salmon-fishing season in Achill was rewarded with abundant catches. Hopes were expressed that the *Achill Fishery* would be a permanent source of local industry and wealth. An extract from the **Achill Herald** in 1856 indicated that the fishery was fully operational but:

"...owing to the remoteness of the island and the difficulties of conveyancing, Mr. Hector has erected an apparatus at Keel for boiling and pickling salmon, where it is dispatched in kits to the London market. Experienced Scotsmen were placed by Mr. Hector as overseers of the various fishing stations, and conductors of the boiling and pickling process . On the propriety of conduct and obliging manner of these men towards the inhabitants of the island, we feel bound to speak in terms of high commendation. This branch of industry, worked by Scottish industry with so much success, is a great benefit to the natives of this island from the large amount of employment, and the liberal wages and remuneration which Mr. Hector is able to give.We understand that the benefit thus conferred is not likely to be interrupted by the close of the salmon fishing season, as Mr. Hector has made arrangements for carrying on the white fishing through the winter, and also for the manufacture on an extensive scale of the purest cod-liver oil." **Achill Herald (1856).**

18. Famous Characters

Socially and economically, Alexander Hector, was popular with both locals and with people at the Settlement. The former were provided with jobs and the latter benefited from his munificence in the provision of school treats for children attending schools on the Mission Estate. His standing with the Achill Mission was high and they could not praise him enough: "*Mr. Hector since coming to the island has used his utmost energy and made every attempt to elevate and benefit, temporally and morally, all who have come within range of his influence.*" Rare praise indeed coming from Edward Nangle! Within a short time the following advertisement appeared in the *Achill Herald*:

" *By Royal Appointment, Alexander Hector, Fish Curer to the Queen for Scotland. Can supply Pickled Salmon, caught and cured in Achill @ 30s per large kit, or @ 20s for a lesser kit, on receipt of a Postal order in Dugort Post Office.*"

The *bag-net* used by Hector consisted of a long piece of net suspended on a string rope, to which, at intervals of about two feet, large pieces of cork were attached to make it buoyant. One end of this rope was secured to the shore, from which it projected into the sea at right angles and the other end was secured by an anchor. From the extreme end of the net, two other nets were secured in the form indicated in the drawing on page 236. The space contained within the nets diverging from the seabed end of the long net had a ceiling and floor of network. When the salmon in pursuing their course along the net, in either direction, came to the long net, they naturally swam along it in search of a breach through which they might pass, and in seeking to accomplish this objective, they went into the netted chambers and from there into the narrow part of the chamber where they could neither turn nor effect an escape. The fishermen examined the nets three times per day, taking up the small end of the bag or chamber into the boat, where they took out the fish by untying a running string. Seemingly, these nets, together with the boats, were expensive, requiring, as the *Achill Herald* pointed out *"expenditure of a large amount of capital."* The nets were also said to be very perishable, susceptible to damage and/or being carried away by storms and other casualties; this along with the payment of wages of the boats crews, entailed a large daily expenditure.

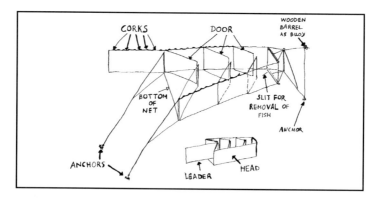

38. Sketch Plan of Bag Net, after Went (1964)

Salmon were plentiful and large catches were made possible by the use of the *bag net* but storage and preservation became a problem, and conveying the fish fresh to market incurred exorbitant carriage costs. Hector quickly solved both problems: *"..He erected a large boiler, had the fish dressed, preserved in vinegar and packed in small kegs or kits, and sent to London by water carriage at low cost." Achill Herald (1859).* Next he acquired from the trustees of the Achill Mission a building formerly used as a Hotel at Achill Sound, where he set up a fish processing plant. He then began to preserve vegetables, particularly carrots, which he exported to all parts of the world. He encouraged the people to grow carrots, having noted that the soil in Achill was *"peculiarly suited, when properly cultivated, to the growth of this vegetable!"* Four *tin* workers were employed in making tin canisters; part of this work was performed by machinery and there was a reputed output of c.900 canisters per day. *Salmon, trout, turbot, lobsters, oysters and cockles* were also preserved and deposited in their raw state in the canisters which was then closely soldered; to make them perfectly airtight a small hole was punched in the top of each canister and closed again with solder. *"A number of the cans placed in an iron frame are then immersed in the boiler which is kept up to the highest boiling heat. They are then taken out, the small hole in the cover is opened and when the steam and expanded air have rushed out, the aperture is instantly closed*

18. Famous Characters

by the application of a heated soldering iron. Articles thus preserved are warranted to keep fresh in any climate for twenty years. Fish taken on Achill shores are exported to the East Indies and Australia."

Hector richly deserved the title *"enterprising Scotsman ,"* for he also secured a contract from the trustees of the Achill Mission to purchase within the island, all the game he required for export to foreign markets. Hector's enterprise undoubtedly provided varied and extensive employment both in the salmon fishery and preserving stations, and in labelling and painting canisters. Vast quantities of peat had to be cut and dried to fuel the boilers; nets had to be made and repaired; crews were employed to man the boats; the fish had to be washed and fires constantly tended. Men, women and children were employed by Hector and he is rightly remembered as the founder of the *Achill Fishing Industry*. It was subsequently claimed that he had provided employment for between one and two people out of every house on the island. As a result of his operations a prediction came true that *"a populous village will grow in the neighbourhood of Alexander Hector's Estate at Achill Sound! "*

Hector also repaired the old *salt-pans* in Achill Sound and erected new buildings in their vicinity. A pier was erected and a boat made available to ferry passengers across the Sound. This was followed by the construction of a floating bridge to convey carriages and loaded carts across this 200 yards wide stretch of water. A new Fishery Bill, enacted in 1860, placed Alexander Hector's Scottish and Irish operations in jeopardy. It was claimed that fishing by *bag-net* was destroying rivers and fisheries, and that salmon intercepted *en route* to their spawning grounds were being exterminated. Hector forcefully disputed this and failing to have his case heard in the British House of Commons, he published a pamphlet outlining the efficiency of the *bag-net*, claiming that salmon stocks had increased rather than decreased since its introduction, and he produced figures to back up his statement:

1851	Salmon take	969 lbs
1862	Salmon take	1290 lbs
1851	June 1-12	44 salmon (290 lbs)
1862	June 1-12	80 salmon (425 lbs)

Achill

Concern was expressed in the Achill Herald over Hector's predicament but the Mission was also worried about the loss of revenue to the estate should there be a cessation of salmon fishing. In a reference to the bag-net, Edward Nangle said:

"the Bill now before the House will deprive Mr. Hector of his living, confiscate a portion of the Mission property by depriving trustees of the Achill Mission Estate of rent and cause massive unemployment."

The prohibition led to a decline in the fishery and in the early 20th century the Achill Fishery was sold to Sweeney's of Achill Sound who after some time expanded the operation to fish for the basking shark. An extract from the Valuation Registers (1855-1894), shows Alexander Hector as the lessee from William Blacker of Ocean Fisheries. A comment in the margin says:

" I have heard this fishery is very valuable. I wrote to Mr. Hector and append his reply (missing!). From the evasive manner which he has written, I could form no idea of its value, but I have casually heard the rent was about £79." J. Scanlan.

The *bag-net* continued in use in Achill and was used by Seán Kilbane and John McNamara (Taxi) to fish for salmon around Purteen in the 1960's but, seemingly, because of licence restrictions it was not used in Keem Bay (Michael Gielty, *pers. comm.*). Shark fishing provided valuable jobs for local fishermen until the operation was disbanded in the 1970's.

Today, individual fishermen and small co-operatives fish for salmon and lobster, exporting the fish to the Continent as well as providing the local hotels etc. with supplies throughout the summer months. The days of large fish catches are over, at least for the present, the waters of both Clew Bay and Blacksod Bay have been grossly over-fished by non-native fishermen (John McNamara (Taxi), *pers. comm.*) who also says that a conservation policy is long overdue.

18. Famous Characters

Lynchehaun - The Playboy

Lynchehaun, the infamous hero in Professor James Carney's book, *"The Playboy and the Yellow Lady "* (1986), and also the character upon which Synge's *"The Playboy of the Western World "* is supposedly based, was born in Polranny near Achill Sound between 1858 and 1860. He had a keen sense of history and listened avidly to fire-side tales of cruel deeds perpetrated by English soldiers against Catholics during the Penal Times. The hanging of Fr. Manus Sweeney in Newport during the 1798 rebellion was particularly repulsive to Lynchehaun and he pledged to be a patriot when he grew to manhood. He went to school in Tonragee and after several examination failures eventually became a school teacher, and almost immediately acquired a teaching post in Belfarsad. This did not last too long as Lynchehaun fell foul of a school inspector, Mr. MacElwain, who did not take kindly to Lynchehaun falsifying the school roll-book so as to increase his income! His next job was in Roundstone, Co. Galway. This too ended in disaster when Lynchehaun seemingly beat up a pickpocket who had tried to relieve him of a quarter year's salary. This incident led to his arrest and confinement in Clifden and, after being freed on bail, he absconded. *En route* to Achill, he called in to a National School near Westport and pretending to be a schools' inspector wrote a very damaging report; the poor teacher fearful of his imminent dismissal was glad to provide a loan of £2 to £3 to the bogus inspector in the hope that this gesture of goodwill would result in him modifying the report. After a short stay in Achill he headed for Birkenhead in England where he got a job as a bus conductor and later joined the Metropolitan Police where he was dismissed for drinking on duty. Returning to Achill like the prodigal son, he was set up in business by his father, settled down and married Catherine Gallagher, a local girl. Living in harmony with his fellow men was not a Lynchehaun characteristic and before long he was involved in several local skirmishes. Having moved to the Valley it was not long before he came into contact with his new employer, Mrs. Agnes McDonnell, who was to feature prominently in his life. One of his first ventures involved cutting *bent-grass* which had been sown on the shore to prevent sand being blown over the pasture land and secondly helping himself from the prolific rabbit warren which Mrs. McDonnell had previously sold to a rabbit-catcher. Adding insult to injury he refused to pay rent and defeated all efforts made by Mrs. McDonnell to redress the situation in law. Hearing that she was selling seaweed to local people without putting the Revenue stamp on the sale docket, he acquired one of these dockets and posted it to the Revenue Commissioners which resulted in Mrs. McDonnell eventually having to pay back taxes on all her seaweed transactions. According to Brother Paul Carney's diary-notes on Lynchehaun, Mrs. McDonnell was an eccentric character, having dismissed several land agents in a short space of time, namely, Josiah Salt, an Englishman, Mr. Patrick Sweeney, contractor for the Swivel Bridge at Achill Sound and Mr. Harry Veriker, a West Mayo land agent. Without the services of a land agent, Mrs. McDonnell found herself in serious difficulty and probably for expediency sake, employed Lynchehaun, not as land agent because she did not think him suitable, but as land steward. Lynchehaun was initially delighted with his new-found respectability but it was not long before he aspired to higher office, i.e. that of land agent. Mrs. McDonnell was unwilling to grant him this position and it seems that relations between the two became increasingly hostile, so much so that Mrs. McDonnell had to resort to the Courts where at her instigation Lynchehaun was served with *notice to quit* the house and shop which he had been renting from her. Lynchehaun was livid at this and swore to get even with her. He also began to drink heavily at this time probably knowing that his tenure in the Valley was about to be severed. The row between Lynchehaun and Mrs. McDonnell was nearing its climax and unfortunately for her she decided that her domestic servants would no longer be allowed to sleep on the premises overnight, leaving her, except for a guard dog, virtually defenceless. These altered domestic arrangements were to have serious repercussions for Mrs. McDonnell, particularly as Lynchehaun must have been aware of them within a short space of time. On the night of the 6th October, 1894, Lynchehaun who had been drinking heavily in a local *shebeen* scaled the walls of Mrs. McDonnell's estate and set fire to a number of out-offices. Seeing the flames, local people ran to help and someone roused Mrs. McDonnell who immediately ran outdoors and meeting

18. Famous Characters

Lynchehaun gave him the keys to the stable so as to unlock the door and free the horses who were in danger of suffocation from the smoke. It is not known how or why Mrs. McDonnell suspected Lynchehaun as being the perpetrator of this foul deed but on his return with the keys she seemingly accused him of causing the fire which he denied furiously and attempted to strike her. She is said to have produced a revolver and threatened to shoot him after which he picked her up and attempted to throw her into the flames but she was rescued by a local girl named Mary Gallagher. The row continued nevertheless and ended up with Lynchehaun striking Mrs. McDonnell senseless and also leaving her with fearful injuries. He then proceeded to break into the house and set it on fire so that by the following morning nothing remained but a burnt shell. A doctor was summoned to take care of Mrs. McDonnell's injuries and the police came to arrest Lynchehaun. On his way to the Police station he is said to have called out to his wife in the Irish language asking her to send clean clothes to him at the Police Barracks. A servant boy arrived with the clothes and Lynchehaun on the pretext of putting them on in the *closet,* threw his blood-stained clothes out of the window where the servant-boy, a relative of Lynchehaun, was there to retrieve them and make sure they would not be available as evidence. Lynchehaun was remanded in custody in Castlebar Gaol for two weeks until Mrs. McDonnell was fit enough to make a statement, at which time he was taken back to Achill to confront the lady and hear her deposition against him. He was again remanded to Castlebar Gaol to await his trial at the County Assizes but on the return journey escaped from custody close to his former home in Tonragee and successfully evaded capture, despite the intensive manhunt comprising a large force of policemen who remained in Achill for three months searching for him. A reward of £250 was offered for his capture, a sum increased by an additional £100 by Mrs. McDonnell's husband. The reward, a vast sum by the standards of the day, eventually proved irresistible and Lynchehaun was captured. His trial lasted four days, the verdict a foregone conclusion and Lynchehaun was sentenced to penal servitude for life. He was removed to Mountjoy Gaol in Dublin to serve his sentence. After seven years of incarceration Lynchehaun petitioned the Governor for mitigation of his sentence. In

Achill

July 1902 he was transferred to Maryborough Gaol (Portlaoise), from where he would escape in September of that year, making his way to Belfast, then to Scotland and freedom once again. After a short spell in Glasgow he made his way to Antwerp and from there to the U.S.A. Meanwhile newspapers in both Britain and Ireland carried stories of his attack on Mrs. McDonnell and his daring escape from Maryborough Prison and £100 reward was offered for information leading to his capture. An intensive police search was mounted, particularly near his home in Tonragee and in Achill. However, Lynchehaun was now safely ensconced in Chicago but he would not remain so for long. In August, 1903 he was arrested in Indianapolis. His trial got widespread publicity; the British Government were pressing hard for his extradition but Lynchehaun seemingly had a very good defence lawyer who secured his acquittal on the grounds that his crime was held to be political and therefore not extraditable. After working at various jobs, latterly as a saloon keeper, Lynchehaun once again returned to his native soil, visiting Achill in 1907. He did not remain there very long but went to Scotland where he died in 1937. His *nemesis* Mrs. McDonnell, when close to death is supposed to have said that he was *a "fine, young, strong, dark, animal-looking man."* Carney (1986).

39. House in Bunafahy © Theresa McDonald

Chapter 19

GUIDE TO THE ARCHAEOLOGICAL SITES OF ACHILL

"I now send you the Name Books of Achill which have given me more trouble than any I have yet visited." O'Donovan (1838:177).

In 1834 the first scientific land survey of the island was commenced by the Ordnance Survey; included in this brief was a survey of ancient sites, a task seemingly not completed without some difficulty to judge by the above comment. This survey of the archaeology of Achill included only a small proportion of the sites and monuments now known to exist on the island. Apart from surveys of the megalithic tombs on Slievemore carried out by Col. Wood-Martin in 1898, Professors Piggott and Powell in 1947 and the late Professor Ruadhrí De Valera and Dr. Seán Ó Nualláin in 1950, little of the islands archaeology was explored until 1984 when the author *via* field survey and documentary research compiled a *corpus* of all extant sites on the island as part of a Masters Thesis under the auspices of University College, Galway. Over 200 sites were recorded and are included in the Office of Public Works Sites and Monuments Record (1991). They are now also included in the new (1993) Ordnance Survey Discovery Series Maps (1:50,000: Sheet 30). A local historian, the late Cyril Gray of Dugort and the late Captain Robert Boyd of the Amethyst Hotel in Keel had carried out their own research over a number of years, and the author acknowledges with gratitude their contribution to this book. Folklore material on Achill held by the Irish Folklore Commission in University College, Dublin was perused. Additional material was provided by my uncle, the late John Moran of Dooagh, whose vast knowledge of the island's recent history, was immense and his contribution is gratefully acknowledged. A number of new site types have been added to the Corpus of Sites which do not appear on the map inset in the back cover. The Stone Circle remains unverified; the Round Houses on Slievemore are associated with the pre-bog field systems, while Coastguard Stations, Enclosures, Keem Bay Village, Sheep Pens, Sweat Houses and Vernacular Housing post-date 1700 A.D. which is the official cut-off point for archaeological site types.

Achill

ARCHAEOLOGICAL SITE-TYPES IN ACHILL *(See map inset back cover)*

1. ANCIENT CHURCH SITES

2. BOOLEY VILLAGES

3. CAIRNS AND LEACHTAÍ CUIMHNE CÁIN

4. CAHERS-CASHELS (CATHAIR-CAISEAL)

5. CASTLE (TOWER HOUSE)

6. CAUSEWAY

7. CAVES

8. CILLINÍ

9. CLACHÁNS

10. COASTGUARD STATIONS

11. CRANNÓGS (CRANNÓGA)

12. CROSSING (FORDING) PLACE

13. CURRACH (STANDS) PENS

14. "DANISH DITCH"

15. DESERTED VILLAGE

16. ENCLOSURES

17. FULACHTA FIADH (BURNT MOUNDS)

18. HOLY WELLS

19. HUT FOUNDATIONS

20. ICE HOUSES

21. KEEM BAY VILLAGE

Achill

Catalogue of Sites

1. ANCIENT CHURCH SITES

The Early Christian Period is now known by some archaeologists as the Early Medieval Period to better represent the many new innovations in religious, economic and social activities which characterise the fifth to the twelfth centuries A.D. These innovations included the introduction of a new religion, technological developments in farming and a new social order spearheaded by large and small monasteries, the large having a proto-urban status. A fundamental prerequisite for the development of this new social order was the introduction of literacy, enabling links to be forged with communities abroad. The Early Medieval period beginning with St. Patrick in the mid 5th century A.D. and continuing until the 12th century, is not as well documented in Achill as it is on neighbouring islands where churches, cross slabs and other monuments abound. Early churches were built mainly of wood, called by the Venerable Bede, the *more Scottorum* after the Irish who were then called the Scots. The *Damhliag* (stone church) came later and incorporated within its structure many elements of the *Durthech* (wooden Church). *"The type of all Irish Churches, from the earliest times until the coming of monastic orders, is the rectangular building, gabled at both ends and small in size."* Leask (1955).

The Early Medieval period saw the introduction of writing but the first evidence of literacy is provided by the ogham stones which appear in Ireland around the middle of the 5th century A.D. An ogham stone and a fragment of another were found on the banks of the Bunowna River in Keem Bay. In the same area is a reconstructed Penal altar and the remains of Keem (Cím) village. A *bullaun* stone was also said to have been located near the altar, suggesting perhaps that Keem Bay might have formerly been the location of an Early Medieval site. Ogham stones were generally erected to commemorate the dead and perhaps mark boundaries; they were inscribed in Irish (and Latin) in a *rune-like* cipher based on the Roman alphabet, which gave the dead man's name and line of descent. The ogham script consisted of a series of strokes cut on either side of, or across, a stem-line. de Paor (1958).

19. Guide to the Archaeological Sites of Achill

There is some evidence, admittedly tenuous, which connects St. Patrick with Achill; this is in the place name, *Silva vocluti,* the place of Patrick's captivity, which has been translated by *Tírechán,* a seventh century scribe as *"Achill Wood."* The reason therefore for the dearth of monastic remains in Achill may be a strong Patrician as opposed to a monastic tradition. The Patrician Church was diocesan based with temporal power vested in a bishop who answered to Rome. The Monastic church was headed by an Abbot, who usually came from a local ruling family, with the organisational status similar to that of the former *Tuath* or tribeland. The holy well dedicated to St. Colman in Slievemore graveyard may indicate a 7-8th century date, presupposing that the dedication refers to the Colman who left Lindisfarne after the *Synod of Whitby* in A.D. 664 in protest over, among other things, the conflict between the Columban (Monastic) Church and the Church of Rome over the rites for the observance of Easter and form of tonsure. It is reasonable to assume that *en route* to Inishbofin, and ultimately to *"Mayo of the Saxons "* (Mayo Abbey), Colman and his monks may have put ashore in Achill and other islands in Clew Bay. A stone cross in Slievemore graveyard of Early Medieval date bears a strong resemblance to Cornish stone crosses of the same period; there is a *Killeen* which may originally have contained an oratory; a holy well referred to above is located north-west of this and another small cross is set against the east wall of the graveyard while a third (originally one of a pair), of the equal-armed variety is located on top of a stone pillar flanking the entrance gateway to the graveyard. Early Medieval remains on Achill are confined in the main to three locations: Slievemore, Kildavnet and Achill Beg Island but there are a number of other sites which have less clear-cut evidence e.g. Keem Bay and Dookinella Thulis. The Church at Kildavnet may also be of Early Christian date but successive restorations have obliterated much of the early diagnostic detail. However, some early features were noted by Leask (1937), an expert in Church architecture e.g. the plain rectangular shape of the building, the east-west orientation, the doorway, the sides of the jambs inclining inwards, thereby narrowing the opening under the lintel and the diminution in width being some 3 to 4 inches. *Kil-Da-Mat* (Kildavnet) was the name given to Achill Beg on Petty's map of

1655 and Kildavnet or Kildownet would seem to be a later corruption of this. Within the graveyard at Kildavnet are a number of crude stone crosses, many of which are probably of Early Medieval date.

40. Kildavnet Cross   *41. West Gable, Kildavnet Church*

The Holy well, not in its original position, is located outside the wall of the graveyard. On Achill Beg within a strongly fortified headland is a large enclosure, some two hundred and twenty metres in diameter, containing a variety of remains: *a leacht* (stone altar), a *bullaun* stone (basin/holy water font), two conjoined (figure-of-eight) huts along the western bank and a *cillín* denoted by crude stones set vertically into the ground. On the hillside overlooking the site, with panoramic views to Clare Island and Clew Bay, and reminiscent in many ways of St. Columcille's stone *"chair"* on Iona, is a small crude cross, similar to those in Slievemore, and Kildavnet and on the Penal altar at Keem Bay. The Achill Beg site is set within one of the most massive and spectacular of the western promontory forts, called *Dún Kilmore,* though this name properly belongs to the circular enclosure and its remains; the headlands are called, respectively, the *Dún* and the *Daingean,* referring to the Promontory Fort. In addition to the three ancient Church sites at Slievemore, Kildavnet and Achill Beg Island, another site set within two adjoining villages (clacháns), *Baile Thuas* and *Baile Thios* in Dookinella Thulis, was extant up until the end of the nineteenth century after which it was demolished and the stones removed. In the immediate vicinity is a holy well and a *cillín* (Children's graveyard). The Rev. Edward Nangle frequently mentions this Church in the **Achill Missionary Herald and Western Witness** and it seems to have been the main Church in use in Lower Achill prior to the construction of the new chapel in Dookinella and the present Church in Pollagh. Fr. Manus Sweeney, hanged in Newport in 1798, is said to have been born in Dookinella Thulis and a nearby monument commemorates his death.

Although Leask (1937) attributed a twelfth-century date and the late Professor M. J. O'Kelly (1942) a fourteenth-century date, the upstanding remains of Kildavnet Church suggest an earlier date still, probably of the Early Medieval Period. There is a record of it being renovated in the Middle Ages, probably by the incumbent of the nearby Tower House, locally called Grace O'Malley's Castle. The plain rectangular shape with no distinction between nave and chancel, the east-west orientation and the projecting stones on the east gable, reminiscent of the cruck *(pairs of straight timbers set in the ground and inclined to meet and cross at the upper ends to support the roof-tree)* construction of the Early Medieval timber churches, all suggest a date between the 8th and 10th centuries. The Church measures forty-four feet, three inches in length by twenty-two feet, seven inches in width, the walls roughly six feet, six inches high and two feet, six inches thick. Early features to note are the oblong slit in the west gable, the south-facing door, five feet, nine inches high by three feet, seven inches wide, the overhead lintel and the two small square recesses on either side of the doorway. Although the size of the Church with its south-facing doorway are not particularly early features, the very early churches being generally smaller than Kildavnet and with a doorway set in the east gable, the plain rectangular shape and other early features outlined above, all point to a relatively early date. Three wall niches *(aumbries),* two in the east wall and one at the east corner, were probably used to store books and sacred vessels. The graveyard contains many old unmarked graves and clay pipes, once a feature of this graveyard, are sometimes found inserted into the graveyard wall. The graveyard also contains the remains of the victims of the Clew Bay disaster, while a large headstone east of the church covers the remains of

Fr. Gallagher, a local priest who ministered in Achill during the Great Famine. West of the roadway in an extension of the original graveyard is a monument to the victims of the Kirkintilloch disaster. The dedication is to St. Davnet or Dympna.

2. BOOLEY VILLAGES

" *Booleying*" or Transhumance was practised in Ireland and on the Continent for hundreds, if not thousands, of years. It is defined as the movement of livestock, usually cattle, from a permanent lowland settlement to summer pasture frequently in the mountains. Originally it involved movement by the whole family but in more recent times only certain family members, accompanied the livestock to the booley at the beginning of May, where they remained until September-October. Return to the permanent village was celebrated by a festival, which coincided with the old pagan festival of Lughnasa. Near Annagh Booley Village is a place called Lugh, probably commemorating one of the most famous Gods of the Celtic pantheon. In Dooagh, close to *Abha Teangaí*, a small river commemorates, *Aibhlin*, one of the Celtic female deities. Booley villages are found mainly in the west of the island, and reflect former patterning in the townland system with, for example, a permanent village in Keel East and a booley in Keel West. Other deserted villages reflect once permanent villages which went out of use in the population decline after the Great Famine, some of which were reused as booleys so the settlement pattern cannot be understood unless cognisance is taken of these spatial movements. The place name, *buaile* the Irish word for booley is, however, confined to the Corraun peninsula and reflected in the placenames of *"Boleycloghan"* and *"Bolinglanna."*

Horses and donkeys were taken to the booley to bring down milk and butter and to bring back provisions. The houses or *bothógs* were constructed of stone and sods, the roof of *scraws and creataí*; some houses had chimneys or a *"poll a 'deataig "* (a smoke hole) on the top of the gable. The door was not very high and people had to stoop going in. The houses were of different sizes to accommodate several families or " *kin groups.*" All the houses had a *"sraideoge"* (shakedown or bed) and all had a table. Food consumed at the booley included potatoes, *"churn-*

butter," fish, milk, eggs and limpets. In Corraun, a line of stones led from the village to the booley to guide *"man and horse"* in foggy conditions. Recreational activities at the booley, included dancing and singing. On the last Sunday of October, before *Samhain*, there was a special concert in the booley with people from neighbouring villages attending. The cyclical nature of the celebrations are of interest and probably reflect older, seasonal patterning, remembered now only in folklore.

Booley huts are difficult to date; many are circular of corbelled construction and unmortared stone walls; others are sub-rectangular or transitional types, between the round and the rectangular house. The sub-rectangular type consists of a single-roomed interior ground plan with rounded exterior corners; extant examples have no window or chimney and are often built up against an earthen bank. They are located in remote upland areas where pasture is available for one season only and generally are only accessible on foot, and then only during the summer months.

3. CAIRNS AND LEACHTAÍ CUIMHNE CÁIN

Cairns and *Leachtaí* construction have been a feature of the Irish landscape since the Neolithic period; these structures, consisting as they do of mounds of stone have no diagnostic features and cannot be dated precisely unless associated with other datable structures or by excavation. Cairns and *leachtaí* are commonly found on hill tops like the three groups in Achill - on Keel Hill north of the Achill Island Pottery Shop, on the top of a flat plateau overlooking Kildavnet quartz quarry and along an ancient *"coffin route"* on top of the Minaun Cliffs in Keel. Contemporary references indicate that some of the cairns on Minaun were erected by Mr. Bald, a surveyor who carried out a trigonometrical survey in Achill in 1809. The datum height recorded for Meenan was 1512 feet and 1530 feet from *Myles' Monument*. Although some cairns were specifically constructed to cover burials, it was also common practice to deposit single stones to mark the spot where a coffin rested on its journey to the graveyard, leading ultimately to a sizeable cairn. A similar practice recorded by Bartlett in an engraving used by the Halls was noted in Connemara. The three sites referred to above are all associated with old roadways and local folklore maintains that an old fort was located on Keel Hill in the vicinity of the cairns. There is a tradition in Achill that people from Lower Achill (area west of Bunacurry) were taken to Kildavnet for burial, via an old pathway over the Minaun Cliffs, into Dooega and through Bunafahy. This resulted from intermarriage between people from Upper Achill and Lower Achill, the spouse from Upper Achill seemingly insisting on burial with his/her own people. It may also be that the only Church in use at that time was the one in Kildavnet. A small Church in Dookinella Thulis was in use from the mid to late 19th century but there was no associated graveyard, except for a cillín (children's graveyard) in the vicinity. The great dilapidation of Slievemore Church and the absence of clearly marked grave-slabs of the period make it unlikely that this graveyard was in use at this time. However, a detailed graveyard survey by qualified personnel is necessary to establish the period of usage of the old graveyard in Slievemore. The proximity of this graveyard to the Deserted Village of Slievemore makes it a likely repository of important information relating to the village.

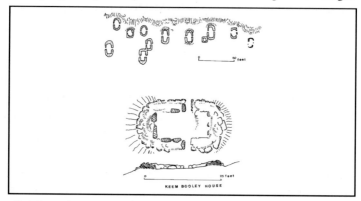

42. Plan of Keem Bay Village, after Piggott (1954).

Records relating to the Great Famine contain harrowing tales of people endeavouring to carry corpses from Lower Achill along the *"Coffin Route-Mass Path"* from Keel to Kildavnet, many never completing the journey and many of the stone cairns along this routeway may mark the burial places of these famine victims. The Kildavnet cairns, some twenty one in all with a larger central example, may well commemorate a major tragic event. These cairns are small, between two and three feet in height, the central cairn of more substantial size and construction than the others. There is no commemoration or date but the general construction suggests they may date to the period of the Great Famine. Most of the *leachtaí* on top of Minaun may represent stations where the coffin rested *en route* to Kildavnet for burial. The labour involved in transporting a coffin up the slopes of a steep mountain is formidable and would have been undertaken only in response to a long-held tradition. There is a small but most unusual cairn, pyramidical in shape, located in dense undergrowth in an old graveyard, west of the Slievemore Hotel. It is said to have been erected by Dr. Adams of the Achill Mission in the late 19th century for the purpose of interring his wife's body in an overground stone vault prior to her removal for burial to her native Cavan.

4. CAHERS-CASHELS (CATHAIR-CAISEAL)

"On this island there are three cyclopean cahirs but their stones have been nearly all removed to build the modern little houses which are nearly in as rude a style as the Cahirs ever were. One of these Cahirs is on the summit of a hill in the townland of Cashel and is called Cathair-a-Caiseal, I could trace the foundations only, but I met old men who saw their own height of the wall standing. It was 75 feet in diameter. The second Cathair lies in the townland of Tóin a tSean Bháile on a point of the island called Rinn na Leanbh lying opposite Doohoma Point, the stones of this were also removed and the ring of it barely traceable." O'Donovan (1838).

Ringforts, *raths, caiseals* and *cathairs* were contemporary site types, the difference being in the material used in construction: rath and ringforts had earthen banks and *caiseals* and *cathairs,* stone banks. However, it is not unusual to find elements of both combined, the distinction being arbitrary in many cases. These sites would have been the home of the well-to-do farmer practising a mixed farming economy. A wide range of building and agricultural skills was available at this period as well as advanced technology which included metalworking and glass-making. The area enclosed by the Cashel was between eighty and two hundred feet, surrounded by a wall ten feet thick in which was set a single gateway, through which a flagged path led to the dwelling house. The *ringfort/rath/caiseal/cathair* are the most characteristic site of the Iron Age and Early Christian Period.

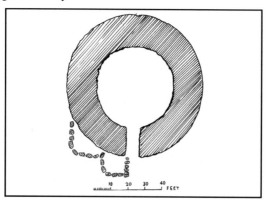

43. Slievemore Caher, after Wood-Martin (1898)

Of the three *caiseal/cathairs* recorded in Achill, two have survived to the present day, the *caiseal* on Cashel Hill and the *cathair* at Caher Point in Dugort; in 1996 a blue glass bead was found in the midden at Caher Point and the site was subsequently excavated by Dr. Ned Kelly of the National Museum. The remains of a wealthy 17th century village was found and recorded. Cashel Hill is strategically located overlooking Salia Bay and Doohoma in Erris. Caher Point and Cashel Hill saw subsequent usage as *cilliní* or childrens' graveyards, while local people claim that bones were noted at the Catháir of Slievemore during demolition. Large " *stone coffins*" not unlike " *lintel graves*" were associated with Cashel Hill, and local legend also attributes a souterrain to this site. Small perforated stone discs (spindle whorls) were noted by a local resident in a nearby field in the 1950's but none survived. Caher Point is a multi-period site and the area recently excavated was probably the remains of *Tóin an tSean Bháile*. Stone-lined graves are aligned in a semi-circle around the perimeter of the Caher and during the National Museum excavation, a grave marker with an inscribed date of 1683, was found, suggesting perhaps that this area may have also been the burial place of the inhabitants of *Tóin an tSean Bháile*. The *cathair* of Slievemore was described by Wood-Martin as more akin to a sepulchre than a fort; *"it had walls four to five feet high, an internal diameter of forty three feet, and walls six feet thick ." Wood-Martin (1898).* A long lintel over the gateway measured six feet six inches long by twenty eight inches wide by ten inches thick. Westropp, who visited the site in 1910, said that the diameter was thirty nine feet and the structure was oval, not circular. The late Professor M. J. O'Kelly visited the site in 1942 and noted that the County Council had removed the stones for roadworks. He described the site as an irregular, circular area of approximately one hundred square feet located close to *"a hard stony track across the bog,"* (now known to be the remains of a pre-bog field wall), which extended southwards.

44. Tower House, Kildavnet © Theresa McDonald

5. CASTLE (TOWER HOUSE)

The Tower House at Kildavnet, locally attributed to Grace O'Malley (1530-1603), is probably an O'Malley Castle but was constructed at least one hundred years before her time c.1429. It is a classic Tower House, representing the home of the strong farmer or local lord. Tower Houses, although a Norman invention were widely copied by the Gaelic Chiefs, so much so that a recent inventory by Barry (1987), indicates that the majority of Tower Houses in the West were owned, not by Norman Lords, but by Gaelic Chieftains. Carrickildavnet was probably one of the £10 castles for which Henry VI provided a grant of £10. This grant was given: *"to every liege-man who would build a castle twenty feet long by sixteen feet wide and forty feet high."*

The Kildavnet Tower House conforms with this description being a rectangular three-storey building, some forty feet (12 metres) high with the remains of a miniature bawn (walled enclosure) on the west side. The tower is neatly battlemented and on the north side over the doorway can be seen the remains of *machicolation*. Small window slits, provided light for the interior rooms and at the same time prevented attackers from gaining entrance. The ground floor is vaulted. The Castle originally had a winding stair, providing access to the floors above, which would have obtained light by the small windows. On the south side there was a *"slop hole,"* a cavity in the wall which allowed the *garderobe* (medieval toilet) to be drained. Defence seems to have been a prime consideration at Kildavnet, indicated by features such as *machicolation,* projecting buttresses along the top of the building which enabled the inhabitants to pour boiling oil or other unpleasant items upon the heads of the attacking force; it is subtly battered and has crenellated parapets. The extremely small bawn probably had a turret attached. These Tower Houses were usually constructed in isolated areas, and in this respect differed from the nucleated settlement preferred by the Anglo-Normans. The Tower House in Kildavnet stands sentinel over the Sound, strategically located to guard entrance to Achill from either Blacksod Bay on the north or Clew Bay on the south. The Tower House in Kildavnet was probably constructed during the period when the O'Malleys were involved in skirmishes with other tribes in *Lorge Owle O'Máille* (end of Ó Máilles Umhall) a large area of thirty six quarters, including *Ilane ní Moghere* (great island, probably Clare Island) which was owned by the O'Malleys. The Ó Máilles, as we have seen, are said to be descended from *Clann Umóir* being called after *Maille*, grandson of Cosgrach. *(Obit A.D. 812).*

The most famous Ó Máille was of course Gráinne (Grace O'Malley) a remarkable woman, whose *"name has been recorded for posterity in Elizabethan State papers and in the Sidney, Salisbury and Carew manuscripts and the Dictionary of National Biography. "* Chambers (1983). Her name is carved in legend in the West of Ireland, and her daring sea-faring exploits are perhaps tinged with some nostalgia, for she witnessed, and fought against, the subjugation of the old Irish order by the British Empire.

6. CAUSEWAY

A causeway differs from a crossing-place (*Coir*) in that it is an artificial construction, commonly found all over Ireland but particularly in marshy areas or in bogs. *Cnoc-na-Ceassaighe* (Hill of the Kesh or wicker causeway) is located south-west of Bolinglanna townland in the Corraun Peninsula. This causeway appears to be heading in a westerly direction and may have provided access across the Sound at *Gubnahardia* before the sea cut its way through to separate the Corraun peninsula from Achill. A promontory fort *Gubnahardin,* located north east of Darby's Point in Cloughmore, was almost totally eroded by this occurrence and, consequently, would seem to indicate that Achill was joined to the mainland in the not so distant past. Other landscape features such as the peat banks bordering the shore also indicate submergence in the recent past. *Beál-na-gGliath (Gob na nGliad)* was the former name of Darby's Point. A sandbank, *na gCliath Mhór,* is a treacherous sandbank located between the north-eastern end of Achill Beg Island and Corraun, and great care has to be taken by fishermen, both when leaving and returning to harbour in order to avoid being marooned on this sandbank. Prior to the introduction of the road system, stepping-stones or fords were used to cross (ford) shallow streams and rivers and are depicted on many of the early Ordnance Survey maps.

7. CAVES

The Ordnance Survey Letters of 1838 briefly mention *Ooghgowan* (Smiths' Cave) in Dooagh. The cave in question is now quite shallow and has no particular features. Nearby is a well which provided water for the village of Dooagh up until the introduction of the community water

Scheme in the 1960's. The cave is located east of Dooagh Village, bordering an old road leading to Keel *via Gob al'Fionáinn* (Gubelennaun) west of Purteen harbour. The *"Priest's Cave"* in Keem Bay, an angular-entranced cave, is located in the cliff face overlooking a small sandy inlet east of Keem Bay strand. Recent cliff collapse in the immediate area prevents entry and exploration should be avoided because of the unstable nature of the cliff which is continually being undermined by erosion. Harris Stone (1906), who lived in Dooagh at the beginning of the present century, claimed that this cave was the home of a rare species of sea otter, *"nearly black, both on upper and under surfaces, with paler colour beneath the throat."* A stagnant pool with leafy ferns at the back of the cave was said to be the pool used by the otter, but the elevation of this cave relative to present-day sea-level makes it an unlikely home for any sea creature. Priests, during Penal times, were prevented by law from carrying out their ministry and were executed if caught so doing; to avoid this fate, they tended to say Mass in out-of-the way places, like Keem Bay, where in the event of detection, rapid escape could be effected. The Penal altar in Keem Bay located north of the Coastguard Station was where Mass was said during the Penal times. Many place names in the area, including the *Priest's Cave,* and *Gaoi Saggart* reflect this activity.

In the Ordnance Survey Name Books Mayo, *Uaim na Bhaocan* (Cave of the Periwinkles) south-west of Dooega is mentioned but nothing is known about this particular cave. Caesar Otway mentioned a cave on Slievemore, probably *Daras Mór* where Fr. Manus Sweeney supposedly hid while trying to avoid capture in 1798. Local folklore is full of tales about caves, some said to be located near the Napoleonic Tower, others *en route* to Annagh and several others along the coast from Slievemore to Saddle Head.

8. CILLINÍ

Cilliní represent the graveyards of unbaptised children who were denied Christian burial because of the Catholic Church's adherence to archaic customs and because of this the children were, until recently, denied burial in consecrated ground. Resulting from this, sites with a folk memory of sanctity or ritual were chosen for internment of the infants; ringforts, caiseals and former graveyards being the preferred choices in Achill. Clusters of crude, uninscribed small boulders or slabs are all that remain to testify to the burial place of these infants. O'Donovan in the Ordnance Survey Letters (1838-40) says: *"In the townland of Slievemore there is a Killeen or small graveyard which contained a Church dedicated to St. Colman, in the north east part stands a mutilated cross, the arms of which are said to have been broken off by four tyrants, Coman, Cuimin, Henry and Puca, who made an incursion into Achill and at the same time burned down the house of one Dubhdara O'Malley which stood near the western extremity of the churchyard, but I could get no account of who they were or where or when they lived."* There is an obituary notice for a Dubhdara Ó Máille in 1219 A.D. which may suggest that the Henry referred to was Henry Butler, later Lord of Aikill and Umhall. The presence of a *Cillín* in Slievemore graveyard is unusual and suggests that the graveyard and Church were no longer in use, otherwise such internments would have been prohibited.

9. CLACHÁNS

The clachán emerged from the old tribal system where related family units shared land in common. It had evolved as a result of family expansion, when sons and daughters grouped their houses around the original homestead. Even a cursory examination of family units in any of the Achill villages today will show how the practice has continued to the present day. The clachán is defined as *"a group of dwellings clustered together without formal plan, having no associated church or school."* Proudfoot (1959). Place name evidence can indicate the location of former clacháns e.g. *Tóin an tSean Bháile* (bottom of the old town), although recent excavation at this site produced artifacts which indicate, not clachán dwellers, but a wealthy community, having Manganese and Buckley ware, elaborate clay pipes and alcohol. They kept cattle, sheep and pigs, and lived in relatively comfortable houses. (Dr. Ned Kelly, *pers. comm.*). *Baile Ailt* in Cloughmore, is another substantial settlement, the size of the houses suggesting a well-to-do community. *Baile Thuas* and *Baile Thios* in Dookinella Thulis were associated with a Church which contravenes Proudfoot's definition of a clachán. Therefore, few, if any, of the Achill sites conform to the classic definition of a clachán. *Leath Baile* north-west of Slievemore, Old Dugort and Cabán in Dookinella may qualify on the grounds of size, arrangement and the absence of a Church. *Tuar* and *Tuar Riábhach* in The Deserted Village in Slievemore have been designated as clacháns by Maginess (1965) but the former presence of a Church in Slievemore graveyard would call this into question. The word clachán is ambiguous in that the word was only introduced into Ireland by a Scot named, John Donaldson, in the eighteenth century, who used it to describe contemporary settlements, while the name clachán has subsequently been applied to settlements of both earlier and later periods.

The *baile* place-name is commonly associated with the clachán but as has been outlined above, the term clachán is of recent date. *Baile* is also synonymous with a homestead or a cluster of houses. Recent investigations in the Deserted Village in Slievemore, by the **Achill Archaeological Summer School,** indicates multi-period construction in *Tuar,* the earliest example probably dating to the Late Medieval Period. Bearing this in mind, and taking into consideration the presence of a Church in the nearby graveyard of Slievemore, the only phase that could conceivably conform to Proudfoot's (1959) hypothesis would be that of the nineteenth century settlement, after the graveyard had gone out of use. More work needs to be carried out on clacháns to determine their precise chronology and association. The Achill examples would seem to confirm the hypothesis of Barry, (1987), that there is no secure evidence that clacháns existed in Ireland prior to the nineteenth century. An integral part of the clachán was the associated Rundale system where land was held in common, the strips or plots being periodically redistributed as population increased. After the Great Famine, when the population decreased, there was need for consolidation of farms into single holdings and many clacháns disappeared.

10. COASTGUARD STATIONS

Coastguard Stations were constructed by the British Government prior to the First World War (World War I) to guard strategic locations in Ireland and to serve as *"lookout points ."* Many were also built in the 1880's -1890's. The first coastguard station in Achill was built in

Bolinglanna in Corraun, a second at Achill Sound and a third at Darby's Point in Cloughmore. The latter, a beautiful building, was demolished to make way for a Salmon Farming Station. Others were erected at Keel and Keem Bay. The Keel station was later acquired by Alexander Hector of the Achill Fishery and subsequently became a Hotel called The Bervie after Hector's place of birth in Scotland.

11. CRANNÓGS (CRANNÓGA)

Crannógs are the lacustrine equivalents of the ringfort and caiseal, the homes of the rich farmer or wealthy lord. Their complexity and size suggest a large and skilled labour force, competent in wood-working, craftsmanship and construction methods. Crannógs are artificial islands set in small marshy lakes and difficult to access; natural islands were also utilised as crannógs. There are over twelve hundred crannógs in Ireland. They were constructed by embedding vertical stakes in the lake bottom bed to anchor a compacted radial timber platform with criss-crossed layers of brushwood, on top of which was constructed a wooden building(s). The term *crannóg* comes from *crann*, the Irish word meaning a tree. An associated feature of the crannóg was an enclosing perimeter palisade which provided a stable encompassing framework as well as a close-set fence, giving additional protection to the inhabitants. Edwards (1990). Some had a wooden causeway to provide access to dryland, others were accessed by boat and had small jetty's constructed to tie up canoes and boats.

The crannóg in Dookinella Calvy is locally called Loughannaderriga (lakelet of the oaks) and likewise by Wood-Martin who partially excavated it in 1888, but it is depicted as Loughannascaddy on the Ordnance Survey maps, causing some confusion between this lake and another of the same name in the Valley. At Loughannaderriga, dense foliage of rowan and bilberry provide exotic colouring in summer, contrasting markedly with the bare and barren surrounding bog. The crannóg is surrounded by a marshy lake and quaking bog, the latter akin to quicksand and to be avoided at all costs. Wood-Martin described Loughannaderriga as an "imperium in imperio", and the only authenticated crannóg in Mayo! A substantial palisade surrounding this crannóg was visible during the exceptionally dry summer of 1984 which would suggest a much larger crannóg than that currently visible. There is some slight evidence that access to this crannóg was *via* a causeway and jetty; in addition, a canoe blade was found here by Wood-Martin as well as a fragment of a beam, *"mortised at one extremity, its quadrangular incision which did not penetrate the plank, was saucer-shaped at the bottom, and a unique arrangement of a peg-hole in each corner shows the firm manner in which it had been originally secured; it probably belonged to the framework of a wooden hut. "* Wood-Martin (1886).

Lakeside dwellings, the forerunners of crannógs, originated in the Late Bronze Age but crannógs as described on page 261, only came into use in the Early Medieval Period, continuing in use up until the 16th century A.D. in some areas. Defended crannógs may belong to the early part of the Medieval Period c.A.D.500. Artifacts recovered from *Loughannaderriga* by Wood-Martin include a bronze pin, numerous pointed ends of stakes dressed with a sharp metal tool, a whetstone, and numerous white sling-stones consisting of water-worn sea-beach pebbles. There is a reference in the **Annals of Connacht** in A.D. 1415 concerning the plunder by Hugh Ó Máille of Dermot Ó Máille' s island: *" Diarmait thereupon took possession of Clare Island. Ó Maille, King of Umhall was killed there and Diarmait Ó Maille was afterwards made king, and from this time the kingship and lordship departed from the seed of Aed."* *Loughannaderriga* was the home of a wealthy lord, probably an O'Malley, but whether or not it was the island referred to in the Annals in unclear. Wood-Martin, during his excavations at *Loughannaderriga*, found pieces of charred wood as well as burn marks on a wooden vessel. No trace of bone or pottery was found at the level excavated. The crannóg is about eighteen metres in diameter, set in a small lake and surrounded by bog. A local prophesy foretells that three children will be drowned here so local people tend to keep their distance. Crannógs are important repositories of environmental information and *Loughannaderriga,* if scientifically excavated, would no doubt provide important botanical and zoological information, as well as a chronology of environmental change in Achill stretching back over thousands of years. This information is presently sealed within the lake mud and will remain so for as long as the present water-logged conditions apply. However, quarrying operations and drainage connected with turf-cutting are increasingly encroaching upon this very important site and, if allowed to continue, will destroy an important part of Achill's heritage. The area bordering the main road in the immediate vicinity of the crannóg, where recent quarrying operations took place, is unsightly and takes away from the beauty of the crannóg and needs urgent attention.

12. CROSSING (FORDING) PLACE

Before the Achill Sound Bridge was constructed, people crossed from Corraun to Achill *via* stretches of firm sand at low tide. *Gob a'Choire*, is the name given to this area where two opposing tides meet daily. *Caol* (Keel), as in narrow-water, may denote a crossing (fording) while *fersait* (Belfarsad), means a sandbank.Other fording places were at the Mill Stream beside *The Shanty* in Dooagh; at Owenavally River beside The Pub, Dooagh and at the Chongie (Teangaí) River near the present bridge.

Tradition maintains that the demise of the wildlife on Achill (a Deer Drive on Slievemore was mentioned by the Halls in 1841-43) occurred when the bridge was first opened in 1888, allowing the fox access to the island. However, if people could cross *via* a sandbank, so too could the fox and other wildlife. Alexander Hector, of the Achill Fishery, acquired from the trustees of the Achill Mission Estate the right to hunt wildlife throughout the island and this no doubt contributed to the demise of many species in the late nineteenth century. Numerous nineteenth century photographs show seal hunters displaying their trophys outside Seal caves in Dugort and Keel.

13. CURRACH (STANDS) PENS

Professors Stuart Piggott and Terence Powell looking at these structures in the 1940's were intrigued by their shape and construction and wondered what future archaeologists would make of them. Currach pens are long rectangular structures made up of beach pebbles and local stone and can be seen north-west of Dooagh Pier and at Purteen Harbour. The currach, constructed of light planking on wooden ribs, covered outside with tarred canvas, was widely used in Achill. The craft of currach-making has now largely died out although there was some attempt made at a revival in recent years. The origin of the Achill currach is unknown but it differs from that formerly used on Inishkea Island as well as on other nearby islands. This is another site-type that deserves attention; documenting the types of currachs and currach pens in different locations throughout Ireland would no doubt produce some interesting material in the area of vernacular studies! During the Great Famine the Quakers were instrumental in providing funds to have a dozen or more currachs constructed on the island, suggesting that local expertise was available for the task.

14. "DANISH DITCH"

The *"Danish Ditch"* located in the townland of Keel East was first recorded by the Ordnance Survey in 1838-40 and probably had nothing whatever to do with the Danes. The only known excursion of the Vikings into the Achill area was in A.D.812 when King Cosgragh Ó Máille of Umhall was killed. The *" Danish Ditch,"* is a stone-lined bank, now grass covered, extending in an east-west direction immediately south of two megalithic monuments on the eastern end of Slievemore Mountain. On the Ordnance Survey map of 1838-40 it is shown as emanating east of (Keel East (i) MA 62), a probable megalithic tomb, and extending eastwards from this site for about one hundred and forty yards (128 metres), after which it forked northward towards a Court Tomb (Keel East I MA 61) before turning abruptly southward for about two hundred yards (183 metres), along the line of the present access pathway.

Colonel Wood-Martin, who surveyed the Achill tombs in the late nineteenth century, shows the court tomb (MA 61) as having a double court; this was later disputed by the late Professor Ruadhrí de Valéra and Dr. Seán Ó Nualláin in the Survey of the Megalithic Tombs of Ireland, Vol.11. (1950) who said they could find no evidence of a second court and that Wood-Martin may have wrongly interpreted some loose cairn material south of the tomb for a second court. It is also possible that stones from the *Danish Ditch,* which form a curve as it turns southwards, may have misled Wood-Martin to misinterpret this as a second court. The *Danish Ditch* is a pre-bog field wall, similar to those excavated at the Céide Fields in North Mayo. The Keel East example appears to be linking two megalithic structures, one of which has been much altered and therefore designated *"unclassified"* in the **Megalithic Survey of Ireland**. de Valéra & ÓNualláin, (1964) Vol 11 Mayo.

15. DESERTED VILLAGE

The Deserted Village of Slievemore is located at two hundred feet O.D. on the southern slopes of Slievemore mountain, which at 2214 feet (671 m), is the highest mountain in Achill. The village is divided into three distinct groups Tuar, Tuar Riábhach and Faiche. There are a total of about eighty houses in Tuar and Tuar Riábhach and between ten and twenty in Faiche. Over 90% of the houses are aligned north-south, parallel to each other and with their long axis running downhill. The most striking feature of the village is the dominant south-facing gables of the houses which stand in many cases to a height of some 2-3 m. The houses were constructed of unmortared stone, with east-facing doorways and a small, splayed window, located in the north-east wall. The house, was basically a one-roomed rectangular structure, although sometimes an additional room was built-on which was used as a stable or outhouse. Some of the houses are constructed on a platform of stone which was either an earlier dwelling which had been levelled or a terrace to make the site level. Dr. Lucas (1947) noted that this platform extended two feet beyond the southern gable and was about two feet high, and built of small rounded stones:

"This platform was never high enough to level the site completely so that in order to keep the tops of the walls horizontal, the southern end of the houses was higher than the northern, the difference being a foot in one of the best preserved examples." Lucas (1947).

During the last occupation phase of the village in the nineteenth century, the cows were tethered at the southern end of the house, evidenced by stone and wooden tethering rings which can still be seen in the walls. This typical *western* house is the same as the Mayo House which has been reconstructed at Bunratty Folk Park. A channel sloping towards the front door drained liquid effluent into a manure pit, where it remained until sufficient had accumulated to manure the nearby fields and potato beds *(lazy beds)*. These stone-lined manure pits and other constructional features noted may represent the remains of an older building phase. The opposing doorways seen in many of the houses were to facilitate the milking of cattle as cows were taken in one door, milked, and then taken out through the back door.

45. House in Deserted Village © Ursula Kavanagh

Houses containing this ancient constructional feature may belong to an earlier building phase. The earliest documented occurrence of the *"double-doorway"* feature in Ireland is at Leacanabuaile, a site containing two constructional phases, with a round house followed by a rectangular house. This same feature was noted at Gateholm Island in Wales and dated to the Late Roman period, perhaps suggesting a transition of this feature from Britain.

A study of the field systems and the *"lazy beds"* surrounding the Deserted Village indicate several occupation phases, substantiated in the recent excavations at the Deserted Village. McDonald, Interim Report (1996). John O'Donovan in the Ordnance Survey letters, (1838-40) refers to the plunder and burning of the house of Dubhdara O' Máille (Obit.A.D. 1219) west of the churchyard, indicating settlement here during the Anglo-Norman period. A major research project involving intensive field survey, selective excavation, together with palynological and geological research should be a priority, in this Achill's premier

19. Guide to the Archaeological Sites of Achill

tourist attraction, and should be incorporated *via* a structured Research Design within the proposed plans to provide an Interpretative Centre for this site.

The desertion of the village was brought about by a combination of circumstances over a long period of time. Sir Richard O'Donnell, who had inherited an almost bankrupt estate in 1827 saw his family's fortunes decline still further through mismanagement, famine etc. resulting in him having to dispose of two-thirds of his Achill Estate through the Encumbered Estates Court to the Achill Mission and others in 1851-52. Eviction for non-payment of rent, especially during Sir Richard's tenure of Achill would have hastened the demise of the village. The 1845-49 famines with the consequent failure of the potato crop in each of five successive years, resulted in the inhabitants moving to Dooagh, a village close to the sea on the south side of the island which had been occupied simultaneously with the Deserted Village in Slievemore. Emigration during and after the various famines and again in the 1880's further accelerated demographic movement of population. When the Achill Mission Estate became the landlords in 1851-52, it is possible that further pressures would have been brought to bear on the tenants. That this was indeed the case is reflected in an eye-witness account of the village in 1855-56, 3-4 years after the Mission acquired ownership:

"In approaching the Colony, the road winds along the base of Slievemore. Here the ruins of a Deserted Village strike the eye unpleasantly, and should be removed, as they disadvantageously occupy the ground." Howard (1855).

The Deserted Village of Slievemore was used as a booley up until the 1940's, the last area in Ireland where this practice was documented. Graham (1953). The late Heinrich Böll (1957) provided a description of Slievemore that ensures that virtually all German tourists coming to Ireland visit this site: *" Suddenly, as we reached the brow of the mountain, we saw the skeleton of the Deserted Village lying on the nearest slope. Nobody had told us about it, nobody had warned us; there are so many deserted villages in Ireland. The Church, the shortest way to the strand had been pointed out to us and the shop in which teas, bread, butter and cigarettes could be had, also the news agent, the Post Office and the little harbour in which the harpooned sharks lay in the mud by the tide like upturned boats with their backs uppermost if the latest tide had not by chance turned over their white bellies from which the liver had been cut out - that seemed worth noting but not the deserted village: grey -like shaped stone gables which we saw without deep perspective, like set-up scenes for a ghost film: with bated breath we tried to count them, gave up at forty, a hundred would be more correct. The next curve of the path brought us to another distance and now we saw it from the side: awaiting the carpenter: grey stone walls, dark window spaces, not a bit of wood, no waste stuff, nothing coloured; like a corpse without hair, without eyes, without flesh and blood; the skeleton of a village, shuddering in its structure, there the main street; and the curve where there is a round space must have been a pub. An adjoining alley, still another. All that was not stone, eaten away from rain, sun and wind - and from time, which patiently dripped over all: twenty-four great drops per day: the acid which eats all away go unnoticed like resignation..."* (translated from the German by the late Brother Angelo Holmes).

16. ENCLOSURES

Enclosures, distinguished from ringforts by their larger size, are found throughout Achill; some may have been sheep or cattle folds, while others may have a prehistoric origin. They can be either round or rectangular in shape and of various sizes. Some of these enclosures date to the pre-Norman period. A large oval-shaped enclosure on Cashel Hill uncovered after peat clearance may be prehistoric in origin. Other smaller, rectangular examples can be seen on Keel Hill, adjacent to a river bank north of Dooagh village, in a field close to the beach at Dooniver and at Baile Ailt north of Kildavnet Church.

17. FULACHTA FIADH (BURNT MOUNDS)

Only one *fulachta fiadh* has been noted in Achill, in a remote area close beside Lough Bunnafreva East near Saddle Head, though others undoubtedly exist.The Bunnafreva example is a roughly oval or kidney-shaped grass-covered depression located on the northern edge of the lake. *fulachta fiadh* were ancient cooking places supposedly used by the

19. Guide to the Archaeological Sites of Achill

Fianna, a band of young warriors led by the celebrated Fionn Mac Cumaill. However, there is increasing evidence to suggest that they may represent former settlement sites, dating between the Early Bronze Age and the early historic period. Experiments carried out at Ballyvourney in Co. Cork. O'Kelly (1954), indicate that cooking practised at *fulachta fiadh* was similar to that described by Geoffrey Keating in his ***History of Ireland*** in the seventeenth century. The stone-lined trough was filled with water and a fire lit in the immediate vicinity. Stones were placed in the fire and when red-hot were thrown into the trough where the water was quickly brought to boiling point. A joint of meat, usually wrapped in straw was placed in the boiling water until fully cooked. Hot stones added at intervals maintained the heat necessary to cook the meat. Repeated usage of the *fulachta fiadh* eventually resulted in the creation of a horse-shoe-shaped mound, the result of stones being thrown up on three sides of the trough, the fourth side being left open for access. The majority of these structures both in Britain and Ireland date to the Bronze Age. Archaeologists, Christy Lawless and Gerry Walsh, found more than a dozen in one field on the outskirts of Castlebar. Buckley & Lawless (1987). This may give credence to Mick Monk's (U.C.C.)theory (*pers.comm.*) that *fulachta fiadh* may be associated with feasting upon return from the booley in the autumn.

18. HOLY WELLS

"As regards the blessed or holy wells, there was one on a farm at the foot of Slievemore at which the islanders performed stations, by going around twenty one times on their bare knees until the blood made its way through the skin; and each time they went round the well they would put a piece of red cloth in a hole in the wall and take up a small stone in lieu of the same." Howard (1855).

The holy wells in Achill are associated with Early Medieval sites or *Cilliní* and the two are probably connected.*Tobar Colman* in Slievemore graveyard has been reconstructed and is circular in shape and edged with flat slabs of stone and surrounded by a low circular stone wall about five feet in height. The entrance is *via* a gap on the south about three feet wide. In 1947, Dr. Lucas noted an empty rectangular recess inside the wall which was covered by a lintel, or a slab of stone, upon which stood a small concrete cross; a few yards west of the well was an upright stone about one-and-a-half feet high. Associated with the holy well are the remains of a small Church, several ancient stone crosses and a *Killeen (Oratory)*, all of which combined suggests an Early Medieval site. The presence of a *cillín* in this graveyard, however, suggests abandonment of the site sometime in the Late Medieval Period.

Tobar Davnet, not in its original position, is now located outside the eastern graveyard wall at Kildavnet; it too is associated with an early Church and numerous stone crosses in the graveyard. A holy well on Achill Beg Island, called the *Blessed Well,* is located about a quarter of a mile east of Dún Kilmore promontory fort and south of the former village overlooking *Trá Bó Dearg,* a beautiful sandy beach.

Tobar Fionnáin (Finian's Well), reconstructed in 1989 by a local priest, Fr. Cosgrave, is located on the banks of a waterfall, at the far eastern end of Keel beach beside the Minaun cliffs. Local legend claims that a flat stone, with an inscription on it was located here but was removed by persons unknown some years ago. The inscription was supposedly written in Irish and in Latin which may suggest an ogham stone. Another legend, common throughout Ireland, as any perusal of folklore collections will confirm, tells how the well was *"fouled by some of Nangle's lads,"* after which it dried up. Recently, however, the well was revived, blessed and re-opened to visitation. An inscribed stone has been set up beside the well. There is another well located north of house number 42 in *Tuar Ríabhach* which John Toolis, Crumpaun claimed originally had an inscribed flat stone lining the floor of the well. The water in this well is now quite murky and recent examination revealed no trace of this slab.

19. HUT FOUNDATIONS

The most common site type in Achill is the ubiquitous hut site, of round or rectangular form and probably ranging in date from the prehistoric to the post famine period. Westropp (1914) noted the foundations of two hut

19.   Guide to the Archaeological Sites of Achill

sites north of the road at Camport near Dooega which have now almost
completely disappeared, but the field systems in the immediate area are
of interest and may well be prehistoric in origin. One of these hut sites
consisted of a circle of turf-sods with stone facings, ten feet thick and ten
feet in diameter, reminiscent of medieval examples. A second group of
roughly circular hut sites can be seen in the townland of Keel East and
Bal of Dookinella and may represent pre-famine settlements or the
remains of former clacháns. In the same area, north of the main road in
Bal of Dookinella is another group of large, roughly rectangular
structures which may represent the remains of the former village of Bal
mentioned in the Irish Folklore Commission files (U.C.D.) as being
occupied prior to the advent of the Achill Mission. At Bellanasally, near
Dugort, are the remains of several hut structures, probably the remains of
a former pre-famine village. On Cashel Hill, at the two hundred foot
contour are the remains of several, relatively well preserved unmortared
stone houses, aligned along an old roadway, locally called *An Bótar
Mhór,* probably the route-way taken by J. B.Trotter in 1815 on his way
to Minaun and the village of Keel. Another group is located south-west
of the Napoleonic Tower which are probably of eighteenth century date.
Nearly all of the promontory forts have associated hut sites, some
conjoined, others either round or rectangular in shape. On the southern
side of the road, south-west of Corrymore House in Dooagh, are the
remains of a group of primitive houses of unknown date. They may also
have been associated with an old road, running along the sea shore which
connected Dooagh with Keem Bay.

At Gubelennaun (*"Gob Aill Fhionnáin, the other Minaun"*) close to
Ooghgowan (Smith's Cave) are the foundations of two rectangular hut
sites, aligned along an extension of the old roadway in Dooagh, which
connected this village with that of Keel. All of the old roadways in Achill,
apart from the one traversing the hillside from Dookinella to Cashel and
the old pathway on Slievemore mountain which connects the Deserted
Village with the megalithic tombs, were coastal based of necessity, due
to the interior of the island probably being heavily wooded or peat

covered. The present road system was laid down by Mr. Bald, an engineer, in 1836.

In Annagh, beside the remains of a Portal Tomb, is a stone hut, locally called the Scotch House, which was erected by Alexander Hector, a Scotsman involved in salmon fishing in Achill in the mid to late 19th century. The late Cyril Gray, Dugort, claimed that Hector robbed stones from the nearby tomb and used some in the foundations of his hut and a large orthostat as an overhead door lintel. West of the Bervie Hotel in Keel are the foundation marks of a beehive hut which survived into the present century. This was described by Morton (1930) as " *one of the few primitive huts still in occupation is in this part of Achill. This beehive hut is circular and the smoke of the turf fire drifts from a hole in the roof. It is really a stone tent.*" Morton compares this beehive hut to the *"black houses"* on the Isle of Skye in Scotland. Harris Stone (1906) thought that this was the oldest house in Achill and probably in Mayo for *"unlike other cottages it has rounded corners and a pole supporting the turf roof. The only attempt at a window being a hole in the roof about six inches in diameter."* A different type of house was described by the late Professor M.J. O'Kelly (1942), which he reconstructed, conjecturally, from descriptions given locally and appears to describe the extant booley houses: " *this type would seem to have been circular in plan and built of stone on the corbelled principle until a height of about 5 feet was reached. There was then a conical roof of thatch held down with grass ropes weighted with stones. It is not clear what the exact arrangements of the timbers was, but there was not a central post! The lower ends of the timbers rested on the top of the wall and the upper ends were crossed and bound with grass rope. On the roof outside, a layer of "scraws" was laid on, followed by thatch, and the whole secured with ropes. There was no window or chimney and the smoke found its way out through the door."* Teach Briste (the*"broken"* or *"poor house"*) is located under a grassy mound beside Keel Caravan Park Office on Keel Sandybanks.

20. ICE HOUSES

In Bolinglanna close to the sea is a house locally known as the *Ice House* which was used by Alexander Hector to preserve salmon prior to exportation. In winter, the ice was collected in blocks and transported by local women from a lake high on Corraun Hill. They were paid the princely sum of one shilling per bucket of ice by Hector, who now had several fish processing and preserving stations throughout the island. There was another Ice House at the Bervie Hotel and ice taken from Keel Lake during the winter was used here to preserve salmon. Mrs. Colohan of the Achill Island Pottery Shop, claims that carts, pulled by horses were backed on to Keel Lake where the ice was cut in blocks and loaded on to the carts and transported to a semi-underground chamber at what is now the Bervie Hotel. Both of the above operations suggest much colder winters than apply at the present time, for it is rare sight today to see Keel Lake frozen to the extent described.

21. KEEM BAY VILLAGE

The late John Moran, born in 1900, was unaware of the existence of a village in Keem Bay so it must have gone out of use prior to the 19th century. Drawings exist which show the village apparently occupied into the early 1900's while *"the village of Kim, a little to the east of the diamond amethyst quarry"* is mentioned in the Ordnance Survey Letters (1838-40). Harris Stone (1906) described Keem as *" totally uninhabited, ruined cabins used by boys and girls for summer booleys."* When William Blacker acquired the lands of Keel West townland from the Achill Mission Estate around 1855 grazing livestock and booleying was prohibited in this area. The similarity in the morphology of the houses in Keem Bay and Bunowna Booley village suggest contemporaneity.

The grass-covered foundation marks of some twelve houses can be clearly seen north of the former Coastguard Station, which is now owned by Michael and Zoe O'Connor and their family.The Ordnance Survey map (Sheet 41) shows a total of 41 houses here originally. The O' Malleys (Pub) in Dooagh claim that ancestors of theirs lived in Keem up until the mid 19th century but the houses above suggest a much older tenancy, a view substantiated by Professor Stuart Piggott who surveyed and planned this village during a visit to the island in 1946-47 and, according to him: *"their grass-grown ruins suggest an antiquity far beyond the last century."* The houses in Keem are of great interest for they appear to have been substantial buildings, all had opposing (double) doorways, and interestingly enough their location is close to the re-constructed Penal Altar and the area where two ogham stones were found in the 1940's.

22. MANOR HOUSE

When Captain Charles Cunningham Boycott arrived in Achill in 1857, he and a friend (cousin?), Murray MacGregor Blacker, leased the townland of Keel West from William Blacker who had previously acquired the lease from the Achill Mission Estate. They resided first at Keem Bay, prior to the construction of Corrymore House, where they subsequently lived. One of these houses is referred to in folklore and by Howard (1855) as an *"iron house,"* seemingly similar to those pre-fabricated houses shipped to Australia to accommodate the first settlers. The entrance to Corrymore House was formerly called "the Iron Gates", a name that now seems to have gone out of use. We have seen in the Achill Mission section how Boycott was charged with looting a shipwrecked freighter for iron and removing it to his premises.The remains of the small manor house in Keem Bay north of the ruins of Keem Bay village is unusual with cell-like rooms at the rear which may have had a military function at some stage. Captain Boycott abandoned this house when Blacker emigrated to the U.S.A. or else after it was burned down, and moved to Corrymore, which he preferred.

23. MEDIEVAL FIELD SYSTEMS

On Slievemore mountain Late Medieval field systems are intermingled with *"lazy bed"* cultivation ridges, both of which are distinct from the later 19th century strip fields which are superimposed upon them. Field systems are very difficult to date without excavation: the only dated Early Medieval examples are those from Lough Gur in County Limerick Ó Riordáin (1940), which are practically identical to nearby modern field systems. Small square fields are generally associated with the *árd* or wooden plough and elongated fields of *ridge-and-furrow* with the mouldboard plough which was introduced into Ireland around A.D. 600. There are several fine examples of *ridge-and-furrow* near the old village of Bunafahy and in nearby Cloughmore, in Slievemore and on Achill Beg Island.

24. MEGALITHS

" Megalithic remains on the island of Achill are most interesting, and present every variety of ancient sepulchre." Caesar Otway (1839).

Megalith means *"large stone"* and megalithic tombs erected during the Neolithic period by the first farmers to Ireland can be found from Malta to Scandinavia and from Spain and Portugal to the West of Ireland. There are four types of megalithic tomb: Court, Portal, Passage and Wedge; Boulder Burials have recently been added to this category, none of which have been found in Achill. Achill has court and portal tombs, the main concentration of which is located on the southern slopes of Slievemore Mountain. They are usually depicted on maps as *" Giants Grave"*, *"Druids Altar"* etc. They were used for communal burial over many generations, and the burial rites of both inhumation and cremation were practised. There is some evidence also for excarnation, the practice of leaving a dead body exposed to the elements until it had been defleshed, after which the bones, often disarticulated, were inserted into the tomb.

Portal tombs like the one in the townland of Dugort West and another in Annagh were constructed around the same time as the court tombs c.3500 b.c. or about 5000 years ago. In 1996 students of the **Achill Archaeological Summer School** inspected the remains of what appears to be a portal tomb in Cloughmore which was brought to the author's attention by Mrs. Mary Teresa O'Keefe and Mr. Jimmy Kilbane. The site-locational preference for the portal tomb differs slightly from that of the court tomb builders, the former generally preferring locations around the 100 to 150 feet contours, the latter generally higher elevations. Court tombs consist of a circular or oval court, the entrance of which is delineated by two portal or *"door"* stones. At right angles to the court is the gallery, containing between one and three chambers, roofed by a capstone(s). Variation on this basic theme is found north of an east-west line between Dundalk and Galway.

Achill

The Megaliths are the most visible monuments in the countryside and consequently there is a substantial body of folklore associated with them, e.g. the resting places of *Diarmuid and Gráinne,* homes of the ancient Fianna, etc. The Slievemore tombs are concentrated at the eastern end of Slievemore in an area of year-round pasture with excellent clay soils and water supply, the latter contained in the many streams which course down the mountainside. Their location at the margins of present-day cultivation suggest that they may have been constructed just above the tree-line when the island was completely forested. Out of eleven sites recorded by Wood-Martin in 1898, only six sites were located by the late Professor Ruadhrí de Valéra and Dr. Seán Ó Nualláin, in 1950 *i.e.* three court tombs, a portal tomb and two unclassified sites.

46. Bal of Dookinella Court Tomb (MA 63) ©Lawrence Collection

Recently, the remains of a number of almost completely destroyed sites have been located in Bal of Dookinella by students of the **Achill Archaeological Summer School** and plans of these will be published in the near future. There is a also mention in recently collected folklore of Slievemore i.e. *Teach an Liag Mhór* in Tonalorcha, a site diligently searched for by de Valéra and Ó Nualláin but not found. At the apex of the group of megaliths in Slievemore, between the 500 and 600 foot contour, is a magnificent court tomb, aligned north-south, with an oval forecourt set at right angles to the gallery containing two chambers, the southern chamber covered by a huge capstone. This tomb would originally have been covered by a trapezoidal (coffin-shaped) cairn. Immediately south of the tomb and extending in a westerly direction is the *"Danish Ditch" (An Cloidhe Lochhlannach)* which leads to another tomb, presently unclassified. This is a very interesting site and was described by O'Connor of the Ordnance Survey (1838) as a *"cemetery, much disfigured by the natives, who have converted the square graves into fialtáns, or lamb houses. At the west side of this group of graves is a small tumulus, hollowed at the top, and containing a few small loose stones in the hollow. This is said to have been a kiln in ancient times, but I think it is a sepulchral tumulus."* O'Connor (1838-40). I agree with O'Connor! Southward, near an ancient roadway emanating in the Deserted Village, is a portal tomb, marked on the Ordnance Survey maps as a *"Giants Grave."* This tomb is again aligned on a north-south axis and is badly damaged. The remains of what appears to have been a circular cairn can be seen on the eastern side close to the fallen capstone. Also on the east is a large slab with rounded edges which may be the stone referred to by O'Donovan in the Ordnance Survey Letters (1838-40) as the stone which *"an impious miller commenced to make a millstone,"* the miller needless to say died shortly afterwards! The backstone is missing and may have been set into a stone-lined bank to the east where several other large orthostatic stones can be seen. This tomb is the most accessible of the Achill megaliths and replacement of the capstone to its former position would provide a tourist attraction to rival that of Poulnabrone in Co. Clare, one of the most impressive megaliths in Ireland. Another good reason to excavate this site and re-erect the capstone is that no Western portal tomb has yet been excavated. The often debated question as to which is oldest in date, the court or the portal might then be answered satisfactorily. About a quarter of a mile west of the portal tomb and south of the old road is another once-magnificent but now badly damaged tomb, classified by De Valéra and ÓNualláin (1964), as a court tomb but which may belong to the transepted type like the tomb excavated at Behy in North Mayo. In Bal of Dookinella, south of the modern road and a little to the east of McDowell's Hotel, is a very complex tomb, depicted on the Ordnance Survey maps as a *"Pagan Cemetery"* but called *Clochan-na-Stooka* by locals. This site was described by the late Professor M.J. O'Kelly (1942) as a *"group of huts with some sort of enclosing wall"* but was accepted, reluctantly it seems, as a court tomb by the late Ruadhrí de Valéra and Seán Ó Nualláin (1964).

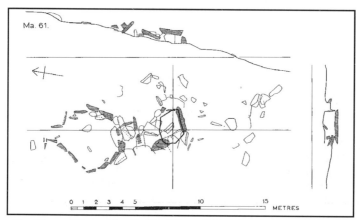

47. Plan of Court Tomb, Keel East (MA 61), after de Valéra & Ó Nualláin (1964)

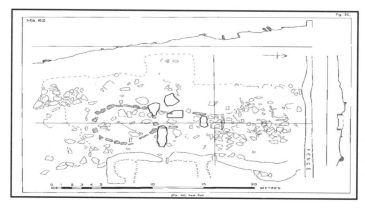

48. Plan of Court Tomb, Keel East (MA 62), after de Valéra & Ó Nualláin (1964)

278

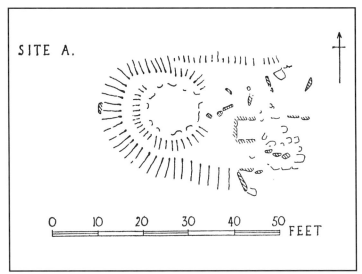

49. Plan of Unclassified Site, Keel East (i), after Piggott & Powell (1947)

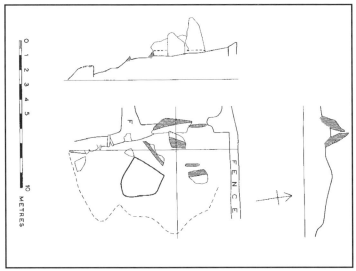

50. Plan of Portal Tomb, Dugort West (MA 64), after de Valéra & Ó Nualláin (1964)

Achill

25. MISSIONARY SETTLEMENT

The contrast between the Settlement in Dugort opposite St. Thomas's Church with that of Keel or Dooagh was stark. The Settlement in Dugort was unlike other settlement forms in Achill, being based on a street plan similar in layout to an English village. It was constructed by the Achill Mission Society in the mid 19th century. Caesar Otway (1839) provided a contemporary description:

" I rose early in the morning and visited the whole range of buildings of which the Settlement is composed. The first of the line to the north is Dr. Adam's house; the next the infant school; then the boys' daily and Sunday school, which has a communion table and reading desk and pulpit, and answers for the present as the chapel; then come the two central houses, forming the residence of the chaplains; next the female school; then the printing office; then the house of the steward; and next the houses of the schoolmasters and scripture-readers." Otway (1839).

A woodcut which was used in February 1846 as a *vignette* for the **Achill Missionary Herald & Western Witness,** a monthly newspaper produced by the Mission which was circulated widely abroad, shows the Settlement as viewed from the new Hotel which John O'Shea (1996) assumes was probably the old Rectory. Some changes had obviously taken place:*"the first house on the left is occupied by the inspecting officer of the Coastguard; the second and third not yet finished, are designed for the assistant Missionary and the converted priests; the next buildings represent the farm offices; and next to them stands the large house, containing, in the lower storey, the kitchen and dining hall of our orphan institution, and in the upper, the male and female school-room and reading room. The range of buildings in the front contain the shop-keeper's residence, the printing office, the home formerly used as the hotel, shop, superintendent's house, the committee room, post office, Church, infant's school and physician's house. The building in the distance behind the flag-staff, is the hospital. The cottages on the mountain represent some of the dwellings of the settlers. The mill and a long line of buildings containing the dormitory and dwelling of the orphans stand to the right of the physician's house and are not* *represented in the sketch."* O'Shea (1996). The illustrations below allow comparison of two contemporary Achill settlements. The Settlement or *"Colony,"* is confined to an area extending from Slievemore, east of the graveyard, to Dugort but does not include Old Dugort.

51. The Settlement c.1850 © National Library of Ireland

52. Keel Village c.1850 © Lawrence Collection

26. NAPOLEONIC TOWER

This Tower, is located on a small hill in Dooagh, appropriately called *Gábhla Fhranca (the French Tower),* with views spanning both Clew Bay and Blacksod Bay, and ideally situated to monitor sea traffic in both areas. It overlooks Dooagh and the Deserted Village in Slievemore and indeed can be seen from most locations in lower Achill. These Towers were built by the British Government during the Napoleonic wars but were later reused during World War I.

Local folklore claims construction materials *e.g.* sand and gravel were brought to the site by horse and cart and the plaster was bonded together using *"ox blood."* North of the tower can be traced the word EÍRE depicted by small quartz boulders, a relic from World War II, visible from the air. South of the tower, at the bottom of the small hill and close to a large rock outcrop, is a linear line of large flag-stones with two short projections at either end on the line, the remains perhaps of an aborted EÍRE sign! Another EÍRE sign can be seen near Rusheen Cove west of Dooagh.

27. OGHAM STONES

The presence of an ogham stone together with a fragment of another is of great importance for it tells us that sometime between the fourth and fifth centuries A.D. and onwards, some people living in Achill were literate. Ogham is based on the Roman alphabet and is represented by parallel lines carved either side of a stem-line, down the sides of tall standing stones, usually commemorating someone of importance. In Ireland, Ogham stones are mainly concentrated in the south-west of the country and may be associated with a pre-Patrician Church. Some would claim that Ogham stones are essentially pagan but many have been found in ecclesiastical sites while others are said to mark tribal boundaries. Bi-lingual (Latin and Old Irish) Ogham stones in Wales testify to Irish settlement by the Deisi in Wales in the 4th century A.D. Ogham stones were also found in Dal Riada, an Irish settlement on the west coast of Scotland.

28. OLD GRAVEYARDS

Old graveyards in Achill are located at Slievemore, Kildavnet, Bunacurry, Caher Point and Dugort. The Slievemore graveyard contains the remains of a small Church, possibly of Early Medieval date. A raised platform in the north-east corner contained a *Killeen* and also a *Cillín* Also located on this platform is a most unusual stone cross, while close by, on the east, are two large orthostats whose presence and function remain unclear.

A small, equal-armed stone cross, can be seen close to the eastern wall of the graveyard while a third (originally one of a pair), also equal-armed, adorn the top of the eastern pillar entrance gatepost. None of the inscribed grave-slabs in the graveyard appear to be earlier than A.D. 1800 but an archaeologically supervised graveyard survey is a necessary prerequisite to the establishment of a precise chronology for the graveyard.

Kildavnet graveyard also contains an early Christian Church, although much of the Early Medieval diagnostic detail has been obliterated during the various renovations to which this Church has been subjected. The Church is a multi-period building, the first known renovation occurring in the Late Medieval Period, the second in recent times. The dedication is to Davnet or Dympna. The graveyard contains gravestones of multi-period date. Early Medieval examples can be seen lying side-by-side with those of eighteenth and nineteenth century date. A large upright monument commemorating the death of a local priest, Fr. Gallagher, *(Obit.* 186*)* who was Parish Priest in Achill during the later famine years, is located east of the Church while a similar monument on the north commemorates a drowning tragedy in Clew Bay. In the adjoining graveyard to the west is a monument to the victims of the Kirkintilloch disaster.

The old graveyard in Bunacurry is now out of use. Grave slabs there indicate a late nineteenth to early twentieth century usage, the last internment being in the 1950's. Two old graveyards on the hillside north of the Slievemore Hotel in Dugort were used by the Achill Mission Society. One of these graveyards may have been the burial place of people from Finsheen, a village now demolished, which was located beside St.Thomas's Church, prior to the arrival of the Achill Mission.

A most unusual monument is located north-west of the above graveyard consisting of a pyramid of earth resting upon a rectangular structure, and secured by cladding of cut, red sandstone, slabs. The pyramid according to local legend covered a casket containing the remains of Mrs. Adams, wife of Dr. Adams who was attached to the Achill Mission. Seemingly, the good doctor not wanting to bury his wife in Achill, had her remains interred above ground and covered by this pyramid, until he himself was leaving Achill and was able to take her with him! Isabella Adams died in 1855 and her husband in 1859. According to the **Achill Missionary Herald**, however, upon Isabella's death, Dr. Adams, had her remains removed to Knockbride, Co. Cavan and there was no mention of a cairn. In addition, if the tale was true, it seems strange that the pyramid was not levelled when the casket was removed! Dr. Adams and his wife were both held in high esteem in Achill and it is possible that the mound was constructed as a *"cenotaph"* to their memory. Other remains in that area suggest a burial ground probably used prior to the arrival of the Achill Mission in 1834.

53. *Caher Point, Dugort* © *Theresa McDonald*

Recently a seventeenth century graveyard was located at Caher Point in Dugort which was probably that used by the inhabitants of the nearby village, *Tóin an tSean Bhaile*, most of which is now covered by sand dunes. A recent (National Museum) excavation here, produced a grave slab dated 1683 and the remains of a midden containing a variety of artifacts and animal bone remains.

29. OLD ROADS

The remains of a former road system, consisting of pathways along the mountain or close to the seashore are still extant in Achill but now rarely used. One of the most prominent is *An tSean mBothair* on Cashel Hill at the 300-400 feet contour. This linked Cashel with Dookinella on the west and Dooega and Kildavnet on the east. Local tradition maintains that many of the large boulders on Cashel Hill were covered with a moss that was eagerly sought after for dyeing the *bainín* wool which was spun and carded locally. Traces of another old road can be seen north of "*The Spout,*" a well in Keel village along which local legend claims was the remains of a stone fort. In the Deserted Village in Slievemore, an old pathway, running from west to east connects the village with a group of megalithic tombs. Traversing an area between the southern field systems of the Deserted Village and the base of Crumpaun Hill is the Green Road which connects Slievemore with the village of Keel and also with Dooagh. This road may have been constructed to provide access to the Napoleonic Tower, but it is more likely to have been one of the Congested District's Board roads, a number of which were constructed during and after the famine. Prior to the construction of the present road system, access around the island was either along the sea shore or *via* these mountain roads. The old road from Keel to Dooagh continued from the Bervie Hotel *via Gob Aill Fhionnáin*, (Gubelennaun), past Ooghagowan Cave and into Dooagh before continuing westwards along the shore towards Keem Bay.

Old roads are of interest in that they can indicate the location of older settlements and are therefore important reminders of past demographic patterns.

30. PENAL ALTAR

During the Penal times (1691-1778) when Catholics were forbidden to practice their religion and priests were banished or had *"a price on their heads,"* crude altars such as the one at Keem Bay were set up so that fugitive priests could say Mass whenever the opportunity arose. Keem Bay was probably selected because of its inaccessibility; access from Dooagh village was *via* a gravel pathway until the 1970's when this roadway was tarmacadamed. The present Penal altar is a modern construction but the stone cross on top is similar to those in Slievemore graveyard and may have come from this site. The original Penal altar had a beautifully made stone cross, seven feet long, with a stem five feet two inches wide; it had no decoration and had been chiselled out of a large slab and was similar to crosses in Burrishoole Abbey near Newport, which was burned down in 1694, shortly after the Penal Laws came into force. The cross was set into a stone cairn of unmortared stone where it remained until broken, accidently, by schoolboys early this century. The present monument is a reconstruction of the original (John Moran, *pers. comm.*), and the stone cross set in the cairn may be one of a pair originally located in the old graveyard in Slievemore. To the east of Keem Strand is a small cave, locally called the *"Priest's Cave"*, while close to the west side of Moyteoge is *"gaoi saggart"* (the *"Priest's Rock"*), where a priest escaping from the *"yeomen"* (British soldiers) leaped to safety on to a waiting boat. Between 1940-42, an ogham stone was found on the banks of the Bunowna river, immediately west of the present Penal altar, and was subsequently deposited in the National Museum of Ireland.

31. PRE-BOG FIELD SYSTEMS

Surrounding the Deserted Village in Slievemore are fields of ridge-and-furrow *(lazy beds),* said to be among the finest in Ireland. Interspersed with these *lazy beds* are older, possibly Late Medieval field systems, while north of the enclosed field walls of the Deserted Village are prehistoric field systems which appear to be associated with the remains of Bronze Age hut sites. In some places the latter extend southwards to meet and mingle with the *lazy beds* and Late Medieval field systems; many of these, which consist of small upright boulders, appear to have been robbed out in antiquity (and/or later), and may, originally have covered the whole area now occupied by the Deserted Village. The prehistoric field walls meander in *zig-zag* fashion downhill; none form straight lines of any length but instead appear to follow the contours of the mountain. There are some co-axial (forming an axis) field walls but the majority are aligned in linear fashion only. Prehistoric field systems at the western end of the mountain are associated with two round houses of possible Bronze Age date and extend across the mountain, seemingly associated with similar hut-platforms of the same date. A field wall known as the *"Danish Ditch"* runs latitudinally across the mountain, appearing to link two megalithic tombs in the townland of Keel East. This prehistoric field bank in shown forking sharply southward on the 1838 Ordnance Survey maps (Sheet Mayo 42). Other pre-bog field walls are located at south of the road past McDowell's Hotel in the vicinity of the former Cathair of Slievemore and slightly north of Bal of Dookinella court tomb. Isolated examples can be seen at *Caisleán* north of Dooagh, and *An Bogagh Mhór*, an area of deep bog north-west of Dooagh. At the latter location, in the 1930's, the late John Moran, Dooagh, found a linear line of stones at the base of a bog, and lying beside them a huge tree trunk (hardwood) measuring some ten feet in length. As nearly two thirds of Achill is still covered by bog it is likely that other pre-bog field walls will be discovered in the future.

32. PROMONTORY FORTS

Promontory forts consist of a projecting headland naturally defended on three sides, the fourth fortified by a rampart extending across the neck of the headland. The artificial defences range in complexity from single to multiple earthen banks, and/or stone walls cutting off the interior from the landward side. Deep fosses or dug-out ditches occur between the embankments or stone walls. A causeway across the ramparts provides access to the interior which sometimes may have a complex entrance passage as at Dún Bunafahy on the Atlantic Drive and Dún Kilmore on Achill Beg Island. Promontory forts are thought to belong to the Iron Age but many were re-used during the Late Medieval period, as appears to have been the case in Achill. The location of the Achill Promontory forts would suggest that defence was a prime consideration. Their re-use in the sometimes turbulent medieval era would appear to confirm this hypothesis. They vary in size and complexity from the *"miniature"* fort of Dún Dooega to the most spectacular of the western promontory forts, Dún Kilmore on Achill Beg Island. They are located on the northern and southern shores of the island, commanding excellent vantage points over sea traffic in Blacksod Bay and Clew Bay respectively. The four on the northern shore at Dugort have been badly eroded by the fierce gales which lash the island in winter. This group is located west of the Golden Strand and are called Dún, Dúnmore, Dúnnagappal and Porteen respectively. The Dún was originally a small triangular level area on the cliff edge and was cut off from the landward side by curving eastern banks, three feet six inches high, between which was a fosse (ditch) twelve feet wide. Most of the site has now disappeared as a result of the erosion of the cliff edge. Dúnmore, a sea stack is separated from land by a narrow channel, making access extremely hazardous. Dúnnagappal, west of Porteen Strand, the latter the location of an unusual stone cist, now disappeared, was recorded by Wood-Martin in 1898. Dúnnagappal had already been severely eroded by 1914 when Westropp surveyed these sites. All that remains now is a small cairn of stones, part of the original mound, set in the centre of a barely discernible circular to oval area. No trace of the ramparts survives. At Porteen, traces of a substantial fosse, nine feet wide by two feet deep is still visible but the inner mound, said by Westropp to have been fifteen feet in diameter and four feet six inches high, has completely disappeared. The promontory forts on the southern side of the island are called Gubnahardin, Dúnnaglas (Dún na Glaise (*"fort of the moving water"*), Dún Bunafahy (*Bono-fo-ia*), Dún Dooega, Dúngubadoon (*Dúntai agus Dúntai Ioctair)* and Dún Kilmore (Dún and Daingean), Dúngurrough (*Dún na gCurrach*) and Dún Beag. The latter three promontory forts are located on Achill Beg Island. Very little remains of Gubnahardin, located north-east of Cloughmore Harbour and overlooking the Blind Sound, the fort having been bisected by the incoming tide when the sea channel cut its way through unresistant rock, sometime after the promontory fort was constructed. Shell midden sites on the opposite shore in Gubnahardia townland were also affected by the incoming tide. A coastguard station which was located beside

Gubnahardin was regrettably demolished about 10 years ago to make way for a Salmon Fish Farm. As the promontory at Gubnahardin was almost completely eroded, leaving only part of an earthen bank, Westropp classified this site as a ringfort. About half a mile west on the Atlantic Drive road, is picturesque Dúnnaglas, a rocky spur cut off from land at high tide, which is encircled on the northern, landward side, by a stone wall, four feet high (1.2 metres), inside of which are the foundations of two adjoining structures, one round, measuring c. twenty two feet north-south (6.8 metres) and the other wedge-shaped measuring fourteen feet (4.45 metres) north-west by fifteen feet (4.65 metres) east-west. The circular structure may be the remains of a Late Medieval tower which local folklore maintains was sited here. Westropp compared this site to the Doon on Inishturk island in Clew Bay and to Daithi's Fort in Gaul (France). On the western end of this promontory, or shore rock, is a terrace, an unusual feature in Irish promontory forts and on the south-eastern side is the remains of a substantial midden inset in the cliff face and difficult to access. Further along the Atlantic Drive is Dún Bunafahy *(Bono-fo-ia)*.

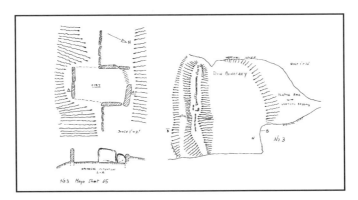

54. Dún Bunafahy Promontory Fort, after O'Kelly (1942)

This fort was strongly fortified with a deep fosse running north-south across the length of the fort. There is a causeway within the fort leading to a most unusual box-like structure, four feet four inches (1.3 metres) wide with a narrow entrance twenty two inches wide (0.06 metres), on top of the mound. This has been variously interpreted as a guard-room, dog kennel, cist grave and souterrain. The latter is probably the best explanation, for traces of a narrow passage, now barely discernible, leads from the box-like structure on the mound to a circular depression bordering the cliff edge. This circular structure, located south of the fosse was recorded by the late Professor M.J. O'Kelly, but only a circular depression now remains. South-west of Dooega village is Dún Dooega, a cone-shaped mound demarcated by a deep fosse thirty four feet (10 metres) long, and six to seven feet (2 metres) wide. The site is located beside a small inlet used by local fishermen to tie up their currachs. About thirty minutes walk, westward and east of Dooega Head, is Dúngubadoon, compared by Westropp (1914) to Dún Kilmore on Achill Beg Island. Two projecting headlands, one named Doonty (*Dúntai)* and the other called Doonty Eighter *(Iochtair)*, the latter inaccessible except by the intrepid climber, make up this impressive headland. The Doonty, was said by Westropp, to contain a group of hut sites and these are faintly visible through the dense crop of sea-pink which covers this headland. The long axis of the fort is orientated north-south; the fosse which cuts off the headland/s measures one hundred and eighty feet (55 metres) long, by nine feet (2.7 metres) wide and runs in an east-west direction; it was originally paved with stone, and some eight feet (2.5 metres) deep, while traces of a dry-stone rampart are visible on the south-east. Recent peat cutting has removed many of the features described by Westropp, while blown sand and sward covers others. On the landward side of the Doonty can be seen traces of a stone wall. On a raised area at the western end of the headland is a small quartz memorial stone commemorating the *"Lios Cearra"* disaster in which three local fishermen were drowned off Dooega Head in July, 1979. On Achill Beg Island there are three promontory forts, Dún Kilmore on the south, and Dúngurrough and Dún Beag on the west. Dún Kilmore, is strongly fortified with two subsidiary headlands, named the Dún and the Daingean, west of which is an isolated grassy rock platform, cut off from the main headland by a deep sea channel. Within the interior of the promontory fort, in the northern quadrant, is a large circular enclosure, described by Westropp as a ringfort but is actually an enclosure, or monastic *vallum* (wall), dating to the Early Medieval period within which are the remains of a *cillín,* a *leacht* (stone slab), a *bullaun* (stone basin), and along the western bank, a series of conjoined hut circles. Multiple, deeply-cut ramparts, one hundred and twenty three feet (37.5 metres) long, originally capped with stone cut off the headland of the Dún, in the centre of which Westropp noted an oval structure, measuring twenty seven feet (8 metres) north-south and thirty two feet (9.8 metres) east-west, with walls between six and ten feet (2-3 metres) thick, are possibly the remains of a Late Medieval tower. The Daingean was fortified across the neck by an outer wall, now vanished, and a fosse twenty eight feet (8.5 metres) wide, by nine feet (2.7 metres) deep. Inside of this was a mound, a drystone wall and the *"mortar-built"* inner wall of the *"gatehouse,"* the later suggesting re-use of the fort in the Late Medieval period. Westropp claimed that *"some resident made a mortar-built Castle in the Daingean in the 15th century."* Dúngurrough is a small promontory fort with a fosse, thirty six feet (11 metres) long, inset in which is a causeway six feet (2 metres) wide. Outside the fort on the east, are the remains of a conjoined hut, now barely visible, but which, during Westropp's visit, stood two feet (0.6 metres) high and had walls six to seven feet (2 metres) wide, the western section measuring fifteen feet (4.5 metres) in diameter and the eastern twelve feet (3.6 metres). Access to Achill Beg is by boat across *Beál-na-Glea (Beál na gCliath),* a narrow sea channel. Dún Beag is a small promontory which may be of late date, and is similar to another small promontory at Gub Grannaghanmore in Salia.

33. RINGFORTS

No ringforts have been recorded or found in Achill. However, documentary sources mention three possible ringforts: Rath Cím, Rath Dookinella and Iubar's Fort *(Dún Inbhir-da-tonn),* the latter probably a promontory fort which featured prominently in *Táin Bó Flidhais.* The absence of ringforts in Achill, which elsewhere are largely composed of earthen banks and ditches is adequately compensated for by a sizable number of stone forts or caiseals, the equivalent of the ringfort and probably reflecting the abundance of stone in the area. The rarity of ringforts is also a feature of Connemara which has about half-a-dozen or so sites, located close to prominent passes and fords. Jim Higgins *(pers.*

comm.) says that this may suggest that there were probably more unenclosed settlements in these areas than elsewhere!

34. ROUND HOUSES

Two round houses are located at the western end of Slievemore mountain, north of the Deserted Village at the 400-500 foot contour, and are substantial structures which are thought to be of Bronze Age date, although Con Manning *(pers.comm.)* thinks they may be of Early Medieval date. This area is locally known as *"The Brion," (Bruighean)* and is said to have been the *fort* of a chief, and to have a *tunnel* or underground passage in the vicinity to enable the *chief* to escape in times of danger! The rocky terrain in the area would make the construction of an underground passage difficult, although not impossible. There is, however, a souterrain, located in the nearby Deserted Village of Slievemore, the entrance of which is now blocked up, and which may be the *tunnel* referred to above.

The entrance in both Round Houses is on the east, the western house exhibiting the remains of a porch or portico, closely resembling a reconstructed Iron Age house at Butzer in England. Reynolds (1979). A geological map of this area indicates that small deposits of tourmaline, rhombus of mica and magnetite, were located in the immediate vicinity of the round houses, while c.500 yards to the west, is a quartz quarry, the location of rare mica schist and limonite, all of which may have had a bearing on settlement in this area.

35. SHELL MIDDENS

Shell middens are mounds or concentrations of sea shells, fish bones, burnt stones and charcoal representing food remains from former settlements of the Mesolithic Period. Middens are also associated with other periods, particularly the era of the Great Famine. They are the equivalent of the modern rubbish dump and when analysed provide valuable information concerning the availability, selection and collection of a variety of marine and terrestrial resources. A study in Tucson, U.S.A. by Rathje (1974) compared the results of two surveys of the lifestyle of a particular population group, one carried out by sociologists using the

19. Guide to the Archaeological Sites of Achill

"questionnaire system," the other by archaeologists who investigated the *"dust-bins"* of the same group; the results were so contradictory that the only conclusion both teams of investigators could come to was that, what people said they did, and what they actually did, were two entirely different matters! The impartiality of the archaeological investigation proved to be more accurate than the sociological survey, reflecting the fact that people are inclined to portray themselves as they would wish to be, rather than what they actually are. Shell midden sites are therefore unbiased records of the economic lifestyle of numerous population groups living at various times in the past, just like dust-bin collections today are of present day habits.

There are many midden sites in Achill, notably on Achill Beg Island, Dugort, Keel and Gubnahardia, the latter on the Corraun Peninsula. In 1898 Colonel Wood-Martin described the shell middens at Keel as *" just above high water mark and in close proximity to one another."* He said that these middens at that time *"were substantial,"* some being forty feet high. One however, had been destroyed because of *"the local practice of crushing shells to make whitewash for houses and to use as manure for the lazy beds."* Artifacts recovered by Wood-Martin from the Keel middens include: *"a hammer stone, a spindle whorl, various glass beads, bones of wild pig and red deer and charcoal."*

Two bronze pins were found on Keel sandybanks by the late Cyril Gray, a local historian, but were subsequently stolen from him. (The author has drawings of these, courtesy of Cyril Gray). A very fine ring-headed pin now in the Ashmolean Museum in Oxford, was also found on Keel Sandybanks. Wood-Martin claimed that *"nothing of metal"* had been recovered from the middens at Gubnahardia, suggesting, perhaps, a prehistoric date for these middens.

The Dugort middens are fairly extensive and probably date to various periods. They are located in deep sand dunes close to Caher Point. Recent excavations of a midden here by the National Museum of Ireland (Dr. N.Kelly, *pers.comm.*) produced evidence of a wealthy community who probably lived in nearby *Tóin an tSean Bhaile* in the seventeenth century A.D. Artifacts recovered included, two glass beads of late date,

Achill

Manganese and Buckley ware, glass bottles in which alcohol was imported, part of an ornate clay pipe, and bones of cattle, pig and sheep indicating a protein rich diet. Previously, two fishing implements were recovered from these middens. In the nearby cillín, located west of the midden, was found a seventeenth century gravestone, suggesting that the cillín may originally have been the burial place of the inhabitants of Tóin an tSean Bhaile, after which it became the burial ground of unbaptised children. The difference between the seventeenth century stone-lined graves and the crude upright stones of the cillín is stark. It is also unusual to find a cillín and a (normal) cemetery at the same location. For this reason, priority should be given to further excavation at this site to determine the relationship between the two burial periods. Regrettably, the substantial archaeological remains here are gradually being eroded by the fierce gales that lash this coast in winter, the bones of the unbaptised babies are clearly visible in section, so stabilisation is a matter of urgency.

T.J. Westropp, who examined the middens at Gubnahardia in 1912, noted the remains of hut sites, hearths and burnt stones. One midden had a clearly laid down stratigraphy:

"a well marked layer of black mould, burned slabs and pebbles; it is in two layers with six inches of sand between, containing shells, vertebrae or spines of fish; a quartzite hammer was also found here; then a layer of oysters, green clay, black mould and charcoal, with a layer of periwinkle on top. The upper stratum was directly under the sward. Mr. Praeger found here a large finely polished bead of blue limestone. The shells were mainly limpets, with only a few periwinkle. Hearth slabs and pebbles, blackened by fire, abound." Westropp (1914).

These middens were forty feet (12 metres) high and one hundred and thirty feet (40 metres) in diameter. Examination of the site by the author in 1984 revealed a stone wall in the sand dunes bisecting the peninsula, inside of which were clear traces of substantial *"lazy bed"* cultivation ridges of unknown date. An interesting phenomenon, here and on the opposite shore at Cloughmore, are huge boulders, strewn out in lines along the shore, which were used in the nineteenth century to *"farm"* seaweed and are known elsewhere as *fucus farms*. During the era of the landlords in the nineteenth century, the shore with its wealth of seaweed was *"striped"* with each tenant entitled to his or her share and, in the Encumbered Estates Court, bankrupt estates with seaweed rights were considered highly marketable. The stones of the *fucus farms* were raised every three years (the time taken for the seaweed to grow) to remove the sand covering them. Local folklore abounds with tales of how *"a Bugler"* on behalf of the landlord, would sound the call for people to come and harvest their strips of seaweed. It was also common practice for *"strips"* to be exchanged in lieu of *"one day's labour!"*

36. SHEEP PENS

Like the currach pens, sheep pens would be difficult to detect archaeologically because they are fairly basic structures, generally square or sub-rectangular in shape, and constructed of unmortared stone. They are found amongst the ruins of the Booley Villages and in areas formerly used for summer pasture. There are several modern day examples sited throughout the island, and these are used primarily to disinfect the sheep and to select those suitable for the market.

37. SOOT HOUSES

These primitive structures were rectangular in plan, of drystone walling, with a door in the southern gable, a roof of timber, and covered by earthen sods. These structures were located at the edge of the settlement to prevent the smoke from circulating within the village. Similar structures located within the village were used as hen houses, but few now remain.

There are a number of examples to be seen in Dooagh and Dookinella. The walls of the average soot house were three feet (c.1 metre) high by twelve feet (3.6 metres) long and five to six feet (c.2 metres) wide. The walls were one and a half feet thick and on them rested the roof timbers. The doorway was set into the southern gable and measured four feet high (1.2 metres) by two feet (c .6 metres) wide. The sods to cover the roof were cut between March and May and were divided into strips one foot by one and a half feet by three feet thick (c.0.3 x 0.5 x 1 metre). They were laid crossways on the timber so that the smoke could penetrate through to the second layer which was placed in the opposite direction. A fire was lit in the middle of the floor in June and allowed to burn slowly for several months or until the roof caved in, after which the potash was transferred to the fields. The fire was renewed as necessary, small lighted coals "caoráns" being best for burning as they smouldered longer. The soot (potash), mixed with stable manure, was used only on root crops e.g. potatoes and vegetables, and was better than seaweed, producing drier potatoes, whereas seaweed, when used as manure, produced a "waxy" potato!

38. SOUTERRAINS

A souterrain consists of an underground passage, or passages, lined with stone walling, and capped by stone lintels. Although souterrains are associated in the public mind with treasure trove, the majority seem to have been used as storage places, or, for refuge in times of danger. They are associated with the ringforts and *caiseals* of the Iron Age and also of the Early Medieval period. Some isolated examples occur, often representing all that remains of the settlement sites of the unfree *(serfs)*, a term used to designate the equivalent of the poor in our society today. The souterrain in Slievemore referred to above was probably associated with Late Medieval settlement in that area. Caesar Otway (1839) referred to a *cave* on Slievemore, this being a euphemism for a souterrain but the location of this site is still unknown, although recent information (Joe Vesey, *pers. comm.*) suggests that it may be close to the Court Tomb, MA 61.

The *Achill Missionary Herald and Western Witness* refers to drainage, reclamation and fencing in Slievemore and no doubt many sites were destroyed as a result. *Teach Fáoi Thalamh* (house under or beneath the ground) is possibly a souterrain and is said to be located east of an old pathway *en route* to Annagh. Another souterrain is said to be located close to the Napoleonic Tower north of Dooagh. A souterrain was probably also associated with the promontory fort at Bunafahy on the

Atlantic Drive (Eoin Halpin, *pers. comm.*).   The Dane's Cave, location unknown, appears to have been another souterrain.

39. STANDING STONES

A standing stone on Crumpaun Hill is known by the name of *Fear Brega* and reference was made to this site in the Ordnance Survey Letters, 1838, and was an appellation given to pagan remains by the Early Christians. St. Patrick is reputed to have been responsible for the destruction of many standing stones; others were christianised or reappear as ogham stones. Standing stones are difficult to date with even excavated examples rarely providing any additional information by way of dating material. They are, however, generally dated to the Bronze Age on the basis of associated structures. However, recent research by Dr. Gabriel Cooney (1996) of U.C.D. suggests that they may have originated in the Neolithic Period and many examples of free-standing stones, sculpted to resemble the human shape *(statue menhirs)* are common in Western Europe. A standing stone is associated with the Keel East (MA61) Court Tomb while a cup-marked large orthostat was noted by Wood-Martin (1887) at nearby, unclassified, Keel East (i).

In some parts of the country standing stones are associated with old roadways, and in other parts of the country with Bronze Age cist graves. Some have been Christianised and inscribed with crosses and other decorations. A standing stone, now prostrate and inscribed with a modern inscription, is located in Uggoole, west of Slievemore. An interesting practice which seems to be confined to Achill, was that stones, considered suitable as grave slabs, were carved *in situ* after which they were brought back to the graveyard. Had the process been reversed, a lot of time and trouble would have been wasted if a stone selected and transported over a long distance was subsequently damaged on site or proved unsuitable.

The *"Letter Stone,"* a long blue-coloured stone (probably limestone) with letters cut out by a chisel, possibly Ordnance Survey Sapper's Marks and therefore likely to have been a Trigonometrical Station or bench mark) was located south of the road to Keem Bay close to an old well near the *"Mearing Cove"* (a boundary line denoting the land division between native and landlord), or according to James McHugh, Dugort, a line dividing the respective properties of Murray MacGregor Blacker and Charles Boycott. James McHugh claims that he and some friends were responsible for the disappearance of the *"Letter Stone"* which they buried *"in a flat area, west of the road going to Keem"* during road construction, between Dooagh and Keem Bay.

A cross-inscribed standing stone was supposedly located on the right-hand side of the road near to the old Church in Belfarsad, but no trace of this now remains; people in the area say it was used in the construction of the new Church in Corraun!

40. STONE CIRCLES

Wood-Martin (1898) recorded what he described as a stone circle on Slievemore. This circle supposedly contained *" a circle within a circle"* and would not have been unlike the plan of Site 27 in the Passage Grave cemetery at Carrowmore in County Sligo. Detailed investigation of this area produced no evidence of a stone circle; the only item of interest was a cairn of different sized stones which could possibly be the remains of a cleared archaeological site.

The remains of a small stone circle (or circle of stones!) was noted in a field, east of Crumpaun and north of Keel village. A quarter of a mile to the north-west and overlooking this site is *Fear Brega (false man)*, a standing stone, together with a number of unclassified sites. In the Irish Folklore Commission files in U.C.D. which relate to Achill, there is a drawing of what appears to be a stone circle, containing eight stones with a *" coffin-shaped"* (recumbent) stone on the north-east, lying prostrate on the ground. The location of this site has not yet been established, the location being described as:

Faoi croc a'Chaibin nGleann na ngad, meaning *"under or on a small hill in the valley of the withe"* (osier/willow)! The remains of what appears to be a stone circle was recently located in Bal of Dookinella (unverified), immediately east of a Court Tomb, locally known as the Pagan Cemetery. A survey of this structure was recently carried out by the author and Gary McGinty, M.E., and will be published soon. It may be one of the sites surveyed by Wood-Martin whose whereabouts have remained unknown since the late 19th century.

Stone circles are normally confined to the south, south-west and north of the country. They are defined as:

" *an uneven number of spaced uprights, symmetrically arranged with the axial stone on the south-western section of the perimeter, standing directly opposite the entrance.*" Ó Nualláin (1984a). Many stone circles are associated with standing stones as in the above examples.

41. STONE CROSSES

Stone crosses in Achill are found in the graveyards at Slievemore and Kildavnet, on the Penal altar at Keem Bay and overlooking Dún Kilmore on Achill Beg Island. Although these crosses exhibit crude workmanship compared with elaborate examples elsewhere, nevertheless they do have intrinsic value. One of a pair of small crosses on top of the boundary wall, either side of the gateway leading to the old graveyard in Slievemore has disappeared. These two crosses were recorded by Dr. Lucas in 1947 who said they were *"more ancient than those in Kildavnet."* He also noted that on both crosses the ends of the arms as well as the top and bottom of the shaft, expanded.

Two other crosses in Slievemore are of interest and would seem to be of ancient date. The example in the north-eastern part of the graveyard where a cillín is also located appears more akin to a standing stone than a cross, but the shape would suggest that some attempt was made to fashion a cross. The Ordnance Survey Letters (1838-40) were probably referring to this cross when they said that four tyrants, of unknown origin and date, broke the arms of a cross in the churchyard, and at the same time burned the house of *Dubhdara Ó Máille*, west of the churchyard. There is an *Obit* for a *Dubhdara ÓMáille* in the ***A. Conn.*** in A.D. 1219, who was killed by King Cathal Crovderg (Red Hand) O'Connor, which probably explains the later animosity between the two families. A second *Dubhdara*, possibly Grace O'Malley's father, in 1589 slew the captain and crew of a Spanish ship which had been wrecked off Clare Island.

Achill

Dubhdara was a relatively common name in the O'Malley family so the *Dubhdara* referred to above remains unknown.

The crosses in the graveyard in Kildavnet could belong either to the Early Medieval Period or to the eighteenth century when the fashioning of small crude crosses was the norm (Higgins, *pers. comm.*) The cross on top of the Penal altar in Keem Bay has a rounded shaft and is of Early Medieval date. It does not appear to be the one described by the late John Moran of Dooagh who said that the original cross on the Keem Bay Penal altar was almost identical to an example in Burrishoole Abbey, near Newport. The Keem Bay cross was accidently broken by schoolboys in the early part of the present century and the remains of this cross may be represented by three large fragments of a pillar-type stone now inset into the floor of the nearby old coastguard station beside the Bunowna River, and close to where other ogham stones were found.

42. SWEAT HOUSES

Sweat-houses were primitive saunas, small huts, built on the corbelled principle which were roughly the same size as the Annagh booley huts. Like the soot-houses, a fire was lit inside to generate sufficient heat before the patient, generally a person with rheumatism, entered the sweat-house to commence treatment. They are usually found close to a water source to enable the patient to have a cold plunge after the sauna! A small corbelled hut, that may have been a *sweat-house,* is located close to Annagh Booley Village and a nearby stream which forms a cataract (water-fall), west of Lough Nakeeroge East.

43. UNCLASSIFIED SITES

There is a whole range of unclassified sites in Achill, some of the most interesting being located on Slievemore mountain and associated with prehistoric field walls. There are also a number of settlement sites, located midway between the permanent villages and the booley sites, which may well be some of the intermediate sites referred to by Wilde (1864). A detailed study of these sites is proposed under the auspices of the **Achill Archaeological Summer School in 1997.**

44. VERNACULAR HOUSING

The Valuation Records are a valuable source of information on vernacular housing containing from 1850 onwards, records of the dimensions of houses and ancillary buildings, as well as the rateable valuation and names of householders. They are also a source of much valuable genealogical information.

The earliest detailed account of housing in Achill comes from Edward Newman (1839) writing about his visit to Achill in 1838. He described Achill as *"more like a foreign land than any I have visited; the natives live in huts which a good deal resemble those of Esquimaux Indians; they are without chimney or windows and the roof seems continuous with the walls; the interior is generally undivided and is tenanted by men, women, children, pigs and poultry, and often goats and cows. These cabins are built in what may be called loose clusters, varying from twenty to thirty in a cluster; these clusters or villages are sixteen in number, some of them are summer residences only and are entirely deserted in winter, others are winter residences only and are entirely deserted in the summer."* The summer residences are of course the booley villages, many of which are still extant and their remains can be seen throughout the island. The following year, the Reverend Caesar Otway, visiting the Missionary Settlement in Dugort, gave a description of an Achill village:

"An Achill village consisted of congeries of hovels thrown indiscriminately together, as if they had fallen in a shower from the sky."

In 1870, Dooagh village was described by William Jack, Assistant Commissioner of Education, as:

"one of the most curious aggregations of miserable huts I have ever seen." As regards layout, he said: *"there was scarcely anything that could be called a street and a stranger set down in the middle of the village would have found it difficult to get out again."*

Local folklore bears out this description of Dooagh, one tale relating how the village was so congested that: *"a donkey with pardógs (creels) could not pass between the houses!"*

Achill

Harris Stone, living in Dooagh in the early part of the century wrote that:

"the majority of rude huts or cabins comprising Dooagh seemed at some time, very long ago, to have been promiscuously thrown out of a gigantic pepper-box on the strand, so extraordinary higgledy-piggledy placed are they being of a similar singular style of architecture and size, it is not easy to find one's way about amongst them." Stone (1906).

Mr. & Mrs. Hall (1841-43) said that the village of Dooagh consisted of about forty cabins, not one with a single chimney.

The earliest house type recorded in Achill was circular or oval in plan with low walls of dry-stone construction and a thatched roof of rye weighted down with stones. There were no windows or chimneys and the only source of ventilation came from the two opposing doorways which were used to regulate the outflow of smoke. The later rectangular house was a single-roomed structure, the western house or byre-dwelling, *"at one end of which he kept his cows and at the other his spouse!"* Achill has a whole range of vernacular structures apart from housing; these include currach pens, turf shelters, outhouses, haggards and small enclosures, all in need of urgent study before they disappear forever.

55. Dooagh Village c.1950

19. Guide to the Archaeological Sites of Achill

Artifacts from Achill

Archaeological artifacts have been found in Achill since the late 19th century, the majority finding their way to various museums. In archaeological parlance, these *"finds"* are of interest for a number of reasons, firstly for their association with known archaeological sites and secondly as indicators of former sites, no longer visible in the landscape.

56. House in Dooniver c.1986 © Theresa McDonald

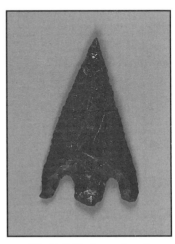

57. Polished Stone Axe-head
© National Museum of Ireland

58. B.& T. Arrowhead,
Maumnaman © N.M.I.

303

Achill

ARTIFACTS	LOCATION
STRAW BOYS HAT	ACHILL SOUND
WOODEN SPADE	BELLANASALLY
STANDING STONE	BELFARSAD
WOODEN VESSELS	CRUMPAUN
JAMES II COPPER COINS	CLOUGHMORE
LATE MEDIEVAL QUERN STONES	CLOUGHMORE
ROTARY QUERN	SLIEVEMORE
FRAGMENTS OF MED. GLASS	SLIEVEMORE (UNVERIFIED)
STONE DISKS	DUGORT
FISHING IMPLEMENT	DUGORT
BRONZE SWORD	DUGORT
STONE CHOPPER	DUGORT
FRAGMENTS OF STONE OBJECT	DUGORT
WHETSTONE	DOOKINELLA
BLADE OF WOODEN PADDLE	DOOKINELLA
BRONZE PIN	DOOKINELLA
WOODEN STAVE	DOOKINELLA
WHITE SLING STONES	DOOKINELLA
FRAGMENTS OF MORTISED BEAM	DOOKINELLA
WORKED TIMBER	DOOKINELLA
WOODEN VESSEL	DOOKINELLA
SHEEPSKIN SIEVE	DOOEGA
IRON KNIFE	DOOEGA
WOODEN OBJECTS	DOOKINELLA
IRON DAGGER	DOOEGA
ROTARY QUERNS (2 + 1)	DOOEGA-KEEL
STONE BEAD OR TOGGLE	GUBNAHARDIA
RED DEER ANTLER	GUBNAHARDIA
FRAGMENTS OF BRONZE & COPPER	KEEL
FRAGMENTS OF BRONZE TUB	KEEL
FRAGMENTS OF SLATE PENCIL	KEEL
BRONZE TWEEZERS	KEEL
QUARTZITE HAMMER	KEEL

19. Guide to the Archaeological Sites of Achill

ARTIFACTS	LOCATION
SPINDLE WHORL	KEEL
FISH BONES	KEEL
RED DEER BONES	KEEL
BLUE GLASS BEAD WITH WHITE INLAY	KEEL
FRAGMENTS OF WHITE GLASS BEAD	KEEL
FLINT FRAGMENT	KEEL
FRAGMENTS OF L. MEDIEVAL BROOCH	KEEL
BRONZE TWEEZERS	KEEL
STEATITE BEAD	KEEL SANDYBANKS
WOODEN LIDS	KEEL (CRUMPAUN)
WILD PIG BONES	KEEL
RINGHEADED PIN	KEEL
STONE DISK	KEEL
FRAGMENTS OF BRONZE PIN	KEEL
SHROUD (COFFIN) PINS	KEEL
POLISHED STONE AXE-HEAD	KEEL (MONYHAIG)
OGHAM STONES	KEEM BAY
STONE CROSS	KEEM BAY
POLISHED STONE AXE HEAD	DERREENS
BARBED & TANGED ARROWHEAD	MAUMNAMAN
WOODEN VESSEL	OWENDUFF
STONE OBJECT	OWENDUFF
SADDLE QUERN	GUBNAHARDIA
POWDER HORN	TONRAGEE
BOG BUTTER	TONRAGEE
UPRIGHT STONE SLABS	TONRAGEE
CLOTHES & TEXTILES	TONRAGEE
SHOVEL-SHAPED STONE	TONRAGEE
5 STONE DISKS	DUGORT
BUCKLEY WARE	DUGORT-SLIEVEMORE
BLUE GLASS BEADS	DUGORT; KEEL
MANGANESE WARE	DUGORT
POLISHED STONE AXEHEADS	UNPROVENANCED
FLINT & QUARTZ FRAGMENTS	SLIEVEMORE-KILDAVNET, ACHILL BEG

Achill

The Achill artifacts span a period of some 5,000 years. Few excavations have been carried out on the island, so it is likely that the above represents only a small percentage of artifacts of the whole. Some of the artifacts e.g. the finds from Keel indicate high status sites, for, undoubtedly, Achill had in the past, many important residents. Surface and chance finds e.g. that of Christy Cunniffe who, on a Field Trip to Achill Beg Island with the **Achill Archaeological Summer School** in 1994, found part of a decorated Medieval quern stone lying in the sand are rare but gratifying. Recent excavations in the Deserted Village in Slievemore have uncovered large quantities of 18th and 19th century pottery, glass and delph which are currently being classified and catalogued.

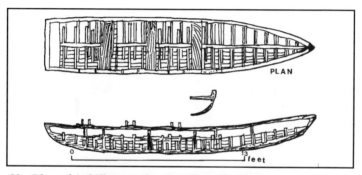

59. Plan of Achill currach, after Hornell (1938)

60. Currach at Keem Bay, c.1950's

306

Chapter 20

THE FOLKLORE OF ACHILL

Folktales are an important part of a community's heritage and represent oral traditions covering several generations. Remote areas like Achill retain old traditions and beliefs because they were never entirely stamped out. Each community has its own tales but some, like the *Fionn Cycle*, are universal and are attached to almost all parts of the country. Folklore is of interest to archaeologists in that it can pinpoint sites of which no visible trace remains and it can also provide explanations for past customs not normally obtained through archaeological research. Folktales relating to former ritual places are common and can be useful indicators of the distribution of particular classes of archaeological monuments. However, caution is needed as stories are often embellished and the same story can be told about several different places. The classification below roughly follows that of O'Suilleabhain (1963).

Achill Villages

Dugort (Old)Village originally contained 40 houses. The name means *Dubh Gort (black field)*. *Duitce Guirt,* referred to in the folklore files in U.C.D. is said to be derived from men bringing in fish and salting them on the *Dubac* or sandy bank. The main surnames in Dugort were Lavelle and Fadian. The surname, Lavelle, is supposed to be of French origin and may have been introduced to the island *via* this sort of contact. It is not known how old the village of Old Dugort is but it conforms to the designation, clachán, particularly as it appears on old photographs. The ruins of houses or huts were located on *Dún Mór* (promontory fort) where *Darby the Runner* was said to have lived.

Molly Vesey who featured in ***Ireland's Welcome to the Stranger*** Nicholson (1847), had a *sibín* (shebeen-pub) in Finsheen. She had been married twice, once to a Lavelle man and secondly to Keane, a native of Doohoma in North Mayo. Dugort women made stockings and flannel and sold them to the French who came to Dugort, in their boats, every two weeks. Dr. Pococke referred to the above industry in 1752: *"the inhabitants have a kind of sheep here with a coarse wool fit for yarn* *stockins, which they spin and knit, and sell the stockins for about ten pence a pair - and with this produce they pay their rent."* Stokes (1891).

The Valley

The village contained 46 houses, most of which had slate roofs. The commonest surnames were Grealis and Gallagher. The former village, *Tóin an tSean Bháile* was located west of the present village and may have been deserted upon the change of ownership in 1776 involving the Duke of Ormond and Thomas Medlycott.

Dookinella

Dookinella village was said to be prosperous when the Flax mill was in operation there in the 19th century. This mill was said to be located in *Garai an Mhuilinn,* a plot *"Sweeney and McLoughlin"* (c.1776) had originally bought for their horses. The area in question was Dookinella Thulis, for the tale says, that when Thulis died, Sweeney and McLoughlin were evicted but Farrell Gallagher, a local man, set them up on his estate by the river. This gave rise to a placename called River, a small village midway between the crossroads at Dookinella and the Minaun cliffs. However, the pair seemingly did not stay here too long as we are told they eventually went to live in *Tóin an tSean Bháile*, from where their ancestors had come! McLoughlin is presumably one of the McLoughlins who purchased parts of the lands of Achill from Thomas Medlycott in 1776. Sweeney was probably a local man. A small chapel was located in Dookinella Thulis but when Thulis (Toland), after whom this townland was named, died, the Rev. Edward Nangle purchased the estate and the chapel was destroyed. Farrell Gallagher, a man seemingly of some importance, gave a site for a new Church to Archbishop McHale of Tuam. Although strongly opposed by Nangle and his bailiffs the Church was eventually built. An amusing tale is told about a landlord named McNamara who had a servant boy named Thulis. One day while on the beach at Dookinella, Thulis found what he thought were shiny buttons which he took to his master, who readily identified them as gold sovereigns. The story goes that McNamara emigrated to England to spend his new-found wealth, while Thulis became the landlord and gave his name to the present townland of Dookinella Thulis.

20. The Folklore of Achill

The Neptune was wrecked on the rocks near Minaun on the 21st January, 1860. She was carrying a cargo of buffalo hides, rum and brandy. The coastguards at Keel were ordered to stand guard over the cargo but seemingly there was some pilfering, the Dookinella and Cashel people getting some of the cargo. A watch from this boat was later sold in England for £21 while an anchor from *The Neptune* was left lying on the beach. Later that night, Reynolds, one of the coastguards became involved in a row with neighbours and was killed.

Óidhe Randal

This night is so-called because a Coastguard in Keel named Reynolds died a violent death, seemingly being murdered by his neighbours. The story goes that Reynolds wanted someone killed and approached a certain person who refused to do the foul deed and during an ensuing fight the Coastguard was killed. A subsequent court case acquitted the man who killed Reynolds. He was buried in Dugort but when news reached the authorities the body was exhumed; coincidentally, that night a great storm blew up and continued to the following morning and has been called *Óidhe Randal* ever since.

Slievemore

Many stories are told about the Great Ó Máille of Slievemore Hill who seemingly owned a large tract of land between Slievemore graveyard and McDowell's Hotel, an area known as Fahy *(Faiche)*, because it was the alleged field of the giants, a euphemism for megalithic monuments. This Ó Máille was not connected with Grace O'Malley or the Clare Island O'Malleys but was descended from the *"first man in Achill."* Another version of this story tells how Ó Máille, upon arriving in Achill, built a small house for his wife and son in Slievemore. Some time later a man named Lavelle arrived, killed Ó Máille and lived with his widow with whom he had three sons. When Ó Máille's son was 15 years of age he encouraged his stepfather to go to Dirk on the pretext of collecting birds' eggs, and there he killed him. This boy, when he grew up, became known as *"Dermot (Darby) the Runner "* and earned quite a reputation for himself, ridding the island of cattle raiders from Erris and elsewhere.The land in Fahy later became the property of the Achill Mission Estate and

Achill

a field here is still known as *"Jamesie McHale's field."* Jamesie was a brother of Archbishop McHale of Tuam, and the story goes that the two *"fell out"* over the ownership of some land in Crossmolina and to *"spite"* the Archbishop, Jamesie came to Achill and joined the Reverend Edward Nangle and the Achill Mission. This story seems to have some basis in fact, for a David McHale, and also an Honor McHale, are registered owners of land in this area in the mid 19th century. In addition, a Bridget McHale, said to be a cousin of the Archbishop also defected to the Achill Mission in the 1850's.

Cattle were brought to Slievemore *"for a change"* i.e. a change of grass and water. The soil in Slievemore was a reddish sandy, soil, rich in cobalt and other minerals, while that in Dooagh was black (reclaimed bog) and low in nutrients. Potatoes and vegetables grew extremely well in Slievemore. Houses in Slievemore were thatched; there was no chimney but a fire was kept constantly going and located against the northern interior gable wall, set between two large flagstones. The smoke filtered through to the thatch and every second year the roof was removed, broken up, and used as manure on the fields. Roofing material consisted of *"scraws,"* measuring some six feet long by three feet wide and two inches thick, cut from the mountainside. The cows were brought indoors during the night and also during the day, in very hot weather and heather was gathered on the mountainside and used as bedding for the cattle. Furniture in the houses consisted of a bed, a table, chairs, an oil lamp and a churn for making butter. Spinning and carding of wool was done by women. The *bed-out-shot,* a recessed area in the wall was located to the left of the fire and the bed platform itself was made of timber planks. Seating was hand-made of wood, not unlike timber boxes. Timber was soaked in the rivers to strengthen it.The water in Slievemore was said to be excellent and old people said that tea was made in a large open-necked jug and tasted much better than tea made in a teapot!

Cattle were the mainstay of the economy but were superseded by sheep. In the era of the landlords from the middle to the late 19th century, a *"herd"* was employed by the Achill Mission Estate to prevent cattle trespassing or grazing on lands in Slievemore. After the village was deserted the people from Dooagh brought their cattle to Slievemore on a daily basis, leaving as early as 5 a.m. in the morning and returning with cans of milk in the evening. During the day, milk was kept cool by storing it in the the many shallow streams which course down the mountainside. The months of May and June were said to be extremely hot and during this period cattle were kept indoors after milking, and returned to the fields in the cool of the evening. Seaweed (wrack), was brought from Annagh to manure the fields. It was first dried there and then transported by cart, or on horseback, to Slievemore. Salmon were caught in Annagh and brought back in a bag, on people's backs. Food in Slievemore consisted of fish: bream, cod, herring, together with *carraigín moss*, *tripodai* and *sloughcan*. On special occasions a sheep or a pig would be killed. The majority of houses and lands in Slievemore are owned, at the present time, by the inhabitants of Dooagh Village, and by a lesser number in Pollagh Village.

Dooniver

Resourcefulness in times of adversity is a particular characteristic of Mayo people. A village in Dooniver was named *Bastapool*, (after Sebastapol), the scene of many battles between tenant and landlord. A story is told of Sally Rua McTigue who lived in a small house very close to the shore in Dooniver and was to be evicted. A plan was drawn up by local people to thwart the bailiffs; turf, stones and seaweed, were collected and inserted into all the chimney places in the house; a fire was started and when the bailiffs arrived they could not get into the house because of the smoke from the burning seaweed etc. and they had to abandon the eviction.

The Breen (Bruigheán, meaning a fort)

The Breen, located at the 400 foot contour at the north-western end of Slievemore mountain was (is) regarded as a fairy fort. Breen is a variant of *Brú (Brú na Bóinne* =Newgrange). Cattle grazing near the Breen often mysteriously disappeared only to reappear sometimes one week later. Claims of sightings of fairies in and around the Breen were common. Music was often heard coming from the Breen, usually the violin (fiddle). A stone-mason was said to keep his gold in a cow's horn in the Breen. Latterly, The Breen was used as a pound for straying cattle and tenants of the Achill Mission Estate had to pay a fine to obtain the release of their cattle (John McNamara, *pers. comm.*).

Many tales are told of the *Creagaharlui*, not far from The Breen, where it was claimed gold was buried (J. Vesey, *pers. comm.*). Seemingly, an old man found a cache of gold sovereigns there, melted them down, and stored them in a cave. He died without telling his wife where he had hidden the gold and people have been looking for it ever since!

The land " *An talamh*"

Glimpses of landscape changes are incorporated in folklore items e.g. *"before the land was striped by Joynt in 1862, the tenants in Achill were all in co."* meaning that prior to Joynt's Survey, the farming practice was based on Rundale where land was held in common by related family units. The absence of fences is mentioned by Spenser writing in 1596 A.D.:

"one neighbour encroach upon the others metes and bounds and endangereth one another with their cattle."

Associated with the Rundale system was the clachán, a cluster of houses grouped together without formal plan. Around the clachán was the *"Scaoth"* (infield), where cattle were grazed after the crops had been harvested.

Agriculture

Spad or *Laidhe* (loy) was the name of the spade in Achill. The handle was called, *cos lamh chrann or feal*, while the area where the foot was placed to help drive the spade was called the broigin or *cluaisin*. The loy had a handle and contained more timber and less metal than the spade and was much lighter. The *crann-ghob* (probably the *gowl gob*) was used in Achill for the cultivation of very sandy soil or bogland. The points were more prominent than in the Kerry fack! Creels *(cleib)* made of *"sally rods"* with ropes of straw were strung over the shoulders and used to carry turf, hard manure, gravel, and seaweed. No shoulder yokes were used. Animals had a pack saddle and *pardogaí* (creels), on the horse or donkey which transported heavy loads of farm produce, seaweed and manure. No sledges were used and there were no slide carts, or carts with solid wooden wheels. A *meitheal* (group of workers) came together for turf cutting, threshing, cutting hay, and making haystacks.

Fishing

Fishing for herrings was carried out between August and Christmas. Nearly every house had a boat and the fish were plentiful. Herrings were salted in barrels; as the barrels had previously been used to store paraffin oil, they were filled with soil and left for several weeks to get rid of the smell of paraffin. The barrels cost one shilling to buy. The herrings were sold at Achill Sound on Fair Days. West of Keem Bay at Achill Head is a rock called " *Carraig a' pota"* where fishermen used to boil pots, or cook a meal, usually of fish, sometimes salted fish, which they brought with them to sea as well as a bag of turf with which to make a fire.

61. Bringing in the Catch, Purteen Harbour c.1950

62. Shark Fishing in Keem Bay c.1960's

Dredging for oysters was carried out at Inishbiggle Island with drift nets, a net like a trawl, (a bag-shaped net) with a groundbar to keep the

Achill

net on the sea bed and to keep the mouth open. The oysters were sold to
agents who sent them to County Clare, but early this century the oyster
beds were destroyed by men from Murrisk and although several attempts
have been made to revive this industry, all have failed. Darrell Figgis,
T.D., resided in Achill for a number of years and was interested in setting
up a fishing industry, but this was not favoured by the Congested
Districts Board because the Board's Inspectors considered the coast too
exposed, and felt that enormous sums of money would have to be
expended on providing sheltered landing places. (Micks, 1925).

Industry

Several attempts were made at setting up industries in Achill. Edward
Nangle, upon arriving in Achill Sound referred to a " *salt factory*" in that
locality which had gone out of use prior to his arrival. There were two
mills at Belfarsad, one for grinding corn and one for thickening flannel,
both of which ceased operations at the beginning of the present century.
Keel sandybanks, Dookinella and Dooniver, were once said to have been
covered with flax, which was collected and spun into various garments.
Sir Neal O'Donnell encouraged his tenants to grow flax, and there was a
large concentration of flax close to his estate near Newport. There was a
Flax mill in Dookinella and possibly another in Keel, but the
whereabouts of both are unknown. Lloyd Praeger (1904) recorded flax
growing here in his paper relating to the survey of the Achill flora.

Knitting Industry

A Miss Chevasse gave knitting classes in Keel, and upon her marriage
to a Colonel Wright she suggested to Fr. Colleran that the classes be
continued. Fr. Colleran, in conjunction with the Congested Districts
Board Inspector, employed a Miss Loughran to continue giving the
classes, even though there were now some expert knitters in the village.

In Dooagh, Miss Eva O'Flaherty started a knitting industry using
knitting machines and very soon had a *coterie* of expert knitters and an
impressive *clientel*e from all over Ireland.

20. The Folklore of Achill

Landlords

The Earl of Cavan was said to have built a fence from *Maum to the bottom of Dugort* to divide his property from that of the Achill Mission Estate. He constructed a bathing house, a canal and a pier, plus a roadway with a gate at the end of it. He used to export turf from the Valley in a big sailing boat. Mrs. McDonnell, a landlord in the Valley:

"took the good land off the people and made a big house on it. She was easily incited and when a complaint was made against tenants, she usually had them evicted. When she died, her body was taken to England for burial and her estate was inherited by her son, Leslie Elliott in January, 1856 ." Irish Folklore Commission Files, U.C.D.

Mr. Saly was a landlord in Dugort who was said to be *"greedy for money."* He built houses in Dugort and he was succeeded by Mr. Grierson, who, was heartily disliked by all who came into contact with him.

Captain Boycott

Captain Boycott was said to be responsible for bringing goats into Achill, and upon his departure for Ballinrobe, he sold them to Mr. Weldon. They later went wild (feral) and remnants of the herd can be seen today near Saddle Head.

Edward Nangle and the Achill Mission

An extract from the Irish Folklore Commission files in U.C.D. describes the ancestors of the Dooagh people as having their *"head village"* in Bal before they were *"banished"* from there by Nangle so that he could make a Pound for cattle and sheep! The remains of a Pound can be seen in the townland of Bal of Dookinella, on the south side of the road, 500 yards past McDowell's Hotel in Dugort. The writer continued: *"...To the old people, the land of Slievemore was like a blessed place: they had their houses and living, and their graveyard and everything else there, and everything was taken off them."* The people of Dooagh claimed ownership of the land between Tuar and Bal, the phrase *"Dooagh extended to McDowell's "* may be significant. (John Moran,

Achill

pers. comm.). When the people were banished from Bal the writer said: *"they went and made those simple houses (in Slievemore):these simple houses were not adequate, so the people came back to Dooagh to live and there make a bigger house ."* In Bal the people had: *"...a farm with fine fields, cattle and sheep, but a landlord named O'Donnell, from Newport, told the people they now had to pay rent to the new owners, the Achill Mission, and if they could do that all would be well! "*(John Moran, J.). In practice, this proved impossible as the rents were increased substantially, tenancies were held *"at will"* i.e. for short periods, and eviction was common. Bogland was reclaimed and the village of Dooagh became one of the most congested villages on the island until the Congested Districts Board re-organised holdings, reclaimed some additional land, and resettled families on new holdings. Thus it is that former neighbours in Slievemore were now resettled side by side in Dooagh.

An Réilt (The Star)

Located at around 800-900 feet on the southern slopes of Slievemore mountain is a huge white quartz boulder called The Star *(An Réilt)*, claimed to be a special place, or place of former ritual. A droveway, marked out by quartz boulders leads the way up to it; a lush, grassy area midway along this droveway is called the *Builg* meaning a full stomach, (John Toolis, *pers. comm.*), and a favourite place for cattle grazing.

Achill Land War

The successors of Edward Nangle, the Trustees of the Achill Mission Estate, had their headquarters in Dublin but kept their Rent Office in Dugort. Various Agents looked after the estate, notably Mr. Whelan, Mr. Weldon, Mr. O'Donnell, Mr. Salt and Mr. Grierson, nicknamed *The Cooley,* because he had spent some time in Ceylon!

Early in the 20th century, the people wanted to buy land and when the Achill Mission Estate refused to sell, agitation commenced. The leaders of this agitation were the Rev. Fr. Colleran, Mr. Darrell Figgis, T.D. Mr. William Egan, a Protestant from Slievemore and Mr. Walter Bourke.

20. The Folklore of Achill

One of the tactics adopted by the leaders of the agitation was *"boycotting."* The landlords involved were the Achill Mission Estate, William Pike, Mrs. Agnes McDonnell and Mr. Scott, owner of lands in Keem and Corrymore House.

Livelihood and Household Support

Bog Deal (Scot's Pine) was usually found under the bog and easily detected as the early morning dew dissolves faster over ground covering tree trunk-beams. A metal probe could determine the length of the beam and whether or not it was worthwhile digging it up. Bog deal dug up in Achill, showed evidence of burning, suggesting forest fires or deliberate conflagration. The bog deal was cut and left to dry on a bank and was often used for roofing houses; in fact all thatched houses were roofed with bog deal. Household furniture was also made from bog deal and bog deal candles were widely used. The procedure for the latter is of interest and involved obtaining a long, straight piece of bogdeal which was split into strips about half an inch wide and one eighth inches thick. Twenty of these would be grouped together in a bundle and secured with *sugán* rope, which was wound round the full length of the candle. Water was sprinkled on the *sugán* to slow down the flames.

Forges

At the beginning of the present century there were four forges in Achill: Keel, Cabán, Cashel and the Valley. People had to bring their own iron and coal or fuel, usually *" hard turf "* which seemingly burned to a high heat. Blacksmiths were located in various villages:

1. John Lavelle, Valley   2. Thomas Toolis, (Cabán) River

3. John Barrett, Keel   4. Michael Gallagher, Cashel

Tools used by the Blacksmith included hammers, sledges, pincers and an anvil.

Fairs

Up until the early part of the present century pig farming was common in Achill. The Fair at Achill Sound, which still takes place on the last

Friday of each month, was originally a Pig Fair which commenced after the Bridge was built at Achill Sound in 1888. Records indicate that Achill Sound once had a major Fair with buyers coming from all parts of County Mayo; it is now little more than a market for *"street traders."*

"Womens Work"

Womens work consisted of everything except cutting turf, *"milking cows and sowing potatoes was beneath the dignity of men!"*

Bread-making

A *losset (losaid?)* was a utensil used to make bread. It was made of light timber, two feet long by one foot wide, with a back and two ends about four inches high; the ends were slightly sloped towards the front so that there were no awkward corners to catch sleeves when making dough. Sourdough was made with flour, salt and soda and mixed with either water or milk, sometimes mashed potatoes were added and the whole left for a few days to sour.

Firewood

Bog-deal (*Cipiní guise*) was plentiful all over Achill. There was a lot of this in the bog at *MoTaidg* (Moyteoge). Large blocks of bog deal were collected for fuel and left to dry beside the fire. After it had been dried, splinters were peeled off and *cipiní* made into little bundles which were left on the hob or stuck into a *poll-a-baic* (a small recess in the wall beside the fire), to dry. People used to *spin and card* wool with no other light except that from a bog-deal fire.

Mining

Copper and sulphur were mined in *Buaile a Ghleanna* (Bolinglanna). Details of this industry are covered under the Encumbered Estates section. Copper mines were located between Gubroe and Carricknahelty, south-west of Bolinglanna and others to the east near Benderg.

Smuggling

In the eighteenth and nineteenth century, smuggling between Tóin na Dumaca harbour in Corraun and Flushing in Holland was common. Caiptín Seoirse Ó Máille and Paídin (ban) Mac Cormaic were, it seems, heavily involved. Legend has it that Paídin was a fine, tall, strong man who used to wear shoes of Spanish leather up to his knees! Once, when smuggled goods were being transferred to Newport for distribution, Captain Ó Máille's ship was sunk at *Poll na Raite (Polranny)* by a Revenue Commissioner's ship called *"The Sloopeen Vaughan"* (Slúipín Mhahon) about which a song was subsequently composed. Another story relates to Pat McNeela, nicknamed Patchaco, who also sailed with Captain Ó Máille and was *"a better sailor, but hadn't the navigational skills!"*

Duty Days

Duty days involved the giving of so many days free work, by the tenant, to the landlord which was offset against rent. Duty days could be avoided by the payment of livestock to the landlord. The same practice was later adopted by the tenants: *"stripes of seaweed being exchanged for a day's labour."* In Leck, the location of the old harbour in Dooagh, seaweed on the shore was divided into "stripes" (strips).

Shoemakers

There were twelve Shoemakers in Achill between 1920-30. In 1930 mass production of cheap shoes, together with wellingtons and sandals flooded the market and homemade shoes became a thing of the past.

63. Dooagh Pipe Band, St. Patrick's Day © Douglas Duggan

Achill

The first Pipe Band consisted of two flute players and a drummer with a homemade drum. Dooagh Pipe Band will celebrate its 50th anniversary in 1997 and plans a big celebration in Cleveland, Ohio.

64. Pollagh Church on St. Patrick's Day © *Douglas Duggan*

Political Fugitives

Prior to the 1798 Rising, a Dookinella man used to drill men on Dookinella Strand, sea rods being used as dummy guns! A spy reported him and he was arrested and marched to Achill Sound prior to being moved to Newport to be tried before the magistrate, Sir Neal O'Donnell. There was no bridge at Achill Sound then, and as the group waited for a ferry to take them across the Sound, a Galway Hooker passed by and the *"drill master"* jumped on board and escaped *via* Darby's Point in Cloughmore, despite efforts by the coastguards there who tried to stop him. Later he went to America to join O'Donovan Rossa.

320

20. The Folklore of Achill

Many ships docked at Darby's Point during the days of the " *free emigration*" when people could work their passage to America. Some of these ships passed through Bullsmouth in Dooniver and legend has it that a man, delighted to be one of the lucky ones going to America threw his old clothes from the ship to a poor man on shore at *Gob Rua na bhFeannóg*, so that he too could emigrate. A tale is told of a priest hiding in a cave in Keem Bay during the Penal Times who was helped by a Dooagh man who brought him food. The man's wife apparently told the *"military"* and got a reward of £100. Her husband is said to have hated her afterwards, and she later drowned herself. The priest was subsequently killed outside the cave and legend has it that traces of his blood can still be seen on the rocks there. This cave is the Priest's Cave in Keem Bay. In recent times cliff collapse has made this cave dangerous and access hazardous.

1916

During 1916 British soldiers, nicknamed *Black and Tans*, because of their mixed khaki and black uniforms, (supposedly nicknamed after a famous group of pack-hounds), were sent to Ireland. They were intensely disliked for their brutality to the people at large and many were killed by Irish mercenary soldiers. A number of young Achill men were members of the I.R.A. (Irish Republican Army), and the *Black and Tans*, on information received *via* an informer, arrested several of these young men who were sent to prison in England. Upon their release, all but one died *en route* to Ireland, the result, it was claimed, of starvation, or, as some would claim, *"slow poisoning."* A grave-slab in Slievemore marks the burial site of one of these young men and has the following inscription:

In Loving Memory of Michael Moran, Dooagh, Achill, late of Liverpool Company, I.R.A. who died 19th January, 1922, aged 25 years.

"The prison's deepest gloom he bore,

to keep the oath he swore"

Erected by *Clann-na-Gael*, his comrades and friends in Cleveland, Ohio, U.S.A.

Achill

Monuments

Other legends relate to conspicuous monuments in the countryside, many of which have long since disappeared, like the *"Stacaí Móra"*, possibly the remains of a stone circle. Seemingly, on a platform near this site *"the chieftain would address his army before going into battle."* Another story which may relate to this site tells of how people from Erris, in North Mayo, used to come to Achill looking for treasure near Dugort *" ...where there were three or four stones standing 4 feet high."* Under a grassy mound on Keel sandybanks is *Teach Briste* (the broken house). It is also called *Teach na daoine boict ("poorhouse")* and was once the home of an old scholar whom legend claims was raided and wrecked by one *Donnead Ropa,* both of unknown origin and date.

Megaliths

In Tonalorcha, *(Tamhnach Luachra)* in Dugort townland, is a place called *Teach a liag mhór,* meaning the house of large stones, probably a former megalithic tomb, now destroyed. De Valéra & Ó Nualláin (1964) searched for this site but could not find it, although they did say that based on Wood-Martin's (1887-88) description it was not a megalithic tomb.

Standing stones

According to folklore there was a standing stone on the north-west point of Inishkea Island which was said to be associated with the *Children of Lir* when they were banished to the Bay of Erris. Nearby Inishglora is traditionally thought to be the island to which the *Children of Lir* were banished. The people of Inishkea used to worship a stone called *Naomhóg*, and a particular family customarily made a dress of flannel for the stones so that it could be displayed when a favour was required. A new Curate to the island heard about this pagan practice and arranged for the stone to be thrown into the sea.

The Dane's Cave

This cave was supposedly under (near) Pat Dever's land, going to the Castle? Both cave and castle are unknown. The cave consisted of two rooms, one of which had a stone bed. This description would seem to suggest a souterrain. Caves or souterrains were well documented or remembered in oral tradition, mainly because of their association with mythological characters or as places of refuge. For example, *"Teach an tSagairt,"* midway up the south side of Slievemore is said to have been *" made by men who knew how to tunnel,"* and *" inside were lots of burned sticks."* (wood). This was probably the cave in which Fr. Manus Sweeney hid when he was *"on the run"* after the 1798 rebellion. Another cave which was said to be located west of the Achill Mission Settlement in Dugort, on the eastern side of Slievemore mountain, was called *Daras Mór*. Yet another is called *Druinnineach* and is said to be located west of Slievemore going towards Annagh. Attempts to find this cave have so far been unsuccessful.

Famine Graves

There are famine graves in the Valley, in Kildavnet and in Keel:

(1) Gob Bass

(2) Below the pier in the Valley

(3) Kildavnet

(4) Keel Sandybanks

Graveyards

In Achill, long ago, all the people were buried in Kildavnet. There is an elaborate tomb in this graveyard containing the remains of Fr. Michael Gallagher who came to Achill in 1847 and who died in 1867. According to folklore, when Fr. Gallagher first came to Achill, there were only two chapels on the island, one at Dookinella and another in Kildavnet. This may be the same Fr. Gallagher, referred to elsewhere in this book, who was ordained in the United States and who set up a scholarship for other members of the family to become priests. However, as none of them did, the people said there must have been some *" mallacht "* (curse) on the scholarship money. According to local folklore, this priest was *"so mean, he wouldn't spend a penny ! "* When he came to Achill he lived in a small house in Cashel until *"The Jumpers"* got the land and he had to leave it!

Achill

He then went to live on the Pike Estate at Achill Sound where seemingly he became great friends with Pike, from whom he received eight acres of land at Kildavnet chapel. A painting of him riding a horse was supposed to hang in Pike's house. Fr. Gallagher is mentioned several times in the *Achill Missionary Herald and Western Witness*, as he was a fierce opponent of Edward Nangle.

The Tower

There is a Tower (Napoleonic) located on a small hill to the east of Croaghaun mountain. It is square in shape, very sturdy, although no cement was used in its construction. It was supposed to have been built by *Gráinne Ní Mháille*. It is in fact the Napoleonic Tower referred to elsewhere in this book. It was the residence of the coastguards in the early nineteenth century and an ideal place to watch for smugglers.

Cillíní

There is a place in Dugort called *Cillín na Leaní* where unbaptised children were buried. Another *cillín* is located at *Carraic Hughie* in Upper Achill, a few hundred yards east of the present Church in Derreens. The origin of this custom is not known but its demise came about when the clergy lifted the ban and allowed these unbaptised infants to have christian burial. Adults also, were sometimes buried in the *cillín*; a sailor washed ashore in Dookinella was buried in the *cillín* near Minaun, because it was not known to which denomination they belonged! Another man, six feet six inches tall, is supposed to be buried in *Goban na bPaistí* (point of land) in Corraun. During World War II the bodies of ship-wrecked sailors washed ashore in Achill were generally buried in the graveyard at St. Thomas's Church in Dugort and their graves subsequently maintained by the Ministry of Defence in London.

RELIGIOUS TRADITION

Feast days

The preparation of a feast to celebrate St. Brigid's day on the first of February (Imbolg) was common in Achill. To honour the Saint, special crosses called St. Brigid's Crosses, were made in nearly all the villages and hung from the ceiling in all the houses. Another tradition which survived was the killing of fowl in honour of St. Martin, the blood of which was "sprinkled on the four corners of the house." The Achill festivals all seem to co-incide with earlier pagan festivals, albeit with different names, Imbolg, Beltaine, Lughnasa and Samhain.

Foretelling the future

At *Tobar Sliabh Mór* (St. Colman's Well) people washed their feet to ensure good health. Fish, which were supposed to live in this well, could foretell coming events if the petitioner walked around the well seven times, said seven rosaries, and threw seven stones into the well; if nothing dire was to happen, the fish appeared; if they remained hidden, calamity was sure to follow. The Holy Well at Minaun, *St. Fionán's Well* was *"fouled by some of Nangle's boys,"* after which it dried up. Similar versions of this story are found in other parts of Ireland. This well was reopened on the 8th September, 1996 (Sr. Paul, *pers. comm.*).

65. Pilgrimage along "Coffin Route" via Minaun © T. McDonald.

Coffin routes and Mass Paths

Folklore records a man seen carrying a corpse, halfway between *Albraca Mionáin* and *Beál na gCliath,* along a roadway called *Bealac na hAisteime* (Ashleam) to *Dub-Eige*. This road was said to have been made in the *"bad times"* (Famine) by men who were paid one penny a day or a *"maimín"* of yellow meal. The corpse had his clothes on and his feet were sweeping the road. He was being taken for burial to Kildavnet. On many occasions, however, the people were too tired to carry the corpses all the way to Kildavnet and they were buried at the side of the road.

Tragedies

In 1894, people on their way to the *"tattie hoking"* (picking potatoes) in Scotland left Achill on two *"Hookers"* to meet up with the Glasgow ship at Westport. Seeing their ship moored near Westport Quay they crowded to one side to have a better look, when at the same time a huge *"squall,"* or gust of wind, capsized the Hooker, and thirty two people drowned, the sail trapping many of them. The bodies, when recovered, were laid out in Westport, and were later brought to Achill, travelling on the very first train to Achill and fulfilling the prophesy of Brian Rua Ó Cearbháin that *"carriages on iron wheels, emitting smoke and fire would carry coffins to Achill on both its first and last train journey."*

The second part of the prophesy was fulfilled when the last passenger train to Achill carried the bodies of the victims of the Kirkintilloch disaster: ten young people who were burned alive in a *" bothy"* (hut) in Scotland, were brought home. Although the railway had been closed in 1934 it was reopened so that all the bodies could be transported together to Mulranny and on to Achill Sound. In 1953, a boat containing a film crew while shooting scenes for *"Shark Island"* close to the *"The Daisies,"* capsized, and all lives were lost except for Hugh Falkus, an actor, who swam into Keem Bay to raise the alarm. Another member of the cast, actress Clare Mullen, who had not been feeling well, did not accompany the others on that fateful voyage and escaped with her life. Hugh Falkus died in early 1996.

On the 12th-13th July, 1979, the *Lios Cearra* went down off Dooega Head and three fishermen drowned, the Skipper, Seán Kilbane and two crew members, Patrick Kilcoyne and John McGeady, all natives of Dooagh. All three are buried together in Slievemore graveyard.

20.   The Folklore of Achill

66.   Purteen Harbour

The Great Famine (*An Feár Gortach*)

A folk tale relates how a Priest warned people *"against planting seed potatoes in 1847, when the general belief was that the blight would continue. Those who disregarded this advice are said to have had a good crop and this is advanced as one reason why people turned Protestant."* This tale is obviously connected to the Achill Mission in Dugort. On the Corraun road is the resting place of *Nancy an Jaillinir,* murdered during *" the bad times (Famine), for a stone of meal!"*

During the famine, cargos of turf from Achill were exchanged for cargos of potatoes in Rathfran, near Ballina. When *The Neptune* was wrecked off Achill Head, the cargo was taken to Annagh and dumped in a deep hole at *Poll a'Mhadaigh* (for safe keeping!). This was later recovered by the Coastguard and sold in Dooagh.

Famine Food

Fucus (seaweed) farms, consisted of large stones arranged in linear fashion along the sea shore which were colonised by seaweed. When sufficient seaweed had accumulated on these boulders, usually after about three years, the seaweed was harvested. It was then used alone as

Achill

a fertiliser or mixed with sea-sand to make *plaggen* soil. Lines of these boulders can still be seen at Cloughmore and at Árds in Corraun. The success of the fucus farms was enhanced by the collection of different varieties of seaweeds, many extremely nutritious, and is one reason given for the fact that few people in Corraun died during the famine. This vast harvest of food from the sea, included *Dilisk, Creannac and Triopadaoi*, together with weeds like *Carraigin, Cuirdíns*, a weed like a parsnip, *Caisearbain* (dandelion), and *Sayna* (senna) which was made into tea.

Roads

William McCormack who arrived in Achill in the mid-19th century is credited with initiating a major road-building scheme in Corraun. He was a well-to-do man, and a member of the *"Irish Beetroot and Sugar Manufacturing Company."* However, he did not survive in Achill and his estate was subsequently sold in the Encumbered Estates Court and purchased by a Mr. Dickens, who built Corraun House.

In Corraun near *" Poll a Bric"* where the Corraun road joins the road to Achill Sound, there are foundation marks of a former Achill Mission school which was demolished by a landlord named Mr. Ryan, who was a bit of a fire-brand and a staunch Catholic and intensely disliked by Edward Nangle. The fact that one was Catholic and the other Protestant probably did not help! Ryan was one-time editor of the **Catholic Vindicator**, and a member of the *Irish Mineral Trading Company.* He built a road in Corraun which is now called *Boitrín Ryan.*

Early in the nineteenth century, Dr. Tanner, the M.P. for Cork, came to address a meeting in Corraun and a *"crumpaun,"* a rough block of bog deal, was set up to mark the occasion. Elsewhere on the island, the old pathways traversed the sea shore or followed trackways across the mountains e.g. *An tSean mBothair.* Travel was by boat or on horseback. During this time people from the West of Ireland had to go to Drogheda to catch the boat to England. The Achill Mission built a number of roads, prior to and during the Great Famine, *via* grants from the Board of Works

20. The Folklore of Achill

to operate relief schemes. Over one hundred men were regularly employed on road construction.

Evictions

Baile Ailt, "once a fine village with a street plan like a town" with houses arranged in terraces in semi-detached fashion, was deserted in the mid 19th century when the landlord, William Pike, is said to have evicted some of the tenants. Along a laneway leading to Kildavnet quarry is a house called:

"Teac na mBaintreac" (Widow's house) where a group of widows from *Baile Ailt* were housed after the eviction, because *" it was cheaper to house them here than pay for them in the Poorhouse!"*

Burials

During the Famine, corpses were buried where they fell, the nearest graveyard being in Kildavnet, which involved the corpse being brought *via* the Minaun cliffs to Kildavnet. Local folklore maintains that there are famine graves on Keel sandybanks and in many other places.

Customs (Marriage)

The Halls (1841-43) described a strange custom relating to love and marriage which seemingly was peculiar to Achill:

"a few days before our arrival, an occurrence took place which is by no means uncommon - a race for a wife. A young man, a carpenter, named Linchigan (Lynchehaun), applied to the father of a girl named Corrigan, for his daughter in marriage. A rival, called Lavelle, asked for her also, on the the plea that he was richer he wouldn't ask so much with her. Whereupon, the factions of the swains were about to join issue and fight, a peacemaker suggested that the boys should run for her. The race was run, a distance of some miles up and down a mountain; Linchigan (Lynchehaun) won, and wedded the maiden." Halls (1841-43).

Wakes

In Achill, men were waked in their best clothes and women in habits, long brown gowns similar to those worn by nuns in the past. Most people were waked in a coffin:*"overboard" (os cionn clair)* is the usual term for being waked. Wake games were played in Achill. When someone died, work was suspended for three days, the corpse was not touched for six hours, continuous candles were lit beside the corpse, and a plate of tobacco, cigarettes and clay pipes were set out for the mourners. Four men with the same surname would take the corpse for burial. The coffin was always carried with the corpse's feet to the front. It was the custom for people to remain at the wake until after cockcrow and, when leaving the wake, they always carried the remains of a *"lighted coal" (caorán)* with them, as protection against evil spirits.

Before people emigrated to the United States they had an *"American Wake"* which was a euphemism for a party the night before the person in question emigrated. Alice McGinty of Salia, aged 87 years in 1855 had two sisters in the U.S.A. who *"were able to do farm work"* and who settled in Chicago. Many emigrants, unable to speak English, returned home after a short while. House work and farm work, were the main types of employment available to emigrants.

Thomas O'Malley born in Keel in November, 1865 said most people from Keel went to Cleveland to work in the Steel Mills and on the Ohio and Erie Canal. Money was sent from the U.S.A. to pay the passage of later emigrants. Letters from the U.S.A. were the property of the community at large: when a letter arrived from the U.S.A. all the neighbours would congregate in the recipients house and the letter was read aloud. The Rev. Stoney of Rosturk used to send people on the *Free Emigration*. They went from Achill Sound or Bullsmouth where the ships used to anchor.

The Supernatural

One, **Paidín Anna**, saw the "fetches" (shades-ghosts) of a group of young women dancing at 3 a.m. on the Green in front of his house! He stood watching them *"with nothing on but his shirt."* Recognising the girls as local, he visited each of them the next day and advised them to go to Keem Bay and to gather a certain herb, boil it, and then drink it. He

20. The Folklore of Achill

told them that if they did not do as he asked, they would be dead within twelve months as *" the fairies had got hold of them."* The girls laughed at him, but within twelve months all were dead.

A cock crowing, and a dog barking at the same time, is a sign of death. A bird coming into a house is a sign of death; to avoid this, three feathers must be plucked from its tail and burned. The bird is then set free.

Answering a knock at the door and then discovering that there is no one there is a warning of impending death for whoever answers the knock. The person should immediately put three grains of salt on the tongue and scatter a few grains of salt over the shoulder in order to ward off death. People cutting turf often came upon little mounds or hillocks, called *"sídh grogíni "* which they avoided cutting into, because these mounds were said to be the homes of the banshees, who also sat on them when *"keening"* their death laments.

A man, whose family came from Dooagh, was said to be descended from a mermaid. His father had hidden her tail in the thatch of the house but when the house caught fire the mermaid found the tail, and disappeared.The mermaid story is widely distributed in Ireland (Higgins, 1996). If a mermaid sees you before you see her, you will not live long!

Hauntings

Many stories are told about hauntings at the booley, no doubt a result of the booley sites usually remote location! For example, even today, few people would volunteer to stay overnight in Annagh. People who did, were kept awake by the noise of *"riderless horses"* galloping round them all night long, together with the unnerving presence of a tall thin man, wearing a hat and dark clothes!

A group of girls sleeping overnight in one of the booley huts had their dog physically thrown in on top of them by a person(s) unknown (John McNamara, *pers. comm.*). Several *"sightings"* were noted in Annagh, including one where a group of young women staying at the booley, noticed a young woman, on the mountainside near Lugh whom they

331

thought was a servant-girl recently come to work in the area. Although they called up to her to join them, she suddenly disappeared; on their way back to Dooagh, one of the young women, twenty two years of age and recently married, collapsed and had to be carried home, her hip dislocated, and who remained, thereafter, a cripple. The appearance of the girl was taken to be a sign or warning of coming disaster, which in this case proved too true. Another involved three young men who upon spying three girls on the beach at Annagh, waved down to them but got no response. Six months later one of three young men died unexpectedly. A rather amusing tale is told about a " *Herd*" who lived with his wife in a house south-east of Lake Bunnafreva East. While tending cattle and sheep for his employer, a local landlord, he returned home to find his wife had left and taken all their possessions with her. Searching the area, he saw her in the distance, climbing up towards Lugh, on her way to Dooagh, carrying her bed (mattress) on her back. It seems that she was scared " *out of her wits*" by something she saw in Annagh and thereafter refused to set foot in the place. The remains of their house and *"lazy bed"* ridges are now almost completely overgrown with ferns, but the area has spectacular scenery and is well worth a visit.

The Devil

The Devil, or Big Fellah, seems to have been a frequent visitor to the booley: the following tale being common to booley sites throughout Achill:

" *Once when the Slievemore people booleyed in Dirk on the north-west side of Slievemore hill, facing Inishkea, a woman, and her baby were alone in the booley waiting for her husband who had gone fishing, when a man, covered from head to toe in black hair, came and sat by the fire. The frightened woman hoping to get rid of the demon , kept saying " nach fada atá siad seo amuich" (aren't they a long time away) while the man replied: " ní tiocfáid siad go deo"* (they will never return).

In desperation, she dipped a*"noggin"* (a small mug) into a pot of brocan (broth) on the fire and threw it over the man, who with an unearthly scream, ran out the door. The woman, grabbed her baby and ran back to Slievemore. Later, men from the village went back to the booley, but all they found was timber chewed up and torn to pieces. The woman said the man was the Devil *(Big Fellah)* and that the salt in the broth had saved her. The woman's husband and sons returned, but were drowned shortly afterwards, bringing to pass the devil's prediction! This story probably dates to the pre-famine period during occupation of the Deserted Village. It also shows that Dirk was being used as a booley by the Slievemore people. This same story is told about a booley village in *Cóire,* a glen on the east side of Corraun Hill where women and young girls lived in *"botógs "* (sod houses) from June to September.

The Banshee, as elsewhere in Ireland, follows certain families and will be heard *"keening"* shortly before a death occurs. Seemingly, she can often be seen sitting on the *Sidh Groigín,* small raised mounds in the bogs from which turf is never cut.

Butter stolen from Churns

A story is told of a man who had butter stolen from a churn. Taking a gun, he set off in pursuit of the thief and approaching a byre he saw a hare which he shot at *"with a bit of silver"* so as not to kill it. He followed the injured hare which went into a local farmhouse and there on the bed was a young woman combing her hair which was covered in blood. This story also forms an element within the Banshee legend. This lady was well-off, had a side-car in which she used to go to market to sell large quantities of butter, but seemingly after this she took no more butter to market!

Fairies

A lady who lived alone owned a spinning wheel with which she made woollen clothes. One night as she was making *" stirabout"* (porridge) a lady walked in and sat down beside her. The woman of the house offered her some stirabout which she took, and later, when she asked for more and was told there was none, she asked the woman if she had made the stirabout with water and from where had she had got the water. Being told that the water was obtained from a well, she advised the woman of

Achill

the house to go to the well next morning where she would find a coin but to tell nobody. The woman continued to collect the coin each morning until, breaking her promise, told a neighbour of her good fortune, and immediately the coins ceased to appear.

Ghosts

A woman seeing a boy crossing the mountain near Corrymore lake late one evening became worried when she did not see him return. What she had seen was his *"shade"* (ghost). Soon after the boy collapsed on the road to Keem Bay having lost the use of his legs and died shortly afterwards. This incident, together with that relating to the young woman who collapsed on the way home from Annagh may suggest a vitamin deficiency leading to *rickets* (a disease which causes softening of the bone), which may explain the above supposedly supernatural events.

A Dooagh woman rising early one morning saw six people dancing on The Green behind her house; some she recognised as neighbours, others had earlier emigrated to the U.S.A. Within a short space of time the woman herself died. This is a common story found throughout Ireland.

Elf shots

When cattle were affected with ailments e.g. *"drooping ears,"* the only cure was to give them three drinks of water in which sídhes (also called elf-darts) or fairy stones had been placed. They were also called fairy darts which were frequently prehistoric implements, collected and sometimes hung in a bag in a byre (stable) to protect animals. The sídhes used in Achill and Erris were generally barbed-and-tanged arrowheads of Bronze Age date. They were kept by people in each locality and could not be touched by any person other than the owner. The stones had to be wrapped in cloth and dropped into a bucket of water together with a " *two-shilling"* (10p) coin with a cross on it. If the water *"fizzled"* up and boiled with large bubbles appearing, the cattle were supposed to get well. The *"elf shots"* (sídhes), were described as small stones of a dark blue colour, probably chert or flint, darker than limestone, and of various sizes, about one inch each way. Others had hollows, said to be the tracks of fairy fingers!

20. The Folklore of Achill

Superstition

The bodies of persons who drowned at sea, upon being brought ashore, were carefully placed in a particular location because superstition maintained that wherever the body rested would be haunted by the *"fetch"* or ghost of the person who had drowned. When bodies of sailors were washed ashore, the local people were afraid to go near that place after dark. However, if clothes belonging to a person who had drowned were thrown into the water near where the drowning occurred, the body would be found more easily.

Natural Medicine

Folk Medicine has once again gained popularity and people tend to forget that it was widely practised in Ireland before the advent of modern medicine. The following are some plants used in Achill in olden times to cure various ailments: *Meiriní na mban sidhe* (foxglove), which had to be gathered when they were in full bloom and were used as a cure for stomach ache and to bathe boils. The root and top of the dandelion when boiled was used for ailments of the heart, or to prevent consumption. Mountain sedge was boiled and used as a cough medicine; brown moss from coarse hilly land was said to be great for the kidneys as well as lily of the valley, and ivy, though not common, was also used. *Buachaill an tí* (house leek) which grows on thatch was said to be good for the eyes. Roots of the blackberry briar were good for diarrhoea.

The crádán (*Dinneen crádán* - lesser burdock) - of which there were two kinds, male and female, and marshmallow plants were dug and boiled, after which vinegar, sugar and egg shells were added. This was considered a good cough mixture. Garlic added to whiskey was used to cure tuberculosis. Boiled broom, to which gin was added, was good for ailments of the kidneys. Juniper berries were collected by women only on Juniper Sunday, the last Sunday of July, which also happens to be the festival of *Lughnasa,* and were believed to help with problems of infertility, but which could also cause abortion.

Achill

Other natural medicines

One of the reasons given for taking livestock to the booley was to avoid *crupán,* a disease afflicting cattle if they were kept too long in one grazing area. Cream, fresh or sour, was said to be good for cuts, burns or sores that had turned septic. Asses milk was excellent for *"whooping cough."* The inside of an onion, toasted for a minute and placed inside the ear cured ear-ache. Grey wool from a black sheep was also good for ear-ache or any severe pain. *Tae na nGarranrtai* (self-heal), a couple of handfuls of this plant was boiled in a quart of water, strained and kept in a bottle. A half-a-cup taken three times per day for nine to fifteen days helped those suffering from angina or palpitations. The herb, *bugoir,* was scorched in fire on St. John's Night (24th June), dried and kept as a cure for many ailments. Cabbage leaves, heated and placed against the face were said to be a great cure for mumps.

Special Days

May Day was a great day for many things: women washing their faces in the dew on May morning to ensure they would not get *wrinkles* that year. I remember my Mother doing this and I in turn have followed suit, with some success! On May Day no " *lighted"* coal could leave the house or bad luck would ensue.

St. John's Night

On St. John's Night, bonfires were lit all over the island, usually at former cross-roads or old roads no longer in use. The bonfire was a communal effort in which everyone joined, particularly in the two weeks beforehand when groups of young people would gather huge stacks of *gorse* and *whin (furze)* to be transported on St. John's Night to the bonfire sites. In the village of Dooagh, one bonfire is sited at the junction of a former crossroads.

336

20. The Folklore of Achill

Michaelmas

"Summer is Summer to Michaelmas Day" was an old saying. Tradition dictated that all crops had to be gathered before Michaelmas. There was a belief that whichever way the wind blew at Michaelmas, so it would blow for the rest of the year. Blackberries were never eaten after Michaelmas. Boxty (grated raw potatoes, fried in butter) was a particular treat at this time. The cows were taken from the booley at Michaelmas and allowed to graze on the *"aftergrass"* around the various villages. The herring season began at Michaelmas with a special ceremony.

Halloween

Customs practised at Halloween were numerous. One of the most popular was one in which curious young boys and girls tried to find out who their future spouses were likely to be. This involved acquiring a fresh herring, which had to be boiled or fried without cleaning. This was taken to the bedroom and eaten before going to bed. Sometime during the night the future spouse was supposed to come and offer a glass of water, which was no doubt eagerly sought! This custom was often abused and many tricks were played, particularly on elderly bachelors in the community. Another custom involved *"throwing cabbage"* at doorways and moving *"farm carts"* from one location to another.

The Wren boys:

Wren boys had to be aged between seven and fourteen years. A furze or veronica bush tied with brightly coloured pieces of cloth or a board with a tiny cage on it was substituted for a live wren, which were difficult to catch. The wren boys went out on St. Stephen's Day (Boxing Day) reciting the following poem, on the doorstep of each house, collecting money as they went:

> *The wren, the wren, the king of all birds,*
> *St. Stephen's Day was caught in the furze,*
> *Up with the kettle, down with the pan,*
> *Give me a penny to bury the wren.*
> *If you haven't a penny, a halfpenny will do,*
> *If you haven't a halfpenny, God bless you.*

Achill

The Penal Times

After the Penal Laws were enacted in 1691, many Catholic landowners in Connacht changed their allegiance to the Protestant faith because they had been forbidden to stand for Parliament, vote, or join the army or navy, practice law, or buy land. Mass had to be held in out-of-the-way places e.g. Keem Bay in Achill where a replica of a Penal Altar still stands.

The White Boys

In 1831 secret societies went under the general name of *Ribbonism* and included the White Boys, Steel Boys, Terry Alts and others. They offered protection to the people against rack-renting, by unscrupulous landlords by threatening them with violence. The penalty for membership was transportation to Van Dieman's Land (Tasmania).

Notable characters

Andrew Mór McTigue from Salia, said to be the strongest man in Achill, lived around A.D. 1800 and was a seaman and mason by trade. It seems that a ship carrying a negro docked in Westport, and he sent out a challenge for someone to come and fight against him. The negro in question was probably *John The Moor Molyneux* who was a black freed slave who died in Galway of the flu c.1805-1810 and is buried in St. James Cemetery, Gleninagh Heights in an unmarked grave. (Jim Higgins, *pers. comm.*). Andrew Mór accepted the challenge and won the fight which was fought aboard ship. Later on, Andrew decided to build a barn but hurt himself putting a huge lintel in place over the doorway which was said to be *"twice the length of a man and two feet thick."* He died not having seen the building completed.

Pat Bourke from Dooagh fought in three wars, World War I, World War II and the Spanish Civil War. He returned penniless to Westport where he died. He was buried in Slievemore graveyard at the expense of Tom McNamara, Boley House, Keel.

20. The Folklore of Achill

THE MYTHOLOGICAL TRADITION

Fionn Mac Cummal

Tales of Fionn Mac Cumaill (son of the slave) appear both in folklore and in legend. Tales of Fionn and the Fianna are associated with most parts of Ireland. An older Fionn, called Fintan, a name meaning *"ancient knowledge,"* who, it was said, survived the Flood and was therefore *"an indispensable witness in matters relating to pre-history."* (Mac Allister, 1939).*" The Colloquy of Fintan and the Old Hawk of Eacaill"*, translated by Eleanor Knott (1957), from a 15th century text, ***The Book of Fermoy:*** Fintan and the Hawk swop tales about their respective adventures since the Flood:

Fintan
" That is the ancient O Bird of Eacaill, tell us the cause of thy journey. I can converse with thee expertly in bird language. "

Bird
"As for thee, thy body is not young; it is long since it shrivelled in Dún Tuleha by the sea; O Fintan, thou learned man. "

Fintan
"More strange is it that I should be living; gloom has settled on my heart; the sorrow of Ros Grecha has maimed me; the tragic death of Illann has grieved me even more. O Bird from Eacaill of the hunters, I have been seeking to behold thee; now that I see thee, tell me why doest thou cling to Achill? "

Bird
"The brightness of its sky, the beauty of its harbours, the warmth of its never chill woods, the fruitfulness of its chase, the freedom of its streams and the quiet solitude of its bays. O Fintan, I was never a night in Eacaill to the west that I could not get by my skill all I devour of fish, of game, of venison."

Fintan
"There came a crow from old Eacaill over the river mouth at Eas Ruaid, I will not hide it though it be a mystery, he robbed me of one eye."

Bird
"It was I the grey hawk that dwells alone in the bosum of Eacaill, who swallowed thine eye O Fintan." Knott, (1957).

Achill

The Celtic God, *Lugh,* is also associated with certain birds in Irish tradition, particularly the raven, a bird said to possess outstanding intelligence and knowledge! In the above poem, the bird also tells Fintan that he has seen " *...full many a raven and crow along with Lugh of the hero's hands."* Ross (1974). Ross interprets this as meaning a reference to *Lugh's* heroic qualities, in that he provided plenty of corpses for the ravens to feed on, and to his own special connection with these birds.

Conn of the Hundred Battles

Prior to the **Battle of Moylena**, " *Conn came from Connacht with Conall Cruachna's sons, Eochy Whitenee and Fiachaidh Whitehand, sons of Crimhthann Culbuide, King of Aicill and Umhall, and of Gairech, daughter of Criomall, and other allies and saved Tara by defeating and killing Eochy (Muinderg) King of Munster."* Knox (1908:12). Crimhthann's two sons were sent as emissaries by Conn to Eógan who had them hanged. Goll mac Morna, chief of the Gamanrad of Iorrus later went to Eógan Mór's camp and killed him.

Cormac Mac Airt

Cormac Mac Airt (A.D.227-266), was the grandson of *Conn Cétchathach* (Hundred Battles), victor at the **Battle of Moylena** and was, according to legend, closely connected with Corraun, having been brought up there by his Druid step-father. Legends about him are found mainly in *Leath Cuinn,* (Conn's half). Cormac's mother, *Achtan,* was the daughter of a Druid and Cormac was supposedly conceived before a great battle *(Mucramha)* and born after Airt, his father, had been killed. He was fostered in Corraun and when he was thirty years of age, his Druid grandfather told him to go to Tara and claim the high kingship.

THE HISTORICAL TRADITION

The French at Killala

During the Rebellion of 1798, the French fleet were reputedly supposed to land in Achill (John Moran, *pers. comm.)* , but being advised that British ships were patrolling in Clew Bay, they endeavoured to avoid them and in the process went too far out to sea, by-passing Achill, and ending up in Killala. Some men from Achill went to join the French army when General Humbert landed in Killala, their names were Molloy and Sweeney, but they never returned.

Fr. Manus Sweeney

Fr. Manus Sweeney is said to have been born in Achill in 1763-64, although his birth-place is disputed. Prior to his birth, it was prophesied that he would be hanged. A beggarman lodging in a mid-wife's house in Dookinella prophesied that a baby born that night would be a great man but would be hanged. The baby's parents, who were well off, sent their son, Manus Sweeney, to France to be educated for the Priesthood. Upon his return to Ireland during the 1798 Rebellion, he was seen greeting a former classmate, a French officer, at Skerdagh, between Newport and Castlebar. This was reported to the English garrison and a warrant was issued for his arrest. He escaped to Achill where he supposedly hid in a cave *(Daras Mór)* on Slievemore, but he was captured either in Dugort or the Valley and later hanged from an old crane in Market Square in Newport. He was buried in Burrishoole Abbey on June 9th, 1799. The people of Achill decided to build a monument to commemorate his death, but could not agree on a suitable location. One evening, two men saw a bright light down on the shore beside Fr. Manus's old home in Dookinella and, needless to say, the monument was erected there, where it stands to the present day.

16th Century Settlement

Between 1654 and 1660 an influx of new settlers, evicted by Cromwell from Ulster, arrived in Tonragee, Ballycroy and Achill. These were: O'Donnells, Gallaghers, O'Clearys, McDaids (Davitt), Cafferkeys, Devers, Ginnellys, McNallys, McManamons, McGintys, McNultys, McLoughlins, McNeas, Pattens, McNeelas, Mulloys, Keanes, Corrigans and O'Neills. According to the Halls (1843), there were four main families in Achill: The Lavelles of French extraction; the O'Malleys indigenous inhabitants of Connacht; the Morans, of Danish extraction;

341

and the Caulfields of English origin. Ó Móráin (1957) lists Ó Máille (O'Malley), Ó Fearghusa (O'Fergus), Mac an Mháistir (Masterson) and Ó Móráin (O'Moran) as four branches of the one stock.

67. The Atlantic Drive © Theresa McDonald

Chapter 21

PLACE NAMES - *LOG-AINMNEACHA*

Annagh (Eanach, narrow path or a strand or marshy place)

Ashleam (léam = leap, water-fall)

Bal of Dookinella (Bal Duma Cin Áille - Bal Dhumhach Chinn Aille = sandbank at the head of the cliff or Dumha = burial place)

Béal na gCliath (Mouth of the Hurdles)

Bealnasolla (Beál an ath salaig = mouth of dirty-ford)

Belfarsad (tidal ford or mouth of the pass-ferry)

Bleanaskill (A narrow tongue of land, shaped like an armpit)

Bolinglanna (Booley in the valley)

Bunacurry (Bun a Curraig = lower wet part of the swamp or moor)

Bunafahy (Bono-fa-ia = lower part of the swamp: faiche = field: Bottom of the open fields)

Bunanioo (Bottom of the wood where the wise man lived)

Bunnafreva Lough West (Loch Bhun na Freimh, lake of the bottom of the root-outlet)

Carrowgarve (Ceatramad Garb-Ceathrú Garbh = rough quarter)

Cashel (Caisial = stone fort)

Claggan (Claigean = round, rocky hill)

Cloughmore (An Cloch Mhór - Cloch Mór = big or great stone)

Cornaclea Point (Corr na Cléithe = the round hill of the hurdle)

Corraun (An Corran = hook or crescent shaped place)

Corryndoberleen (Cóire an Doibirlin = hollow, or place difficult of access: a tight corner, or corrie of the dark, mysterious pool or Coire an Dobairlinn = corrie of the dark, or shady lake)

Derreens (Doirín = little oak wood)

Dooagh (comes from Dumha (Dubh) Acha meaning mound of the field or a sandbank)

Dooega (Dubh Eige, means black surface land. Could also mean Éige's fort, Dún Éige, or Éige's burial mound)

Dookinella (Duma Cin Áille-Dumhach Chinn Aille = means sandbank at the head of the cliff)

Dooniver (Dubh Ibir = means Ivir's fort)

Achill

Dugort (Dubh Gort, means black garden/cultivated field or mound in a field)

Finsheen (Síochán Fionn, meaning ash trees and also by tradition Fionn's seat. Could also mean 'white')

Glacknagloghraha - Glaic na gCloch Reatha (Recess (hollow) or ravine of the rolling stones)

Gubfoheratawy (Gob Fothar an tSamhaidh (Tamhnaigh) = point/headland of the sorrell/wood, or possibly a fertile, grass-grown surface sloping down to a cliff)

Gubnahardia (Gob Na hÁirde = Beak or snout of the hill/lookout point)

Inishbiggle (Inis Bigil = vigil island). Inishbiggle does not appear on either Petty's 1685 map or Strafford's 1635 Inquisition of County Mayo, nor in the 1636 County Mayo Book of Survey and Distribution.

Keel (An Caol means the strait or narrow neck or quarter)

Kildavnet (Carraig Cille Damnaite = rock of Kildavnet; Cill Damhnait = Davnet's Church)

Kilmore (Great Church)

Lough Nakeeroge West (Loch na Ciaroige=the lake of the cockroach or Lake of the Mountain Ash). Locally, this name is pronounced, caoróg, meaning a small berry, and could refer to the rowan trees or the solitary strawberry tree beside the lake.

Maumnaman (Maum na Mbán - Mám na mBan = elevated pass of the women)

Mweelin Muig Muillin (Maoileann Bhig Mhuileann = Plain of the hill. Mweelin- Maoilin = peak/summit of hill - or summit of the little Mill)

O'Connor's Rock (Carraig Uí Conchuir's rock -Cregín Conchubhair), a small hill north of Dooagh and east of Annagh, said to be near the spot where a chieftain named O'Connor and his crew were shipwrecked. The bodies were buried in the graveyard in Slievemore.

Ooghbleannaghallbaud (Óichín Bléan an Ghall Bhád = Cave or cove of the English boats: the location of this area is between the Benmore cliffs and Achill Head)

21. Placenames

Ooghnadirka (Uaimh na Deirce = cave or cove of the cave)
Owenduff (Abhainn Dubh = Black river)
Polranny (Poll Raithní = Hole of the ferns)
Roenacoragh (Ró na Córach= Point or headland)
Salia (Sáile = brine or salt water)
Slievemore (Sliabh Mór = Great mountain), pronounced *Slé Mór*. The Ordnance Survey Letters describe it as a large village to the east of the townland, the houses of stone, and poorly constructed)
Sraheens (Na Sraithíní = small holms/little marshy fields)
The Sound (Gob an Choire- = point/headland of the cauldron and of the fair wind - head of the corrie)
Tinny Lough (Loch na Tine = lake of the fire or loch a'tsionnaigh = lake of the foxes. *Lough Mullach an Bhaile,* however, may be its real name and if so, it is associated with Annagh Booley Village)
Tonragee (Tóin re Gaoth = windy hill or low ground facing an inlet)
Uggoole (Ogúl = a hollow or a connecting piece of land). Occurs only in Mayo and Galway.
The Valley (Tóin an tSean Bhaile - ar rinn na leanbh = Bottom of the old town); (ar rinn na leanbh = cillín = children's graveyard)
Sources: *Ordnance Survey Name Books*, Mayo, 1838-40; ***The Back of Beyond****.* Barry, (1973); ***Mayo Places*** *.* Ó Muraíle (1985); John Toolis, Keel, John McNamara, N.T., Dooagh and Tom McNamara, Boley House, Keel.

> *"Have you ever heard of the Land of Beyond,*
> *That dreams at the gates of the day?*
> *Alluring it lies at the skirts of the skies*
> *and ever so far away;*
> *Alluring its calls: O ye the yoke galls,*
> *And ye of the trail overfond,*
> *With saddle and pack, by paddle and track,*
> *Let's go to the Land of Beyond!"*

> *Robert Service, 1948.*

345

Achill

Bibliography

Aalen, F.H.A.1983 "Perspectives on the Irish Landscape in Prehistory and History," Reeves-Smyth, T. & Hammond, F. *Landscape Archaeology in Ireland, B.A.R. British Series* **116**:357-377. Oxford.

Aldridge, R.B. 1969 "Notes on Children's Burial Grounds in Mayo," *Journal of the Royal Society of Antiquaries of Ireland*, **99**: 83-87.

Anderson, C. 1830 **Historical sketches of the native Irish and their descendants illustrative of their past and present state with regard to literature, education and oral instruction**. London.

Armstrong, Rev. T. 1906 **My Life in Connacht with sketches of Mission Work in the West.** Dublin.

Bald, W. 1836-40 "An account of the Model of the Island of Achill, Clare Island and the south-west district of Mayo," *Proceedings of the Royal Irish Academy,* Vol.**1**:263-64.

Barrow, J. 1836 **A Tour Round Ireland through sea-coast counties**. London.

Barry, T. 1973 " The Back of Beyond," *Cappuchin Annual:* 151-162.

Barry, T. B. 1981 "Archaeological excavations at Dunbeg Promontory Fort, Co. Kerry," *Proceedings of the Royal Irish Academy,* **81C**:295-329.

Barry, T.B. 1987 **The Archaeology of Medieval Ireland.** London/New York.

Bieler. L. 1949 **The Life and Legend of St. Patrick.** Dublin.

Bieler, L. 1979 **The Patrician Texts in the Book of Armagh**. London and New York.

Binchy, D. 1962 "Patrick and his biographers: ancient and modern," *Studia Hibernica* **2**:7-173.

Blacker, W. 1834 **Prize essay addressed to the agricultural committee of the Royal Dublin Society on the management of landed property in Ireland**. Dublin.

Böll, H. 1957 **Irische Tagebuch (Irish Journal).** First English edition, 1967.

Bowen, D. 1970 **Souperism: myth or reality.** Dublin.

Bowen, H. J. 1961 **Ancient Fields.** London.

Brady, N. 1990 "A glimpse of Early Irish Agriculture," *Archaeology Ireland,* Vol. **4**. No. 4:18-19.

Buckley, V. M. & Lawless, C. 1987 "Prehistoric Cooking in Co. Mayo," *Cathair Na Mart, Journal of the Westport Historical Society,* Vol. **7**. No. 1:33-34.

Byrne, F.J. 1973 **Irish Kings and High Kings**. London. Paperback Edition, London, 1987.

Byrne, M.E. & Dillon, M. 1937 "Táin Bó Fraích," *Études Celtique,* **2**, 1-27.

22. Bibliography

Cambrensis, Giraldus, 1980 **The History and Topography of Ireland** *translated* **by John J. O'Meara from the Latin**. Dublin.

Campbell, A.1937 "Notes on the Irish House," *Folklife* **1**:207.

Carney, J. 1986 **The Playboy and the Yellow Lady**. Dublin.

Caulfield, S. 1978 "Neolithic fields: the Irish evidence, " In H.C. Bowen and P.J. Fowler (eds.) **Early Land Allotment in the British Isles**, *B.A.R. British Series* **48**:137-144. Oxford.

Caulfield, S. 1983 " The Neolithic Settlement of North Connacht," In Reeves-Smyth, T. and Hammond, F.(Eds.), **Landscape Archaeology in Ireland**. *B.A.R. British Series 116*:195-215. Oxford:

Census of Population, 1841-1991 (Central Statistics Office), Dublin.

Chambers, A. 1979 **Granuaile, the life and times of Grace O'Malley, c.1530-1603.** Dublin.

Chapman, R. 1979 "Transhumance and Megalithic Tombs in Iberia," *Antiquity* **53**:15-152. London.

Charlesworth, J.K. 1930 "Some geological observations on the origin of the Irish flora and fauna," *Proceedings of the Royal Irish Academy,* Vol. **39B**:358-90.

Charlesworth, J.K. 1952 " The History of the Irish Flora and Fauna," *The Advancement of Science, Vol.* **10**. *No. 37:39-44.*

Congested Districts Board for Ireland. First Annual Reports, 1893-1923. 4 Vols.

Conroy, M.J. 1974 " Plaggen Soils: A Review of man-made raised soils." *An Foras Talúntais* No. **11**:319-324.

Cooney, G. & Grogan, E. 1994 **Irish Prehistory: A Social Landscape**. Dublin.

Cooney, G. 1996 "Standing Stones: marking the Neolithic landscape," *Archaeology Ireland*, Vol. **10**, No. 2:29-30.

Costello, N.1939 **John McHale, Archbishop of Tuam**. Dublin.

Curtis, E. 1931-33 "Original Documents relating to the Butler Lordship of Achill, Burrishoole and Aughrim (1236-1640),"*Journal of the Galway Archaeological and Historical Society,* Vol.**15**:121-8.

Curtis, E. 1932 "Seventeenth Century Documents relating to the Manors of Aughrim & Burrishoole," *Journal of the Galway Archaeological & Historical Society. Vol* .**16**. *No.1:48-56.*

Curtis, E. 1932 (ed.) **Calendar of Ormond Deeds**. Vol. **I**, 1172-1350. Irish Manuscript Collection.

Curtis, E. 1934(ed.) **Calendar of Ormond Deeds**. Vol. **II**, 1350-1413. Irish MS. Commission.

Curtis, E. 1935 (ed.) **Calendar of Ormond Deeds.** Vol. **III**, 1413-1509. Dublin.

Curtis, E. 1937 (ed.) **Calendar of Ormond Deeds.** Vol. **IV**, 1509-1547. Dublin.

Curtis, E. 1941 (ed.) **Calendar of Ormond Deeds**. Vol. **V**, 1547-1584. Dublin Stationary Office

Achill

Curtis. E. 1978 **A History of Medieval Ireland**. London.

Curwen, J.C. 1818 **Observations on the State of Ireland**. Vol. **I** and **II**. Dublin.

Dalton, E.A. Rev. 1911 **History of Ireland**. Half-Vol **I**. London.

D'Arcy Sirr, J. 1845 **A memoir of the Hon. and most Reverend Power le Poer-Trench, Last Archbishop of Tuam**. Dublin.

de Paor, L. & M. 1958 **Early Christian Ireland**. London and New York.

de Valéra R. and Ó Nualláin, S.1950 " The Megalithic Tombs of the Island of Achill," *Journal of the Royal Society of Antiquaries of Ireland*. Vol. **80**: 199-227.

de Valéra, R. 1961"The Court Cairns of Ireland", *Proceedings of the Royal Irish Academy*, Vol. **60C**:9-140.

de Valéra, R. & Ó Nualláin, S. 1964 **Survey of the Megalithic Tombs of Ireland**, Vol **11. County Mayo**. Dublin.

Devon Commission,1847 **Digest of Evidence Taken Before Her Majesty's Commissioners of Inquiry into the State of the Law and Practice in respect of the Occupation of land in Ireland**, Vol.**I**. Dublin.

Donnelly, J.S. " Irish agrarian rebellion: the Whiteboys of 1769-76, "*Proceedings of the Royal Irish Academy*, Vol. **83C:**293-331.

Duignan, M.V. 1944 "Irish agriculture in early historic times," *Journal of the Royal Society of Antiquaries of Ireland*, Vol. **64** :124-145.

Edwards, N. 1990 **The Archaeology of Early Medieval Ireland**. Batsford, London.

Edwards, R. Dudley & Williams, T. (eds.) 1957. **The Great Irish Famine:studies in Irish History, 1845-52. Dublin**. Reprinted 1994.

Evans, E. E. 1957 **Irish Folkways**. London.

Farrington, A. 1932 "Origin of the Irish flora and fauna," *Irish Naturalist's Journal*, **4**. No. 4:1-3.

Farrington, A. 1953 " Local Pleistocene Glaciation and the level of the snowline of Croaghaun mountain in Achill Island," *Journal of Glaciology: 2*:262-67.

Fitzpatrick, Rev. W. 1886 **Achill as it is compared to what it was**. Dublin.

Fleming, A. 1988 **The Dartmoor Reaves.** London.

Fowler, P. J. 1966-67 "Ridge and furrow cultivation at Cush, Co. Limerick," *North Munster Antiquarian Journal*, **10**:69-71.

Freeman, T.W. 1957 **Pre-Famine Ireland**. London.

22. Bibliography

Freeman, A. M.1983 **Annála Connacht: The Annals of Connacht** (A.D. 1224-1544), Dublin.

Gailey, A. & Ó hÓgáin D. (eds.) 1982 **Gold under the Furze**. Dublin.

Gibbons, M. & Higgins, J. 1988 "Connemara's emerging pre-history" *Archaeology Ireland,* Vol. **2** No. 2:62-6.

Goodbody, R. 1995 **Quaker Relief work in Ireland's Great Hunger**. Bray, Co.Wicklow.

Graham, J. 1953 "Transhumance in Ireland," *The Advancement of Science,* Vol. **10**. No. 37: 74-79.

Graham, J. 1970 "Rural Society in Connacht, 1600-1640, " In Stephens, & Glasscock, R.E. (eds.) **Irish Geographical Studies in honour of Estyn Evans**:192-208 Belfast.

Green, E.R.R. 1967 "The Great Famine (1845-50)," **The Course of Irish History**, Moody, T.W. & Martin, F.X. (eds):263-274.

Griffith, Sir Richard, 1845 **General Valuation of Rateable Property in Ireland (Co. Mayo), 1848-1864**. Dublin.

Groenman-van-Waateringe,W. 1981 "Field boundaries in Ireland," In Ó Corráin, D. (ed.), **Irish Antiquity***: 285- 290. Tower Books, Cork.

Halbert, J.N. 1898 "Impressions of Achill by members of an Easter Party," *The Irish Naturalist ,* Vol. **7**: 135-143.

Halls, S.C. & A.M. 1841-43 **Ireland: its scenery and character**. Vol. **3**:293-401. London.

Halpin, E. 1994 "Setting the Parameters," *Archaeology Ireland,* Vol. **8** No. 3:36-37.

Harbison, P. 1987b "The date of the crucifixion slabs from Duvillaun More and Inishkea North, Co. Mayo," In Rynne, E. (ed.), **Figures from the Past**:73-91. Dublin.

Harbison, P. 1988. **Pre-Christian Ireland**. London.

Hennessy, W. M. 1871 (ed.) **The Annals of Lough Cé: a Chronicle of Irish affairs, 1014-1690**. 2 Vols. London.

Hennessy, W.M. & MacCarthy, B. 1887-1901 (eds.) **Annals of Ulster**. 4 Vols. Dublin.

Henry, F. 1945 "Remains of the Early Christian period on Inishkea North, Co. Mayo," *Journal of the Royal Society of Antiquaries of Ireland,* **75C**:127-55.

Henry, P. 1951 **An Irish Portrait**. London.

Higgins, J.G. 1987 **The Early Christian cross slabs, pillar stones and related monuments of Co. Galway, Ireland (2 vols)**, *B.A.R . British Archaeological Reports,* **375**.Oxford.

Higgins, J. 1996. **Irish Mermaids**. Crow's Rock Press, Galway.

Hornell, J. 1938 **British Coracles and Irish Currachs.** London.

Achill

Howard, J.E. 1855 **The Island of Saints**. London.

Jackson, J. (ed.) 1886 **Miscellanea Genealogica et Heraldica**. Dublin.

Jackson, K. 1938 and Reprint 1990 **Cath Maighe Léna**. Dublin.

Jackson, K. 1953 **Language and History in Early Britain**. Edinburgh.

Jackson, K. 1964a **The Oldest Irish tradition: a window on the Iron Age**. Cambridge, England.

Joyce, P.J.1910 **A Forgotten Part of Ireland**. Philadelphia.

Kenney, J. F. 1929 **The Sources for the Early History of Ireland**. Reprinted Dublin 1968.

Kennedy, M.J. 1969 " The metamorphic history of north Achill Island, Co. Mayo, and the problem
of the origin of the Albite Schists," *Proceedings of the Royal Irish Academy*, Vol.**67B:**261-280.

Kerr, B.M. 1943 "Irish seasonal migration to Great Britain, 1800-1838," Irish Historical Studies **3,**
No.12:365-380.

Kidson, C. & Heywood, A. 1978 "Holocene Eustatic sea-level change," *Nature*, (London),Vol. **273**.

Kingston, B. 1990 **The Deserted Village at Slievemore: a study**. Castlebar, Co. Mayo.

Knott, E. 1957 "Fintan and the Old Eagle of Achill," *Irish Classical Poetry,* **21**. Commonly
called Bardic Poetry. Dublin.

Knox, H.T. 1908 **The History of the County of Mayo to the close of the 16th century.** Castlebar,
Co. Mayo.

Lane, P.G. 1992 "Corraun Mountain, Mayo and the 1850's: a socio-economic study, " In *Cathair na
Mart,* Vol **12**. No.1:75-89. Westport, Co. Mayo.

Leask, H.C. 1936 "Irish Castles 1180-1310, " *Archaeological Journal* **93**:143-198.

Leask, H.C. 1936-39 "Characteristic features of Irish architecture from early times to the 12th
century" *North Munster Antiquarian Journal,* Vol.**1**:10-21.

Leask, H.C. 1941 **Irish Castles and castellated houses**. Dundalk.

Leask, H.C. 1955 **Irish churches and monastic buildings: the first phases and the Romanesque.**
Dundalk. Reprinted Dundalk, 1977.

Lewis, S.A. 1837 **Topographical Dictionary of Ireland. 3 Vols**. London.

Lucas, A.T. 1947 "Field-Notes made on Achill on 5th and 6th August," 1-12. Unpublished. Rynne,
Athenry, Co. Galway.

Lucas, A.T. 1960 "Irish food before the Famine,"*Gwerin* **3**, 1-36.

Lucas, A.T. 1969 "Sea-sand and Shells as manure, " **Studies in Folklife** (ed.) G.Jenkins. **Essays in
Honour of I.C. Peate:**184-203. London.

22. Bibliography

Lucas, A.T. 1970 "Contributions to the History of the Irish house: A possible ancestry to the Bed Outshot" (*Cúilteach*), Folklife **8**:81-98.

Lucas, A.T. 1971-73 "Souterrains: the literary evidence," *Béaloideas,* 39-41, 165-191.

Lucas, A.T 1972 "Irish ploughing practices," In *Tools & Tillage,* Vol. **2**:52-62, 67-83.

Lucas, A.T.1978 " The Gowl Gob: an extinct spade type from Co. Mayo, " *Tools and Tillage,* Vol. **8**: 191-199.

Lynn, C. J. 1978 "Early Christian period domestic structures: a change from round to rectangular," *Irish Archaeological Research Forum* **5**:29-45.

Lynn, C. J. 1983 "Some 'early' Ringforts and Crannógs," *Journal of Irish Archaeology,* Vol.1:47-58.

MacAirt, 1951 **Annals of Inishfallen.** Dublin Institute of Advanced Studies. Dublin.

MacAirt, S. 1955 "Co. Armagh, Toponymy and History," *Proceedings of the Irish Catholic Historical Commission:*1-5.

MacAllister, R.A.S. 1928 **The Archaeology of Ireland.** London.

McErlean, T. 1983 "The Irish townland system of landscape organisation,"*Landscape Archaeology in Ireland,* Reeves- Smyth, T. E. & Hammond, F. *B.A.R. British Archaeological Reports,***116***: 315-340. Oxford.

MacPhilbin, 1951 **Misé Padráig.** Dublin.

McDonald, T. 1989 "Achill Island," *Archaeology Ireland,* Vol. **4**. No.3:7-9.

McDonald, T. 1992 **Achill 5000 B.C. to 1900 A.D. Archaeology, History, Folklore.** Dublin.

McDonald, T. & Halpin, E. 1991-93 Survey of the Historic and Prehistoric landscape of Slievemore Interim Reports (Unpublished). Office of Public Works, Dublin.

McDonald, T. 1993-96 Survey of the Historic and Prehistoric landscape of Slievemore. Interim Reports (Unpublished). Office of Public Works, Dublin.

McGrath, F. 1991 "Emigration and the landscape: the case of Achill Island," *Trinity Papers in Geography,* No. **4**:1-18. Department of Geography, Trinity College, Dublin.

McNally, K. 1973 **Achill.** 1973. Newton Abbot.

McNally, K. 1975 **The Batsford Colour Book of Ireland.** London.

McNally, K 1978 **The Islands of Ireland.** London.

McNeill. T.E. 1991 **The Archaeology of Ulster.** Institute of Irish Studies, Queen's University, Belfast.

McParlan, J. 1802 **Statistical Survey of County Mayo.** Dublin.

Achill

McQuaid, Brother. 1960 "Education in the Diocese of Tuam in the 19th Century." Unpublished Thesis, Maynooth.

Maginess, M.R. 1965 " Achill Island: aspects of social geography."
Unpublished Thesis 1965: Geography Department, Queens University Belfast.

Mallory, J.P. 1984b "The origins of the Irish,"*Journal of Irish Archaeology*. **2,** 65-9. Belfast.

Manning, C. 1984 "The excavation of the Early Christian enclosure Killederdadrum in Lackenavorna, Co. Tipperary,"*Proceedings of the Royal Irish Academy,* Vol. **84C**:237-68.

Mason, T.H. 1936 **The Islands of Ireland: their scenery, people, life and antiquities**. Dublin. Reprinted 1938, 1950 and 1967. Dublin.

Max, M.D. 1972-73 "A note on the stratigraphy and structure of Achill Island," *The Geological Survey of Ireland Bulletin,* Vol. **1.** No. 3:223-30.

Max, M.D.1974 "A reply to discussion on the paper: A note on the stratigraphy and structure of Achill Island,"*The Geological Survey of Ireland Bulletin,* Vol **1**. No. 4:485-90.

Maxwell, W. 1832 **Wild Sports of the West**. London.

Meid, W. (ed.)1974 **Táin Bó Fraech**. Dublin Institute of Advanced Studies, Vol. **22**. Medieval and Modern Irish Series. Dublin.

Mellars, P. & Payne, S. 1971 " Excavation of two Mesolithic Shell Middens on the Island of Oronsay *Nature,* Vol. **23**:397-398.

Mellars, P.A. 1978 "Excavation and economic analysis of Mesolithic shell middens on the island of Oronsay" in Mellars P. (ed.), **The Early Postglacial Settlement of Northern Europe**:371-396. London.

Micks, W.L. 1925 **History of the Congested Districts Board from 1891 to 1923**. Dublin.

Mitchell, F. 1976 **The Irish Landscape**. Glasgow.

Morton, H.V. 1930 **In Search of Ireland.** London.

Mulchrone, K. 1939 (ed.) *Bethu Phátraic*. **The Tripartite Life of Patrick**. London.

Mulloy, S. 1991 **O'Malley. People & Places**. Westport, Co. Mayo.

Mulloy, S. 1994 "Fr. Manus Sweeney," *Cathair Na Mart,* No.**14**:27-38.

Nangle, Rev. E. 1838 **The origin, progress and difficulties of the Achill Mission**. Achill.

Nangle. Rev. E. 1864 **The case of the Achill Mission Estate as plainly stated by Edward Nangle, in reply to the Hon. Joseph Napier**. Achill.

Napier J. & Hamilton G.A. 1864 **Case of the Achill Mission Estate**. Dublin.

22. Bibliography

Neilson, Rev. W. 1808 **An introduction to the Irish language. In three parts, with copious tables of the contractions**. Dublin. Reprinted Achill, 1843.

Newman, E. 1839 "The Natural History of Ireland, " *The Magazine of Natural History,* Vol. **3**: 571-574. London.

Nicholson, A. 1847 **Ireland's welcome to the stranger or excursions through Ireland in 1844 and 1845, for the purpose of personally investigating the conditions of the poor**. Dublin.

Noel, Baptist W. 1837 **Notes on a short tour through the Midland counties of Ireland, in the summer of 1836, with observations on the state of the peasantry**. London.

Ordnance Survey Letters Mayo by John O'Donovan and Thomas O'Conor, et. al. **Vol. I and II** Dublin 1862.

Orme, A.R. 1970 **The World's Landscapes 4. Ireland.** Vol. **1**:56-57. London.

Orpen, 1911-20 **Ireland Under the Normans, 1169-1333.** 4 Vols. Oxford. Reprint 1968.

O'Connell, M. 1990 "Early Land Use in north-east Co. Mayo-the palaeoecological evidence," *Proceedings of the Royal Irish Academy,* Vol. **90**:259-279.

Ó Corráin, D. (ed.).1981 **Irish Antiquity: Essays and Studies presented to Professor M.J. O'Kelly,** Cork.

Ó Danacháir, C. 1972 "Traditional forms of the Dwelling House in Ireland," *Journal of the Royal Society of Antiquaries of Ireland*, Vol.**102**:77-96.

O'Donnell, P. 1937 **The Bothy Fire & all that**. Dublin.

O'Donovan, J. *et. al.*, 1838-40 **Ordnance Survey Field Name Books of County Mayo**. No. 46.

O'Donovan, J. (ed.). 1847 **The Book of Rights (Leabhar na gCeart)**. Dublin.

O'Donovan, J. 1851 **The Tribes, Genealogies and Customs of Hy Fiachrach**. Dublin.

O'Donovan, J. 1851 **Annals of the Four Masters: Annala Rioghachta Eireann. Annals of the Kingdom of Ireland by the Four Masters from the earliest period to the year 1616**. 7 Vols. Dublin.

O'Dowd, A. 1991 **Spalpeens and Tattie Hokers: history of the folklore of the migratory agricultural worker in Ireland and Britain**. Dublin.

O'Floinn, R. 1995 "Sandhills, Silver and Shrines; fine metal works of the Medieval Period in Donegal," In **Donegal: History and Society. Interdisciplinary Essays on the History of an Irish County**. (eds.) William Nolan, Liam Ronayne and Mairead Dunleavy: 85-148. Geography Publications, Dublin.

Achill

O' Kelly, M.J. 1942 " Antiquities and Folk Culture, Achill Island." Unpublished pamphlet. National Museum Topographical Files.

O'Kelly, M.J. 1954 "Excavations and experiments in ancient Irish cooking places," *Journal of the Royal Society of Antiquaries of Ireland*, **84**:105-55.

Ó Máille, S. 1958 "Aicill in Ainmneacha"*Journal of the Royal Society of Antiquaries of Ireland*, **88**:1-10.

O'Malley, E. 1936 **On Another man's wound**. Richard & Cowan.

Ó Móráin, P. 1957 **A short account of the history of Burrishoole Parish**. Mayo News, Westport.

O Muirithe, D. 1972 **A Seat behind the Coachman**. Dublin.

Ó Muráile, N. 1985 **Mayo Places: Their names & origins.** Westport.

Ó Nualláin, S. 1984a " A study of Stone Circles in Cork and Kerry, *Proceedings of the Royal Irish Academy*, Vol **84C**:1-77.

Ó hOgáin, D. 1991 **Myth, Legend and Romance**. London.

O'Rahilly, T. F. 1946 **Early Irish History & Mythology.** Dublin. Reprinted Dublin, 1976.

O' Reilly, B. 1991 "The vernacular architecture of North Co. Dublin," *Archaeology Ireland*, Vol.**5**. No. 2:24-26.

O'Ríordáin, S. 1940 "Excavations at Cush, Co. Limerick," *Proceedings of the Royal Irish Academy*, **45C**, 83-181.

O'Ríordáin, S. 1942 **Antiquities of the Irish Countryside.** Cork. Reprinted, 1979, London.

O'Ríordáin, S. & Rynne, E. 1961"A settlement Site in the sandhills at Dooey, County Donegal," *Journal of the Royal Society of Antiquaries,* Vol.**91**,58-64, 1961.

O'Shea, J. 1996 "Achill: the Famine and religious conflict, " *Muintir Acla,* **003** :21-26.

Ó Súilleabháin, S.1963 **A Handbook of Irish Folklore**. Pennsylvania.

O'Sullivan, W.M. (ed). 1958 **The Strafford Inquisition of Co. Mayo**. Dublin (Irish MSS.Comm). Cal Pat. Rolls, Ireland.

Otway, C.1839 **A Tour in Connacht**. Dublin.

Petty, W. 1720 **A Geographical description of the Kingdom of Ireland**. Dublin.

Piggott, S. and Powell, T.G.E. 1947 " Notes on the Megalithic Tombs of Sligo and Achill, " *Journal of the Royal Society of Antiquaries of Ireland,* Vol. **77**:136-46.

Piggott, S. 1954" Some primitive structures in Achill Island, " *Antiquity* **28***:*19-24.

22.   Bibliography

Praeger, R.L, Kane, W.F. Tatlow, E.M. Hanna, H. and Halbert, J. N. 1898 "Impressions of Achill by members of an Easter Party,"*The Irish Naturalist*. Vol. **7**:135-143.

Praeger, R.L. 1904 " The Flora of Achill Island," *The Irish Naturalist,* Vol.**13**:265-289.

Praeger, R. L. 1909 **A Tourist's Flora of the West of Ireland.** Hodges Figgis, Dublin.

Praeger, R. L. 1915 "Clare Island Survey, " *Proceedings of the Royal Irish Academy,* 2 Vols.

Praeger, R. L. 1974 **The Botanist in Ireland.** Hodges Figgis, Dublin.

Praeger, R.L. 1969. **The Way That I Went.** Dublin.

Price, L. 1963 "A Note on the use of the word *'Baile'* in Place-Names" *Celtica,* **6**:119-126.

Prichard, M. 1987 **A Sporting Angler.** London.

Proudfoot, V.B. 1958 "Ancient Irish Field Systems, " *Jn. Advancement of Science* **56**:369-71.

Proudfoot, V.B. 1959 " Clacháns in Ireland, " *Gwerin* **2**:110-122.

Raftery, B. 1981"Iron Age burials in Ireland, " In **Irish Antiquity** (ed.) Ó Corráin, D:173-204. Cork.

Raftery, B. 1982 **La Tène in Ireland: problems of origin, and chronology.** Marburg.

Rathje, W. 1974 "The Garbage Project" *Archaeology,* Vol. **27**.

Reed, R. C. 1987-8 "Irish Court Tombs: A Minimum Colonisation Model," *The Journal of Irish Archaeology.* Vol.**4**:*1-6.*

Renwick, W. L. 1934 (ed.) **Complete Works of Edmund Spenser (which contains "A View of the Present State of Ireland.").** London.

Reynolds, P.J. 1979 **Butzer Iron Age Farm.** London.

Royal Commission, 1870 Royal Commission of Enquiry into Primary Education in Ireland. Vol. 2. Reports of the Assistant Commissioners. Dublin.

Ross, A. 1974 **Pagan Celtic Britain.** London.

Ruthledge, R.F. 1951. "Some notes on Achill birds, " *The Irish Naturalists Journal,* **10** :205-207.

Rynne, E. 1961 "The Introduction of La Tène into Ireland" In G. Bersu (ed.) *Bericht Über den V. Internationalen Kongress für Vor-und Frühgeschichte, Hamburg 1958,* 705-09.

Rynne, E. (ed). 1987 **Figures from the Past: Studies of Figurative Art in Early Christian Ireland.** Dublin.

Scally, B. 1988 "A Journey to Achill," *Cathair na Mart, Journal of the Westport Historical Society,* Vol. **8**. No 1:118-122.

Seddall, H. 1884 **Edward Nangle: The Apostle of Achill:A memoir and a history, with an introduction by the Most Rev. Lord Plunket,** D.D., Dublin.

Achill

Simmington, R.C.1956 (ed.) **Books of Survey and Distribution: being abstracts of various surveys and instruments of title, 1636-1703 Vol. II, County of Mayo with maps of the county from Petty's Atlas, 1683, and of Tirawley barony from the Down Survey, 1657**. Dublin Stationery Office.

Simms, J.G. 1958-59 "Connacht in the 18th Century," *Irish Historical Studies, 9: 116-133.*

Simms, J.G. 1965 "Mayo Landowners in the 17th Century, " *Journal of the Royal Society of Antiquaries of Ireland.* Vol.**95**:237-239.

Stephens, N. & Glasscock , R.E. 1970 **Irish Geographical Studies in honour of E.Estyn Evans.** Belfast.

Stockman, G. 1974 **The Irish of Achill.** Institute of Irish Studies, The Queens' University, Belfast.

Stokes, G.T. 1891 **Pocockes Tour in Ireland in 1752.** London.

Stokes, W. 1887 **Vita Tripartita.** 2 Vols. London.

Stone, H. 1906 **Connemara and the neighbouring places of beauty and interest in Co. Clare, Co. Sligo and Achill**. London.

Strachan, J. 1944 **Stories from the Táin**, 3rd Ed. Revised D. Bergin. Dublin.

Sweetman, D.1992 "Dating Irish Castles," *Archaeology Ireland,* Vol. **6**. No. 4:8-9.

Synge, F.M.1968 "The Glaciation of West Mayo," *Irish Geography* 5:372-386.

Thomas, C. 1971 **The Early Christian Archaeology of North Britain.** Oxford University Press, Oxford.

Thomas, L. 1857 "Beehive houses, "*Proceedings of the Scottish Archaeological Society ,* **3**:127-144.

Tierney, J.J. 1976 "The Greek Geographic tradition & Ptolemy's evidence for Irish geography," *Proceedings of the Royal Irish Academy,* **76B**:257-65.

Tithe Applotment Books, 1824-1838. Dublin.

Trotter, J.B. 1819 **Walks through Ireland in 1812, 1814 and 1817; described in a series of letters to an English gentleman, with biographical memoirs of J.B. Trotter**. London.

Tuke, J.H. 1848 **A visit to Connaught in the autumn of 1847 with notes of a subsequent visit to Erris. A letter addressed to the Central Relief Committee of the Society of Friends**. Dublin

Tuke, J.H.1880 **Irish Distress and its Remedies, the land question: a visit to Donegal in the Spring of 1880.** London.

Waddell, J. 1970 "Irish Bronze Age Cists: a survey," *Journal of the Royal Society of Antiquaries of Ireland,* **100**:91-139.

22. Bibliography

Wall, M. 1967 "The Age of the Penal Laws (1691-1778)", In T.W.Moody & Martin, F.X. **The Course of Irish History,** (Eds):217-231. Cork.

Wallace, P.F. 1985a "The Archaeology of Viking Dublin," In Clarke, H.B. & Simms, A.(eds.),**The Comparative History of Urban Origins in Non-Roman Europe. Part 1**:103-45. Dublin.

Walsh, Rev. P. 1936"Christian Kings of Connacht," In *Journal of the Galway Archaeological and Historical Society,* Vol.**17**:124-43.

Walsh, Fr. P. 1940 "Connacht in the Book of Rights," *Journal of the Galway Historical and Archaeological Society,* Vol. **20**:191-95.

Walsh, Fr. P. 1947 " The Annals attributed to Tigernach," In **Irish Men of Learning** *(ed.)* Colm O'Lochlainn:219-225.

Walsh, J. & Freeman, J. 1982 "Ten Irish boys trapped in a blazing shed - a disaster that appalled the world," *Evening Press*, 3rd December, 1982.

Went, A.E. J. 1948-50 " Movement of salmon around Ireland, " *Proceedings of the Royal Irish Academy,* Vol. **54C**.

Went, A.E.J. 1964 "The pursuit of salmon in Ireland" *Proceedings of the Royal Irish Academy,* **63C**.

Went, A.E.J. and Ó Súilleabháin, S. 1967 " Fishing for the Sun Fish or Basking Shark in Irish Waters," *Proceedings of the Royal Irish Academy,* Vol.**65C**.

Westropp, T.J. 1911-15. "Clare Island Survey," *Proceedings of the Royal Irish Academy,* Pt. 2.Vol.**31**.

Westropp, T.J. 1912-13 "Brazil and the legendary islands of the North Atlantic: their history and fable. A contribution to the ' Atlantis 'problem," *Proceedings of the Royal Irish Academy,* Vol. **8**. No. 30: 223-260.

Westropp, T.J. 1912-13 "Early Italian maps of Ireland from 1300 to 1600 A.D. with notes on foreign settlers and trade," *Proceedings of the Royal Irish Academy,* Vol **30C**. No. 16:412-420.

Westropp, T.J. 1914 "The promontory forts and early remains of the islands of Connacht," *Journal of the Royal Society of Antiquaries of Ireland,* Vol **4**. Part 1.-Achill:297-317.

Westropp, T.J. 1914 "Notes on *Táin Bó Flidhais*, in connection with Forts at Rathcroaghaun (Dún Flidhais) and others in Co. Mayo, "*Journal of the Royal Society of Antiquaries of Ireland,* Pt. 2. Vol **44**.

Whittow, J.B. 1974 **Geology and scenery in Ireland**. London.

Wilde, Sir W. 1864 "Ireland, past and present; the land and the people: A lecture," *Journal of the Royal Society of Antiquaries of Ireland,* Vol **3**:367.

Williams, A. 1897 **Something about Achill.** Dublin.

Achill

Williams, B.B. & Robinson, P.S. 1983 "Excavations of a Bronze Age Cist and Medieval Booley Houses in Glenmakeran, Co. Antrim and a discussion on Booleying in North Antrim," *Ulster Journal of Archaeology,* **41**:29-45.

Williams, B.B. 1984 "Excavations at Ballyutoag, Co. Antrim," *Ulster Journal of Archaeology:* **47**:37-149.

Woodham-Smith, C.1962 **The Great Hunger:Ireland 1845-49**. London.

Wood-Martin, W.G. 1886 **The Lake Dwellings of Ireland**. Dublin.

Wood-Martin, W.G. 1887 "On certain rude stone monuments in the island of Achill, "*Journal of the Royal Society of Antiquaries of Ireland:* Vol**18**: 367-381.

Wood-Martin, W.G. 1888 **The Rude Stone Monuments of Ireland** Dublin.

Wood-Martin, W.G. 1895 **Pagan Ireland**. London.

Wood-Martin, W.G. 1902 **Traces of the Elder Faiths of Ireland. 2 Vols**. Dublin.

Young, A. 1780 **A Tour in Ireland 1776-79**. 2 Vols. London.

Abbreviations

A.F.M.	*Annals of the Four Masters*
A. Conn.	*Annals of Connacht*
A.U.	*Annals of Ulster*
A.L.Cé	*Annals of Lough Cé*

INDEX

Abha Teangaí, 250
Achill Archaeological Summer
School, **45**,260,275-76,301,306
Achill Beg,16-19,29-30,32,35,
49,52, **53**,72,88,104,108,137,
143,173,219,247-48,257,270,
274,287-91,293, 299,306
Achill Fishery,174,233-38, 261,
263,272-73
Achill Head,18,25-26,40,43,
101,152,232,313,327
Achill Head Hotel, 24
Achill Island Pottery, 251, 273
Achill Mission, 34,43-44,70,90,
98,100-03,106-213,221-22,
230-37,253,263,267,271,273
280,283-84,301,309-10,312,
315,317,323,328

    Dispensary, 116,120,147,
    149-50,159
    Farm,93,114-15,123,128,
    134,136,148,150-53,158-
    59,162,190
    Hospital,149,181-83,190
    Hotel,43,100,137,182
    Mills,120,124,130
    Orphanage,125-26,128,
    134,137,161-62,165,174,
    176,179,190,194,199
    Printing Shop, 137,166,
    190,237
    Schools, 103,112-13,118,
    124,133,137,141,148,
    154,158-59,162-66,172,

179-82,189-90,193
    Settlement (The Colony),
    27, 42,102,114-120,123,
    128,130,132,134,139-41,
    147-50,152,159,162,164,
    169,171-72,181-82,**185**,
    186,190,192,220,235,
    267, 280, **281**
Achill Missionary Herald &
Western Witness, 91,101,110,
113,118-204,206,209,223,233,
235-36,249,280,284,296,324
Achill Relief Committee,104,
119,144-45,148,156,176,199,
203
Achill Sound,16,18-19,29,32,
88,99-100,110,112,128,138,155,
162-63,165,169,177,179,182,
187,189,194,207, 236-37,257,
260,262-63,313,317,320,323,
326-30
Achill Sound Bridge,29,263
Achill Sound Hotel, 128,132,
134,174,195,207
Achill Tourism (see
Turasóireacht Acla)
Act of Union, 77,80
Adams, Dr. Neason, 101,104,
112,116,137,144,147,149,150-
51,156-58,161,163,165,176,183,
188,194-6,209, 253,284
    Isabella, 116,188,196,284
Amethyst, 25,243
Anglo-Norman, 1,2,9,**12**,56,74,

23. Index

23. Index

363

23. Index

23. Index

McNulty, Margo, 42
McParlan, James, 88
Mail Car, 138,147,162,189
Marriage Customs, 75,222,329
Mayo Abbey, 52,247
Mayo Butlers, (See Butlers)
Mayo Constitution, 100-01,166,
180-82
Mayo Naturally, 46
Mayo Telegraph, 125,139,160,
167,178,182-83
Malbie, Sir Nicholas, 11
Manning, C., 292
Marshall, William, 56-57,60
Maumnaman, 28,86,303,305
Maynard, Samuel, 182
Maynooth, 142
Maxwell, Somerset, 170,204
Maxwell, W., 36
Medlycott Estate,11,54,62,70,
81,108,124,214-17,308
Megalithic Tombs, 2,27,48,111,
146,264,271,275-77,**278,279**,
285,287,309,322
Meitheal,79,313
Mesolithic, 20,47, 292
Migratory labour, 20, 224-28
Mills, 124,146,217,314
Minaun,18,24,29,32,39,91,125,
198,251-53,270-71,308-9,324,
325,329
Mining, 219, 318
Monk, Mick, 269
Monyhaig, 48,305
Moran, John, 243,273,286-87,

300,315,340
Moran, John (J.), 316
Moran, Lieut. Michael ,321
Morrison, M., 42
Mount Sandel, 47
Moyteoge, 24-25,44,286,318
Mulloy, Sheila, 68
Mulranny,16,138,164,179,326
Murrisk, 5-6,8,11,15,60,62,
65,67,314
Mweelin, 28-9,117,142,162-66,
172,179,181,186,190,194-98,
206,216,218,220
    Agricultural College,173,
    190
    Hospital,173,176,190
    Training School, 29,164,
    173,176,179,190,193,
    196-97
Mweewillin, 216-220

Nangle, Rev. Edward,34,43,90,
93-4,100,104,106-213,217,219,
231-34,238,249,270,308-10,
314-16,324,328
    Eliza, 111,116
Napier, Rt. Hon. Joseph,130,
170,200,204-06
Napoleonic Tower, 26,258,271,
282,285,296,324,
    wars, 77-80,106,108,228
National Board of Education,
108,116,141,205
National Museum,48,254,285-6,
293

23. Index

23. Index